If This Be Treason

The American Rogues and Rebels Who Walked the Line Between Dissent and Betrayal

Jeremy Duda

Guilford, Connecticut

To Robyn, my partner in life, whose love, support, and encouragement helped make this book possible.

An imprint of Globe Pequot

Distributed by NATIONAL BOOK NETWORK

British Library Cataloguing in Publication Information Available

Library of Congress Cataloging-in-Publication Data Available

ISBN 978-1-4930-2401-8 (cloth)
ISBN 978-1-4930-2402-5 (e-book)

∞™ The paper used in this publication meets the minimum requirements of American National Standard for Information Sciences—Permanence of Paper for Printed Library Materials, ANSI/NISO Z39.48-1992.

Contents

Introduction

If this be treason, make the most of it.

—Attributed to Patrick Henry

Legend holds that Patrick Henry, when accused of treason by his colleagues in Virginia's House of Burgesses for implying in a speech against the Stamp Act that King George III should be assassinated, proudly replied, "If this be treason, make the most of it."

Modern historians believe that Henry did not actually utter those famous words, though the myth, if that is indeed what it is, has lived on for more than 250 years as a testament to his passion for liberty. Contemporary observers wrote that Henry parried the accusation against him with an insincere apology to the slighted king, which was enough to calm the nerves of his startled colleagues.[1] Recalling the episode years later, after the United States had won its independence from Great Britain, Edmund Pendleton remarked in a letter to James Madison that Henry had been commended for his "dexterity in playing on the line of treason, without passing it."[2]

The exact location of that line, separating dissent, disloyalty, and defiance from outright treason, has been difficult to discern ever since.

Treason is the only crime explicitly defined in the Constitution of the United States. Article III, Section 3 states, "Treason against the United States shall consist only in levying war against them, or in adhering to their enemies, giving them aid and comfort." Relatively few Americans have actually been punished for violating those twenty-four words.

Far more common have been those who had the poisonous word hurled in their faces for acts that, while not treasonous, were perilously close to that line, or at least viewed as such by many of their fellow Americans. For those who make such accusations, treason is not necessarily the crime defined in Article III. To them, it is more like Supreme Court Justice Potter Stewart's famous definition of obscenity: "I know it when I see it."

But where exactly is that line?

Was it somewhere along George Logan's voyage to France, as the Philadelphia doctor aroused the wrath of the ruling Federalists by striving to keep his country out of war? Perhaps it stood before the negotiating table at Guadalupe-Hidalgo as Nicholas Trist defied his president's orders so he could salvage the least dishonorable peace treaty he could forge with a vanquished Mexico.

Most certainly that line stood between Richard Nixon and the South Vietnamese as he secretly undermined Lyndon Johnson's last hope for peace in order to clinch his election as president. It may well have been at the National Security Council as Oliver North and John Poindexter defied Congress to ensure that the Nicaraguan Contras could continue their fight against communism. And for Daniel Ellsberg and Edward Snowden, America's greatest whistle-blowers, it unquestionably stood between the secrets they knew and the newspapers they revealed them to.

Some crossed the line out of love of country, to do what they truly believed was in the best interests of their fellow Americans. Others found that they had crossed the line by doing nothing more than subscribing to unpopular views, such as those who fell victim to the Sedition Act, Espionage Act, and the excesses of McCarthyism.

Still others crossed it for nothing more than personal gain. One would be hard-pressed to argue, for example, what good William Walker could have believed he was doing for his country when he subverted its laws and foreign policy to become the conqueror of Nicaragua.

The Founding Fathers withheld the power to define treason from Congress by design. They knew that leaving the Congress to define the greatest crime one can commit against his or her country could have dire consequences for the rights of the citizens of their fledgling republic. Congress may decide how to punish treason; it may even word the laws against it as it desires. But the ceiling was set by Americans who knew how easily the crime could be abused by the government.

James Wilson, a delegate to the Constitutional Convention of 1787, thought it prudent to define treason narrowly and to prevent Congress from expanding it further in order to safeguard the people's liberty. "If we have recourse to the history of the different governments that have hitherto subsisted, we shall find that a very great part of their tyranny over the people has arisen from the extension of the definition of treason," he told the convention. Wilson recalled that "some very remarkable instances of the definition of treason have occurred, even in so free a country as England." In one of those instances, Wilson said, a man had wished death on the unknown person who had killed his favorite buck, only to later find that the perpetrator was the king. For wishing the king's death, the man was convicted of treason. "I speak only of free governments, for in despotic ones, treason depends entirely upon the will of the prince. Let this subject be attended to, and it will be discovered where the dangerous power of the government operates to the oppression of the people. Sensible of this, the Convention has guarded the people against it, by a particular and accurate definition of treason."[3]

In *The Federalist* No. 43, Madison praised the convention's work in narrowly defining the crime of treason. As treason may be committed against the United

States, Madison wrote, the United States must be empowered to punish it. "But as new-fangled and artificial treasons have been the great engines by which violent factions, the natural offspring of free government, have usually wreaked their alternate malignity on each other, the convention have, with great judgment, opposed a barrier to this peculiar danger, by inserting a constitutional definition of the crime, fixing the proof necessary for conviction of it, and restraining the Congress, even in punishing it, from extending the consequences of guilt beyond the person of its author."[4]

Certainly there are those Americans who have committed actual treason against the United States, but their numbers are few, and they are subjects for another book. The purpose of *If This Be Treason* is not to examine their lives, their crimes, or their fates. Nor is it the purpose of this book to debate the wisdom of policy. Probably every president from George Washington to Barack Obama has been called treasonous for pursuing policies their critics thought detrimental to the well-being of the United States and its citizens. I will leave it to the partisans to decide such questions for themselves.

It is the purpose of this book to examine those who fell into the gray area between dissent and betrayal, who could be said, at least by some, to have committed acts that would be almost treason. For whatever reason, and in whatever fashion, those are the Americans who have set their foot on the same blurry line as Patrick Henry.

Chapter 1

The Unauthorized Peacemaker

To defend and support the rights of our country as an independent commonwealth is certainly the first duty of every good citizen.

—George Logan

The line between patriot and traitor is so often a matter of partisan perspective. That lesson was as true during the earliest days of the Republic as it is today. And one of the first Americans to learn it was a Pennsylvania doctor named George Logan.

As he attempted to stave off war between the young United States and its erstwhile ally, France, Logan aroused the ire of President John Adams's administration and his Federalist allies in Congress to such a degree that his unauthorized peace mission would inspire a law that still today inspires cries of "treason."

Logan was born to a prominent Pennsylvania family. His grandfather, James Logan, had emigrated from Ireland to Pennsylvania in 1699, sailing with colony founder William Penn, whom he would serve as his secretary. James Logan found success in fur trading, land, and shipping, and would become a member of the Pennsylvania elite, serving as mayor of Philadelphia and later the colony's chief justice. His success would allow him in 1728 to build Stenton, the Logan family estate that still stands in Philadelphia to this day. It was at Stenton where George Logan was born to James Logan's eldest son, William, in 1753.[1] George Logan achieved prominence befitting of his famous family. He became a doctor during the Revolutionary War and served in the Pennsylvania Legislature from 1785 to 1789. He was also renowned as a farmer, with a lifelong love of agriculture instilled in him by his father. Thomas Jefferson once described him as "the best farmer in Pennsylvania, both in theory and in practice."[2]

Despite being dubbed the best farmer in Pennsylvania, belonging to a prominent and respected family, serving two stints in the Pennsylvania Legislature, and even a term in the United States Senate, it is Logan's 1798 journey to France that engraved his name in the annals of American history. That voyage took

Philadelphia doctor George Logan's unsanctioned peace mission to France, taken with the intent of heading off a war with the United States, led the Federalist-controlled Congress to pass the namesake Logan Act.
U.S. NATIONAL LIBRARY OF MEDICINE

place amid precarious times, as the United States suffered political strife at home and the threat of war abroad.

It is popular today to bemoan the state of distrust and animosity between Democrats and Republicans by declaring that never before in American history has its populace been so divided among partisan lines. Those who make such statements, however, would be shocked to see the partisan venom that existed during the United States' infancy. During the administrations of George Washington and Adams, political passions between the ruling Federalists and the opposition, the Democratic-Republicans, were at a fever pitch. As political warfare erupted over the extent of federal power, interpretations of the Constitution, economic policy, and the role of manufacturing and agriculture, the two sides' passions were inflamed by a virulently partisan press and the emergence of Democratic-Republican societies that formed the backbone of the opposition. The Federalists, led by Adams and Alexander Hamilton, and Democratic-Republicans, led by Jefferson, saw nothing but the worst of intentions in each other.

Throughout the 1790s, the discord between the Federalists and Democratic-Republicans played out against the backdrop of America's "quasi-war" with France, which had become one of the biggest points of contention between the two parties. The former ally of the rebellious colonists was now in the throes of its own revolution, with American public opinion sharply divided between the Democratic-Republicans, who looked fondly upon France's revolution as a welcome continuation of America's own experiment in liberty, and those on the Federalist side, who deplored the mob rule and violent excesses that led a parade of the revolution's enemies to the guillotine. The Jeffersonians viewed the Federalists, whom they already thought too favorable toward Britain, as betraying the cause of America's greatest ally. To the Federalists, the Democratic-Republicans' embrace of France's revolution threatened to bring its atrocities to the United

States. The revolutionary government in France exploited that schism to the best of its ability. When Edmond-Charles Genêt reached America as France's minister to the United States in 1793, Citizen Genêt, as he became known, stirred emotions and whipped French sympathizers into a lather as he traveled from Charleston to Philadelphia. Along the way, he recruited Americans to serve as privateers against British ships, jeopardizing the neutrality proclamation that President Washington issued shortly after his arrival.*

The alarming deterioration of relations between America and France reached a new low with the Senate's passage of Jay's Treaty in 1795. Negotiated by John Jay, the first chief justice of the Supreme Court and a loyal Federalist, the treaty sought to resolve years' worth of postwar grievances. The United States objected to Britain's continued occupation of forts on its territory, the impressment of American seamen, and the status of trade relations between the United States, while both sides demanded payment of outstanding debts from during, and even before, the Revolutionary War.

Under the treaty, Britain agreed to evacuate the disputed forts and grant the United States additional trading rights, and the United States agreed to guarantee the payment of prerevolutionary debts owed to Great Britain by its citizens. Few Americans, even Washington himself, were exceptionally pleased with the treaty, which failed to resolve a number of issues, including the impressment of sailors, which would ultimately help lead the two nations back to war nearly twenty years later. Democratic-Republicans reviled the treaty, which they thought gave up too much to Great Britain, such as consenting to harsh British policies against French shipping that sometimes led to the seizure of American ships, as well as the treaty's failure to provide compensation to slaveholders, whose human property was emancipated by the English. In addition, the Democratic-Republicans viewed Jay's Treaty as a slap in the face to America's ally of France.

Unfortunately for America, that view was shared by the French. The United States had already stopped paying its wartime debts to France on the grounds that the money was owed to the monarchy that was deposed in 1792, not the revolutionary government. Jay's Treaty was the last straw. France began attacking and seizing American ships. In response, the United States rescinded its treaties with France and used its newly reconstituted navy to attack French vessels. No declaration of war had been issued by either country. But in all but name, war had come to the United States.

In April 1798, Adams attempted to ease the hostilities by sending three commissioners to negotiate with the French. Elbridge Gerry and John Marshall

* In 1794 Citizen Genêt fell out of favor with the revolutionary government, which recalled him back to France. Knowing he would face the guillotine upon his return, he begged the Washington administration to grant him amnesty in the United States. His wish was granted, and Genêt lived out the rest of his days in America, dying in 1834.

were to join Charles Cotesworth Pinckney, the American ambassador in Paris, to iron out the countries' differences and restore peace between them. However, the negotiations were unsuccessful, and the envoys were dismayed by requests from three French officials, who became known in the United States as X, Y, and Z, for a "loan" from the commissioners. Marshall and Pinckney returned to the United States, leaving behind Gerry, who was viewed as friendlier toward the French, to hopefully continue the negotiations. Adams announced the failure of the mission without disclosing the attempt to solicit bribes from the Americans. But when Democratic-Republicans obtained the Adams administration's correspondence about the peace mission, the insult to America's honor incensed the nation. Due to Adams's decision to replace the three French officials' names with letters, the infamous incident became known to history as the XYZ Affair.

The XYZ Affair had not yet become public knowledge when Logan decided to take action. But the United States and France were already perilously close to a war, and Logan hoped to avert it. In addition to the ominous news from Adams's commissioners in France and the American war preparations that were gaining steam every day, Logan possessed three traits that would lend themselves to a desire to undertake a mission of peace. First, he was a Republican in the mold of Jefferson, with whom he was close. Furthermore, Logan, like other Republicans of his time, had a great affection for France, which for many of his countrymen was coupled with an aversion to Great Britain. Not only was France America's indispensable ally during its long fight for independence, but it had now thrown off the shackles of its own despotic monarchy and embraced many of the very principles of liberty it had helped the United States to attain. Logan was no stranger to Britain, and indeed, had reason to look fondly upon America's former mother country. As a teenager, his father had sent him to Bristol to study at a Quaker school where his grandfather had once been a teacher. And for the first four years of the colonies' revolt against the crown, Logan lived and studied as a medical student in Edinburgh, returning home to Stenton in 1779.[3] But despite his natural affections for Great Britain, Logan's sympathies lay with France. And he shared in the Republican enthusiasm for the principles of the French Revolution. "To this Republican party Dr. Logan, in common with many conspicuous men, belonged, and he advocated their doctrines of sympathy with France with great earnestness," Deborah Norris Logan wrote in her memoir of her husband's life.[4]

Finally, like his father, grandfather, and great-grandparents before him, George Logan was a Quaker. Though he had been expelled from the Society of Friends in 1791 because he "appeared in a military way"—in reality, his only martial activity had been to join a militia—he never cast off his strict Quaker upbringing, and for the rest of his life he shared the values it instilled in him, including an aversion to war. He never sought to rejoin the Society of Friends, but later in life he would often accompany his wife, Deborah, to its meetings.

His Quaker heritage would make Logan a popular figure in France during his mission of peace.[5]

Logan, Democratic-Republican, Francophile, and Quaker that he was, decided that something had to be done to avert war with France, and he was perhaps the man to do it. Logan believed the French to be unaware of the United States' "growing importance," and felt they should be warned that their actions may push Americans into the arms of their common antagonist, Great Britain. Logan sold two parcels of land to finance his trip and made preparations in case the Federalists tried to seize other property in his absence. He had his friend, Thomas McKean, chief justice of the Pennsylvania Supreme Court, draw up documents giving Deborah power of attorney to manage his affairs while he was gone, possibly even to sell Stenton if needed to prevent the Federalists from seizing it.[6] With his affairs in order, Logan set sail on the *Iris* on June 12, 1798.

Logan traveled without a passport but with certificates affirming his United States citizenship from his two powerful friends, Jefferson and McKean. Their assistance, especially Jefferson's, would soon arouse immense suspicion on the part of the Federalists. Deborah Norris Logan later wrote that she was never able to determine how it became publicly known that her husband had obtained the credentials, but once the Federalists learned of that fact, Jefferson and McKean became "objects of the most furious obloquy" for assisting his unofficial mission. "Among other things," Deborah wrote, "it was said in the Federal prints that it was believed to be 'the first instance where chief judge of any place had furnished credentials to a traitor.'" Logan also took with him two letters of introduction from Philippe-André Joseph de Létombe, the French consul in Philadelphia, for Philippe-Antoine Merlin and Charles Maurice de Talleyrand, two of the leading political figures in France.[7]

The voyage across the Atlantic was uneventful and, after stopping to dine in Dover, where he observed soldiers lining the English coastline, with more garrisoned in a nearby castle to defend against the French, Logan disembarked in Hamburg, then a common transit point for those journeying to France.[8] But upon inquiring with French officials in Hamburg, he was told that the government in Paris had forbade the issuance of any more passports to Americans. His insistence that he must deliver to Citizen Merlin, a member of the five-person executive council of the French Directory, a letter entrusted to him by Létombe did nothing to persuade the French chargé d'affaires. But Logan soon found an ally who could smooth his passage into France: the Marquis de Lafayette.[9]

Lafayette, the French aristocrat who made himself a hero in the United States by joining the American cause and taking up arms against Britain during the Revolutionary War, had not fared as well under his own country's revolution. After his troops, who were under the sway of the radicals who had seized power in Paris, rebelled against him, Lafayette attempted to flee back to France, only to be captured by the Austrians, who imprisoned him for more than five years at Olmütz, in the present-day Czech Republic. Lafayette won his release in 1797 at the insistence of Napoleon Bonaparte, then a rising young general in France's revolutionary wars. Since then, Lafayette and his family had taken up residence near Hamburg, a fortuitous turn of events for Logan.

Logan called upon Lafayette and explained the situation, and the marquis, who had watched the gathering war clouds between the United States and France with apprehension, agreed to help secure for Logan a passport that would get him into France.[10] "He said that he was sincerely attached to our country," Logan wrote his wife of Lafayette, "and had for some time viewed with great anxiety the misunderstandings which had taken place between the sister republics." Lafayette managed to convince a member of the French legation in Hamburg to violate the prohibition on new passports for Americans and get Logan into Paris, on the grounds that the doctor carried letters from Létombe and could help restore friendship between the United States and France.[11]

Word of Logan's voyage hadn't yet spread from the Federalists across the Atlantic, but his activities soon caught the attention of Adams's loyalists in Europe. William Vans Murray, a Federalist who served as America's ambassador to the Batavian Republic, as the Netherlands had been rechristened in 1795, caught wind of Logan's plans from The Hague, though the initial information he received was not completely accurate. Vans Murray wrote to John Quincy Adams in Berlin, where he served as America's minister to Prussia, informing him that a Mr. Droghan—based on the incorrectly spelled name; Vans Murray initially believed him to be Irish—was on his way to Paris with letters from Jefferson to Merlin and Talleyrand, which the vice president hoped would avert war between their countries. He also informed the younger Adams that the Dutch government had ordered its minister in Paris to help mediate the burgeoning Franco-American conflict.[12]

On August 6, Vans Murray updated John Quincy Adams that the true identity of the mystery Irishman was the Philadelphia doctor, Logan, "a propagandist of sedition and philosophy." Vans Murray's suspicions were heightened by the word he'd received that Logan carried passports from Jefferson and McKean. Vans Murray actually tried to have Logan detained by Dutch authorities in Rotterdam so the Americans could ascertain the purpose of his trip, but was unsuccessful in heading him off before the doctor left the Netherlands for France. By the time Vans Murray reached Rotterdam himself in the hope of speaking with the suspicious envoy, Logan was already gone.[13]

Upon arriving in Paris on August 7, Logan learned that Marshall and Pinckney had long since departed, and that Gerry, the last of Adams's peace commissioners, had just set sail for the United States. It appears that Logan was intent on communicating at least with Gerry, if not the other commissioners he expected to still find in Paris. "My object in coming to France was to state such circumstances to Mr. Gerry respecting the situation of our Country, as might have induced him to conclude a Peace before his return to the United States," Logan wrote to Merlin at the end of his trip. Regardless of what Logan had planned for his arrival in Paris, he would now have to improvise. Since Gerry had already taken his leave, Logan informed Merlin, he considered it his duty to urge France to act with "justice and magnanimity" toward the United States.[14]

In lieu of the ability to meet with Adams's commissioners, Logan made his first contact with a fellow American, and it was his good fortune to find a countryman who was outside the Federalists' orbit. Fulwar Skipwith, the American consul general in Paris, who had been appointed by his distant cousin, Jefferson, during the latter's time as Washington's secretary of state, informed Logan that the Directory had recently enacted an embargo against all American shipping in French ports. American ships had been seized and their crews imprisoned, Skipwith told Logan. The frayed relations between the United States and France had taken a turn for the worse, and the stakes of Logan's journey had just become higher, he learned. But this ominous news provided some clarity to Logan, whose already vague plans had been thrown into disarray by the news of the peace commissioners' departure. He must convince the Directory to lift the embargo and release the hundreds of jailed seamen.[15]

Logan's first meeting with a representative of the French government threatened to test the bounds of his amateur diplomacy skills. Armed with Létombe's letter, he secured an interview with Talleyrand, foreign minister of the French republic. Talleyrand is perhaps one of the greatest political survivors in history. Through the decades of upheaval that began with the storming of the Bastille in 1789, Talleyrand had not only survived but flourished amid the turmoil in France. Despite his aristocratic background, he held high office in the Directory through the darkest days of the revolution, and beyond. He became a close confidant of Bonaparte's, assisting him during his 1799 coup, though they broke in 1807, leading to Talleyrand's resignation as foreign minister. After Bonaparte's downfall, Talleyrand played a key role in the restoration of the Bourbon monarchy under Louis XVIII, and took the lead role in representing France during the Congress of Vienna.

The meeting with Talleyrand was disappointing and unproductive. The master diplomat revealed nothing as Logan expounded upon public opinion in the United States and the dangers of war between the two countries. Logan presented a gift he'd brought for Talleyrand, an essay he'd written on crop rotation. But Talleyrand offered only his own agrarian advice to the Pennsylvania farmer, and sent Logan on his way with nothing else to show for his efforts. Instead, the crafty foreign minister sent others to probe Logan and discern the purpose of his trip, though they were prudent enough to not ask for bribes this time, as they had with Gerry, Marshall, and Pinckney. Under the guise of generosity, they offered to save Logan the trouble of delivering Létombe's letter to Merlin themselves. Knowing that the letter was the greatest tool—perhaps even the only one—that he could use to get a face-to-face meeting with the leader of the French republic, which Talleyrand seemed determined to prevent, Logan declined the offer.[16]

Once again, Logan found a way around French obstruction, this time in the form of Rutger Jan Schimmelpenninck, the Batavian minister in Paris. Schimmelpenninck told Logan that his country was eager to help restore peace between the United States and France, and offered to personally introduce Logan to Merlin.[17] Two days later, Logan and Schimmelpenninck set out for the Luxembourg Palace, the seat of the French Directory.

Before Logan got his opportunity to meet the head of the republic, he received welcome news from one of Talleyrand's top subordinates: The French would raise the embargo and free the imprisoned seamen. On August 11, the prisoners were ordered free in a memorandum signed by Talleyrand and Étienne Eustache Bruix, a minister of the Directory. A second memorandum signed by Merlin and Talleyrand, dated five days later, officially lifted the embargo against American shipping. The Directory noted in the August 16 memorandum that the continuation of the embargo threatened to drive the United States into the arms of the British, a great fear of an unstable country already embroiled in war.[18] Logan was overjoyed, writing to Skipwith that "everything will be done in accordance with our wishes." He told Skipwith that Gideon Gardner, one of the imprisoned captains, would receive permission to sail that day, and urged the consul general to return to Paris immediately.[19] Talleyrand informed Skipwith of the decision in a letter the next day, transmitting copies of the two directives.[20] The doctor's work, however, was not yet finished. He still must sit down with Merlin.

Logan and Schimmelpenninck met Merlin at the Petit-Luxembourg, a hotel adjacent to the palace. After Merlin read the letter that Logan had delivered from Létombe, Schimmelpenninck withdrew so the two could discuss the situation at hand between America and France. Logan told Merlin that he was not there to justify the United States' actions or to criticize those of France, but he explained why he believed it was in France's best interest to make peace with the United States. Logan warned that Britain, and especially Prime Minister William Pitt the Younger, was trying to drive a wedge between its wayward colonies and their French allies, aided in America by the likes of William Cobbett, publisher of the Federalist *Porcupine's Gazette*. As a nation more committed to the "manly pursuit of agriculture" than to manufacturing, Logan said France would be well advised to respect neutral shipping that allowed it to exchange its agricultural goods for the manufactured wares of other nations. If France and the United States continued down their precarious path and French troops found themselves on American shores, Logan told Merlin, "every citizen of our country should become her enemy."[21]

Merlin replied that France had no desire to interfere with the internal affairs of the United States, nor to disgrace its own revolution or diminish the reputation it had earned by helping America to achieve its independence. France had been driven to hostilities against neutral shipping by Great Britain's example, Merlin told Logan, and had done so only to avoid giving any advantage to its wartime enemy. But he assured Logan that he was willing to rectify the situation.[22]

The day after their meeting, Logan, Schimmelpenninck, and other diplomats attended a dinner with Merlin at the Petit-Luxembourg. Merlin espoused nothing but goodwill toward the United States. After a round of toasts to the Republic of France, the Batavian Republic, and the Cisalpine Republic, created the year before in Northern Italy as a French client state, Logan, noting the absence of a toast to the United States, requested that he be allowed to raise a toast to, "The United States of America, and a speedy restoration of amity between them and France." Merlin stopped him. "Sir, I wished myself to give that toast, and will now do it in your words," he said.[23] Logan left the dinner with copies of the decrees ending the embargo and freeing the American sailors. French newspapers hailed "le brave Logan," with one joyfully declaring "that war between the United States and France will not take place."[24] Logan continued his stay in Paris, where he ultimately spent three weeks sightseeing, as well as meeting with Merlin and other members of the Directory.

Despite his earlier assurances from Talleyrand and the copies of the directives he'd provided to Skipwith, Deborah Logan writes that her husband continued to seek pledges of France's willingness to ease the pressure on his country. When asked during one meeting by members of the Directory what France could do to convince the United States that it meant to restore relations to their previously amicable state, Logan replied that it must raise the embargo, free the imprisoned seamen, and assure the United States that any minister it sent "would be received in France as one from the most favoured people would be." One director told him, "That is more than we would do for the most favoured nation in Europe," to which Logan replied, "But nevertheless, it is what you must do, if you wish to conciliate my country."[25]

Convinced that the Directory had seen the error of its ways, Logan on August 29 left Paris for Bordeaux, where the *Perseverance* would ferry him back across the Atlantic to the United States. He wrote Deborah on September 9, the day he left, that the American ships and sailors captured by the French had been released, the Directory had assured him that it was ready to treat with the United States, and that he carried dispatches from the French government "calculated to restore that harmony, the loss which has been so sensibly felt by both countries."[26] News of Logan's exploits would reach American shores before he did, though its impact would not be greeted with the universal elation he must have hoped for.

Since the moment he'd set foot on the *Iris*, Logan had been cut off from his home country and was unaware of the maelstrom that had erupted in the wake of his departure. On the Federalist side, Logan's mission was viewed with suspicion from the beginning. Why would a man traveling as an unauthorized envoy believe he would succeed when Adams's own diplomats had been refused even an audience with the leaders of revolutionary France? Adams saw political motives in Logan's sojourn, writing to Secretary of State Timothy Pickering that Logan's trip appeared to have been taken with an eye toward the upcoming elections. "The object of Logan, in his unauthorized embassy, seems to have been to do or obtain something which might give opportunity for the 'true American character to blaze forth in the approaching elections,'" Adams said, quoting a dispatch that had been recently attributed to Logan, though he denied being the author. "Is this constitutional for a party of opposition to send embassies to foreign nations to obtain their interference in elections?"[27] Several days after Logan's departure, a Federalist ally informed Washington of the doctor's trip, lamenting that despite his "mischievous" intentions, no law allowed the government to prevent his departure.[28]

Others saw far greater conspiracies in Logan's actions. No sooner had Logan departed from Philadelphia than the Federalist press tarred him with the most odious of brushes. The *Philadelphia Gazette*, a Federalist newspaper, published a "Communication" to its readers, warning them of what the paper described as a treacherous mission aimed at selling out the United States to a demagogic France and its sympathizers in the Democratic-Republican faction led by Jefferson, whom its opponents had described with the epithet "Jacobins." Several days after Logan sailed for Hamburg on *Iris*, the *Philadelphia Gazette* wrote:

> *We are assured from the best authority that Dr. Logan (a noted and violent Democrat) departed from this city on Wednesday or Thursday last, in the ship Iris, for Hamburg, on his route to Paris. There cannot be the least question that the doctor, from his inordinate love of French liberty and hatred to the sacred Constitution of the United States, has gone to the French Directory fraught with intelligence of the most dangerous tendency to this country. The secrecy of his intention (for his very linen was made up out of his own house) and visit by daylight on the day of his departure to the French Consul, announce that his abandonment of wife, children, relatives, and country is of a species of conspiracy most fatal to freedom and abhorrent to humanity. For can any sensible man hesitate to suspect that his infernal design can be anything less than the introduction of a French army to teach us the value of true and essential liberty by reorganizing our government through the blessed*

operations of the bayonet and guillotine? Let every American now gird on his sword. The times are not only critical, but the secret of the Junto is out. Their demagogue is gone to the Directory, for purposes destructive of our lives, property, liberty and holy religion.[29]

The Federalists may have immediately divined the purpose of Logan's trip, but if Jefferson was aware of it at the time he wrote the certificate of citizenship, he gave no indication of it. Jefferson wrote shortly after Logan's departure that Logan had intended for at least a year to go to Europe, with plans to depart as soon as he could get enough money for his trip, and wrote in the certificate that he provided to Logan that he was visiting Europe "on matters of business."[30] He insisted that he had written similar declarations to a hundred others besides Logan, and that the Federalists' claims that he had played some kind of role in Logan's mission was a "calumny."[31]

However, Deborah Logan describes her husband's trip as being conceived with the express intention of heading off a war between the United States and France. "In the midst of this state of things my husband formed the project of his visit to France, with what appeared to me the romantic idea of persuading the rulers of that arrogant government to alter the tone of their conduct towards the United States."[32] Nonetheless, Jefferson said Logan "unwisely made a mystery" of his trip, which led the Federalist war hawks to spread panic over an alleged plot to recruit a French army to land on American shores.[33] Jefferson may have been kept in the dark, but McKean was well aware of Logan's intentions, and expressed his gratitude "that we possess one man who is capable and devoted enough to undertake this task."[34]

Deborah was left alone to suffer the vitriol and suspicion heaped upon her husband, and by extension, upon her as well, though her later recollections focused mostly on her concern for George and his good name. "[W]hen he left me indeed, I was as completely miserable as I could be whilst innocent myself and united to a man whose honour I knew to be without a stain. But I found it necessary, by a strong effort, to control my feelings," she wrote. A "friendly Federalist" informed her that some in the government had considered searching her home for evidence of treason or other wrongdoing by her husband. These, after all, were the days of the Alien and Sedition Acts. Deborah informed him that she and her husband had nothing to hide. Deborah described this as a period of "political excommunication" for her.[35]

Thomas Jefferson visited Deborah shortly after her husband's departure, taking a detour around the main road to Stenton in order to elude the Federalist spies who watched over him. The vice president expressed concern for Deborah's well-being and encouraged her to proudly show her face in public to demonstrate her husband's innocence and the clarity of her conscience. Several days later,

Deborah took Jefferson's advice and went into town. Some people told Deborah that they were surprised to see her out and about, while others who did not express that sentiment to her face told others of "their astonishment that I could look thus gay and cheerful in the circumstances in which I was placed."[36]

By the time Logan boarded the *Perseverance* in Bordeaux for his return voyage to the United States, he believed he had made real progress. He had received assurances from Merlin that France desired peace, and carried documents from Talleyrand ordering that the embargo be lifted and America's jailed sailors be released. However, the Federalists were sharpening their knives. Deborah Logan even worried that her husband might be prosecuted under the dreaded Sedition Act, which had been passed during his voyage.[37] Foreshadowing the hostile reception that would greet him in Philadelphia, Cobbett's Federalist newspaper *Porcupine's Gazette* mocked Logan as word spread that the *Perseverance* was on the Delaware River, and the doctor would soon be home:

> *He is come!*
> *He is come!!*
> *He is come!!!*
> *ENVOY LOGAN, THE PEACEMAKER, is come. The* Perseverance *is below, and Logan is very probably in—Germantown. It is reported that he is to make his public entry this afternoon, bearing in his hand an Olive Branch, and accompanied by his secretary of Legation—What a pity that addled eggs are so scarce.*[38]

To the great chagrin of the Federalists, Logan's mission appeared to bear fruit where Adams's envoys had failed. Whether Logan's efforts had anything to do with the Directory's decision to lift the embargo and release the imprisoned seamen is highly debatable. Frederick Tolles, Logan's biographer, wrote that by the time Logan arrived in France, Talleyrand and the Directory had already decided that war with the United States would be only to their detriment, pushing the Americans into the arms of their biggest enemy, Great Britain, and threatening French possessions in North America. Several sources had informed the Directory that American public opinion was inflamed, and the leaders of France had already considered lifting it. But it served France's interest to give credit to Logan, who "for a brief moment . . . was the hero of Paris." "Logan, having arrived at the crucial moment, became the pivot on which French policy swung around—at least for the public, the people of Paris," Tolles wrote.[39] However, Tolles argued that Logan should receive some credit for stopping the "diplomatic imbroglio of 1798" from turning into a full-fledged war with France.[40]

Certainly the captains of the ships seized by the French were grateful to Logan for interjecting on their behalf. In a letter to Logan, delivered as he prepared to sail from Bordeaux, Gideon Gardner and a handful of other captains gave credit where they believed it was due: "We are fully convinced that your exertions and manly remonstrances have already raised the embargo from all the American vessels, and set at liberty all their prisoners, and will probably have a considerable influence in restoring captured vessels and property to their legal owners." Logan deserved the approbation of his countrymen, the captains wrote, and expressed their fervent wish that he be welcomed in the United States with open arms.[41] Jefferson also credited Logan with heading off a war. "That your efforts did much towards preventing declared war with France, I am satisfied," he informed Logan in 1813.[42]

For the Federalists, the success or failure of Logan's mission—they largely considered it futile—was not the primary issue at hand. Even if Logan had possessed concrete proof that he alone had averted war with his unsanctioned voyage, it seems unlikely that the Federalists would have welcomed him back with open arms, given the venom that had spewed forth from Federalist pens during his absence. Within a month of his return, they would use the power of Congress to retaliate against Logan's affront to Federalist rule and policy.

Upon returning to Philadelphia, Logan met with Adams to discuss the details of his trip. Despite rumors that Adams would refuse to meet with him, the president received Logan cordially, and showed none of the "irritability of temper" for which he was well known.[43] Years later, Adams spoke well of Logan and their meeting after the doctor's return from Paris.

> *I had no reason to believe him a corrupt character, or deficient in memory or veracity. After his return he called upon me, and in a polite manner informed me that he had been honoured with conversations with Talleyrand, who had been well acquainted with me, and repeatedly entertained at my house, and now visited me at his request to express to me the desire of the Directory, as well as his own, to accommodate all disputes with America, and to forget all that was past: to request me to send a minister from America, or to give credentials to someone already in Europe to treat; and to assure me that my minister should be received, and all disputes accommodated in a manner that would be satisfactory to me and my country. I knew the magical words* Democrat *and* Jacobin *[emphasis added] were enough to destroy the credibility of any witness with some people; but not so with me. I saw marks of candour and sincerity in this relation that convinced me of its truth.*[44]

Logan described Adams as leaping from his chair at one point and declaring that he would send whichever minister he pleased. But aside from that, the meeting went well. Adams even served his guest tea.[45] The amicability with which Adams received Logan would not last long.

By Logan's account as well, Adams received him cordially as he met with the president to debrief him on his exploits in France. Logan was more coldly received by Adams's secretary of state, Pickering. Visiting Pickering on November 12 in Trenton, where the federal government had temporarily moved to flee from an outbreak of yellow fever in Philadelphia, Logan handed over the papers provided to him by Skipwith, only to be informed that Pickering had already received the documents from other sources. The secretary of state called the Directory's promises "ostensible and illusory," and recited a litany of grievances over France's treatment of neutral—and especially, American—shipping, noting that the most recent embargo against neutrals, which Pickering viewed as specifically targeted at the United States, had actually been approved by the Directory while Gerry, Marshall, and Pinckney were in France to negotiate with the government.[46] Logan recounted that Pickering showed him to the door at the end of the interview and told him bluntly, "Sir, it is my duty to inform you that the government does not thank you for what you have done."[47]

So too was Washington hostile to Logan, who on November 18 went to Rosannah White's boardinghouse in Philadelphia, where the former president was staying, to apprise him of the results of his trip. Washington was already familiar with Logan, having initially met him and his wife in 1787 during the Constitutional Convention. Logan and Robert Blackwell, an Episcopal minister and doctor from Philadelphia, with whom the former president was also acquainted, had arrived separately at White's boardinghouse and called upon Washington at the same time. Washington's written account of the meeting made it clear that he had no desire to see or speak with Logan. Washington in fact did his best to ignore Logan and converse directly with Blackwell, but Logan was determined to be heard. The famously formal Washington wrote that he only reluctantly shook Logan's hand, and that Logan took a seat without being offered one.

When Blackwell took his leave, Washington expected Logan to follow. "[A]s I wished to get quit of him," Washington wrote that he remained standing, "and shewed the utmost inattention to what he was saying."* But the Pennsylvanian remained and described his recently concluded mission to France.[48] Washington wrote contemptuously of the conversation, in which he questioned Logan

* Lafayette wrote to Washington in May 1799, and in his letter described his meeting with Logan and the assistance he provided in Hamburg. Lafayette expressed sympathy for Logan's position, and noted with regret that he'd seen blame heaped on Logan in the newspapers. "It is incumbent on me to let you know what I have to say in his favour," he wrote his former commanding officer (Lafayette to George Washington, May 9, 1799). Considering the high esteem in which Washington held Lafayette, owing to their time together during the Revolutionary War, one must wonder whether the letter did anything to improve Washington's low opinion of Logan.

as to why he would presume he would succeed, where "gentlemen of the first respectability in our Country specially charged under the authority of the Government, were unable to do." Washington continued to express his disdain for Logan, scornfully describing Logan's account of his trip a month later in a letter to Vans Murray. "He says the inclination of France to be upon good terms with the United States is now so strong, that it must be our own mismanagement, & disinclination to Peace, if matters with that Country are not accommodated upon terms honorable & advantageous to this."[49]

Though Logan was initially better-received by Adams than he was by his predecessor, the president's attitude toward him became far less neutral once Federalists in Congress set their sights on the unauthorized envoy. When Congress convened in December 1798, Adams's address to the body made no mention of Logan or the unofficial mission that had captured the Federalists' imaginations. The president devoted most of his address to the state of affairs with France. Though France had sought to impress upon the United States that it wished to repair their relations, Adams was skeptical due to the continuation of its January 1798 embargo against any shipping that carried British-made goods, which he regarded as "an unequivocal act of war against the commerce of the nations." "Hitherto, therefore, nothing is discoverable in the conduct of France which ought to change or relax our measures of defence."[50] Adams urged the Congress to prepare for war as the only way of guaranteeing peace. And while leaving the door open to reconciliation with France, Adams insisted that it must be France that extended the olive branch.

Though Adams did not reference Logan or his mission in the address, he perhaps foreshadowed his willingness to take action against future self-styled ambassadors, and explained why he may have viewed Logan's well-intentioned journey with suspicion. Adams told the lawmakers, "[T]o send another Minister, without determinate assurances that he would be received, would be an act of humiliation to which the United States ought not to submit. It must, therefore, be left to France, if she is indeed desirous of accommodation, to take the requisite steps."[51]

But after the Senate replied with a message to Adams that questioned France's decision to bypass the administration's "constitutional and authorized agents" and deal with the United States "through the medium of individuals without public character or authority," Adams took up their cause.[52] On December 12, Adams issued a reply to Congress that made clear he viewed Logan's conduct as unacceptable. "Although the officious interference of individuals without public character or authority is not entitled to any credit, yet it deserves to be considered whether that temerity and impertinence of individuals attempting to interfere in public affairs between France and the United States, whether by their secret correspondence or otherwise, and intended to impose upon the people and separate them from their Government, ought not to be inquired into and corrected."[53] *

It was Congressman Roger Griswold, a Connecticut Federalist, who turned Adams's words into action. On December 26, Griswold introduced a resolution calling for "an act for the punishment of certain crimes therein specified," seeking to create criminal penalties to match the opprobrium that the Federalists had attached to Logan's mission. The act, his resolution asserted, was aimed at American citizens "who shall usurp the Executive authority of this Government, by commencing or carrying on any correspondence with the Governments of any foreign Prince or State, relating to controversies or disputes which do or shall exist between such Prince or State and the United States."[54]

On January 9, the bill was introduced in the House:

> *Be it enacted . . . That if any person, being a citizen of the United States, whether he be actually resident or abiding within the United States, or in any foreign country, shall, without the permission or authority of the Government of the United States, directly or indirectly, commence or carry on any verbal or written correspondence or intercourse with any foreign Government, or any officer or agent thereof, relating to any dispute or controversy between any foreign Government and the United States, with any intent to influence the measures or conduct of the Government having disputes or controversies with the United States, as aforesaid; or if any person, being a citizen of, or resident within, the United States, and not duly authorized, shall counsel, advise, aid or assist, in any such correspondence, with intent as aforesaid, he or they shall be deemed guilty of a high misdemeanor.*[55]

The proposed penalty was a fine of up to $5,000 and imprisonment of six months to three years.

Logan's name was rarely mentioned in the early days of the debate, and some supporters of the bill insisted that it was not aimed at any particular recent events, though indirect references to Logan permeated the House's proceedings. John Nicholas, a Democratic-Republican from Virginia, spoke of the likelihood that the legislation was "founded upon what had been seen in the public papers relative to the conduct of a certain gentleman who has lately been in France."

Nicholas was one of many Democratic-Republicans who questioned the need for such a law. The Constitution already defined the crime of treason, Nicholas declared. It was not in the power of Congress to create a new

---

* Jefferson mocked his rival Adams for bowing to the Senate's pressure on the Logan issue, writing to James Madison, "when the Senate gratuitously hint Logan to him, you see him in his reply come out in his genuine colours" (Thomas Jefferson to James Madison, January 3, 1799).

offense regarding the issue. And if it could, he said, it would be unnecessary. While declaring that his colleague had been mistaken "in supposing [the bill] had reference to any particular person," Griswold insisted that the grim situation in Europe bespoke the necessity of a law to prevent individuals from interfering with the executive's negotiations with foreign governments. Griswold, however, at least partially dropped the charade by referencing the still-unnamed Logan, saying he "did not know but an interference of this kind might have already taken place; but the object of this motion was prospective, and had nothing to do with what is past."[56]

Though his name usually went unspoken, the debate was rife with offhand references to Logan and his controversial trip. The Federalists painted vivid pictures describing the alleged damage that a man such as Logan could inflict while conducting such freelance diplomacy. Congressman Robert Goodloe Harper, one of the leading voices in the House of Representatives for the passage of the Logan Act, insisted that a freelance diplomat could go to a foreign country under the guise of seeking peace, but instead foment war, which "may happen to suit a faction better than peace." South Carolina's John Rutledge took Harper's argument a few dramatic steps further by suggesting that there could be some who are so zealous in their belief that the Adams administration was hostile to liberty that they believed it necessary to overthrow the government, "to the effect which, they may think a French army and a French invasion necessary."[57]

Even if imbued with the best of intentions, an unauthorized envoy could forge terms of a peace that would be grossly unacceptable to the government, Harper said. "I do admit that there might be a possibility of obtaining peace on terms which the Government would be averse to accepting. I will go further. I will say on terms which it would be criminal in the Government to accept," said Harper, who declared that he would sooner go to war than "suffer our rights to be ravished from us."[58] Delaware Federalist James Bayard questioned what would happen if an unauthorized envoy brought back peace terms that the government was not willing to accept. If one party in the United States, in this case, quite obviously the Democrat-Republicans, urged their acceptance while the government rejected them, it would be a cause of great discord, possibly including civil war, he said. Bayard declared an action such as Logan's to be "separate only by a shade from treason."[59]

Harper argued that Logan's "weak, silly project" had achieved nothing but "a few trifling changes" from the French. But even in the best of circumstances, unsanctioned diplomacy of the type Logan engaged in would represent an intrusion of the very sovereignty of the United States, Harper said. The South Carolinian declared that the government, "if it had any sense of vigor, and is at all worthy of the trust reposed to it," should not allow unauthorized individuals to make peace, "even on terms which it desired." If the government wanted to raise an army or impose taxes, Harper asked, would it allow private clubs to do so on its behalf? And what would it say to a foreign government, asked Connecticut's Samuel Dana, if such an envoy tried to negotiate without the authorization of his government? "He must say, 'I have no power, I am undelegated; but our Administration is either weak or wicked, and will not do what is for the interest of the country,'" he alleged.[60]

Congressional Federalists didn't stick exclusively to the substance of the bill or the debate surrounding it, in some cases taking turns defaming the character of any person who would have the "incredible nonsense" to imagine that he could bring Merlin and Talleyrand in line with nothing more than a set of unofficial credentials. "To me it is incredible, nor can I ever be led to believe it until I am forced to adopt a lower opinion of human intellect than even the conduct of this person had yet been able to inspire," declared South Carolina's Charles Pinckney.[61] * One congressman even compared Logan to Don Quixote, insisting that the doctor would have to be as foolish as the Man of La Mancha if he believed he could restore the tattered relationship between France and the United States, "by the mere force of his own private remonstrances or personal influence."[62]

To no avail, the Democratic-Republicans, led by Albert Gallatin of Pennsylvania and John Nicholas of Virginia, fought back with all their oratorical abilities. Nicholas asserted that he would have been proud to undertake a mission such as Logan's. And how, he asked, could it be considered a criminal act to restore peace to one's nation? "The endeavors of an individual to procure peace for a nation could surely never be construed into treason," the Virginian stated. In fact, he said, the time may come when it becomes necessary to force peace upon the executive branch.[63]

Gallatin agreed that some correspondence with foreign governments would constitute criminal interference, such as an individual who sought to bring his country into a war. He noted that such a situation, already cited by the law's supporters, had occurred in Gallatin's native land of Switzerland, when partisans had invited the French to seize the country. But what purpose would it serve to do the same with all correspondence between American citizens and foreign governments, even in cases where an individual had nothing but the best of intentions, Gallatin asked. If an individual American, "out of a sincere desire for peace, or out of his hatred for war," were to go to France and prevail upon the government to end its hostilities toward the United States, "he saw nothing either criminal or improper in such a conduct, but the contrary."[64]

The Democratic-Republicans vented their myriad grievances against the Federalist Party and its recent conduct. Just as the Federalists accused their

* Not to be confused with Charles Cotesworth Pinckney, the American minister to France who was involved in the XYZ Affair, who was a cousin of the congressman.

enemies of siding with the French in an attempt to undermine the Federalists and the policies of their duly elected government, the Democratic-Republicans chastised them as the party of war. If, Nicholas asked, "all individual interference is to be prohibited, the President having declared all negotiation to be at an end, how is peace to be procured?"[65] Nicholas said the proposed law would attach guilt not only to "the person who was lately in France," but to all who shared his views and his desire for peace. It may, he said, "excite a suspicion" against any peace overtures by the French government, giving the Adams administration an excuse to reject them.[66]

To the Democratic-Republicans, it was clear that the Federalists' motives extended far beyond their irritation with Logan. As with the notorious Alien and Sedition Acts, they viewed the Logan Act as nothing more than a vicious attempt to stifle dissent. Nicholas said he had no doubt that the true intent of the law was to "excite suspicion and clamor throughout the United States" against the Federalists' political enemies. William Claiborne, who had replaced Andrew Jackson as Tennessee's at-large representative, asked if the time had arrived when it had become a crime to simply be a Republican. Claiborne "believed this to be a law for the punishment of republicans," especially by leaving the courts so much discretion in determining someone's guilt.[67] Harper, by declaring that, were he in France and Talleyrand asked him for his opinion on the state of relations between their countries, he would not hesitate to tell him that France's conduct was "highly impolitic" without fear of running afoul of the law, gave Gallatin a perfect opening to describe how he expected the law to be enforced. "If a man is a Federalist, he will be innocent, but if he is an anti-Federalist he will be guilty," Gallatin said.[68]

Early in the debate, Gallatin pondered the extent to which the government may use the law to punish "indirect" correspondence with a foreign nation. Suppose someone wrote a book arguing that the United States should make peace on certain terms. Would that individual, he asked, now be subject to prosecution?[69] He wondered aloud how far the Federalists would go in passing new laws to stamp out opposition to their policies. Only a few months earlier, the Federalists had insisted that Congress must pass the Alien and Sedition Acts because they were necessary for the nation's defense. Now they wanted to go a step further. "If . . . we are to legislate on such arguments as these, what is the kind of measure we may not be called upon to adopt," Gallatin asked.[70]

As Congress debated the law aimed at his unauthorized mission, Logan defended himself from the critics who had maligned his name and patriotism. On January 12, the staunchly Democratic-Republican *Aurora General Advertiser* published an editorial from Logan in which he described his journey to France and defended his honor. The Federalist newspapers were "unworthy of notice," Logan wrote, but he could not ignore the slander of those in high office who had impugned his motives. "To defend and support the rights of our country as an independent commonwealth is certainly the first duty of every good citizen. But a state of war is inevitably attended with so many calamities that an enlightened nation will seek every honourable means to avoid it. With France the situation of the United States appears to me peculiarly delicate, having received from that nation the most essential services during our arduous struggle against the wanton injuries and oppressions of the British government. Under these impressions I embarked for Europe," Logan wrote.[71]

Logan recounted for the readers of the *Aurora* his arrival in Hamburg, the assistance provided by "that distinguished friend to our country," Lafayette, his discovery that President Adams's commissioners had left France just as he arrived in Paris, and his learning of the embargo that had been placed on American ships and had led to the imprisonment of the country's seamen. "Unacquainted with any law, moral or political, by which I was prohibited from benefitting my country, I availed myself of every legal means to procure an interview with influential characters, when, as a private citizen of the United States, I gave it as my opinion that it was in the power of France, by acts of justice and magnanimity worthy of her elevated situation, to restore harmony between the two republics," Logan wrote. He described his pleadings with French officials to lift the embargo against neutral American shipping and to release its seamen. And he emphasized that he went only as a private citizen, and not at the direction or request of "the most respectable citizens of the United States" who had been "implicated with myself respecting my late journey to Europe," a reference to the unnamed Jefferson and McKean. "If after these declarations, which I aver to be true, any person shall think fit without proof to assert or insinuate to the contrary, I shall regard or rather consider him as a contemptible propagator of falsehood and calumny; convinced that, upon the strictest examination, my conduct whilst in Europe will be found neither dishonourable to myself nor injurious to my country."[72]

But among the Federalists in Congress, Logan's missive fell upon deaf ears. The extent of the Federalists' distrust of the Democratic-Republicans was on full display as Harper wondered aloud what mischief could be done if an envoy simply used peace negotiations as a cover for more odious motives. Will it be denied, Harper asked, that "the agent of a faction" could go to France under the pretense of peace and advise the Directory how to act in order to "lull the country into security, increase its influence among us, and strengthen the hands of its own party?"[73]

Outnumbered, the Democratic-Republicans were unable to defeat the Logan Act. Adams signed the bill into law on January 30, 1799. But they achieved at least one victory in convincing their Federalist foes to add a provision to the law excluding people who sought redress for private grievances against foreign governments, such as those whose property had been seized. On January 16, the day before the House passed the measure, Massachusetts Representative Isaac Parker addressed the concerns of Gallatin and others that the bill was too broad and would inadvertently include American citizens who pressed their claims against foreign nations. Though Parker said he did not believe such people would face punishment under the act, he was willing to explicitly exempt such cases from the proposed law. Parker's amendment stated: "Provided always, That nothing in this act contained shall be construed to abridge the right of any citizens of the United States to apply by themselves, or their lawful agents, to any foreign Government, or agent thereof, for the redress of any injury in relation to person or property, which such individuals may have sustained from such Government, any of its agents, citizens or subjects."[74]

The Federalists' scorn and the passage of the Logan Act appear to have done nothing to diminish Logan's standing in the eyes of his fellow Pennsylvanians. The former lawmaker, who had served in the Pennsylvania Legislature from 1785 to 1789, was once again elected to that body shortly after his return. And in 1800, the Legislature elected him to the United States Senate, where he declined reelection after one term. Adams forged a treaty with France that formally ended the quasi-war in 1800, before Logan's election to the Senate.

During Logan's second year in the Senate, the Democratic-Republicans in Congress made an attempt to repeal the Logan Act, part of a larger effort to erase partisan laws left behind by the Federalists when they lost power. Senator Stevens Thomson Mason, of Virginia, introduced a resolution to repeal the act. Despite the Democratic-Republican majority in the chamber, the Senate voted against bringing the bill up for a third and final reading, defeating the measure. Logan was recovering from an illness at Stenton during the failed repeal effort, and learned the disappointing news upon returning to Washington.[75]

Logan never lost his Quaker's devotion to peace, nor did he let the dubious honor of the Logan Act prevent him from once more seeking it in a foreign land. As Logan left office in 1807, war clouds again loomed over his country, this time with its old nemesis Great Britain, setting the stage for his second mission of peace. Much as it had been when Logan traveled to France in 1798, the United States was still caught in the middle of Britain and France's wars against each other, which had spurred British attacks against American shipping as it sought to choke off France's maritime trade. The year Logan left office, the situation grew more precarious, as the British man-of-war *Leopard* fired on an American ship, *Chesapeake*, near Hampton Roads, Virginia, killing several sailors and seizing several more. Jefferson, who was nearing the end of his presidency, responded with his Embargo Act, which barred American ships from trading in foreign ports. By 1810, the policy had done nothing to bring the United States and Great Britain back from the edge of the abyss.

As Jefferson's presidency gave way to James Madison's, Logan implored the new president to keep America out of war. He didn't mince words with Madison.

"During the federal administration under Mr. Adams, a desperate faction was anxious to involve our country in a war with France. The people viewing the calamities of war with horror, entrusted the fate of their country in the hands of Men who professed maxims of peace, as the best policy to promote the happiness and prosperity of the United States. This desirable situation of our Country is like to be jeopardized by our republican administration, giving up their sound judgment, founded on deliberate reflection, to the temporary feelings of popular resentment, roused into energy by the clamor of unprincipled demagogues," Logan wrote to the president shortly before his trip to England. Logan expressed optimism that both the United States and Great Britain "would substitute a just and magnanimous policy, to suspicion, jealousy and cupidity." Much as George Washington had averted war with England when he sent John Jay to conclude a treaty of peace, and even Adams had made peace with France, "an act of magnanimity which obliterates many of his political blunders," Logan implored Madison to send two or three peace commissioners to Britain. "My heart mourns on account of the political insanity of my Country—Make use of your power and your influence, as the first magistrate of the United States, to arrest the progress of the destruction of your country—A war with Britain, at once unites us as an ally to Bonaparte, and will dissolve the union."[76]

Madison shared Logan's desire for peace, but warned that it would ultimately be up to Britain, not the United States, as to whether peace reigned. "[T]he question may be decided for us, by actual hostilities against us, or by proceedings, leaving no choice but between absolute disgrace & resistance by force. May not also manifestations of patience under injuries & indignities, be carried so far, as to invite this very dilemma?" Madison replied to Logan. If Britain would make reparations for firing on the *Chesapeake*, "[t]he way will then be open for negotiation at large." He impressed upon Logan the notion that the United States desired peace, but it was up to Britain to make that happen. "From this view of the subject, I cannot but persuade myself, that you will concur in opinion, that if unfortunately, the calamity you so benevolently dread, should visit this hitherto favoured Country, the fault will not lie where you would wish it not to lie."[77]

Once again, Logan decided to take action. He informed Madison that he planned to visit Great Britain, and that he would be happy to bring with him any communications the president had for the American minister in London. Madison took him up on the offer.[78] Logan did not expressly tell Madison that his trip to England was intended to help restore peace between the two nations, but the president must have at least suspected what Logan had planned, given his famed trip of 1798 and his fervor for keeping the United States from again taking up arms against Great Britain. And once he was in Britain, Logan didn't refrain from informing Madison about his activities.[79] Certainly others divined Logan's intentions as he prepared to depart. Phineas Bond, the British consul in Philadelphia, wrote to Francis J. Jackson, Britain's recently appointed minister to the United States, that Logan "has taken up his old Trade of diplomatic volunteering."[80]

Logan sailed from New York in February 1810 to gauge British public opinion and hopefully convince British leaders to call off their nation's atrocities against the United States and revoke the decrees that brought attacks on America's ships and impressment against its seamen. He met with cabinet officials and members of Parliament, discussing the state of affairs between the United States and Great Britain, as well as, of course, the latest agricultural practices in Europe. Many of the officials and other prominent Brits whom Logan met with shared his desire for peace, and he informed Madison that "a general anxiety prevails to preserve peace" with the United States. Unable to secure an interview with Prime Minister Spencer Perceval after several months in the country, Logan wrote him a letter, pleading that he lift the orders against American shipping and "declare herself the advocate of neutral rights." The fate of the struggle against Napoleon was at stake, he reminded the prime minister.[81]

Needless to say, Logan's mission was unsuccessful, despite committing five months of his life to a trip in which he traveled "one thousand miles thro' that country."[82] Without a doubt, Logan's expedition violated the law that the Federalists had passed to prevent just such a trip. But unlike John Adams and his Federalist allies, Madison made no move to punish Logan under his namesake law. Deborah Logan claimed that Madison "afforded him every facility" when he went to Britain.[83]

After the War of 1812 began, Logan was still adamant that it could have been averted, had the United States taken a different course of action.[84] Logan believed that both sides were at fault for the "unnecessary war."[85] Rather than blame his old friend, he decided that Madison "was influenced by men as devoid of principle, as of genuine patriotism."[86] To Madison, he warned of the horrors of a protracted war, comparing the ongoing conflict with Britain to the ruinous wars of Sweden's Charles XII and France's Louis XIV.[87] He counseled against the invasion of Canada, saying any territory the United States acquired would be "baneful monuments of our ambition, and injustice."[88] He also urged Jefferson to talk sense into Madison and persuade him to bring forward an offer of peace to Great Britain. Jefferson laid the blame for the "justly declared" war squarely at Britain's feet. But if Logan could suggest a true path to peace, Jefferson said he would forward it to the proper authorities. "[I]n the meantime its object will be best promoted by a vigorous & unanimous prosecution of the war," Jefferson replied.[89] Tragically, Logan's attempts to bring peace were no more successful in America than they were in Britain.

Never in American history has George Logan's act been used to convict anyone, and only once has an American citizen even been charged for an alleged violation. In 1803, a Kentucky farmer named Francis Flournoy wrote an article in the Frankfort newspaper *Guardian of Freedom* under the pseudonym "A Western American" advocating that Kentucky and other parts of the West, some of whose inhabitants viewed the Eastern states with suspicion, secede from the United States and form an independent country to be allied with France, which then still controlled the vast territory west of Kentucky, that would shortly become known to Americans as the Louisiana Purchase. The United States attorney for Kentucky, a Federalist holdover from the Adams administration, considered the article to be "indirect" correspondence with a foreign government, and had him indicted under the Logan Act. The case was quietly dismissed and became a moot point after the Louisiana Purchase made the Western lands Flournoy eyed as an ally to his proposed country official territory of the United States.[90]

But rarely has the Logan Act's laughable ineffectiveness stopped Americans from accusing their rivals of violating the law, which occasionally finds itself in the news still today. During World War II, former president Herbert Hoover's negotiations over food relief to war-ravaged Europe led Franklin Roosevelt's administration to accuse him of violating the act. Former vice president Henry Wallace faced accusations after railing against the Truman Doctrine and Marshall Plan during a 1947 tour of Europe. After Jane Fonda's infamous visit to North Vietnam, outraged Americans, including members of the Nixon administration, suggested that the actress could be charged under the act. Ronald Reagan accused Jesse Jackson of violating the act with his 1984 trips to Cuba, Nicaragua, and Syria, and later accused House Speaker Jim Wright of violating it during unauthorized negotiations with Nicaragua's Sandinista government. Angry Republicans lobbed accusations at Nancy Pelosi in 2007 after a trip to Syria, and Democrats returned the favor a few years later when forty-seven GOP senators wrote their letter to the mullahs of Iran. Ironically, Timothy Pickering, who, as John Adams's secretary of state was part of the Federalist frenzy against Logan, was himself accused of violating the act a decade after Logan's trip.[91]

The Federalists who passed the Logan Act in 1799 thought they were drawing a line in the sand against the usurpation of executive power and preventing subversives in America from collaborating with the nation's foreign enemies. In reality, they created nothing more than a popular empty threat for American politicians. All that, because a Pennsylvania Quaker tried to keep his country out of war.

Chapter 2

Speech Becomes Sedition

The Freedom of the Press is the Bulwark of Liberty.
—Benjamin Franklin Bache, in the inaugural edition of the *Aurora General Advertiser*

Imagine a blogger going on trial for writing that Barack Obama or George W. Bush was the worst president of all time. With his freedom hanging in the balance, what better proof could he offer of his own opinion than a subjective view of the incidents that led him to that conclusion? If nothing more was needed to convict a writer of political opinion than malicious intent to defame the nation's commander in chief, our federal prisons would overflow with columnists, bloggers, and cable-news pundits. But this was the very situation that many newspapermen found themselves in during the dark days of the Sedition Act.

It has been an unfortunate theme in America's history that when its people, or at least its leaders, feel besieged, the government has too often hastened to sacrifice its citizens' civil liberties. Lincoln did it as he strove to keep a fractured Union together during the Civil War. The Espionage Act reared its head during World War I, as the United States cracked down on agitators at home while fighting the Germans across the Atlantic. Uncounted Americans fell victim to McCarthyism and other excesses of Cold War hysteria. Many argue now that the government has done it again in the wake of the September 11, 2001, terror attacks.

But it happened first in 1798 during the administration of President John Adams, under the aegis of the infamous Sedition Act. At least fourteen people were indicted under the Sedition Act, ten of whom were convicted, with many victims coming from the ranks of the Republican press. Others who avoided the Sedition Act still faced common-law charges or other forms of harassment at the hands of the Federalists.[1]

The Sedition Act took an especially heavy toll on those who were associated with Philadelphia's *Aurora General Advertiser*. Three of its writers—Benjamin

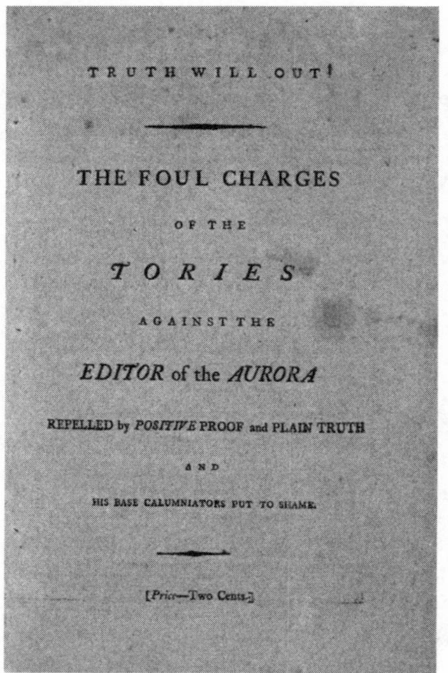
TRUTH WILL OUT!

THE FOUL CHARGES

OF THE

TORIES

AGAINST THE

EDITOR of the *AURORA*

REPELLED by *POSITIVE* PROOF and PLAIN TRUTH

AND

HIS BASE CALUMNIATORS PUT TO SHAME.

[*Price*—Two Cents.]

Benjamin Franklin Bache, publisher of the *Aurora*, rankled Federalists and helped inspire the passage of the Sedition Act with tracts such as Truth Will Out!

Franklin Bache, James Callender, and William Duane—would both inspire and fall prey to the act during the final three years of the Federalists' control of America's national government.

Like many of America's leaders during the Civil War, the two world wars, the Cold War, and beyond, Adams and the Federalists in Congress felt that mortal danger lurked for the republic, then still in its infancy. Abroad, that danger manifested itself in the form of an increasingly belligerent France. At home, in their eyes, it took the form of the Democratic-Republicans, whom they believed to be a "French faction" in America. That threat was most visible in the form of an increasingly vituperative Republican press. To the Federalists, no one epitomized that evil as much as Benjamin Franklin Bache.

Bache would never face charges under the controversial Sedition Act, likely saved from future indictment only by his untimely death at the age of twenty-nine. But his newspaper, the *Aurora General Advertiser*, would help to inspire the Federalists to pass the law in the first place. And his comrades at the *Aurora* who outlived him would be among the scores of journalists of the era who felt the wrath of the Federalists and their anti-sedition law.

Thomas Jefferson's anti-Federalist followers formed America's first opposition party, the Democratic-Republicans. They bemoaned what they described as the monarchical tendencies of the Federalists, whom they viewed as too favorable to Britain and its way of government. More to their liking was revolutionary France. Jefferson believed that "The tree of liberty must be refreshed from time to time with the blood of patriots and tyrants."[2] France watered the tree of liberty with gusto. And the Federalists, to whom revolutionary France represented nothing more than anarchy, decadence, and godlessness, worried that the Jeffersonians would import those bloody practices to the United States.

The bitter divide between them played out on the pages of bombastically partisan newspapers. The Federalists had their voice in newspapers like John Fenno's *Gazette of the United States* and the caustic William Cobbett's *Porcupine's Gazette*. The Democratic-Republicans found their standard-bearer in Bache's *Aurora General Advertiser*.

Bache was the grandson of Benjamin Franklin, born to his only daughter, Sarah. His larger-than-life grandfather had a tremendous impact on young Bache's life. When Franklin sailed for France in 1776 to win the country's backing for the colonies' revolution, he brought the seven-year-old Bache with him, along with his teenage grandson William Temple Bache. For more than nine years while he grew up in Europe, Franklin was the only parent Bache had. Franklin saw to his education—Bache attended the same boarding school as a young John Quincy Adams, who would later become a target of the *Aurora*'s vitriol—and taught him printing and typesetting, skills that would allow him to follow in his grandfather's footsteps.[3] Years later, his enemies would see the influence that Franklin had on his grandson, though they didn't necessarily believe Bache had lived up to his illustrious grandfather's name. "So it is to have had a philosopher for a grandfather, for the idea that was the food of much of his extravagance of mind, and placed him in a state of pretence where he was obliged to act a part for which he had not the talents," the Federalist William Vans Murray wrote after Bache's death from yellow fever.[4]

In 1790, Bache put his printing and typesetting skills to use for the first time. The first edition of the *General Advertiser* came out on October 2, declaring its mission to the world: "The Freedom of the Press is the Bulwark of Liberty. An impartial Newspaper is the useful offspring of that Freedom. Its object is to inform." The *General Advertiser* did not begin as a strictly political newspaper, but within a year of its founding, Bache shifted the newspaper's focus primarily to politics and world news. He would sit in the listening area on the floor of the House of Representatives, where he would diligently follow the debates of the earliest congressional sessions. The transformation of his newspaper would be completed in 1794, when he renamed it the *Aurora General Advertiser*.* In the November 1794 announcement of the rechristening of his newspaper, Bache said it would "diffuse light within the sphere of its influence—dispel the shades of ignorance and gloom of error, and thus tend to strengthen the fair fabric of freedom on its surest foundation, publicity and information." Bache also added a new slogan to the paper's masthead, *Surgo ut prosim*, which roughly translates into "I rise that I might serve," or "I rise to be useful."[5]

The political tone of Bache's newspaper reflected his own Republican beliefs. As the *Aurora*'s prominence increased, the Federalists grew vexed both by Bache's

* Bache's newspaper would more commonly be known as the *Philadelphia Aurora*, or simply as the *Aurora*.

gibes at Federalist leaders like Adams, Alexander Hamilton, and even George Washington, and by his ability to obtain documents and information that revealed information they would prefer stay hidden. The Republican press as a whole was despised by the Federalists, but the *Aurora* held a special place in many Federalists' hearts. So jarring and incessant were Bache's attacks that Abigail Adams said he had the "malice and falsehood of Satan."[6] Washington called Bache's livelihood a "malignant industry" that had assailed him with falsehoods "in order to weaken, if not to destroy, the confidence of the Public." And William Cobbett, who possessed perhaps the most poisonous pen in the early republic, called out his "notorious Jacobin" rival in the pages of *Porcupine's Gazette* as "Printer to the French Directory, Distributor General of the principles of insurrection, anarchy, and confusion—the greatest fool, and most stubborn Sans Culotte in the United States."[7] The Federalists' deep-seated hatred of the *Aurora* would continue long after Bache's death, as his successors carried his mantle through the turbulent election of 1800 and beyond.

The abuse heaped on Bache would not be limited to the printed word or, near the end of his life, criminal charges. Bache suffered physical assaults as well. In 1797, while touring a ship on the Philadelphia waterfront, Bache was attacked by a Federalist named Clement Humphries. The assailant was fined in court, but to the Adams administration, assaulting someone like Bache apparently did not constitute much of a crime, considering that the president appointed him as a bearer of diplomatic dispatches to France. And in May of 1798, a drunken mob attacked Bache's house while he was away. Bache's wife Margaret and their children hid inside the house until neighbors chased the riotous crowd away.[8]

Jefferson knew the importance of the press to the Republican cause, at one point urging James Madison to help find new subscribers to the newspapers, "for if these papers fall, republicanism will be entirely brow-beaten."[9] Surely the Federalists hoped so as well. Some Federalists considered trying to shut down Bache's press as early as at least 1796, when he published a letter from Pierre Adet, the French minister to the United States, to Secretary of State Timothy Pickering, which contained a litany of France's grievances against America.[10] It would be another two years, however, before the Federalists took drastic action.

While Bache's name is often associated with the injustices of the Sedition Act, it was a simpler common-law charge of seditious libel that finally brought him into court. In fact, the Sedition Act was still being debated in Congress when Bache was charged. The charge would be brought in response to one of Bache's greatest and most politically charged scoops: the publication of a letter, until then unknown to the public, from French foreign minister Charles Maurice de Talleyrand to America's envoys. The letter was a laundry list of French outrage over the United States' treaty with Great Britain, American newspapers' invective against France, and an alleged desire by the United States to force war upon his country, which, at the time, seemed a very real possibility.[11] For Federalists who had long alleged that Bache was nothing more than a French agent, his publication of the Talleyrand letter on June 18, 1798, was the smoking gun they needed.

Abigail Adams had declared that the actions of Bache and others were so criminal that they should be brought before a grand jury, and predicted that they would provoke a backlash that would silence them. "[T]he wrath of an insulted people will by & by break upon him," the First Lady wrote. Those words would soon prove prophetic.[12]

In the case of Bache and the Talleyrand letter, there was no need to wait for Congress to pass a Sedition Act. On June 26, 1798, Richard Peters, a Federalist judge, issued an arrest warrant for Bache on a charge of seditious libel, a common-law crime, stating that he had libeled the president and his administration "in a manner tending to excite sedition, and opposition to the laws, by sundry publications and re-publications." Bache was released from jail after two friends posted a $1,000 bond, and set to work defending himself from the charge.[13] The next day, the *Aurora* announced the arrest to its readers. Bache's newspaper insisted that the case was bogus because federal courts had no jurisdiction over a common-law libel case.* But the ultimate decision, the *Aurora* declared, would rest not on jurisdiction, but on the freedom of the press.[14]

The Federalists finally had Bache right where they wanted him. But there was more work to be done, more of his kind who needed to be chastened. Congress had already taken up the Naturalization Act, which dramatically increased the amount of time a foreigner must live in the United States before becoming eligible for citizenship, and the Alien Friends Act, which gave the president carte blanche to deport any foreigner he deemed dangerous to the country. Now they were ready to set the final piece of their repressive machinery that would collectively become known as the Alien and Sedition Acts.

On June 26, the same day as Bache's arrest, Maryland senator James Lloyd introduced a bill to "define and punish the crime of sedition."** The act's notorious Section 2 stated:

---

* Ironically, Robert Goodloe Harper, a Federalist congressman and a supporter of the Sedition Act, would state several weeks later, during the House of Representatives' debate on the bill, that he believed federal courts had no jurisdiction over common-law libel offenses. The comment was unrelated to Bache's case. Harper was rebutting a comment from John Nicholas, a Democratic-Republican congressman, in which he'd asserted that a common-law libel offense could not be committed against the United States government, which Harper denied (*Annals of Congress*, House of Representatives, 5th Congress, 2nd Session, 2141).

** The Senate would vote on the final passage of the Sedition Act on July 4. The perverted symbolism of the date of the bill's passage would not be lost on Bache, who responded by reprinting the Declaration of Independence in the *Aurora* (Tagg, 372).

> *And be it farther enacted, That if any person shall write, print, utter or publish, or shall cause or procure to be written, printed, uttered or published, or shall knowingly and willingly assist or aid in writing, printing, uttering or publishing any false, scandalous and malicious writing or writings against the government of the United States, or either house of the Congress of the United States, or the President of the United States, with intent to defame the said government, or either house of the said Congress, or the said President, or to bring them, or either of them, into contempt or disrepute; or to excite against them, or either or any of them, the hatred of the good people of the United States, or to stir up sedition within the United States, or to excite any unlawful combinations therein, for opposing or resisting any law of the United States, or any act of the President of the United States, done in pursuance of any such law, or of the powers in him vested by the constitution of the United States, or to resist, oppose, or defeat any such law or act, or to aid, encourage or abet any hostile designs of any foreign nation against United States, their people or government, then such person, being thereof convicted before any court of the United States having jurisdiction thereof, shall be punished by a fine not exceeding two thousand dollars, and by imprisonment not exceeding two years.*[15]

Under the law, people accused of violating the act could exonerate themselves by providing evidence of the truth of their words, a difficult proposition for those who were dragged into court for vilifying their opponents as tyrants and closet monarchists. Failure to do so could land violators in prison for up to two years. The act was set to expire on March 1, 1801, which would be three days before the inauguration of Jefferson, whose victory in the presidential contest was at least partly attributable to public anger over the Sedition Act.

Federalists had bandied about the idea of the Sedition Act for months, and there was no murkiness surrounding its intention: to clamp down on the Republican press. In April, Jefferson warned Madison that the Federalists had their hearts set on an anti-sedition law, and that, "The object of that is the suppression of the whig presses. Bache's has been particularly named."[16] Shortly before Bache published the Talleyrand letter in the *Aurora*, Massachusetts Federalist Stephen Higginson told Secretary of State Pickering that "seditions, conspiracies, seductions, and all the Arts which the French use to fraternize and overturn nations, must be guarded against by strong and specific acts of Congress."[17]

In Congress, the Federalists made no effort to disguise the target of the Sedition Act. Connecticut congressman John Allen, who would lead the charge for the act in the House, opened the discussion by warning of newspapers that sought to "overturn and ruin the Government" by printing falsehoods against the people's elected representatives out of hostility to liberty and free government. As if anyone in the chamber were unclear about whom he was referring to, Allen demonstrated his case by reading several passages from the *Aurora*. A June 28 article, Allen noted, accused the government of seeking war against France, whose peace overtures it rejected while threatening hostilities for refusing to treat. "Such paragraphs need but little comment. The public agents are charged with crimes, for which, if true, they ought to be hung," Allen sneered. In another piece, by mockingly suggesting that the Sedition Act would soon make Philadelphia less free than Constantinople, Bache sought to convince his "poor, deluded readers" that a vast conspiracy was at hand, the congressman asserted. After referencing the opprobrium recently heaped on President Adams in New York's *Time-Piece*, another Republican paper, Allen offered a perverse antecedent to Supreme Court Justice Oliver Wendell Holmes's famous declaration that the First Amendment did not grant the right to yell "fire" in a crowded theater,* questioning whether the freedom of the press guaranteed by the Constitution allowed newspapers to simply cast whatever aspersions they wanted against anyone, regardless of the truth. "Because I have the liberty of locomotion, of going where I please, have I a right to ride over the footman in the path?" he asked.[18]

The very act of urging resistance to the Sedition Act and trying to "render it odious among the people," among other statements, were no less than "deadly thrusts at our liberty," Allen proclaimed. Had the term *Orwellian* existed at that time, it surely would have been applied to Allen's thesis: To publicly oppose the Sedition Act was an act of sedition in and of itself.[19]

The Democratic-Republicans pointed out the obvious—that the bill would be used to silence critics of the "temporary majority" in Congress. Democratic-Republican congressman Albert Gallatin chided Allen. In order to prove a conspiracy against the government, he said, Allen had provided nothing more than a few newspaper articles that were not seditious, and at worst, were perhaps in some cases erroneous. And even those would not be punishable by the Sedition Act, Gallatin said. The Swiss-born Gallatin would, of course, be incorrect in that prediction. However, he was quite prescient in predicting how and why the Sedition Act would be employed against the Federalists' enemies by men such as Allen. "His idea was to punish men for stating facts which he happened to disbelieve, or for enacting and avowing opinions, not criminal, but perhaps erroneous," Gallatin alleged. Asked Gallatin, "For by what rule of evidence could he discover and know what was really the writer's belief?" By singling out Bache's claim that Philadelphia would soon be less free than Constantinople, Gallatin told Allen that he would only prove the *Aurora* right. "In order to convince the writer of his error, that gentleman not only supports the bill, but avows principles perfectly calculated to justify the assertions contained in the paragraph," he said.[20]

---

* Holmes would make that comment in defense of the 1917 Espionage Act, whose suppression of civil liberties has often been compared to the Sedition Act.

And the Democratic-Republicans vainly protested that the bill was unconstitutional. "No gentleman in support of this bill has gone into the constitutional question. No one has shown what part of the Constitution will authorize the passage of a law like this," North Carolina's Nathaniel Macon said. Of course, the Supreme Court would not establish the principle of judicial review until its landmark ruling in *Marbury v. Madison* five years later. As such, the constitutionality of the Sedition Act was never challenged in court.[21]

Perhaps seeing at least some of the realities of what the law would really do, the Federalists sought to mildly soften the blow. Harper briefly proposed an amendment stating that nothing in the Sedition Act was intended to curtail Americans' freedom of speech. After a discussion with Delaware's James Bayard, he withdrew the amendment and replaced it with another of Bayard's making, stating that anyone prosecuted under the law could present "the truth of the matter" in his defense, with the job of determining that truth ultimately falling to the jury.[22] It was to have little effect when defendants pleaded their cases.

Adams signed the Sedition Act on July 14, and Bache responded by warning his readers to "hold their tongues and make toothpicks of their pens." It was not advice that he would follow personally. With Adams's signature on the act, the *Aurora* trumpeted, it was now a federal crime to print, write, or speak any criticism of the federal government, the president, or the Congress, though Bache wryly noted that it was still permissible to criticize Vice President Jefferson. "Like the British monarch, John Adams now has Alien and Sedition Acts to silence his critics," Bache wrote on the day of the signing. Bache continued to yank at Adams's tail. Under the heading, "Something like treason by the new bill," Bache observed in the July 19 edition that it wasn't so long ago that some thought America could not have a worse man as president than George Washington. "[B]ut we learn that they have since, from the most complete conviction, acknowledged the error of their opinion."[23]

Several days later, Bache ominously reported the first arrest under the Sedition Act: William Durrell, the Republican editor of the *Mount Pleasant Register* in upstate New York. "Today's edition of the *Mount Pleasant Register* is the last that will ever appear," he informed his readers. He also reported that the *Time-Piece* had ceased publication, announcing "that no libelous or inflammatory matter shall be inserted in [this] paper in [the] future."[24] The Republicans' worst fears would quickly come to pass.

Meanwhile, Federalist newspapers cheered the passage of the new sedition law. The *Columbian Centinel*, a Federalist newspaper, praised supporters of the Adams administration as true patriots while decrying the Federalists' opponents as anarchists, Jacobins, and traitors. "It is patriotism to write in favor of our government—it is sedition to write against it."[25] Cobbett helpfully included a list of seditious newspapers he thought worthy of prosecution in *Porcupine's Gazette*.[26]

Bache would not live long enough to fall prey to the Sedition Act, though his writings in the weeks after the bill's passage would have provided the Federalists with ample opportunities. On September 10, 1798, Bache would fall instead to a far greater threat—the yellow fever outbreak then raging through Philadelphia. "In ordinary times the loss of such a man would be a source of public sorrow—in these times men who see, and think, and feel for their country and posterity can alone appreciate the loss—the loss of a man inflexible in virtue, unappalled by power or persecution—and who in dying knew no anxieties but what were excited by his apprehensions for his country—and for his young family," his widow, Margaret, who was pregnant with their fourth child at the time, would write in the *Aurora*.

Fewer tears were shed by the Federalists. Cobbett did not spare the grieving Margaret from the cruel words he'd for years directed at her husband. "Whether bearded or not bearded, whether dressed in breeches or petticoats . . . shall receive no quarter from me," he announced in *Porcupine's Gazette*. He made good on his claim, often including heavy doses of sexual innuendo in his attacks on "Mother Bache."[27]

In death, Bache would escape his charge of seditious libel, and likely prosecution under the Sedition Act, whose passage he had inspired. But his colleagues from the *Aurora* would bear the brunt for him. One of those comrades was William Duane, whom Bache's wife, Margaret, placed in charge of her husband's beloved newspaper after his death.

Long before he became a journalistic thorn in the Federalists' side, Duane had a storied history of causing trouble at newspapers in other countries. Born to recent immigrants from Ireland near Lake Champlain in upstate New York, Duane moved with his mother to her native land at the age of eleven, after his father died. When he was twenty-one years old, Duane got a job as a parliamentary reporter for a London newspaper, but was fired for including comments in an article that were deemed libelous to the government. So the young American enlisted in the East India Company's private military service and moved to Calcutta. But the quarrelsome Duane quickly clashed with his superiors, and left to become editor of the *Bengal Journal*, where he devoted himself to the cause of liberty.[28]

Duane's second newspaper job ended even worse than his first. Duane wrote an article implying that Colonel Canaple, the royalist commander of a French outpost near Calcutta, who had taken refuge with the British after fleeing from French revolutionaries who had threatened to execute him, had spread false rumors about the death of Earl Cornwallis, the commander in chief of British India, who at the time was on a military campaign. The commander filed a complaint against Duane and the British authorities, eager to maintain good relations with French royalists, arrested him. Duane informed his captors that he was "born and bred in the bosom of America and confirmed in my love of freedom by a long residence under the British Government."

Facing deportation, Duane was saved when the French commander he'd offended died and was replaced by a figure more sympathetic to both the French Revolution and to him, who asked that the charges be dropped.[29] After the Canaple incident, Duane started a new newspaper, *Indian World*. His final expulsion from India would result not from his writings, but from an assault conviction against two British colonists. "Englishmen, I have experienced the blessings of Liberty in your country and for a time I wished to be as one of you," Duane wrote in a final message to his readers on December 26, 1794. Now he would return to America where, "I shall be received with esteem. . . . I left them without disgrace, I return without disgrace, I trust in God I shall find them free, that I may forget if possible that Slavery exists anywhere." Before leaving the country, Duane accepted an invitation to what he thought would be a conciliatory meeting with the British governor of the colony. Instead, the governor's Indian sepoys brutally beat him, and Duane was deported back to England.[30]

Back in Britain, Duane became editor of the *Telegraph*, the official newspaper of the London Corresponding Society. Three days after a peaceful October 1795 rally hosted by the society, a mob attacked King George III in St. James Park, and because the attackers yelled radical slogans from the society's event, the crown blamed it for the violent outburst. More ominously, Parliament passed an anti-treason and anti-sedition act in response. After Duane spoke to a crowd of three hundred thousand at another rally hosted by the society a couple weeks later, Duane was charged under the new law. Before he could be tried, Duane left Britain to return to his native country.[31]

In July 1798, Bache hired Duane to replace James Callender, an acerbic writer for the *Aurora* who had fled Philadelphia during the congressional debates over the Sedition Act, which he was certain would be used against him. On November 1, the *Aurora* resumed printing with its new chief at the helm.* It would not be long before he became as troublesome to the Federalists as his departed boss.

Duane was at the center of several contentious episodes before ultimately facing charges under the Sedition Act. The first occurred as he and several comrades protested against another of the Federalists' repressive laws. One Sunday in February 1799, Duane, whose enemies had already dubbed him an "Irish revolutionary" due to his heritage, went with three Irish militants to St. Mary's Roman Catholic Church in Philadelphia to collect signatures on a petition denouncing the Alien Friends Act. The group had posted flyers on the doors and gates of the church,

---

* Duane would take Bache's place not only at his newspaper, but in his family, marrying the widow Margaret Bache in 1800.

urging parishioners to sign the petition. After the service, Duane's comrade, James Reynolds, was standing on a tombstone and speaking to a group of twenty or thirty people when a fifteen-year-old boy insulted him. The incident escalated rapidly from there. Witnesses said Reynolds responded by pulling a gun on the teenager and holding it to his chest. A crowd disarmed Reynolds and dragged him to the mayor's office, where he was charged with inciting a riot. Duane and his three friends were cleared of the charges, but more serious trouble loomed.[32]

About two months after the St. Mary's fracas, Duane published an editorial criticizing a Pennsylvania militia unit for its conduct in suppressing Fries's Rebellion, an armed revolt by farmers who were protesting against a federal property tax. Thirty members of the militia regiment, led by Captain Joseph McKean, marched into Duane's second-floor pressroom and demanded to know which unit he'd insulted in his article. When Duane refused, an angry McKean slapped him and Duane punched back, sparking a brawl. The woefully outnumbered Duane was dragged by soldiers downstairs and into a courtyard, where they beat him severely.[33]

The article criticizing the militia didn't result in any Sedition Act charges, though as far as the Federalists were concerned, Duane had been pressing his luck. That luck ran out on June 24, 1799, when Duane published an article accusing Pickering of being under the influence, and maybe even in the pay, of the British. Pickering told President Adams that he wanted Duane charged under the Sedition Act and deported under the Alien Friends Act. Before President Adams could act on his secretary of state's request, Pickering had Duane arrested for seditious libel, as Bache had been before him. Federalists, including Washington, cheered the arrest. The secretary of state also planned Sedition Act charges as well, clipping newspaper articles from the *Aurora* in support of a future case.

Duane's trial was set for October 1799. But within a week, the charges were dropped. Many presumed Adams had called it off himself to prevent the public disclosure of a 1792 letter in which the then vice president had aired his own suspicions that the English held sway over Pickering, whose appointment as ambassador to England he suspected to be the result of "much British influence." The wheels of justice were not moving nearly fast enough for Pickering, who decided to take a new route against Duane.[34]

The result was a bizarre courtroom drama that played out in the United States Senate. A vengeful Pickering convinced the Senate to convene a court of its own against the *Aurora* publisher on a new charge of sedition, for publishing a still-secret elections law that the upper chamber had been considering, which would have created a Federalist-dominated congressional committee to count electoral votes—a flagrant attempt to help Adams in the looming election against Jefferson. The Senate found Duane guilty of a "high breach of the privileges of this house" without even calling him to appear in his own defense.[35] The Federalist lawmakers would not bring Duane into their impromptu court to defend himself until several months later, when he was scheduled to receive his sentence.

With Jefferson presiding over the Senate, Duane appeared to receive his punishment. But the Federalists would not allow his attorneys to present the defense they wanted to make, which challenged the Senate's jurisdiction to hear his case. Duane and his attorneys, Thomas Cooper and Alexander James Dallas, had anticipated this; they decided beforehand that rather than submit to these intolerable restrictions from what they already considered a kangaroo court, his counsel would simply resign in protest and Duane would refuse to appear again. "I will not degrade myself by submitting to appear before the senate with their gag in my mouth," Cooper declared.[36] Two days later, on March 26, Jefferson, the Senate's presiding officer, was left with no choice but to issue an arrest warrant against Duane for contempt of court. Duane went into hiding until the Senate adjourned for the session and the warrant expired.[37]

The fugitive Duane did not run far. He claimed to have continued staying mostly at his own home while he ran out the clock on the warrant. He even continued writing his scathing editorials for the *Aurora*, defying a law intended "to terrify printers into silence or servility."[38] But while Duane may have figured out how to evade the Senate's warrant, the Federalists were not prepared to leave things at that. The Adams administration had grumbled for months about the need to charge him under the Sedition Act. The day before Duane's arrest, the president vented to Pickering about the reluctance of William Rawle, United States attorney for Pennsylvania, to charge Duane under the Sedition Act for his attacks against the secretary of state, noting, "If Mr. Rawle does not think this paper Libellous he is not fit for his office, and if he does not prosecute it, he will not do his Duty."[39]

Now was the time to bring the full weight of the Sedition Act to bear against Duane. Adams wrote to Pennsylvania's attorney general and the federal district attorney for Philadelphia and told them to bring charges for Duane's criticism of the Electoral College bill.[40]

On October 17, Duane was finally indicted under the Sedition Act, though justice was not as sweet or as swift as the Federalists would have liked. Rather, the indictment simply fizzled out over time. Dallas, Duane's attorney, convinced the judge to postpone the trial on the grounds that about twenty witnesses who could testify in the publisher's defense had left town. The new date was set for May 1801, after the inauguration of the upcoming presidential election's winner. By the time the new date approached, Jefferson was in office, the Federalists had been swept from power in Congress, and Duane simply wrote to Jefferson asking that the charge be dropped.[41] Jefferson asked Duane for a list of pending public charges against him, "observing that whenever in the line of my functions I should be met by the Sedition law, I should treat it as a nullity."[42] Jefferson took a similar view toward other outstanding Sedition Act cases, which died with the loss of Federalist control.

Even without their weapon of choice or the power that came with control of the national government, the Federalists did not let up on Duane. In May 1801, a Federalist flour merchant named Levi Hollingsworth sued the publisher for libel. The suit was part of a larger Federalist plot to get a judge to declare that Duane was not a United States citizen, on the grounds that, though he was born in New York, he did not qualify for citizenship because he and his mother had left the country for Great Britain before the signing of the Declaration of Independence. The judge agreed, though fortunately for Duane, with the advent of a Democratic-Republican administration, he no longer faced the threat of deportation under the Alien Friends Act.[43] * Furthermore, Duane was unable to evade the jail sentence that the Federalists had long sought for him, and the publisher spent thirty days behind bars. Jefferson contemplated pardoning Duane, but even many Republicans thought he'd pushed his luck with his broadside against Hollingsworth, and persuaded the new president otherwise.[44]

Though Duane eventually slipped through their fingers, the Federalists still got their pound of flesh from his attorney, Thomas Cooper. In lieu of Sedition Act charges against his client Duane, the Federalists took out their frustration on Cooper for an anti-Adams article he'd written, arresting him on April 19, 1800. He was fined $400 and received a six-month jail sentence, during which he would continue to write letters to the *Aurora*, datelined "Prison of Philadelphia." Cooper would later express his disappointment that the Democratic-Republicans settled for allowing the Sedition Act to expire and halting all ongoing cases instead of repealing and repudiating it, which would have rehabilitated the reputations of people like him, who had already paid their dues.[45]

James Callender, who had quit the *Aurora* and fled Philadelphia on the eve of the Sedition Act's passage, was correct in predicting that the law would be used against him. However, he was mistaken in believing that Virginia was far enough away to escape its insidious reach.

Like Duane, Callender had long history of defiance that had forced him to flee Great Britain to escape charges of his home country's sedition laws. In his native Scotland, Callender had run afoul of British authorities for his advocacy in the Scottish reform movement under the tutelage of Francis Garden, Lord Gardenstone. The authorities investigated him for his authorship of an anonymous tract, *The Political Progress of Britain*, which detailed abuses of the British government and promoted Scottish nationalism and independence.[46] In January 1793, the government issued a warrant for Callender's arrest, and he fled to the United States. The following year, he began writing editorials for Bache's *Aurora*, where

---

* Duane became a naturalized citizen in 1802 (Phillips, 155).

his scathing polemics made him one of the Federalists' most hated members of the Republican press. He lambasted Washington for Jay's Treaty, which Republicans viewed as a vile accord with America's enemy, Great Britain, accusing the president of cloaking himself in the "marque of patriotism . . . to conceal the foulest designs against the liberties of the people." He revealed Alexander Hamilton's affair with Maria Reynolds in his *The History of the United States for 1796*. And he began ripping into Adams from the moment he replaced Washington as president.[47]

Callender's time at the *Aurora* came to an end in 1798 as the Congress prepared to pass the Sedition Act, which he believed to be especially designed to target him. He'd already become a naturalized citizen on June 4 to escape deportation as an enemy alien. To escape the new sedition law, Callender decided he'd have to leave town. Temporarily leaving behind his wife and children, Callender fled Philadelphia, never to return.[48] The Federalist *Gazette of the United States* announced the departure of the notoriously hard-drinking "Envoy Callender" to its readers: "Left this city on a tour to the westward. His business or destination is not known. But he was seen a few days since, near the 22nd milestone, on the Lancaster road . . . DRUNK."[49] *

After arriving in Virginia, Callender joined the staff of Richmond's *Examiner*, a leading Democratic-Republican newspaper in the South, where he again caught the attention of local Federalists, who formed an Anti-Callender Society, which was, in effect, a vigilante group that tried to run him out of town.[50] Being out of sight hadn't put him out of mind for his old enemies in Philadelphia either.

In the heat of the presidential campaign, the Federalists were eager to shut down their opponents with the Sedition Act. Callender gave them the opening they needed in January 1800, when he published a pro-Jefferson tract called *The Prospect Before Us*. The pamphlet castigated Adams, whose reign "has been one continued tempest of malignant passions." He alleged that Adams, whom he said presided over a venal and corrupt administration, sought to bring the United States into war with France, "for the sake of yoking us into an alliance with the British tyrant." Callender ended his jeremiad with an exhortation that the choice between Jefferson and Adams was a choice "between paradise and perdition." "Take your choice, then, between Adams, war and beggary, and Jefferson, peace and competency," he wrote.[51]

A copy of *The Prospect Before Us* soon found its way into Pickering's hands. Callender personally sent a copy to Adams as well, though the president could have picked up a copy for himself in any number of Philadelphia's bookstores. Abigail Adams became livid when she encountered the tract at a local bookstore, which she derided as "abuse and scandel [sic]," and said was "all the host of Callender's lies."[52]

---

* Callender's drinking would ultimately cause his death several years later. In 1803, he accidentally drowned in the James River while drunk (Tise, 291).

Supreme Court Justice Samuel Chase, who presided over many a Sedition Act trial due to his Federalist loyalty and his belief that "a licentious press is the bane of freedom, and the peril of Society," personally traveled to Virginia to secure an indictment against Callender and prosecute him for his offending pamphlet.[53] On May 23, he persuaded a grand jury in Richmond to bring charges under the Sedition Act. The indictment cited twenty passages from *The Prospect Before Us*.[54]

James Monroe, then the governor of Virginia, pledged not to interfere with the enforcement of the Sedition Act, expressing his hope that "the people will behave with dignity on the occasion and give no pretext for comments to their discredit." But nor did he stand idly by while Chase persecuted Callender. The writer was popular in Virginia, and the Sedition Act was not. The state's legislature had voted twice to condemn the offensive law. Monroe contemplated providing Callender with counsel, though former senator John Taylor rendered state assistance unnecessary after he raised $100 from the people of Caroline County to pay for Callender's attorneys, both of whom had ties to Monroe and the state government. Attorneys William Wirt, the clerk of Virginia's House of Delegates, and George Hay, Monroe's son-in-law, stood at Callender's side as he pleaded not guilty on May 28.[55]

The prosecution's case against Callender laid bare the absurdities of trying to defend one's self from a law intended to stifle dissent in the manner of the Sedition Act. Thomas Nelson, the prosecutor in the case, grilled Callender over his insistence that Adams's tenure had been a "tempest of malignant passions." "Is this true? What evidence is there of its truth? If not true, with what intention has he published it? Was it not to excite the contempt and hatred of the people against him?" Nelson exclaimed to the jury. Nelson also questioned how Callender could say with certainty, as he had in his pamphlet, that Adams would bring the United States into war with France. "You cannot say this is true, therefore, it must be false, scandalous, and malicious," he said. Adding to Callender's woes was the resignation of his attorneys, who had quit in disgust due to Chase's frequent interruptions and haranguing. An all-Federalist jury returned a guilty verdict in two hours. Callender was fined $200 and sentenced to nine months in prison. The sentence would reach its natural end on March 3, 1801, the very day the Sedition Act expired, arguably making him the law's final victim.[56] *

---

* When Callender later turned against Jefferson, he would again face charges of libel, this time for criticizing his former defense attorney, George Hay. The charge was an insult to add to previous injury. In December 1802, Hay, outraged over Callender's attacks against him, as well as for the publication of rumors that Jefferson was having an affair with his slave, Sally Hemings, approached Callender from behind at a drugstore and beat him with a cane (Slack, Charles. 2015. *Liberty's First Crisis: Adams, Jefferson, and the Misfits Who Saved Free Speech*. New York: Atlantic Monthly Press, 243–44).

Though many of the Sedition Act's victims were publishers, the law drew in Republicans from other walks of life as well. The most severe sentence handed down under the law wasn't to a newspaperman, but rather, to a laborer and Revolutionary War veteran named David Brown. The Connecticut-born Brown had become an itinerant evangelist for Jeffersonian Republicanism, traveling throughout New England preaching his anti-tax, anti-Federalist message.[57]

The law caught up with Brown's Republican road show in November 1798, on the road to Dedham, Massachusetts. Local Federalists were enraged when someone erected a "liberty pole"—a popular form of protest at the time—adorned with a placard reading, "Liberty and Equality—No Stamp Act—No Sedition—No Alien Bills—No Land Tax—Downfall to the Tyrants of America—Peace and Retirement to the President—Long Live the Vice-President and the Minority—May Moral Virtue be the basis of Civil Government." Despite the prevalence of similar liberty poles at the time, Federalist newspapers called it an "outbreak of sedition" that threatened to bring insurrection and civil war. Angry Federalists had already taken down the pole by the time a federal judge ordered its removal. On the orders of Adams and Pickering, the authorities set out to determine who was responsible for this affront.[58]

Benjamin Fairbanks, a prominent Dedham resident, was arrested for putting up the liberty pole. But the authorities soon determined that Brown, "a vagabond ragged fellow, [who] has lurked about in Dedham, telling everybody the sins and enormities of the Government," was the chief culprit. Brown was arrested in Andover, Massachusetts, and, unable to pay the $4,000 bond, was jailed in Salem to await trial. Fairbanks took at least some of the blame for the liberty pole incident, admitting to being present when the pole was erected, though he told Justice Samuel Chase, again presiding, that he'd been misled and did not realize how serious the offense was. For his honesty, he paid fifteen shillings and spent a meager six hours in jail for his crime. Fisher Ames, a Federalist Massachusetts congressman who served as a character witness for Fairbanks, shifted the blame to Brown, a "wandering apostle of sedition."* Chase decided to make more of an example of Brown, an outside agitator who'd come to "create discontent and to excite among the people hatred and opposition to their Government." Brown

---

* Ames's brother, Nathaniel, a local physician, was called to testify on Brown's behalf. After he twice ignored subpoenas to appear in court, which he argued had not been properly served, Nathaniel Ames was arrested for contempt and dragged into court. Historian Larry Tise described the Ames brothers' involvement in Brown's case as "little more than a political tug-of-war between two brothers who hated each other." Nathaniel Ames hated his brother and his Federalist friends, and had worked with both Brown and Fairbanks to advance the Republican cause. Thirteen years after the incident, the *Columbian Centinel* revealed that it was Nathaniel Ames who originally came up with the idea to erect the liberty pole outside of Dedham (Tise, 422–23).

also refused Chase's demand that he name his other coconspirators, further earning the judge's enmity.[59]

Brown was fined $480 and sentenced to eighteen months in jail. When his sentence ended in December 1800, Brown was still unable to pay the fine, and remained behind bars. His release wouldn't come until Jefferson pardoned him a few weeks after his inauguration, at which point Brown had spent a full two years behind bars, making him the most harshly penalized victim of the Sedition Act.[60]

The Alien and Sedition Acts would spark a tremendous amount of backlash against Adams and the Federalists. The laws prompted the legislatures of Kentucky and Virginia in 1798 to pass protests against the acts, known to history as the Virginia and Kentucky Resolutions. The resolutions, penned by Thomas Jefferson and James Madison, accused the Federalists of exercising authority not granted to the federal government by the Constitution. The Kentucky Resolution declared the unconstitutional acts to be "altogether void, and of no force."

If the Federalists hoped that the Alien and Sedition Acts would help them to maintain control in the election of 1800 and help Adams to fend off his challenge from Jefferson, they were sorely mistaken. The laws would become a key issue in the race, and would contribute to Jefferson's victory over his nemesis. The Democratic-Republicans would also take control of Congress, relegating the Federalists to the status of perpetual minority party until finally disbanded in 1824, years after it had ceased to be a relevant force in American politics.

Three days before Thomas Jefferson's inauguration as president, the Alien and Sedition Acts expired as scheduled. Thus ended the American government's first great exercise in restricting its citizens' civil liberties. Tragically, it would be far from the last.

Chapter 3

The Federalists' Last Stand

These kind of men, although called Federalists, are really monarchists, and traitors to the constituted government.

—Andrew Jackson

When asked what he thought an upcoming convention of Federalist opponents of the War of 1812 would accomplish, former congressman Josiah Quincy, one of the party's more radical members, joked that it would produce nothing more than "a great pamphlet."[1]

Quincy's prediction would prove prescient. But those who attended the gathering that became known as the Hartford Convention would spend the rest of their lives defending themselves from accusations that they had, at the very least, walked to the brink of treason, if not vaulted clear over it.

Federalist frustrations over more than two years of war culminated in December 1814 in the Hartford Convention, a meeting of the party's leaders from across New England. But the convention was so much more than just an airing of grievances about the war, which was deeply unpopular in New England. It was also a venting over the result of nearly fourteen years that the Federalists had spent in the political wilderness following the rise of Thomas Jefferson and his Democratic-Republicans.

As Quincy had predicted, the convention did produce a great pamphlet. The Federalists made a slew of proposals to ameliorate New England's suffering and concerns, and pitched several proposed constitutional amendments designed to recalibrate the balance of power, which had been tilting away from them since Jefferson had won the presidency in 1800. The ascendancy of Jefferson and the continuation of his Democratic-Republican policies under James Madison heralded the end of the Federalist Party as a national force. In New England the Federalists still held the levers of power and the hearts of the voters. But in the rest of the country, they had long ago been relegated to the margins of American

A Democratic-Republican political cartoon portrays King George III urging prominent Federalist delegates to the Hartford Convention to turn their backs on their country and leap into his arms.
LIBRARY OF CONGRESS

politics. Madison left no doubt that he viewed the Federalists as a political afterthought when he told a journalist in 1811, "The Republicans are the nation."[2]

Well before the War of 1812 began, Federalists became objects of deep suspicion in the eyes of the Democratic-Republicans, and the war exacerbated those concerns. Some believed that Federalists were actively aiding the British. In December 1813, Captain Stephen Decatur was trying to sneak his naval squadron out of New London harbor when two blue lights began shining on both sides of the Thames River, alerting the British, whose ships arrived to block his exit. New Londoners defended their honor amid accusations that they had tipped off the British, speculating that the signals could have been given by British spies on the coast, or could have been innocently lit by fishermen, or were perhaps the product of Decatur's own imagination.[3]

Decatur was certain of the source, and informed Navy Secretary William Jones that at least twenty other sailors in his squadron had seen those signals, or similar lights. "There is not a doubt, but that they [the British] have, by signals and otherwise, instantaneous information of our movements," Decatur informed Jones. He was indignant at the denials from the people of New

London, writing, "There are men in New London who have the hardihood to affect to disbelieve it, and the effrontery to avow their disbelief."[4] In his response to Decatur, Jones declared, "I . . . am truly astonished at the turpitude you have witnessed in the bosom of our own happy country."[5] The epithet "blue light federalist" entered the American vocabulary as a synonym for the treasonous New Englanders.

Some New England Federalists even contemplated forging a separate peace with Great Britain and leaving Madison and the Democratic-Republicans who started the war to fight it out themselves. In November of 1814, Massachusetts governor Caleb Strong sent a trusted ally, Thomas Adams, a General Court member who represented the British-occupied town of Castine (now in Maine), to Halifax to discuss the possibility with the British general, Sir John Sherbrooke. Adams was sent to find out how the British would respond if there should be a direct confrontation between Madison and Strong. The following month, after receiving instructions from Lord Bathurst, the British colonial secretary, Sherbrooke informed Adams that if the United States didn't ratify a proposed peace treaty with Great Britain, he was authorized to sign an armistice with the New England states and provide logistical support, though no troops, to defend themselves from the "resentment of the American executive." Thanks to Congress's swift ratification of the Treaty of Ghent, we will never know how far either the Federalists or the British would have been willing to go to uphold that agreement.[6]

Whether some Federalists in New England pined for secession is not in question. Some had been advocating in favor of separation for years, and the war only inflamed those passions further. Far more important to history is the question of whether the participants of the Hartford Convention did so. Modern historians believe the answer to be an unequivocal "no." The evidence points to the conventioneers actively eschewing disunion in favor of relatively moderate proposals, though their recommendations were still quite radical at the time. Nonetheless, that question dogged the participants and their children and grandchildren for decades to come. In many circles, the convention's members were branded as traitors, a charge that would stick with some for the rest of their lives.

Perhaps the stench of disloyalty would not have clung for so long had the Hartford Convention not followed more than a decade of machinations by radical Federalists, some of whom began agitating for a separate "northern confederacy" of New England states shortly after Jefferson and his Democratic-Republicans won control of the federal government in 1800.

Life in the political minority was a shock to the Federalists, as were the actions of the new president. Jefferson and his allies in Congress replaced Federalist officeholders with Republicans, repealed the Judiciary Act that John Adams had pushed through Congress in the last days of his presidency, sacked the judges whom Adams had appointed on his way out the door, and impeached Supreme Court Justice Samuel Chase.* While some actions, such as the ousting of political opponents from federal offices, would become commonplace in future generations when new presidential administrations took control, there was yet no template for how such transitions should work.

Judges and federal offices could be reclaimed under a future Federalist administration, but the Federalists first had to win back the power they'd lost. And developments under Jefferson would make it more difficult to reverse their political fortunes. When Jefferson purchased the vast territory of Louisiana from the French in 1803, Federalists saw that the inevitable addition of new states in the West, especially new slave states, would diminish their already-diluted power in Congress. As Congress in 1811 debated the admission of Louisiana to become the eighteenth state, and the first new state since Jefferson's historic purchase—the last new state admitted to the Union had been Ohio in 1803—Josiah Quincy warned of troubling ramifications. "If this bill passes, it is virtually a dissolution of the Union; that it will free the states from their moral obligation, and as it will be the right of all, so it will be the duty of some to prepare for separation, amicably if they can, violently if they must."[7]

The 1804 ratification of the Twelfth Amendment to the Constitution—which eliminated the system in which the runner-up in presidential elections became vice president and replaced it with the system in place today, where nominees for president and vice president run on a unified ticket—further curtailed the Federalists' ability to reclaim their lost influence in the national government. Whereas previously the Federalists could at least hope to win the vice presidency as a consolation prize in presidential elections and potentially use it as a springboard to the White House—the only two men to follow George Washington into the nation's highest office, after all, had been the sitting vice presidents at the time of their elections—the Republicans could now deny that prize to the Federalists as well.

Given the setbacks that the Federalists had suffered, the timing of the first New England secession movement in 1803 and 1804 should come as no surprise. Timothy Pickering, John Adams's former secretary of state who had recently been elected as a United States senator for Massachusetts, wrote to his fellow Bay State Federalist George Cabot in January 1804 that "separation" was the solution to the Federalists' problems. "If, I say, Federalism is crumbling away in New England, there is no time to be lost, lest it should be overwhelmed, and become unable to attempt its own relief. Its last refuge is New England; and immediate exertion, perhaps, its only hope."[8] Pickering began rounding up allies for a plot to separate New England from the Union and create a "northern

* Chase was impeached by the House of Representatives but acquitted by the Senate.

confederacy." He drew his support from a core group of Massachusetts Federalist leaders known as the Essex Junto.

The term *Essex Junto* was coined by John Hancock around 1778 during the fight over a new Massachusetts state constitution to describe a group of political opponents who largely lived in Essex County. The Junto disapproved of the original proposed constitution from 1776 in large part because of the weak executive branch it would have created, a defect they remedied in a later state constitution that was adopted. The term later came to be applied to Pickering and others from the radical wing of the Federalist Party with which John Adams feuded.[9] *

To many Republicans, the Essex Junto became a byword for disloyalty and treachery. Jefferson, distrustful though he was of Federalists in general, didn't blame the party as a whole for the separatist sentiments of some. "The 'Essex Junto' alone desire separation," he said of the 1803 plot. "The majority of the Federalists do not aim at separation. Monarchy and separation is the policy of the Essex Federalists." Late in the War of 1812, as Federalist delegates went to Hartford, Jefferson described to a friend what he viewed as the three types of Federalists: "1. [T]he Essex junto who are Anglomen, Monarchists, & Separatists. 2. [T]he Hamiltonians, who are Anglomen & Monarchists, but not Separatists. 3. [T]he common mass of federalists who are Anglomen, but neither Monarchists nor Separatists."[10]

Pickering and his allies tried to persuade Federalists in New York to support Vice President Aaron Burr in the state's upcoming governor's race in the hope of joining him to their secessionist cause. Indeed, such a plot was discussed at a dinner at Burr's home. Many years later, William Plumer, then a Federalist United States senator who later defected to the Democratic-Republicans, recounted plotter James Hillhouse telling him during the dinner, "The Eastern States must, and will, dissolve the Union, and form a separate government of their own; and the sooner they do this the better."[11] The central pillar of their plan was to entice Alexander Hamilton, the spiritual leader of the Federalist Party, to lead their movement. They invited Hamilton to a planned meeting in Boston in the autumn of 1804.[12]

Hamilton had no desire to see the republic he'd helped create dismantled. "I view the suggestion of such a project with horror," Hamilton told a friend. But he agreed to attend the Boston meeting in order to dissuade the plotters from bringing their plan to fruition. Hamilton never made it to Boston. His death at Burr's hands in their famous July 1804 duel saw to that. But Hamilton's death may have had more influence in squashing the secession plot than his presence in Boston would have. Without the man they had counted on to lead their revolt,

---

* The term is sometimes attributed to Adams, though it appears to have originated with Hancock long before the advent of the Federalist Party.

the plotters canceled their meeting and their secession plans petered out. But some intended the delay to be only temporary.[13]

Talk of disunion reared its head again in 1808. John Quincy Adams, writing of the rumors that had reached his ears, said he didn't doubt that some Federalists were entertaining the idea, given the aborted 1804 plot. But he predicted that the idea would fizzle out because it had not "sufficiently matured" and was intended only as a threat. "The policy of separation is, indeed, avowed in some quarters, with a sort of ostentation which indicates rather an expectation that it will produce its effect as a menace, than a deliberate purpose for execution. They who use it in this view have not yet learnt the necessary political lesson, never to threaten where you do not intend to strike." Adams was correct that the secession movement hadn't matured. Massachusetts Federalists proposed a convention in New Haven to discuss the possibility, but found no takers among its fellow New England States.[14]

The Federalists had taken their lumps in the years since Jefferson expelled them from the White House. Their political power had waned, and their New England heartland had borne the brunt of Jefferson's 1807 embargo. But for them, the worst would not come until 1812, when the United States once again went to war with Great Britain in what some would dub America's second war of independence.

War with America's mother country had been building for years. Neutrality in the successive wars between Britain and Napoleonic France had been no protection for American commerce, and in fact had earned it the enmity of both nations, who targeted the United States' shipping in order to prevent American goods from reaching their enemies' ports. The maritime threat, brought to a head by a British attack on the American ship *Chesapeake* off the coast of Virginia, led Jefferson to implement the Embargo Act of 1807, which prohibited American ships from conducting international trade—though it still allowed foreign ships to trade in American ports, as long as they did not take back any goods from the United States. Two years later, Madison grudgingly scrapped the embargo and replaced it with his Non-Intercourse Act, which allowed Americans to trade with most of the world but left in place the embargo against commerce with the British and French. Madison's act included a provision allowing trade to be reopened with either country if they recognized America's neutrality and shipping rights. An 1810 law allowed trade with both nations, but stipulated that if either Britain or France lifted its restrictions on neutral shipping, the United States would reimpose restrictions on the other.[15]

Eventually, France backed off, at least enough for the Francophile Madison to focus on Britain's depredations against American shipping,* which included

* France offered to remove its restrictions on American shipping only if the United States would reimpose its own restrictions against the British, which many Federalists argued did not meet the criteria of the 1810 law, known as Macon's Bill No. 2 (Wood, 665–66).

blockades, frequent seizures of American vessels, and the impressment of their sailors, who would be kidnapped and forced into British naval service. Amid the continuation of Britain's commercial warfare against the United States, Madison in 1811 signed a new law barring British ships from trading in American ports. But the British outrages continued. By mid-1812, Madison and the "war hawks" in Congress had had enough. Madison asked for a declaration of war to defend America's neutrality, commercial rights, and indeed, its rights as a sovereign, independent country, a status of its former colony to which Britain had never quite reconciled itself or respected.[16]

"Whether the United States shall continue passive under these progressive usurpations, and these accumulating wrongs; or, opposing force to force in defence of their national rights, shall commit a just cause into the hands of the Almighty disposer of events; avoiding all connections which might entangle it in the contests or views of other powers, and preserving a constant readiness to concur in an honorable reestablishment of peace and friendship, is a solemn question, which the Constitution wisely confides to the Legislative Department of the Government," Madison told Congress in his war message. Congress displayed the wisdom that Madison wanted to see, voting in favor of a declaration of war. The Federalists voted unanimously against it.[17]

Ironically, Britain had actually repealed its odious orders-in-council, the decrees authorizing attacks on American shipping, just days before the declaration of war. But by the time Madison learned of it, the iron dice had already been rolled and there was no going back. America's national honor had to be defended.

Historian Samuel Eliot Morison would call the War of 1812 America's most unpopular war, a bold statement considering that he made it while anti-Vietnam protests erupted across the nation.[18] The locus of that discontent would be New England, which had already suffered mightily under the successive embargo acts.

Republican suspicions of the Federalists, which dated back to the presidency of George Washington, were roused by concerns about where their loyalties would lie in a war against England. One of the greatest philosophical schisms between the two parties had long been their respective attitudes toward Britain and France. The Republicans, sympathetic to France because of its invaluable assistance to the colonies during the Revolutionary War, and its own revolution in defense of the ideals they cherished, were intensely hostile to Britain and distrusted the Anglophile tendencies of the Federalists, whom they viewed as closet monarchists, at best. The Federalists looked upon Britain as America's mother country, not only in the colonial sense but in terms of the values, traditions, and institutions it had bequeathed to the United States, and viewed postrevolutionary France as a hotbed of anarchy and atheism that the Republicans hoped to import to America. As the United States careened toward war with Britain in 1810, Joseph Varnum, a Republican congressman from Massachusetts, lamented the presence of "a party in our Country, fully determined to do everything in their power, to Subvert the principles of our happy government, and to establish a Monarchy on its ruins."[19]

Indeed, some Federalists viewed the outbreak of war as the signal to pursue the "northern confederacy" they'd long yearned for. After Congress declared war, Massachusetts Federalist Thomas Dawes wrote to Noah Webster, later of dictionary fame, that there was "but one way left to save us from the yoke of Bonaparte and Virginia." "You know what I mean," Dawes obliquely wrote. "And tho' late, I think with you, it is not too late." Robert Goodloe Harper, a South Carolina Federalist who would later represent Maryland in the Senate, had no doubts that the war would split up the Union, and seemed to embrace the likelihood. "The Eastern States will soon relieve themselves from a burden which they will consider as no longer tolerable, by erecting a separate government for themselves. Thus the dissolution of the Union, and all the direful evils attendant upon it, must, as we believe, be the last and necessary consequence of continuing the present war," he wrote in October 1812, just a few months into the war. The *Columbian Centinel*, the Federalist Boston newspaper, declared in February 1813, "The determination that was necessary in 1776 . . . is necessary now."[20]

Talk of disunion heated up as the war dragged on. After Federalist leaders decided to convene in Hartford, Pickering wrote in December 1814, " 'Union' is the talisman of the dominant party; and many Federalists, enchanted by the magic sound, are alarmed at every appearance of opposition to the measures of the faction, lest it should endanger the 'Union.' I have never entertained such fears. On the contrary . . . I have said: 'Let the ship run aground.'" Pickering suggested that secession would only be a temporary measure because the Southern states, in their desire to preserve the Union, would redress New England's grievances.[21] To another correspondent, Pickering said he "uniformly disclaimed" the idea of secession, as long as the liberty and safety of the Union as a whole could be guaranteed. "At the same time, I have considered that there may be evils more to be deprecated than a separation," he said.[22]

Some of the loudest and most radical antiwar voices emanated from the pulpits. New England clergy voiced fierce opposition to the war and to any participation in it. One Byfield, Massachusetts, clergyman, Elijah Parish, advocated an "honorable neutrality" after war was declared. "Let the southern heroes fight their own battles, and guard . . . against the just vengeance of their lacerated slaves," proclaimed Parish, who urged his parishioners to "once more breathe that free, commercial air of New England which your fathers always enjoyed," and to "Forbid this war to proceed in New England."[23]

Federalists were adamantly opposed to a war against Britain, which still held a special place in their hearts and was an important trading partner for the maritime commerce–dependent region. In Congress, the Federalist bloc unanimously voted against the declaration of war against Britain and mustered near-unanimous votes against most war-related bills. The only exceptions were legislation considered necessary for the defense of New England, such as coastal fortifications. The Federalists viewed it as a Republican war fought for Republican goals. They worried about the possibility of an American alliance with the tyrant Napoleon, and morally opposed the invasion of Canada.* Though essentially powerless in Congress, the Federalists used their control at the state level to frustrate the federal government's war efforts, passing laws to silence pro-war demonstrations by army recruiters, placing quarantines on newly arrived privateers and threatening to seize federal tax money. Politicians, newspapers, and clergymen discouraged military enlistment and subscriptions to war loans.[24]

But the most damaging step that the New England states took to obstruct the war effort was their refusal to provide badly needed soldiers to fight the British. The United States had only 6,774 active-duty soldiers when the war broke out in 1812, and the Republicans, ever fearful of standing armies that could pose a threat to liberty, had done little to expand the country's armed forces, even as war with Britain grew nearer. The New England Federalists, hostile to and suspicious of the Madison administration, didn't want its soldiers fighting for anything but their own defense, and certainly didn't want them fighting under the command of federal officers.

Shortly after the outbreak of the war, Major General Henry Dearborn, the United States Army's ranking officer in New England, ran up against the Federalists' first major roadblock. Dearborn ordered Massachusetts to provide forty-one companies of militia troops, along with five from Connecticut and four from Rhode Island. Dearborn wanted detached companies, without their full contingents of officers, to ensure that federal officers wouldn't be outranked by those from the state militias. The Federalist governors of New England, who were deeply opposed to any invasion of Canada, and especially, to their troops participating in it, wanted to keep their militias under their control. They refused to put their militia under federal command, which they justified on the grounds that the Constitution only gave the national government the power to call out militias to suppress insurrections or repel invasions, a condition they did not think the war had met. Furthermore, they claimed the constitutional right of the states to appoint militia officers. Connecticut lieutenant governor John Cotton Smith's response was typical of the New Englanders. "The Governor is not informed of any declaration made by the President of the United States, or of notice by him given, that the militia are required 'to execute the laws of the

---

* Troops from outside of New England sometimes shared that sentiment. In July 1812, two hundred Ohio militia members under the command of William Hull refused to cross the border, proclaiming that their purpose was defensive only, and that they would not fight in another country (Wood, 667).

Union, suppress insurrections, or repel invasions.' As, therefore, none of the contingencies enumerated in the constitution, and recognized by the laws, are shown to have taken place, his Excellence considers that, under existing circumstances, no portion of the militia of this State can be withdrawn from his authority."[25]

Madison, in his November 1812 message to Congress, said, "The refusal was founded on a novel and unfortunate exposition, of the provisions of the Constitution relating to the Militia."[26] Novel and unfortunate it may have been to Madison, but the governors were stubborn. The relationship between federal officers and state militia soldiers would be a source of constant friction in New England throughout the war.

In Connecticut, when state officials called out their militia in June 1813 to protect Decatur's squadron, they appointed Major General William Williams to command the troops. Normally, such a unit wouldn't have warranted an officer of such a high rank, but Massachusetts authorities wanted to ensure that their commanding militia officer would outrank the federal brigadier general Henry Burbeck. Burbeck, a Federalist, was amenable to the arrangement. That compromise continued under Burbeck's successor, but unraveled in July 1814 when Brigadier General Thomas Cushing arrived in Connecticut. Cushing demanded full command of the militia, and indeed, could justify it under the Federalist governors' constitutional criteria, as a squadron of British ships appeared off the coast shortly after his arrival. In response, Smith, now the state's governor, gave command of the unit to one of his own, Major General Augustine Taylor. Cushing objected, but withdrew under threat from Taylor. Cushing would have the last laugh, however, after the state was forced to assume financial responsibility for the militia for the last five months of the war.[27]

Elsewhere, other arrangements kept the peace between the Federalists and the Army, but proved to be only temporary. In Massachusetts, Cushing, who was stationed there prior to his transfer to Connecticut, agreed to keep state and federal troops separate. When Dearborn replaced him, he believed the agreement applied only to Boston. And when Dearborn called up 1,300 militia troops in June 1814 to fend off British attacks, he dismantled the militia's 64-person units, replaced them with 100-man units, as per army regulations imposed in 1813, and put federal officers in charge. The next time Dearborn asked for militia soldiers, this time for 5,000, Governor Caleb Strong demanded that they serve under state officers, leading the Madison administration to saddle Massachusetts, like Connecticut, with the cost of its own defense.[28]

New Hampshire was at first spared the internecine strife that plagued Connecticut, Massachusetts, and Rhode Island because it had a Republican governor at the start of the war. But after Federalist John Taylor Gilman won the governor's office in 1813, he too resisted federal control of the militia. Gilman called up seven companies of militia in April 1814 to defend Portsmouth, but insisted they be kept under state control. In response, the federal government withheld crucial supplies, leading the legislature to order Gilman to send the troops home. A transfer of power from the Republicans to the Federalists had similar effects in Vermont, where the new Federalist governor in 1813 brought home militia troops who'd been seen to take part in an incursion into Canada. The brigadier general whom Governor Martin Chittenden sent to deliver the order was arrested for sedition by the Republicans in Plattsburgh, who wrote back to the governor, "An invitation or order to desert the standard of our country will never be obeyed by us." However, most of Vermont's troops had already come home and the rest were discharged, since the campaign they'd been sent to participate in was over. A Republican newspaper called for Chittenden to be prosecuted for treason, and Solomon Sharp, a Republican congressman from Kentucky, introduced several resolutions in the House of Representatives demanding his prosecution. Fortunately for Chittenden, Congress didn't grant his requests.[29]

Chittenden later took a more conciliatory attitude toward federal officers, but was thwarted in his attempts to cooperate with the war effort by his own soldiers. In April 1814, Chittenden agreed to call up five hundred militia troops to defend Lake Champlain, but the troops, like their counterparts in Massachusetts, were so offended by the reorganization of their cherished state units that they deserted. After Chittenden urged people to volunteer for the defense of Plattsburgh, the Vermont legislature passed a resolution proclaiming that the state's troops could only serve under state officers.[30]

The only New England state to cooperate and agree to put its troops under federal commanders was Rhode Island, whose governor wanted to ensure that the national government would foot the bill. But federal agents in the state couldn't afford to pay for the soldiers' upkeep, leaving Rhode Island, like its neighbors, holding the bill.[31]

The five states of New England weren't the only states that were forced by the cash-strapped federal government to pay for their own defense, but, brimming as they were with antiwar sentiment, they were the angriest. By the war's end, the five New England states had coughed up more than $1 million in defense costs, with Massachusetts running up the largest bill, at $850,000.[32] * "So far as regards the common defence . . . the Genl. Govt. has deserted its duties," wrote Rufus King, a Federalist senator from New York, in September 1814. "Without money, without soldiers & without courage, the President and his Cabinet are the objects of very general execration."[33]

---

* Connecticut and Massachusetts would receive partial reimbursements in 1831, but the full reimbursement wouldn't come until 1861, as the federal government faced a far more serious secessionist threat than any that ever originated in New England (Hickey, 283).

By 1814, prospects for peace looked good. The defeat of Napoleon brought an end to the perpetual war in Europe and, with it, the perceived necessity among the belligerents to target neutral shipping. The United States and Great Britain were preparing for direct negotiations to end the two-year-old war between them. The worst of the war seemed to have bypassed New England. The bulk of the fighting had occurred in the Great Lakes area, Ohio, and New York. Congress had repealed Madison's most recent embargo of 1813. Some Federalists resisted the calls for a convention of New England states, which had been simmering since the war began, on the grounds that it could jeopardize the ongoing peace negotiations with Britain.[34]

But the winds shifted in the summer of 1814. With peace negotiations at a stalemate, the British brought the war directly to New England with a ferocity not yet seen in the Northeast. The war—detested in New England from the beginning, and growing increasingly more so as taxation, blockades, and proposals for conscription (though Madison and Congress never implemented the dreaded proposal) took their toll on the public's already thin patience—became more unpopular than ever as the British raided the New England coast and defense costs soared. Some areas in New England fell under British occupation. As Washington and the White House burned, the war seemed to be taking a turn for the worse across the country. Calls for a New England convention were on the rise, and Federalist leaders were having trouble tamping them down.

Noah Webster insisted that fundamental faults in the Constitution were to blame for New England's ills, and urged the leaders of Old Hampshire to demand that the Massachusetts legislature call a convention of New England states to find remedies for those flaws. The calls for a convention now sprang forth from Hampshire County, in the state's interior. At a town meeting in South Hadley in December 1813, prominent local Federalists instructed officials to go to the state's General Court and propose a convention. More than forty other resolutions and other such requests followed, urging state leaders to take action.[35]

Moderate Federalists initially opposed the idea, but public pressure was reaching a boiling point. Radical Federalist Francis Blake had begun advocating for Massachusetts to withhold federal tax dollars, a suggestion rejected by the legislature but taken up by the residents of Reading, who pledged, "Until the public opinion shall be known, we will not enter our carriages [on the tax rolls], pay our continental taxes—or aid, inform or assist any officer in their collection." To delay the calling of a convention, opponents insisted that the New England states wait until after the 1814 elections in order to ensure that the idea had the public's support. The results of those elections validated the pro-convention sentiment. After Henry Dearborn's clash with Caleb Strong—who had just been reelected as governor over a moderate Republican candidate who opposed many of Madison's war policies, but warned also against wholesale opposition to the war—Strong acceded to the public's demands and called the General Court into a special session on September 7.[36]

In his address to the legislature, Strong decried the federal government's failure to defend New England. Without financial help from Washington, the states of New England could not provide for their own defense and bear the burden of wartime taxes simultaneously. The Constitution, Strong declared, had failed to grant the states of New England their equal rights as parts of the Union. Both chambers of the legislature overwhelmingly voted in favor of a report calling for a convention with Massachusetts's neighbors. Connecticut and Rhode Island quickly followed suit. Due to the opposition of Federalist leaders in New Hampshire and Vermont, those states declined to participate, though some counties sent delegates.* To combat the perception that the convention would be dominated by Massachusetts, the states chose Hartford as its site.[37]

There were high expectations in some Federalist quarters. The *Centinel* suggested that the convention could plant the seeds for a new nation. "Advance boldly. . . . Suffer yourselves not to be entangled by the cobwebs of a compact which has long ceased to exist," the paper wrote. A newspaper article about the selection of Connecticut's delegates boldly declared that the "Second Pillar of a new Federal Edifice reared."[38]

Despite their misgivings, some prominent Federalists eventually warmed to the idea of a convention as, in Harrison Gray Otis's words, a "safety valve . . . not as a boiler," the only way to defuse public opinion and the heated rhetoric permeating New England without actually crossing the Rubicon of secession or nullification. The convention was about taxes, threats of conscription, and the common defense of New England, said Otis, who called secessionist threats "ridiculous," and said the convention was meant "to take measures to defend ourselves against the enemy; as the General Government cannot do it." George Cabot told his more radical compatriots, "We are going to keep you young hot-heads from getting into mischief." The key to preventing mischief lay in the selection of the convention's twenty-six delegates.[39]

Almost to a man, the states chose as their delegates even-keeled, rational moderates who would resist some of the wilder demands of their inflamed constituents. George Cabot, Nathan Dane, and Harrison Gray Otis led the twelve-person Massachusetts delegation. Connecticut sent Chauncey Goodrich and James Hillhouse as part of its seven-man delegation. Daniel Lyman and Samuel Ward led Rhode Island's team of four. The convention unanimously chose Cabot

---

* The convention refused to seat one of the Vermont delegates because he represented a county with a Republican majority. Three other delegates represented the two holdout states, from the New Hampshire counties of Cheshire and Grafton, and the Vermont county of Windham (Hickey, 276; Dwight, Theodore. 1833. *History of the Hartford Convention: With a Review of the Policy of the United States Government Which Led to the War of 1812*. New York: N & J White, 352).

as its president and Connecticut's Theodore Dwight as its secretary. The states took care to omit prominent radicals such as Pickering, Blake, Josiah Quincy, and Samuel Fessenden. Perhaps the only true radical in the bunch was Massachusetts's Timothy Bigelow, who received no committee assignments and played only a minor role in the deliberations.[40]

The "hotheads" whom Cabot had rebuked, seeing the purpose of their exclusion and the nature of the delegates, were wary of the entire enterprise. "I was opposed sincerely and most zealously to the Convention, because I found no one man among its advocates prepared to act. When you ask any of them what the Convention will do, you will find it is expected they will talk: talk of amendments, talk of militia, talk of defence, talk of being out of the national taxes what we advance, but nothing more," Massachusetts radical John Lowell wrote to Pickering. "I was wholly opposed to a premature and feeble effort." Lowell considered the delegates to be good men, but "not calculated for bold measures." Cabot, he said, would not "be in favor of any measures which will disturb our sleep," while Otis, he said, was "naturally timid, and frequently wavering." Bigelow was the only ray of hope that Lowell saw in the group. "Bigelow is really bold on the present question, has a just confidence in the power of Massachusetts, sneers as he ought to do (and as I am sure I do) at all the threats of vengeance of the other States; and, if he was well supported, I have no doubt that measures of dignity and real relief would be adopted," Lowell said.[41]

Suspicions were rife on the Republican side as well. While the Federalist radicals worried that the convention wouldn't go far enough, some Republicans were concerned that it would go too far. William Plumer, the Federalist-turned-Republican, saw trouble ahead, writing to a friend, "I expect no good, but much evil from it. It will embarrass us, aid the enemy, and protract the war. The prime object is to effect a revolution—a dismemberment of the Union. Some of the members, for more than ten years, have considered such a measure necessary." A Republican political cartoon portrayed King George III imploring Otis and other Hartford Convention delegates on a cliff above him to leap into his arms. Below the cliff, Caleb Strong prays to join the British aristocracy as Lord Essex, in honor of the Essex Junto.[42]

Others more accurately predicted a more measured response from the convention. "There will be much smoke and no fire," predicted one Republican newspaper. For the most part, Republicans were largely reassured by the moderate nature of the delegates. Madison made no moves to punish the Federalists or to block the convention, though he sent Colonel Thomas Jessup to Hartford to keep watch over the convention and on the Springfield Armory, a target of Shay's Rebellion nearly thirty years earlier.[43]

Some argued that a convention between the New England states would be unconstitutional, a charge that John Quincy Adams would later lodge against the delegates. At the time of the convention, Adams voiced his concerns about the conventions to his wife. "This is a dangerous measure, but I hope it will not have all the pernicious effects to be apprehended from it," he wrote. His father, the last Federalist to ever hold the presidency, seemed more derisive than concerned, joking in a letter to Plumer that the Hartford Convention was meant to resemble the Congress of Vienna, "at least as much as an ignis fatuus resembles a Vulcano."* "I cannot write Soberly upon this subject. It is ineffably ridiculous," he sneered.[44]

The delegates convened on December 15 at the state house in Hartford. The proceedings of the Hartford Convention were kept secret, contributing to the suspicion it aroused at the time and the rumors of treason that would harry its delegates in later years. Indeed, little is known about what went on behind those closed doors. The "secret journal" of the convention's proceedings provides a recitation of the days' activities and descriptions of the subjects discussed, which some participants and their allies would later point to in defending their loyalty. The delegates were pledged to secrecy, and they honored that commitment in the years to come. Otis gave the opening remarks and led the way in the deliberations. The first draft of the convention's agenda focused on war-related issues such as local defense, the invasion of Canada, fights over the command of state militias, and concerns over conscription. In deference to the more ardent delegates, Otis named a committee to draft a set of proposals, which would include a slew of amendments to the Constitution.[45]

On January 5, 1815, the convention concluded, and its report was published for the first time in the newspapers the following day. "The expectations of those who apprehended it would contain sentiments of a seditious, if not of a treasonable character, were entirely disappointed," Theodore Dwight would write in his history of the convention. Republicans breathed sighs of relief, as did moderate Federalists. Strong praised the convention for avoiding "fatal excess" when "passions of the multitude are inflamed," while Otis said it "had the immediate effect of calming the public mind throughout New England." Even the more-ardent Federalists, such as Pickering, found little to complain about. "I think the report of the Convention bears the high character of wisdom, firmness, and dignity," Pickering wrote to Lowell. "They have explicitly pronounced sentence of condemnation upon a miserable administration, and, stamped as it is with the authority of a body of men so eminently distinguished, that judgment cannot fail of making a just impression where it is needed."[46]

The report opened with a condemnation of the Madison administration's conduct of the war and the resulting consequences suffered by New England.

---

* *Ignis fatuus* refers to the lights caused by gas from decomposed organic matter that sometimes appear over swamps.

The litany of grievances, well aired by the Federalists throughout the course of the war, included "the authority exercised over the militia" by the national government, which the states of New England decried as unconstitutional, and the "destitution of the means of defence in which the eastern states are left"; fears of conscription and a law allowing the enlistment of minors in the military without parental approval; the failure to allow the New England states to provide for their common defense; the conquest of Canadian territory and the resulting manpower shortage that left New England defenseless in the face of repeated British attacks on the coast; the heavy cost of defense left to the states; the disruption of the commerce, "the vital spring of New-England's prosperity" that its states' citizens depended on for their livelihoods; and the burden of high wartime taxes.[47]

To ease the hardships imposed by Madison and the war, the delegates proposed "an arrangement, which may at once be consistent with the honour and interest of the national government, and the security of these states." The states of New England, the report stated, must be permitted to assume their own defense. Furthermore, the states must receive a portion of the taxes they paid to the national government so they could pay for their defense.[48]

Not content to limit their report to war-related issues alone, the delegates included a laundry list of complaints dating back to the beginning of the Jefferson administration, the myriad ways in which the Federalists had been shut out from positions of power and prevented from reclaiming them. The report expressed outrage over the predominant position the South had assumed in shaping the destiny of the nation, decrying the "combination among certain states . . . so as to secure to popular leaders in one section of the Union, the control of public affairs in perpetual succession." The delegates fumed over the removal of Federalist judges and the Republicans' refusal to appoint Federalists to positions of power while granting patronage to their own. They groused about "the easy admission of naturalized foreigners, to places of trust, honour, or profit, operating as an inducement to the malcontent subjects of the old world to come to these States, in quest of executive patronage," revisiting the fears of Jefferson's foreign-born adherents that led John Adams and his Federalist-controlled Congress to pass the repressive Alien Friends Act and Naturalization Act in the late 1790s. They bemoaned the administration's hostility to Britain, and, at times, France, as a sop to "popular prejudice." "Lastly and principally," the report alleged "A visionary and superficial theory in regard to commerce, accompanied by a real hatred but a feigned regard to its interests, and a ruinous perseverance in efforts to render it an instrument of coercion and war."[49]

The report included seven proposed amendments to the Constitution that would provide redress for the Federalists' enumerated grievances. Some proposed amendments were aimed at curbing the growing power of the slaveholding South. One proposed to eliminate the three-fifths compromise that granted

Southern states extra congressional representation for their slaves, while another would limit presidents to one term and prohibit two presidents from the same state from serving in succession, an obvious attempt to halt the continuation of the "Virginia dynasty" that had elected Virginians Jefferson and Madison, and would, after the war, send James Monroe to the White House. Another amendment would require a two-thirds vote in Congress to admit new states, which could have checked the trend of New England being drowned in an expanding congressional sea of Southern and Western representatives and senators.

Other proposed amendments sought to ensure that the evils of the War of 1812 could not easily be repeated. The conventioneers wanted to require a two-thirds vote in Congress to both declare war and impose embargos on foreign shipping or restrictions on American trade. Finally, the Federalists—xenophobic as they often were toward the Republicans and their foreign-born luminaries, such as Albert Gallatin—wanted to prohibit naturalized citizens from serving in Congress or holding civil office.[50]

The most radical nugget to be found in the report, the closest the convention came to advocating for separation and disunion, explained that, while the states of New England would not pursue secession, they wouldn't necessarily rule it out in the future. Should the "causes of our calamities" prove to be permanent and irreversible, the delegates proclaimed that "a separation, by equitable arrangement, will be preferable to an alliance by constraint." But that day had not yet arrived. And except under the direst of circumstances, that day could only come amid agreement from all signatories to the contract that was the Constitution. "A severance of the Union by one or more states, against the will of the rest, and especially in a time of war, can be justified only by absolute necessity." The delegates included a provision granting themselves the right to call themselves back for a future convention in Boston, "if in their judgment the situation of the country shall urgently require it."[51]

By the time the Hartford Convention completed its report, Americans weren't in any mood for dissent against the war. The Treaty of Ghent and Andrew Jackson's stunning victory over the British at New Orleans saw to that. News of Jackson's triumph, greeted with jubilation from the American public, followed the publication of the convention's report by just a few days. A month later, the peace treaty forged at Ghent in December finally reached the country. America's honor had been defended, and its people viewed themselves as the war's winners. There would be no second convention.

Theodore Dwight may have been correct in surmising that nothing in the convention's report would validate the accusations of treason and treachery the Federalists faced when they convened at Hartford, but that didn't stop their political enemies from alleging the foulest of motives and actions. The content of the report "did not stop the clamours of those who were unwilling to lose so powerful an engine of partisan warfare as this had long been," as Dwight later lamented.[52]

Writing to President James Monroe in 1817, Andrew Jackson, the hero of New Orleans, made clear his view of the Federalists' conduct in Hartford. "I am free to declare, had I commanded the military department where the Hartford Convention met, if it had been the last act of my life, I should have punished the three principal leaders of the party," he said. "These kind of men, although called Federalists, are really monarchists, and traitors to the constituted government."[53]

The accusations against the Federalists of the Hartford Convention would persist long after the convention adjourned. Years later, John Quincy Adams, after being accused of complicity in treasonous Federalist plots, lashed out at his former party, which he'd broken with in 1807.

The Hartford Convention, he averred, was the culmination of the conspiracy. "The Hartford Convention was unconstitutional and treasonable, and was the only instance up to that time of State resistance to the general government, and wholly abnormal, hideous, and wicked," he wrote.[54]

The 1820s and 1830s would see a wave of self-defense from the delegates and their heirs against the allegations that haunted them. An anonymous delegate, writing as "one of the convention," published a series of letters between the participants in 1820 in an attempt to achieve vindication against some of the more scurrilous rumors and assumptions floating around. In his *A Short Account of the Hartford Convention*, published in 1823, and "addressed to the fair minded and the well disposed," Theodore Lyman noted that if the official documents of the convention had contained any hint of treason, Republican editors would have gleefully published it. "[H]ave they not shouted Hartford Convention, crucify him! Crucify him! For eight years—and, forsooth, is it not out of kindness and good feeling that they have abstained all that time from publishing this most foul and traitorous journal?" Lyman wrote.[55]

Dwight published his history of the convention in 1833, writing that "the Hartford Convention, from the time of its coming together to the present hour, has been the general topic of reproach and calumny, as well as of the most unfounded and unprincipled misrepresentations and falsehood." Like Lyman, Dwight despaired that no amount of evidence seemed to satisfy the convention's accusers. "If there was any treason, proposed or meditated, against the United States, at the Convention, it must have been hidden in as deep and impenetrable obscurity, as the fabulous secrets of freemasonry are said to be buried, otherwise some traces of it would have been discovered and disclosed to the public before this late period," Dwight wrote. "No such discovery having been made, the inference must necessarily be, that no such treasonable practice or intention existed."[56]

The attendees of the Hartford Convention faced generations of scorn for their falsely alleged secessionist plot and for the Federalists' opposition to the

War of 1812, which accelerated the end of the Federalist Party as a national, and eventually, even a regional, political force. In the 1816 presidential election, Federalist nominee Rufus King mustered only thirty-four electoral votes in Connecticut, Delaware, and Massachusetts. Even the Federalist stronghold of Rhode Island opted for James Monroe. It was the last time the party would nominate a candidate for president. The Republicans won control of Connecticut in 1820, and Massachusetts, three years later, even winning Essex County, home to the infamous junto. Federalists clung to scraps of power in Delaware, Maryland, and North Carolina for a time, but eventually, their flame was extinguished in those states as well.[57]

Even after the Federalists fell completely off the national stage, "blue light federalist" continued as a derogatory term for anyone deemed disloyal. In a speech in which he railed against the Tariff of 1828, Kentucky congressman Henry Daniel derided his opponents as "dirt grubbers," "mud machines," and "blue light federalists."[58] In an 1830 article castigating the Anti-Masons of Little Falls, New York, a Syracuse newspaper took aim at a town officer, alleging, "he was a blue-light federalist; and when this signal was given to the anti-masons, they put forth their best efforts in his behalf."[59]

In his 1915 book *The Northern Confederacy*, Charles Raymond Brown seems to brand the delegates as at least guilty by association. While acknowledging that the Hartford Convention delegates "seem to have had in mind a different method of attack" than the radicals who favored secession, Brown writes, "Now perhaps we can safely say that the Hartford Convention was simply the crowning act of the Essex Junto, whose intrigues began with the Adams administration. The Convention was not a mere product of the War of 1812, because we recognize in these grievances of the very earliest, as well as the latest, grounds for Junto conspiracies. . . . In all of these we have heard the complaining and threatening voices of the 'Essex Junto,' and it seems almost superfluous to add that the Hartford Convention was truly an offspring of Juntoism."[60]

Perhaps the greatest dishonor bestowed upon the attendees of the Hartford Convention is that what little praise they would garner from future generations often came from Confederate veterans of the Civil War and their sympathizers, who for decades were fond of citing Federalist dreams of secession in defense of their lost cause. "They sat with closed doors, but it is known that their object was the discussion of the expediency of those States withdrawing from the Union and setting up a separate Confederation," read the minutes of one Confederate veterans' reunion, held in 1899 in Charleston, South Carolina. "They determined upon its inexpediency then, but published to the world the conditions and circumstances under which its dissolution might become expedient."[61] No doubt they and many others found inspiration in the report's assertion that secession, carried out against the will of the other states, "can be justified only by absolute necessity."

In a sense, one could say it was poetic justice that led the Federalists to be branded traitors to their country. In its heyday in the 1790s, the Federalist Party had no qualms about resorting to cries of "treason" when the Jeffersonians opposed their designs, even criminalizing dissent with the notorious Sedition Act and jailing those who dared to criticize their actions. And surely some Federalists in the years after Jefferson's rise crossed the line. But there is no question that the people of New England had legitimate grievances during the War of 1812, and that the Federalists' grand response, the Hartford Convention, was unfairly demonized. For their successes in fending off the rising tide of extremism at the convention, the delegates were rewarded with a lifetime of accusations and suspicion. Such was the fate of those who opposed America's second war of independence. Their power evaporated. Their names were besmirched. And all they got for their troubles was a great pamphlet.

Chapter 4

The Rogue Diplomat

We are making peace. Let that be our only thought.

—Nicholas Trist

"War is at best a horrid calamity, and those who wage war for the purpose of subjugating nations to their will are guilty of a heinous crime."[1] Those words, written to Nicholas Philip Trist by his grandmother when he was a young man, echoed in his consciousness for the rest of his life, and helped to shape the future of his nation. As an envoy sent to negotiate a treaty of conquest with Mexico, Trist would defy the president he served and, in an act of justice and sympathy for America's vanquished foe, strive to stop his country from imposing a harsher peace. Trist could not stop the United States from subjugating Mexico, as his grandmother surely would have hoped for. But he could stop his country from going further, preempting the schemes hatched by some Democrats in Congress and President James K. Polk's own cabinet to seize more territory, or even the Republic of Mexico as a whole. The result was the Treaty of Guadalupe Hidalgo in 1848, which brought six new states into the country and set the borders of the continental United States as we know them today.

When Polk needed an envoy to go to Mexico and negotiate the inevitable settlement that would follow the United States' roaring victory over its southern neighbor, Secretary of State James Buchanan's suggestion of Trist seemed a safe and reliable choice. Trist served as his friend Buchanan's second-in-command at the Department of State as his chief clerk. He had no political aspirations. He spoke fluent Spanish as a result of his eight-year term as America's consul in Cuba. And he was a Southern, pro-slavery, and pro-expansion Democrat who, Buchanan insisted, could be counted on to support Polk in Mexico as the president grappled with defiant generals abroad and recalcitrant Whig congressmen at home.[2]

Buchanan was adamant that Polk could count on Trist to follow his instructions to the word, which would be of paramount importance as the president

Nicholas Trist at age thirty-five, as portrayed in 1835 by artist John Neagle and then rendered in this lithograph. The portrait was painted twelve years before Trist would earn notoriety as President Polk's renegade peace envoy in Mexico.
NEW YORK PUBLIC LIBRARY, THE MIRIAM AND IRA D. WALLACH DIVISION OF ART, PRINTS, AND PHOTOGRAPHY

looked ahead to the coming peace with Mexico. Polk's goals were becoming grander as General Winfield Scott's army advanced deeper and deeper into Mexico, and still they lagged behind the more active imaginations of some of his fellow Democrats, who were starting to advocate the outright annexation of the entire country.

Trist supported the war, the president, and his friend Buchanan. But he had competing influences on his conscience that had set their roots in him long before Buchanan and Polk called him to the White House to discuss his mission in April 1847. One was his grandmother, Elizabeth House Trist. When Nicholas Trist enrolled at West Point in 1818, his grandmother, known affectionately as Eliza, wrote to him often. While she didn't necessarily oppose his decision to go to the military academy, his pacifistic grandmother made no secret that she had certain hopes and expectations for the kind of man he would, or would not, become. "I hope you will never take up arms but in defence of your Country. I would as soon hear of you turning highwayman as to join an army for ambitious motives," Trist's grandmother wrote in the same letter in which she warned against the "heinous crime" of waging war to subjugate other nations. Trist's father, Hore Browse Trist, had once killed a man in a duel, and Eliza reminded her grandson of the heavy toll it had taken on his conscience. "[H]e did it in justification of his own honor . . . yet it prey'd upon his mind." She concluded her letter, "I should glory in seeing you at the plough tail rather than hearing of your being a general in a foreign service."[3]

Aside from his grandmother, perhaps the greatest influence who shaped Trist's life, as well as his decision to betray his president for the good of his country, was none other than Thomas Jefferson. By the time Trist became acquainted with Jefferson, the former president had long been out of office. In fact, Trist was born in 1800, the year of Jefferson's election, and had little personal recollection of the heady days of the Jefferson presidency that charted a radical new course for republicanism the United States. But years later, Trist would come to know Jefferson through his grandmother. Eliza first met Jefferson in 1782. Jefferson, then a delegate to the Continental Congress, spent two years living at her mother's boardinghouse in Philadelphia. Through the years, they maintained their correspondence, and Jefferson persuaded her to move to Albemarle County, Virginia, where he lived. After Jefferson completed the Louisiana Purchase, he appointed her son, Hore, as port collector for the lower Mississippi River in New Orleans. Hore only held the job for one year before he died of yellow fever. Several years later, Eliza moved back to Virginia.[4]

After accepting an invitation from Jefferson to stay at Monticello following his 1817 graduation from the College of Orleans, Trist fell in love with Virginia Randolph, the ex-president's granddaughter. When he dropped out of West Point, he returned to Monticello to win Virginia's heart, marrying her after a six-year courtship.* The sage of Monticello tutored the young Trist, who served as his private secretary. Jefferson and Trist rode the countryside together, walked the grounds at Monticello, and had countless hours of deep, philosophical conversation. Jefferson trained Trist in the law, continuing his studies from West Point, which Trist had decided to attend largely at Jefferson's urging. And Jefferson passed on many of his own values to his young protégé, imbuing his skepticism of religion, reverence for logic, and, as he would display in Mexico more than twenty years later, a devotion to justice and morality. Trist developed a deep bond with Jefferson, which he described as "an intimacy as close, a familiarity as unreserved, as was permitted by the disparity of years." At the end of Jefferson's life, Trist served as executor of his will and was at the founding father's bedside when he died on July 4, 1826, the fiftieth anniversary of America's independence.[5]

After Jefferson's death, Trist continued to carry on his work in developing the former president's beloved University of Virginia. Through that work, Trist became close with another protégé of Jefferson's, James Madison, who succeeded his mentor as rector of the university. They corresponded for years, sending dozens of letters to each other. In the early 1830s, as an aging Madison decried the nullification movement that had emerged in South Carolina, threatening to drag the country into civil war, Trist quietly assisted Madison in his writings against it.[6]

Eliza must have been pleased when Trist decided he wasn't cut out for a military life and dropped out of West Point after his third year. But he was not quite sure yet what to do with his life. He considered practicing law, a

* In honor of the boy's great-grandfather, the couple named their second child Thomas Jefferson Trist, which they shortened to Jeff (Ohrt, 56).

field of study of his at West Point, but decided against it. He bought a share of a small newspaper in Charlottesville, but succeeded only in fighting with his partners.[7]

Trist's true calling emerged in the fall of 1828, when Henry Clay, then serving as President John Quincy Adams's secretary of state, offered him a job as a clerk at the Department of State. Clay had been a fierce opponent of the Jeffersonians, but took pity on Jefferson's family after his death because of the grim state of its affairs. He offered Trist a job in the hope that it would provide some comfort to his mother-in-law, Jefferson's daughter.[8] Under normal circumstances, Trist's tenure at the State Department would have been short-lived. Andrew Jackson defeated Adams in the 1828 presidential election, shortly after Trist began his work for the administration. The change in administration swept out many federal employees who had won Adams's patronage, and a first-year clerk at the State Department could not have expected to stay on through the tumultuous transition.

But Trist had a knack for making fortuitous connections that would serve him well throughout his life—with Thomas Jefferson, James Madison, and Henry Clay, among others—and that tendency turned what should have been a brief stint at the State Department into a career. At West Point, Trist had befriended Andrew Jackson Donelson, nephew of the hero of New Orleans. And when Old Hickory's administration began, his namesake nephew persuaded Jackson to keep Trist at his post, even though he had been appointed by the Whigs. Trist became an intimate acquaintance of Jackson's, even succeeding Donelson as the president's personal secretary. Jackson often relied on Trist, whom he called "a man of integrity and honor," for advice.[9] And Trist was a great admirer of Jackson, of his certainty and willingness to do what he thought right, regardless of other opinions. Trist found himself in Jackson's cabinet room once when the secretary of state warned that the president's acceptance of a compromise border between Maine and Canada would cause a "clamor" in New England. "I care nothing for clamors, sir," Jackson fired back. "I do precisely what I think just and right."[10] The comment impressed Trist enough for him to record it later that day. Trist's relationship bore professional fruit as he became a fixture in official Washington, and paid off handsomely when Jackson named Trist as America's consul to Spanish Cuba in 1833, a post he held until the Whigs finally unseated the Democrats after William Henry Harrison was elected president in 1840.

As the American consul in Cuba, Trist spent much of his time fending off accusations from the British that he refused to enforce laws against the African slave trade, which, despite the ban, still flourished in Cuba with the aid of the island's Spanish officials. Trist also clashed with American captains due to his insistence on the enforcement of a law requiring captains to pay their men three months' worth of wages if they were discharged in a foreign port. In one case, Trist actually imprisoned an American captain, with help from the Spanish authorities, for refusing to pay a seaman his three months of wages. The law was unpopular with American merchants and captains, but Trist was proud of his insistence on enforcing it anyway.[11]

Following his removal as consul,* Trist bought a thirty-seven-acre farm outside of Havana and stayed in Cuba for the next four years. But the venture was a failure. Fortunately for Trist, Jackson was aware of his plight. After Polk's election in 1844, Jackson urged the president-elect to find a place for his old secretary. Polk's new secretary of state, James Buchanan, who remembered Trist from his time on a congressional committee years earlier that had investigated allegations against him as consul, was happy to oblige, and named him chief clerk at the State Department.[12]

As Trist took up his new post, war loomed over the United States. With American assistance, Texas had won its independence from Mexico in 1836. Polk had been elected partly on a platform of annexing Texas, which had been an independent republic for ten years, and incorporating it as the twenty-eighth state. But Mexico had never reconciled itself to losing its northern territory, and made it clear that it would view annexation as an irreparable breach with the United States. As the conflict deepened, frequent skirmishes erupted on the disputed border between Mexico and Texas.

America's designs on Mexico's vast northern lands were clear. In November 1845, Polk had sent John Slidell, who had just vacated his seat as a Louisiana congressman, to Mexico City to negotiate the purchase of Alta California and New Mexico, for $25 million. Slidell was also to settle the border dispute between Mexico and Texas, which was about to be granted statehood. Texas claimed the Rio Grande as its southern border with Mexico, while Mexico claimed a border farther north, at the Nueces River. The Mexican government, then in the throes of instability and a succession of coups that followed its independence from Spain, rejected Slidell's offer and reaffirmed its claim to Texas.[13]

War seemed imminent as Slidell departed from Mexico and Polk sent troops to occupy the Nueces Strip, as the land between the Nueces and Rio Grande was known. General Mariano Arista, who led Mexico's Division of the North, marched his own troops into the disputed territory in response. The dispute between the United States and Mexico reached its boiling point on April 25, 1846, when a detachment of American soldiers led by Captain Seth Thornton rode into an ambush and was decimated by General Anastasio Torrejon. Between

* Harrison's death just one month into his presidency delayed Trist's removal until November 1841, when Secretary of State Daniel Webster informed him that President John Tyler had relieved him of his post "on general grounds of propriety and expediency," not because of the allegations of inaction in suppressing the slave trade in Havana (Mahin, 15).

Mexico's rejection of Slidell and its attack on American soldiers in the "Thornton Affair," Polk had had enough. On May 11, he asked Congress for a declaration of war against Mexico, which it granted him two days later.

As Mexico steeled itself for the coming war, Antonio Lopez de Santa Anna again seized control. The general, a former president several times over whose most recent ouster had come only a year earlier, offered his services to the government. In a letter written from exile in Cuba, Santa Anna said he had no aspirations to again become president, but that he would offer his military services in defense of his country.

Nothing, however, could have stemmed the onslaught that the United States unleashed. Led by General Zachary Taylor, the Americans crushed Arista's forces at the Battle of Palo Alto, the first major battle of the war, and drove deep into Mexican territory. After Taylor's victory at Monterrey, Santa Anna reneged on his promise and declared himself president in December. But Santa Anna fared no better than his luckless predecessors in turning the tide of the war. Taylor routed a larger army led by Santa Anna at Buena Vista on February 23, 1847. The general's greatest victory of the war was so resounding that some began speaking of Taylor as a candidate for president.

America had seen nothing but success on the battlefield. But the war seemed no closer to an end, the Mexicans no closer to giving up and negotiating a peace. Polk wanted to force Mexico to surrender. The surest way to do that, he decided, would be to advance on Mexico City, which would require landing American troops at Veracruz, at the foot of the National Road that led to the capital. The general he chose for this critical mission was Winfield Scott.

Polk had already named Scott as the commander of American forces in Mexico, only to relieve him of his command shortly afterward. He didn't particularly like the general. Scott, known as Old Fuss and Feathers, was egotistical and vain, in stark contrast to the more reserved and humble president. And he was a Whig, to boot. But Polk and his cabinet did not believe Taylor was capable of carrying out a high-risk amphibious landing at Veracruz, and Scott's military acumen was beyond question. Scott, they determined, was the right general for the job. Their faith in Scott was well-placed. Leading a 12,000-man force, Scott laid siege to the city, which fell on March 29. The road to Mexico City now lay open.[14]

The time was ripe for Polk to negotiate an end to the war—on extremely generous terms for the United States, of course—but not for Buchanan to head south and settle accounts himself. After all, as long as Mexico refused to name peace commissioners of its own, the United States could not send its top diplomat to negotiate the terms. And Polk needed not only an envoy, but one who would satisfy, or at least not offend, all the squabbling factions of his Democratic Party. Buchanan presented Trist as the ideal man for the job.[15]

Polk's instructions were clear: The United States–Mexico border would be set at the Rio Grande, extending west to the Pacific from the point where the river met with southwestern New Mexico. The United States would take New Mexico, Alta California, and Baja California. Mexico would grant the United States transit rights across the Isthmus of Tehuantepec, the narrowest point across Mexico, which, in the days before the Panama Canal, served as the easiest way to pass from the Gulf of Mexico and Pacific Ocean. American investors hoped to build a railroad across it. And the United States would assume its citizens' claims against Mexico for $15 million, to be paid in five annual installments.

Polk acknowledged that he might not get all he sought, so he set some conditions for Trist. If the envoy was able to achieve all of his goals, he was authorized to pay Mexico as much as $30 million, which was still far less than the land was worth. If he could not obtain American access to the Isthmus of Tehuantepec, he could pay only up to $25 million. And if Baja California were unobtainable, that number dropped to $20 million.[16]

Trist set out for Mexico with three letters: One, from William Marcy, the secretary of war, explained Trist's mission to Scott. If Trist informed Scott that he had reached an agreement with Mexico, Marcy told the general, Scott was to regard that as an order from Polk himself to suspend all military activity. The second was a sealed letter from Buchanan to Manuel Baranda, the Mexican foreign minister, informing him that Trist would be available to negotiate based on the terms that Polk had outlined for his envoy. Finally, Trist carried a copy of Buchanan's letter for Scott, so he could stay informed of the details of Trist's mission.[17]

The peace mission was off to a rocky start before Trist even reached Mexico. Polk had wanted Trist's mission and departure to be a secret. If knowledge of Trist's mission became public, Polk believed antiwar Whigs would send their own agents to Mexico to sabotage it. "This they would do rather than suffer my administration to have the credit of concluding a just and honourable peace," Polk wrote.[18]

But on April 20, the *New York Herald* revealed the plan, down to the last detail of Polk's instructions. Polk blamed a State Department clerk named William Derrick, the lone clerk who had been privy to the details of Trist's mission. Buchanan did not escape Polk's wrath, receiving a fierce tongue-lashing from the enraged president. In turn, Buchanan suggested that Virginia Trist was the source of the leak. Polk, who wrote in his diary, "I have not been more vexed or excited since I have been president," questioned whether Trist himself could have leaked the information. Or he wondered whether it possibly could have come from Buchanan, whose presidential ambitions were well-known. Polk never learned the source of the leak, but whoever it was continued plying the newspapers with information. And American journalists covering the war in Mexico reported extensively on his mission. Trist became such a celebrity after his departure that a fictional version of him featured prominently in Charles Averill's novel of the war, *The Mexican Ranchero.*[19] *

Once Trist arrived in Veracruz on May 6, his mission deteriorated further when he ignited a feud with General Scott. In retrospect, it should have not have been surprising that the stubborn, thin-skinned, and vainglorious Scott would clash with the argumentative and self-righteous Trist. Based on their incompatible personalities, they seemed almost destined to come into conflict.

The arrogant and suspicious Scott needed little help in conjuring up affronts from Washington, and Trist did plenty to fan the flames as well. Etiquette and protocol demanded that Trist present himself to the general when he reached Veracruz. Instead, he sent a letter to Scott at his headquarters announcing his arrival and informing the general that he would provide Scott with instructions regarding Buchanan's diplomatic dispatch. He also sent along Marcy's letter to Scott, as well as the sealed copy of Buchanan's dispatch to the Mexican foreign minister, though not the unsealed copy meant for Scott's eyes.[20]

Scott was immediately wary of Trist and his mission. After his repeated clashes with Polk, he was convinced that the president wanted to replace him with a loyal Democratic general who would not challenge him. Certainly Polk had considered as much, and likely would have followed through had he been able to find a suitable replacement so early. And a friend in Washington had written Scott to inform him of what the source claimed was Trist's "well-known prejudice against me."[21]

Trist's actions after his arrival in Veracruz further stoked those suspicions. Scott was furious with both Trist's conduct and his superiors' decision to foist this diplomat upon him. "I see that the Secretary of War proposes to degrade me, by requiring that I, the commander of this army, shall defer to you, the chief clerk at the Department of State, the question of continuing or discontinuing hostilities," he wrote to Trist. As the commander of American forces in Mexico, Scott saw no reason why he should play second fiddle to a clerk from the State Department. "The question of an armistice or no armistice is most peculiarly a military question, appertaining, of necessity, if not of universal right, in the absence of direct instructions, to the commander of the invading forces," he wrote.[22]

Along with his reply to Trist, Scott returned Buchanan's dispatch, which he said he could not deliver. "I very much doubt whether I can so far commit the honor of my government as to take any direct agency in forwarding the sealed dispatch," he told Trist.[23] Furthermore, he sent a copy of his letter back to Marcy in Washington, telling the secretary of war that he did not have the time to

* More than sixty years after Trist went to Mexico, he was again immortalized in fiction as a character in Emerson Hough's novel, *54–40 or Fight.*

deliver the dispatch to the foreign minister. To Buchanan and Polk, Scott railed against what he alleged was a lack of support from Washington, and asked to be recalled from his command after learning of Trist's instructions, saying he could not properly carry out his duties with "such a flank battery planted against me."[24]

Trist, failing to see his own fault in antagonizing Scott, took great umbrage at the general's refusal to follow the orders that Polk, through him, had given. He wrote to his wife from Veracruz to describe the state affairs and his intentions toward the imperious general. "If I have not demolished him, then I give up," he said.[25]

Marcy tried to ease Scott's concerns and salve his wounded ego in a letter that faulted Trist for not visiting him in person to deliver the letters. He also emphasized that Trist could only force Scott to accept an armistice after Mexico's Congress had ratified a peace treaty, assuring the general that his role had not been superseded by a diplomatic envoy.[26]

But Marcy reminded Scott that it was still his duty to send Buchanan's dispatch to Mexico City and that he must not wait for Trist to arrive in person before he did so. And he pointed out that logic dictated the envoy be able to call a cease-fire if the Mexicans approved a peace treaty. "As the negotiator is the first to know the fact that a treaty has been concluded and so ratified, it is, beyond dispute, proper that he should be directed to communicate the knowledge of that fact to the commanding general." Scott's concerns were far from assuaged. In his view, Marcy might as well have asked him to hand over the command of his army to Trist, so abhorrent did he find the "dishonor" of being "required to obey the orders of the chief clerk of the State Department."[27]

As Marcy tried to placate Scott, Trist searched for a solution to his standoff with the general over Buchanan's dispatch. Scott had sent a courier to return the unsealed dispatch to Trist. Believing he had no authority to deliver it to the Mexican foreign minister himself, Trist was unsure what to do with it. Polk believed Trist lacked even the authority to accept it back from Scott, and that he had "committed a great error in receiving it."[28] So Trist languished in Puebla, where Scott's moving headquarters had relocated, waiting to negotiate with a Mexican government that had not yet been invited to treat with him.

It didn't take long for Polk to decide that he'd made a serious mistake by sending Trist to Mexico, declaring, "Because of the personal controversy between these self-important personages, the golden moment for concluding a peace with Mexico may have passed." After so much frustration with Scott, he was ready to oblige the general's request to remove him from his command, and even went so far as to contemplate a court-martial. So toxic had the environment become that Trist too might have to come back, Polk mused. But while the cabinet agreed with Polk that Scott and Trist's conduct was problematic enough to warrant firing both men, it also saw that removing them would be severely disruptive at a critical juncture in the war. Polk yielded to his cabinet's advice while they awaited further news from Mexico.[29]

Thus far, the news hadn't been promising. The combination of Mexico's wounded pride and deteriorating political structure made it difficult to negotiate. Rather than convince the Mexicans to sue for peace, each new victory by Scott further convinced them to stand their ground. Those who suggested surrender in Mexico's Congress were often castigated as traitors by their colleagues.[30] Presidents and foreign ministers were replaced with alarming regularity, an alternating cast of pro-peace and pro-war leaders, making it difficult for the Americans to even know who they were supposed to negotiate with, let alone whether Mexico's leaders were actually willing to surrender and negotiate an end to the war.

Though he still hadn't found a way to work amicably with Scott, Trist found the solution to the impasse over Buchanan's dispatch by handing it off to Edward Thornton, the head of Britain's legation to Mexico, whom Trist had met years earlier during a British diplomatic mission to Washington. Thornton had come to Puebla to visit Scott and Trist, and agreed to serve as courier for sealed dispatch, which his colleagues delivered to Domingo Ibarra, who had become Mexican foreign minister after pressure from militants in the Mexican Congress forced Baranda's resignation. Shortly afterward, Santa Anna called a special congressional session to discuss a possible end to the war, paving the way for the negotiations that had brought Trist to Mexico.[31]

Trist informed Scott of the revived prospects for peace in a June 25 letter, to which Scott sent a cool response that, as Trist wrote Buchanan, "constituted the commencement of our official intercourse with reference to the duties with which I am charged." Polk's leading general and peace envoy were finally communicating in an official capacity, seemingly indicating a begrudging acceptance by Scott of Trist's presidentially ordained role. But those communications still passed through a veil of hostility that threatened to upend Polk's peace mission.[32]

As Polk struggled for a solution to the problem of his quarreling general and envoy, Scott and Trist not only reached an improbable accord, but fast became friends and coconspirators once they put their differences aside. Their rapprochement began when Trist, a hypochondriac by nature, fell ill in Puebla. About a week after responding to Trist's message about Mexico's willingness to discuss peace, Scott learned that Trist was severely ill and confined to his sickbed. Putting aside his hostility for the envoy, Scott made a gesture of goodwill by sending Trist a jar of guava marmalade, which Trist had become quite fond of during his years in Havana. When Trist received the gift, the acrimony he felt for Scott vanished.[33]

Soon, the two men were meeting on a regular basis, and it didn't take long for their conversations to turn to their superiors in Washington, whom Scott and Trist had both come to view as obstacles that stood in the way of their missions.

If Polk was dismayed by Scott and Trist's feud, he should have been far more alarmed by their reconciliation. Once Scott and Trist joined forces, the prospects for peace improved dramatically, though not on terms that would have pleased Polk or his cabinet. Scott and Trist's first genuine attempt to bring Mexico to the negotiating table was predicated on an act of outright bribery. It was the British diplomat Thornton who first suggested to the pair that Santa Anna might be more open to negotiating in exchange for cash. On July 15, Scott and Trist sat down to discuss the matter, and decided to offer the Mexican president $1 million, of which $10,000, from a contingency fund carried by Scott, would be provided up front, with the rest coming after Mexico's Congress ratified a peace treaty. Trist acknowledged to Scott that they had no authority to make such a payment, but wrote to the general that he felt "a duty to disregard" that lack of authorization. Scott was so enthusiastic about the plan that he sent along the $10,000 immediately, then wrote Trist to let him know that the payment had been made.[34]

However, the bribery plan turned out to be premature. Mexico's Congress, at the time controlled by those who were fiercely opposed to making any concessions to the American invaders, rejected Santa Anna's pleas to rescind a law that prohibited him from negotiating a peace treaty. Santa Anna had Thornton deliver a message to Scott at his headquarters in Puebla, informing the general of the unwelcome development. Scott would have to send a clearer message to the Mexican government before it was willing to sit down at the negotiating table.[35]

That message came in the form of two resounding battlefield victories for the United States. On August 20, two of Scott's colonels, Bennet Riley and Persifor Smith, routed a numerically superior Mexican force at the town of Contreras, just miles from the entrance to Mexico City. Scott followed quickly with an assault on Santa Anna's remaining positions outside the town of Churubusco, forcing the Mexican generalissimo to fall back to the capital.[36]

As Scott prepared for a final assault on Mexico City, Santa Anna arrived in the capital on August 20 and rallied Congress to his cause. He needed time to organize his defense of the city, and the only way to get it was through a truce with Scott. The American general, wary of the bloodshed that an attack on Mexico City would cause, was a willing partner. Scott agreed to a brief truce. "Too much blood has already been shed in this unnatural war," Scott wrote to Santa Anna. The truce did not last long. Nearly as soon as it went into effect, Santa Anna violated the terms by fortifying his defenses and blocking Americans from obtaining supplies in Mexico City.[37]

But by the time Scott ended the cease-fire on September 7, Trist had begun negotiations with Mexican officials. Hard-liners in the Mexican government were pressuring Santa Anna not to concede too much, and that pressure conflicted with Trist's strict instructions. Mexican negotiators demanded that the border with the United States be set not at the Rio Grande, but at the Nueces River. They would concede Alta California, but only north of San Diego and its exquisite deepwater harbor, and would not give up New Mexico, Baja California, or the right of transit across the Tehuantepec.[38]

Trist knew he could sacrifice Baja California and the Tehuantepec transit rights, but not San Diego and New Mexico, and certainly not the Nueces River line, the disputed boundary that had brought the United States into the war in the first place. But if he held firm, he knew it would likely precipitate an invasion of Mexico City by Scott. Trist's solution was the revival of an old idea of his—a "neutral zone" between the Rio Grande and the Nueces, which could possibly be enforced by European overseers. Trist had initially suggested the neutral zone in passing, not intending it to be a serious offer, but Mexican officials seized upon the idea. It seemed like it might be the only way to forestall an assault on Mexico City. A skeptical Trist agreed to forward the proposal—which would grant Mexico the neutral zone and the harbor of San Diego—to his government, while urging Scott to renew the cease-fire for an additional forty-five days.[39]

Polk and his cabinet were stunned, to say the least. Trist seemed more interested in simply ending the war than in achieving America's war aims. Polk was already distressed by the armistice Scott had negotiated with Santa Anna, and now Trist threatened to deprive the United States of the war spoils it had fought so hard for, just as the president was warming to the idea of taking Sonora and Baja California, telling his cabinet in September that he was "decidedly in favour of insisting on the acquisition of more territory." The president had long been beset by concerns that sending Trist to Mexico was a mistake. He now had all the confirmation he needed. On October 4, Polk instructed Buchanan to recall Trist back to the United States.[40]

Buchanan's letter ordered Trist to return to Washington with any treaty he had already negotiated. If none had been negotiated, he was to return anyway, "by the first safe opportunity."[41]

Unfortunately for Trist, or so it seemed at the time, safe opportunities were hard to come by. Ironically, by the time Trist received Buchanan's letter, Scott had already taken Mexico City on September 14, eliminating the need for the gentle negotiating hand that led Polk to recall Trist in the first place. With his troops holding down the Mexican capital, Scott couldn't spare any soldiers to safely escort Trist on his journey home. Scott said it would be more than two weeks before he could spare the troops for an escort.[42]

By the time Trist received Buchanan's letters on November 16—Buchanan, worried that perhaps his letter hadn't reached its destination, sent a second, which Trist received at the same time as the first—he was eager to conclude his negotiations and hesitant to return to Washington. Before Trist received the letters, developments in Mexico's fractured government provided new hope for a settlement to the war. Mexico's Congress voted down legislation that would have barred the government from sacrificing any of the country's land in a peace deal. Manuel de la Peña y Peña, whom Trist believed to be the best negotiating partner he would get, had assumed the presidency amid the tumult of Mexico's chaotic wartime government. And the pro-peace *moderados* had taken control of Mexico's Congress. But given the instability in Mexico's government, Peña's tenure could end abruptly at any time. Trist didn't want to lose the opportunity.[43]

So Trist made a fateful decision that would alter the course of American history: He would ignore Polk's order and stay in Mexico to negotiate an end to the war.

Upon learning that Trist had disobeyed the order to return home, Buchanan was certain that he did so on Scott's advice. This was partially true, but it was not Scott alone who urged Trist to continue his mission of peace. Scott urged Trist to "finish the good work" he had started. Edward Thornton, the British chargé d'affaires, implored him to bestow "charity for this unhappy nation," and to help preserve Mexico's sovereignty. "I look upon this as the last chance for either party of making peace," Thornton told Trist.[44]

And on December 4, which Scott had earlier set as the soonest date at which his troops could escort Trist out of the country, Trist met with James Freaner, a newspaper reporter who had been covering the war for the *New Orleans Delta*. The two had grown close while stuck in Mexico together, meeting often for drinks and conversation. Trist told Freaner that he was considering disobeying his orders so he could negotiate peace with Mexico behind Polk's back. Freaner was thrilled with the idea. "Mr. Trist, make the treaty," he implored. "Make the treaty, sir. It is not in your power to do your country a greater service than any living man can render her. . . . You are bound to do it. Instructions or no instructions, you are bound to do it. Your country, sir, is entitled to this service from you."[45]

Even Peña seemed to be pushing Trist toward negotiations, though the Mexican president knew he had no authority to act. On November 24, with full knowledge of the recall notice Trist had received a week earlier, Peña wrote to Trist, informing him that a delegation had been appointed to negotiate a treaty with him. With the support of its president and Congress, Mexico was ready to submit.[46]

The decision had been made. Trist, who had a lifetime habit of writing long, rambling letters, now penned a sixty-five-page letter to Buchanan to explain his decision. The influences of his grandmother, Thomas Jefferson, and Andrew Jackson shone through on every page. After explaining that he believed Polk to be unaware of the true details on the ground in Mexico, Trist warned that continuing America's occupation of the country or, even worse, annexing it outright, would bring "incalculable danger to every good principle, moral as well as political, which is cherished among us."

Additionally, he reminded Buchanan of what Polk's preferred treaty terms would cost Mexico. The losses Mexico had incurred so far had not yet convinced it to make peace. Threatening to take more would likely have the same effect. "However helpless a nation may feel, there is necessarily a point beyond which she cannot be expected to go under any circumstances," Trist wrote. "This point is, I believe, here reached."[47] Later, Trist would write that he was "governed by my conscience" and by "a sense of justice" to put an end to America's "abuse of power."[48] An enraged Polk did not see conscience and justice in the actions of his insubordinate envoy. Trist had "acted worse than any man in the public employ whom I have ever known," the president said.[49]

Trist, Thornton, and others had grown concerned that Polk would set his sights on new objectives that far exceeded the goals he had outlined in Trist's initial instructions, and with good cause. Upon learning of Scott's capture of Mexico City, Polk began to rethink his goals. Now that the capital was in American hands and the war was essentially won, the United States could safely increase its demands. And Polk's cabinet had no shortage of ideas about exactly what those demands should be. Polk told his cabinet that the United States should settle for no less than both Californias and transit rights across Tehuantepec; in addition, the United States should consider a border along the twenty-sixth parallel, running west from the southern tip of Texas, which would have taken another 187,000 square miles. For good measure, Polk said, the United States should consider acquiring the port city of Tampico on the Gulf of Mexico, which lay south of the proposed new boundary line. With Trist presumably on his way back to Washington, Polk had no intention of sending another envoy to replace him. If the Mexicans wanted to negotiate, they could reach out to the Americans, Polk decided.

Polk was still opposed to conquering and annexing all of Mexico, though some in his cabinet, such as Treasury Secretary Robert Walker, enthusiastically urged the president to take the entire country. And if the war continued, some believed the annexation advocates would eventually persuade a reluctant president, especially if the war continued until all of Mexico was under American control.[50] For now, that was out of the question, as far as Polk was concerned. But after all the trouble that America had gone through, and considering Mexico's repeated reluctance to negotiate long after it was clear that it had been beaten, Polk believed the United States should exact a greater toll for ending the war. In his annual message to Congress on December 7, Polk held firm on his refusal to annex Mexico as a whole, saying his goal had never been "to make a permanent conquest of the republic of Mexico, or to annihilate her separate existence as an independent nation." However, the United States must gain new territories "in satisfaction of the just and long deferred claims of our citizens," and Mexico must pay for its refusal to negotiate based on the generous terms that Trist had initially offered. So American armies must "press forward our military operations" and seize as much territory as possible.[51]

Had Polk remained adamant about his increased demands, domestic opposition may have scuttled his plans even without Trist's betrayal. Many Whigs had opposed the war on moral grounds, viewing it as a war of conquest unbecoming of the United States. Others were wary of annexing lands occupied by Mexicans, who were viewed by many in those days of unchallenged white supremacy as an inferior race whose influence would corrupt the superior stock of the United States. And the Pandora's box of slavery loomed over every aspect of the war. Would the new states carved from Mexican territory be free or slave? How would the issue be decided? The 1847 failure of the Wilmot Proviso, a proposal to ban slavery in any lands conquered from Mexico, had left the festering issue unresolved.

As Scott and Trist continued their machinations in Mexico, Polk faced increasing pressure at home to conclude the war. The Whigs, who had taken control of the House of Representatives in the 1846 election, had always been hostile to the war effort. As the war dragged on, the Whigs, along with much of the American public at large, grew wearier. Whig congressmen, including an antiwar freshman named Abraham Lincoln, wanted Polk to finally end the war.

Polk was not running for reelection, but hoped to buoy his Democratic Party's prospects through a satisfactory resolution to the war. And as the public grew ever more tired of the war, the Whigs hoped to capitalize on those frustrations in the 1848 presidential race and win the White House for the first time. Many Whigs clamored for Zachary Taylor, whom Polk had inadvertently made into a hero through his exploits in the war, to be their nominee. Although Taylor's politics were virtually unknown, he was a popular war hero, argued many Whigs, who could deliver the White House to them. Politics would come later. Others dreamed of nominating Henry Clay, the thrice-defeated presidential candidate and longtime Kentucky senator whose impact, despite his inability to win the White House, was nonetheless so great that he, along with John C. Calhoun and Daniel Webster, were deemed the Great Triumvirate of American politics.

Clay, by now an elder statesman and revered figure, had hoped to bolster his chances for the Whig nomination with a grand speech of the style he'd been renowned for throughout his long political career. It did not succeed in winning him the presidency, or even the nomination, which would go to Taylor, who had become a wildly popular figure due to his battlefield heroics in Mexico.* But the speech electrified the nation and invigorated the antiwar movement, putting a capstone on Polk's need to bring the war to a close.

---

* Among those who favored Taylor over Clay was Lincoln. The Illinoisan was a lifelong admirer of Clay, but he supported Taylor out of pragmatism, believing the general gave the Whigs their best chance of winning the presidency.

On November 13, in his hometown of Lexington, Kentucky, Clay delivered a blistering critique of Polk and the war, which he called a war of "unnecessary and of offensive aggression." It was Mexico, not the United States, that was defending itself honorably, Clay said. Clay also warned against the growing calls to annex Mexico, asking what exactly would be done with the conquered nation once it became part of the United States. "Does any considerate man believe it is possible that two such immense countries . . . with populations so incongruous, so different in race, in language, in religion, and in laws could be blended together in one harmonious mass, and happily governed by one common authority?"[52]

But the longer American forces remained in Mexico, and especially if they drove deeper—Scott had threatened to bring the war from Mexico City to the countryside if Mexico kept refusing to negotiate—the more all-Mexico advocates in Congress and Polk's cabinet would continue to gain momentum. On December 17, a month after Clay's historic speech, Buchanan told a Democratic Party meeting that if Mexico continued refusing to negotiate, the United States may have no choice but to annex the entire country.[53] Others in Polk's cabinet shared his view on the subject.

By that point, however, Mexico was ready to negotiate. And its American negotiating partners vehemently opposed outright annexation. The illegal negotiations between Trist and three Mexican peace commissioners began officially on January 2, 1848. Trist conceded Baja California and the coveted transit rights across Tehuantepec, but held fast on the harbor of San Diego.* The United States would assume all claims its citizens held against the government of Mexico, while granting American citizenship and property rights to Mexicans who remained in the annexed territories. For that land, which totaled more than a third of Mexico's territory, Trist agreed that his country would pay $15 million—lower even than Polk had authorized.[54]

Though he was negotiating as a renegade diplomat who was no longer constrained by his president's instructions, Trist knew there were still boundaries. Not only Polk but the Senate as well would have to approve the treaty, and anything viewed by the war hawks at home as too lenient toward Mexico would face certain rejection. Trist had to find the proper balance between the maximum amount of fairness toward Mexico—*fairness*, of course, being a relative term for a country that had been invaded and dismembered—and the minimum amount of land and concessions that Polk and Congress would be willing to accept. The Mexican commissioners were not thrilled with the terms, but knew they were unlikely to get anything better. And Trist warned them as well that time was of

---

* Robert E. Lee, Scott's engineering officer and one of his favorite aides, assisted Trist in proving to the Mexican negotiators that the harbor of San Diego, whose acquisition was a top priority for Polk, was indeed part of Upper California (Ohrt, 144).

the essence. If Scott were replaced as the commander of the American forces—Polk had already decided to recall his disloyal general, who would be replaced with William O. Butler—Trist too would be out of the picture, and the Mexicans would almost certainly find any subsequent peace offering to be far more punitive. The commissioners understood and sent the proposal to their provisional government in Queretaro for approval.[55]

Trist and his Mexican counterparts signed the Treaty of Guadalupe Hidalgo on February 2. As he prepared to sign the "Treaty of Peace, Friendship, Limits, and Settlement," as the treaty was officially dubbed, Don Bernardo Couto, one of the Mexican commissioners, turned to Trist and said, "This must be a proud moment for you; no less proud for you than humiliating for us." Trist replied, "We are making peace. Let that be our only thought."[56]

Afterward, Trist would make clear to his wife how wrong Couto was about him feeling proud that day. "Could those Mexicans have seen into my heart at that moment, they would have known that my feeling of shame as an American was far stronger than theirs could be as Mexicans. For though it would not have done for me to say so there, that was a thing for every right-minded American to be ashamed of, and I was ashamed of it, most cordially and intensely ashamed of it," Trist wrote to Virginia. Trist lamented that he had to force the Mexican commissioners to accept terms they loathed. "Had my course at such moments been governed by my conscience as a man, and my sense of justice as an individual American, I should have yielded in every instance."

Trist gave the completed treaty to Freaner, the *New Orleans Delta* reporter who urged him along his course of defiance, to deliver to the White House. When Polk received the Treaty of Guadalupe Hidalgo on February 19, he agonized over whether to accept it. The treaty met all of the unconditional criteria he had set for Trist: Alta California, New Mexico, and a border at the Rio Grande. But it had been negotiated illegally. And while he remained steadfast in his opposition to annexing all of Mexico, Polk had come around to the notion that his original terms were too generous.[57]

Polk concluded that he could not reject a treaty that achieved his goals, no matter how much he wanted to punish Trist for his betrayal. "Mr. Trist has acted very badly," Polk wrote in his diary, after he and Buchanan had spent all night examining the treaty. "But notwithstanding this, if on further examination the Treaty is one that can be accepted, it should not be rejected on account of his bad conduct." He also suspected that Congress would follow through on threats to defund the war effort if he rejected the treaty and continued hostilities. "A majority of one branch of Congress is opposed to my administration. They have falsely charged that the war was brought on and is continued by me with a view to the conquest of Mexico," Polk wrote in his diary, of the Whig-controlled House of Representatives. "If I were now to reject a treaty made upon my own terms . . . the probability is that Congress would not grant either men or money to prosecute the war." If that happened, even Polk's gains of New Mexico and Upper California might be lost.[58]

Opinions were mixed in Polk's fractured cabinet. Marcy, the secretary of war, wanted to send it to the Senate, and he was joined by Secretary of the Navy John Mason, Postmaster General Cave Johnson, and Attorney General Nathan Clifford. Walker, the treasury secretary, still dreamed of annexing all of Mexico, and urged the president to reject Trist's treaty. And Buchanan, who had opposed all territorial gains at the start of the war, now insisted that Polk should hold out for more land, including a southern border set at the Sierra Madre Mountains. Polk, who had long grown tired of Buchanan's vacillations and his obvious angling for a future campaign for the presidency, chastised his secretary of state for his "total change of opinion on the subject." Trist's treaty, Polk decided, would go to the Senate.[59]

Given the divisions that the war had caused in Congress, Senate approval for the treaty was far from a foregone conclusion. Many Whigs were outraged that the United States would seize any territory at all, while some of the more hawkish Democrats demanded that the country take more. And some questioned why they should approve a treaty approved by a renegade diplomat. But after weeks of discussion and disagreement, the Senate on March 10 approved the Treaty of Guadalupe Hidalgo by a vote of 38–14, bringing an end to the divisive war and fulfilling America's Manifest Destiny of extending the nation's borders from sea to shining sea.[60]

Trist did not exactly receive a hero's welcome upon his return to Washington. As he expected, Polk fired Trist immediately. The president not only refused to give Trist any credit, public or private, for his role in ending the war, but even refused to reimburse the now-unemployed envoy for the expenses he had incurred on his mission. The only praise Trist received was from members of the peace party in Mexico's Congress. "Of him there remains in Mexico none but grateful and honoring recollections," one of the peace commissioners said in Congress during the ratification of the peace treaty.[61] Nonetheless, Trist stood strong in his convictions that he had done what was right. Quoting Martin Luther, Trist wrote after his return home in 1848, "If I am to have a fault, I would rather speak too harshly, and thrust forth truth unwisely, than to have played the hypocrite and held truth in."[62]

The high cost of Trist's conscience was years of poverty. After the war, Trist worked as a paymaster for a railroad company, while he and his wife rented out rooms in their house to make ends meet. And as the United States careened toward civil war, few wanted to remember the man whose treaty exacerbated the nation's divisions over slavery and set it on the course to disunion.

Only Scott remembered the service Trist had done to his country. After Lincoln took office in 1861, Scott, then in the twilight of his career, too old even to command troops against the Confederacy, urged the new president to appoint Trist as revenue collector for Philadelphia. Lincoln, who once agitated against the war in Congress as Trist simultaneously struggled to end it in Mexico City, declined to offer the old Democrat a job.[63]

It wasn't until 1870 that Trist finally received, if not the credit he deserved, then at least the money he was owed. Charles Sumner, the abolitionist Massachusetts senator, led the charge in Congress to finally reimburse Trist for his wartime pay and expenses—with interest, no less. Shortly afterward, President Ulysses S. Grant's postmaster general named him postmaster of Alexandria, Virginia.[64]

That post was the lone reward ever granted Nicholas Trist for the tremendous service he provided to his country, and he held it happily for four years, until he died at the age of seventy-three. From the halls of Monticello to the docks of Havana to the battlefields of Mexico, Trist never forgot the lessons passed on by his grandmother, Thomas Jefferson, James Madison, and Andrew Jackson. When the time came to make what he believed to be a choice between betraying either his president or his country, surely it was his grandmother's words that rang out in his mind. "My dear Nicholas, when the hour arrives that you must quit this world, let not your conscience upbraid you with having done anything to dishonour humanity."[65]

Chapter 5

The Gray-Eyed Man of Destiny

Unless a man believes that there is something great for him to do, he can do nothing great.

—William Walker

Rarely in American history has a man been so celebrated for breaking the laws of his own country than William Walker.

The Neutrality Act of 1818 aimed to prevent private citizens from conducting their own foreign policy, which could of course create great complications for America's own, more official foreign policy. And Walker defied it with bravado as he waged wars of conquest in Nicaragua.

In Walker's flouting of those laws, many Americans saw not the acts of an outlaw but the glimmering future of their country and its Manifest Destiny, which they didn't necessarily think should have ended when the Stars and Stripes were raised over the Pacific following the Mexican War. With no room to expand in the West, those Americans looked south, where their imaginations in the 1850s were captured by "filibusters," swashbuckling adventurers who embarked on missions of conquest in the Latin world in the name of fame, riches, glory, and Manifest Destiny.

The term *filibuster* had a far different meaning in the 1850s than it does today. Rather than the time-honored practice of preventing bills from coming to a vote, made famous by Southern senators' obstructionist tactics against civil rights legislation, a filibuster in Walker's day was a soldier of fortune, a mercenary who struck out on his own to conquer foreign lands south of America's borders.*

Many filibusters achieved a level of celebrity reserved today for movie stars, musicians, and professional athletes, and became popular heroes throughout the country. And none was more memorable or more successful, at least for a time,

---

* As a military term, *filibuster* entered the English lexicon by way Spanish and French words that were derived from the Dutch word *vrijbuiter*, which translates to "freebooter" or "pirate" (Caro, Robert A. 2002. *The Years of Lyndon Johnson: Master of the Senate*. New York: Knopf, 92).

William Walker, the greatest of the "filibusters," sought glory in his ill-fated conquest of Nicaragua, becoming a hero to many Americans and a nuisance to others in the process.
LIBRARY OF CONGRESS

than Walker, who, after becoming embroiled in the cross-border civil wars raging in the newly independent nations of Central America, conquered and ruled Nicaragua.

Though he was the most successful of America's filibusters, Walker only ruled Nicaragua for a short time. With every victory, he grew more popular at home. But each step earned him new enemies—inside Nicaragua, in the capitals of the country's neighbors, in Washington, DC, in London, and in the boardroom of America's greatest tycoon, Cornelius Vanderbilt. Once he was ousted by a coalition of Central American governments, angered by both his meddling and his victories, Walker was never again able to regain the success he'd achieved in Nicaragua. Even a once-laudatory press turned against him. Walker didn't let that deter him as he dreamed of ruling an empire in the tropical lands south of Mexico, and he continued plotting his return to power. In the end, his return was far from triumphant, and he met his end before a Honduran firing squad at the age of thirty-six.

By modern standards, Walker would be considered a particularly reprehensible figure. Driven by a lust for power and a disregard for what he believed were the racially inferior inhabitants of the Americas, he set out to invade foreign nations and plant his flag of conquest as the benevolent white ruler who would bring order and American values to the simpleminded natives. In his quest to curry support in America, particularly in the South, he even sought to reestablish the outlawed practice of slavery in Nicaragua. But to many of his fellow Americans at the time, not only were those goals not necessarily disreputable, they were outright laudable. Walker was cheered by the public, lauded by the press, and even encouraged by some political leaders, especially in the South, where the filibusters' wars were often viewed as quests to extend the embattled institution of slavery.

Filibustering was the final of many trades the restless Walker practiced in his short life. Born in Nashville in 1824, Walker's parents, a Scot named James Walker and Kentucky woman named Mary Norvell, wanted their oldest child to become a man of the cloth. After graduating from the University of Nashville at the age of fourteen, Walker decided to pursue a career in medicine instead of in the ministry.

A medical degree from the University of Pennsylvania and a year studying medicine in Paris and Heidelberg propelled the young Walker into what could have been a lifetime career as a successful doctor. He decided instead to abandon medicine to study the law, and moved to New Orleans to practice his new trade. When Walker was engaged to be married in 1848, he decided that a career at the bar couldn't provide for the life he wanted to give his bride-to-be. He turned next to a life in journalism, and helped to found the New Orleans *Crescent*.[1]

Considering both his Southern heritage and his infamous decree reintroducing slavery to Nicaragua, which would catapult the already-famed filibuster to the status of icon among some Americans, one might expect Walker to have been a lifelong supporter of the institution. But that was far from the case. Walker had been raised in a household in which slavery was scorned, and his father, a merchant and insurance salesman, employed free blacks.[2] At the *Crescent*, as well as later in his life, Walker's positions on slavery would stand in stark contrast to the decree he used to generate Southern support for his cause.

The *Crescent* was an unconventional Southern newspaper, with editorial positions that stood out as unusual and even suspicious in antebellum New Orleans.* The paper offered what it called a "broad and less specifically Southern view of the world" than its contemporaries in the city, and Walker adhered to that credo. Walker was part of an editorial team that viewed slavery, if not with overt hostility, then with more subtle disapproval. The newspaper praised Alexis de Tocqueville's masterpiece, *Democracy in America*, using the same coded language that the Frenchman employed regarding "the institutions of this country." The newspaper enthusiastically recounted the slave revolts, murders of slave owners, and insurrections on slave ships that so terrified Southerners. And at times, it even advocated the gradual abolition of slavery, once writing, "If these states [Kentucky, Tennessee, and Virginia] choose to abolish slavery within their own borders—and we confess that the signs of the times indicate they will do it—it is their own concern."[3]

Even more laden with irony than Walker's paper taking an antislavery stance was its editorializing against filibustering. Like many in the South, the *Crescent* supported America's acquisition of Cuba. But it opposed achieving that goal

---

* A colleague of Walker's at the *Crescent* was the poet Walt Whitman, who lampooned New Orleans life under the nom de plume Daggerdraw Bowieknife, paying homage to the city's violent culture.

through force. "Cuba must be independent of Spain, and as an ultimate consequence, a member of our union," the paper wrote. However, Cuba "must win her own freedom. . . . If we wait a little the ripened plum will fall into our laps."[4]

It is for the most part impossible to determine which of the Crescent's editorials came from Walker's pen, but historian Albert Carr writes, "To judge by the internal evidence of content and style, his individual mark was all over it." Pro-slavery editors, even in other Southern states, derided the *Crescent* as a "Yankee paper."[5]

Nothing in Walker's upbringing or early life would indicate the path he would eventually take. A friend of Mary Walker's described him as a sensitive boy who would spend every morning reading to his invalid mother. "He was very intelligent and as refined in his feelings as a girl," Jane H. Thomas wrote decades after Walker's death in her recollections of life in Nashville. As an adult, Walker stood only five-foot-five and weighed less than 120 pounds, with thin lips and emotionless gray eyes. His soft-spoken nature and socially withdrawn personality would belie the ruthlessness and steely determination that would later become known to his allies and foes. Unlike other filibusters, Walker was not driven to conquest by greed, slavery, or Manifest Destiny; rather, he was propelled by the greatness that he believed was his *own* destiny.[6]

The trajectory of Walker's life changed dramatically in 1849 when his fiancée fell victim to the yellow fever epidemic that raged annually through New Orleans. Walker most likely met Helen Martin through his friend and fellow attorney, Edmund Randolph. Exhibiting the tenderness that he was known for as a child, but which would be thoroughly absent later in life, Walker learned sign language so he could communicate with Helen, who was deaf and mute. They got engaged in 1848, inspiring Walker to change careers so he could give Helen the life he believed she deserved.[7]

Quite understandably, Helen's death left Walker a changed man. A colleague from the Crescent remembered Walker as silent, kind, and studious, with his nose always crammed in a book. But sorrow engulfed him after Helen died. The pensive widower wanted to purge himself of his grief "by some deed of violent daring." When the *Crescent* folded shortly afterward, Walker, like so many aimless young men of his era, packed up and headed west to California, where the gold rush drew adventurers from across the world.[8]

After arriving in San Francisco, Walker continued the journalist's trade, joining the *Daily Herald*, which his old friend Edmund Randolph had founded after moving to the city from New Orleans.* In the bustling, lawless city, he made

---

* The *Daily Herald* took a far different editorial stance than the *Crescent* on slavery issues, advocating secession if Northern states refused to enforce the Fugitive Slave Act, and demanding laws to prevent free blacks from moving to California (Brown, 179).

challenging the corruption and ineptitude of San Francisco's police and judiciary his professional calling card. His criticism was so scathing that he quickly aroused the wrath of his targets. A judge whom Walker had criticized came to the newspaper's office with the intention of whipping him, but was unable to find him. He left a note demanding an apology, prompting Walker to challenge the judge's friend to a duel.[9]

On another occasion, Walker and his colleague John Nugent were cited for contempt of court after castigating Levi Parsons, a local judge, for rejecting grand jury indictments for allegedly insufficient evidence, and accusing him of using his position "to aid the escape of criminals." Walker was jailed and fined $500, which he refused to pay. The next day, a crowd of four thousand supporters gathered in the city's plaza and, whipped into a frenzy by Randolph, shouted, "Let's bring the judge out here!" and "Set Walker free!" The crowd got its wish, or at least one part of it, when Walker's lawyers were able to convince a superior court judge to restore him to freedom. In the aftermath of the incident, Walker unsuccessfully tried to convince California's legislature to impeach Parsons.[10]

Walker decided to abandon journalism and return to law after the Parsons episode. But perhaps the affair imparted a lesson upon Walker—that there was glory to be found in defying authority for a popular cause. And two years of mundane legal work in Marysville surely did not give him the excitement he craved. In 1853, he would find his true calling: the life of a filibuster.

America's love affair with filibustering in the 1850s found its beginnings with a much older desire, the acquisition of Cuba. Albert Gallatin, James Monroe, John Quincy Adams, and Henry Clay were among the early American leaders who coveted the island. Some worried that it would fall into the hands of a hostile power, most notably Great Britain. Supporters of slavery fretted that Spain would succumb to pressure to abolish the institution in Cuba, adding to the mounting pressure to do the same in the United States.[11]

As abolitionism spread in America, Southerners eyed Cuba and other Latin American nations as territory where slavery could be expanded to counter the loss of power they experienced as the United States expanded westward. Future Confederate president Jefferson Davis introduced legislation to annex Cuba to "increase the number of slaveholding constituencies." Albert Gallatin Brown, a United States senator from Mississippi, declared, "I want Cuba, and I know that sooner or later we must have it. . . . I want Tamaulipas, Potosi, and one or two other Mexican States; and I want them all for the same reason—for the planting or spreading of slavery. . . . Yes, I want these Countries for the spread of slavery."[12]

President James K. Polk was "decidedly in favour of purchasing Cuba and making it one of the States of [the] Union," and even discussed the possibility with his cabinet. When the proposed purchase of Cuba from Spain didn't come to pass, others moved to fill the void. Narciso López, a Spanish Creole who fled from Venezuela to Cuba, and later to the United States after his wealthy family lost its land in Simón Bolívar's wars of independence, waged several filibustering expeditions to free the island from Spain.[13] *

Filibustering became such a popular phenomenon that supporters would hold memorial masses for deceased adventurers. López's 1851 death inspired a mass at St. Patrick's Cathedral in New York and a torch-lit procession in New Orleans. Composer Henry Thunder wrote the "Filibuster Polka" in tribute to the would-be conquerors in 1852.[14]

Walker's introduction to the world of filibustering came by way of a man named Frederic Emory, whom Walker described as having been paid by a group of men to establish a military outpost in Arizpe, in the Mexican state of Sonora, to protect nearby gold mines from Apaches who had been raiding the area. Local newspapers were filled with accounts of potentially prosperous mines in Sonora that were abandoned in the face of marauding Apaches, and Walker had taken a keen interest in the situation. The Mexican government had had little success in its halfhearted attempts to subdue the Indians in the farthest reaches of its territory, where its power was stretched thin, and two French-led expeditions had failed to do so as well.[15]

Popular sentiment in the United States held that the locals in Sonora could not defend themselves from the Apaches, and local newspapers exhorted hearty Americans to take up what the British would later call the "white man's burden." "They cannot protect themselves and the government cannot protect them. Their only hope is a war and the occupation of their territory by United States troops," wrote the *Alta California*, a San Francisco newspaper.[16]

The twenty-nine-year-old doctor-turned-lawyer-turned-journalist seized the opportunity. He would become the glorious, self-ordained protector of Sonora. And in achieving that goal, he would create a new nation and fulfill his destiny.

That Sonora was the sovereign territory of Mexico made no difference to Walker. If Mexico could not exercise control of its territory, he reasoned, it could not truly lay claim to the land. And Walker aimed to assert the control over the land and the Apaches that Mexico could not. "Northern Sonora was, in fact, more under the dominion of the Apaches than under the laws of Mexico," Walker wrote years later in justification of his mission. "The state of this region furnished the best defense for any American aiming to settle there without the formal consent of Mexico."[17]

---

* López asked Jefferson Davis to lead his first expedition. Davis turned him down and suggested Robert E. Lee, who also rejected the offer, which he believed he could not in good conscience accept while still a commissioned officer in the United States Army (Brown, 48).

From the outset, officials on both sides of the border were wary of Walker's designs. Mexican officials in Guaymas turned away Walker and his partner, Henry Watkins, and sent them back to San Francisco after receiving reports that they were planning an invasion. James Gadsden, the US ambassador to Mexico City, sought to alleviate the Mexicans' fears with an assurance that President Franklin Pierce would enforce American neutrality laws. Beset by concerns that Walker could jeopardize the planned purchase of southern Arizona and New Mexico that would come to bear his name, Gadsden instructed officials in California to hinder the "movements of hostile character by lawless individuals from that state."[18]

Rebuffed in Guaymas, Walker, who was wholly unfamiliar with military matters, determined to seize Sonora by force of arms. For his invading army he assembled a motley collection of failed gold prospectors, barroom brawlers, cutthroats, Mexican War veterans, and assorted adventurers. Walker and his forty-five-man army set sail on October 16 on the *Caroline*, a ship owned by the US consul in Guaymas.[19]

By the time he and his crew had set off from San Francisco, Walker had already suffered multiple setbacks. General Ethan Allen Hitchcock, who commanded the US Army's Pacific Department, had gotten wind of his plans, which he determined were a violation of the Neutrality Act. Hitchcock commandeered the *Caroline* to prevent its departure, but was forced to give up control of the ship and let Walker's expedition depart after being threatened with contempt of court. Leaving most of his food and ammunition on the pier as he hurriedly left Hitchcock behind, Walker set off on his quest to become the ruler of Sonora on October 16.[20] Hitchcock's interference would not be the last, or certainly the most successful, occasion in which federal officials tried to halt one of Walker's expeditions before it began.

On November 3, 1853, Walker recorded the first of his many conquests, modest though it was. His First Independence Battalion, as his crew was dubbed, came ashore at the village of La Paz, near the southern end of the Baja Peninsula on the Gulf of California, after traversing the coast in search of a suitable place to make landfall. Walker took the local governor prisoner, lowered the Mexican flag, and raised one of his own design, bearing two red stripes with a white stripe in the middle, along with two red stars signifying Lower California and Sonora, the not-yet-captured territory of his would-be nation.[21] Walker then issued the first of the myriad decrees that would fill his filibustering career, announcing, "The Republic of Lower California is hereby declared Free, Sovereign, and Independent," with Walker, of course, as its president, "and all allegiance to the Republic of Mexico is forever renounced."[22]

So far, Walker was the master only of the small village of La Paz. Three days into his ostensible reign, the peripatetic Walker moved on to Cabo San Lucas, on the southern tip of the peninsula, as he flitted along the coast in search of a place where he would establish his government. As Walker prepared to depart and head south, he and his First Independence Battalion would face their first military action.

Six of his men who had gone ashore to collect wood came under fire from the Mexicans, and, upon hearing the shots, Walker came to their aid with thirty members of his battalion. The gunfight lasted an hour and a half, after which Walker and his men retreated to the *Caroline*. Walker's men "did not receive so much as a wound, except from cacti."[23] Both sides declared victory in the first battle of Walker's filibustering career.[24] But when Walker's side of the story reached San Francisco, it was a propaganda coup for the aspiring master of Sonora.

The *Alta California* dramatically exaggerated the battle, which it proclaimed as a great victory for Walker. "Thus ended the battle of La Paz, crowning our efforts with victory, releasing Lower California from the tyrannous yoke of declining Mexico, and establishing a new Republic," the newspaper's San Diego correspondent informed its readers.[25]

Cabo San Lucas had little to offer Walker, who decided to head north along the Baja Peninsula's Pacific coast. As he sailed for Ensenada, about ninety miles south of San Diego, Walker's prospects appeared bleak. He had not received the reinforcements he'd been expecting from San Francisco, and he was running low on food to feed the men he already had, some of whom were growing restless.[26]

Walker wouldn't have to wait much longer for his new recruits. When word of the Battle of La Paz reached San Francisco, about 50 men volunteered for service in Walker's army during a meeting at a city fire department. Watkins opened a recruiting office a few blocks from the wharf, at the corner of Kearny and Sacramento Streets, where he was he able to recruit dozens more. Despite openly recruiting—the flag of Walker's new nation fluttered defiantly over the recruiting office—Watkins faced none of the troubles that bedeviled Walker when he first set off for Mexico. Hitchcock had been assigned to a new post, and his replacement had yet to arrive. On December 7, Watkins and a contingent of about 230 men set sail in the *Anita* to rendezvous with Walker in Ensenada, "where the President contemplates establishing the seat of the Government for the present."[27]

After it landed at Ensenada, the First Independence Battalion suffered wounds from more than just cacti when Walker and his men were attacked by a larger force of Mexicans. After several days under fire, Walker sent Timothy Crocker, his second lieutenant, to break the siege. Crocker charged out of the adobe house where the battalion had been holed up with twenty men. After about fifteen minutes of fighting, Crocker managed to force the Mexicans back. But they had suffered several casualties, including the death of First Lieutenant John McKibben. Walker renamed the adobe house Fort McKibben in his honor.[28]

In Walker's mind, he had already established a legitimate government. Now it was time to put those declarations into practice, or at least to put them on paper. He named a full cabinet for his presidency, with Emory serving as secretary of state, John Jernigan as his secretary of war, and Howard Snow as secretary of his navy, which at that point was comprised only of the *Caroline*.[29] In a series of new decrees at Ensenada, Walker declared all customs duties to be lifted, and established the Napoleonic code as the law of the land. And he declared the independent Republic of Sonora, expanding his imaginary empire across northwestern Mexico, with Sonora and Lower California as its two member states.[30]

Walker also issued an address to the people of the United States, stating as justification for his conquest the Mexican government's lack of interest in the region, or its inability to exercise control over it. "The moral and social ties which bound it to Mexico have been even weaker and more dissoluble than the physical. Hence, to develop the resources of Lower California, and to effect a proper social organization thereon, it was necessary to make it Independent," Walker stated. "On such considerations have I and my companions in arms acted in the course we have pursued. And for the success of our enterprise we put our trust in Him Who controls the destiny of nations, and guides them in the way of progress and improvement."[31]

If the Ensenada decrees and Walker's address were meant to rouse the support of his fellow Americans, they failed miserably. The public's adulation of Walker's exploits turned to contempt when he decreed independence for Sonora—not because he had crossed some invisible line of acceptable conduct or decorum, but because he had laid claim to land he had not yet conquered. The *Alta California*, one of Walker's biggest cheerleaders, now mockingly declared the filibuster a "veritable Napoleon." "Santa Anna must feel obliged to the new President that he has not annexed any more of his territory than Sonora. It would have been just as cheap and easy to have annexed the whole of Mexico at once, and would have saved the trouble of making future proclamations," it wrote.[32]

Nonetheless, Walker believed himself the rightful ruler of Sonora, no less surely than if the Mexican president had decreed it himself. And it was time to make good on that claim. About two weeks after the battle in Ensenada, the *Anita* arrived with the reinforcements and ammunition that Walker needed to continue his expedition, but, to the chagrin of the First Independence Battalion, no food. Walker remedied the lack of provisions by seizing cattle, along with horses, from a local bandit whom he had arbitrarily blamed for the attack in Ensenada.[33]

By the time Walker had launched his long-awaited incursion into Sonora, the First Independence Battalion had fallen on hard times. Disenchanted by the lack of food and progress, a number of his men deserted. Walker tried to rein in the mutiny by executing two deserters and flogging two others, exhibiting for the first time the harsh discipline that his men in Nicaragua would come to know.[34]

The battalion fared no better in San Francisco, where Watkins, now officially the vice president of the Republic of Sonora, had returned for more recruits. Major John Wool, Hitchcock's replacement, who had been instructed by Secretary of War Jefferson Davis to "zealously co-operate with the civil authorities in maintaining the neutrality laws," raided the recruiting center and arrested Watkins, along with several others. Emory had also been arrested crossing back into the United States at San Diego.[35]

Unaware of the misfortune that had befallen his men in the United States, Walker began his ill-fated march toward the frontier of Sonora on March 20, 1854. As he made his way toward the Colorado River, dozens of men deserted the battalion, and a group of Cocopah Indians who had joined the expeditionary force absconded with much of Walker's cattle. When the battalion reached the river, fifty more bedraggled men—now hungry, tired, wearing tattered rags, and indignant over the air of moral superiority with which Walker still carried himself as his troops suffered—deserted and headed north for Fort Yuma. Walker and his remaining men were attacked by the Cocopah who had left his army.[36]

Unable to cross the river and devoid of the supplies he needed to forge into Sonora, even Walker, convinced as he was of the exalted role Providence had chosen him to fulfill, could see that the expedition was hopeless. Of the three hundred men under his command when he left Ensenada, only thirty-four remained, the number whittled down by defections and attacks. What was left of the First Independence Battalion was quickly running out of food and ammunition. Walker retreated toward Ensenada, coming under frequent attack along the way by Melendrez, the infamous local bandit whose cattle he'd stolen. He surrendered to the US Army at the border in San Diego.[37]

A hero's welcome awaited Walker from the adoring public in San Francisco that had cheered his departure seven months earlier, and had eagerly followed reports of his exploits in the local press. The local authorities celebrated his return in their own way, charging Walker with a violation the Neutrality Act. Emory and Watkins had already been convicted.[38]

At trial, Walker implausibly told the jury that he hadn't decided to land at La Paz in a "hostile manner" until after he'd left the territorial waters of the United States, a convenient chronology of events that would have put him outside the reach of the neutrality law because he'd violated it outside of American jurisdiction. Although the jurors no doubt saw Walker's lie for what it was, they were as smitten with the would-be conqueror as the rest of the city, and acquitted him of the charges.[39]

Walker, now with the honorific of "Colonel," returned to the newspaper business he'd left behind the year before, joining the staff of the *Commercial Advertiser*. For Walker, it was a fortuitous decision, for one of the newspaper's proprietors, Byron Cole, also dreamed of an empire in Latin America. Cole quickly piqued Walker's interest in a new expedition, this time farther south, in Nicaragua. It was the quest that would make Walker a household name across America.[40]

Nicaragua in 1855 was in the throes of a multistate civil war that raged across the borders of the five Central American nations, which just twenty-four years earlier had won their independence from Spain in the wave of anticolonial revolutions that swept through the once-mighty nation's American empire. The conservative Legitimists, the aristocratic party of the ruling class, battled the populist, liberal Democrats across the borders of Costa Rica, El Salvador, Honduras, Guatemala, and Nicaragua for control of Central America.

Cole left the *Commercial Advertiser* and traveled to Nicaragua in the fall of 1854 to offer his assistance to one of the country's warring factions. He arrived at an opportune time. Francisco Castellon had returned from exile to oust his Legitimist rival, Fruto Chamorro, and installed himself as Nicaragua's provisional director with the help of Democratic-ruled Honduras. When Guatemala's Legitimists invaded Honduras and overthrew its Democratic government, Honduran Legitimists turned on Castellon. Under the command of General Santos Guardiola, known as "the Butcher" due to his savagery against both his enemies and his own men, Honduran forces invaded northern Nicaragua to restore the Legitimists to power.[41]

In desperate need of manpower to fend off the Butcher's invasion, Castellon signed a contract with Cole for three hundred American fighters, who would be paid in gold and land. Upon receiving the contract, Walker, wary of facing further allegations of violating the Neutrality Act, demanded that it be rewritten to specify that the men would be colonists. When he received the new "contract of colonization," Walker brought it to federal district attorney S. W. Inge, the chief prosecutor from the Sonora trial. Inge assured him that the contract would not violate the neutrality act.* Wool approved, agreeing not to hinder Walker's expedition and even wishing him good luck. With Inge and Wool's blessing, Walker signed the contract and prepared for his second expedition.[42]

On June 1, 1855, Walker's dilapidated ship, the *Vesta*, arrived in the bay of Realejo, on the northern end of Nicaragua's Pacific coast, with his army of 300 Immortals, as they would become known. His crew included several veterans, including Crocker, who had led the charge that broke the Mexicans' siege at Ensenada, along with men who had fought in the Mexican War. Walker traveled to León, the Democratic capital, to meet with his benefactor Castellon, who

---

* Secretary of State William Marcy reached the same conclusion. When Nicaraguan officials who had gotten wind of Walker's departure protested to the State Department, Marcy explained that no law forbade Americans to enter into the military service of the government of Nicaragua (*Index to the Executive Documents, Printed by Order of the Senate of the United States, First and Second Sessions, Thirty-Fourth Congress, 1855–'56.* Washington, DC: A. O. P. Nicholson, Senate Printer, 1856, 22).

instructed him to use his army to take the Legitimist-held city of Rivas, near the shores of Lake Nicaragua.[43]

Ponciano Corral, the Legitimist officer who controlled Rivas, had received word of Walker's march, and dispatched some of his troops to meet Walker's *falange*, as the Nicaraguans called his forces, using the Spanish word for "phalanx." After a skirmish at the village of Tola, Walker's troops advanced toward Rivas, which Corral had fortified in anticipation of the Immortals' arrival.[44]

By most standards, the battle of Rivas was a failure for Walker. Fifteen of his fifty-five men were killed or wounded in their initial charge into the town plaza, and about one hundred native troops provided by Castellon fled, with Walker and his remaining soldiers forced the take cover in hilltop houses. Colonel Felix Ramirez, a Democratic officer who had accompanied the Immortals, deserted Walker rather than join the battle. After four hours of fighting, Walker was forced to withdraw. Among Walker's dead was Crocker, his trusted subordinate from the Sonoran campaign, and Achilles Kewen, another key member of his *falange.* Nonetheless, the Immortals acquitted themselves well, holding their position against a force of more than five hundred soldiers for several hours, and suffering only eighteen casualties. Walker claimed to have killed at least seventy Legitimists and wounded at least as many.[45]

Walker retreated to León, where he learned that cholera had broken out in Rivas. Rather than let the disease decimate his troops, Corral marched his men to Granada. Walker had the opening he needed. But he was obstructed by José Trinidad Muñoz, Castellon's top general, who denied his request for two hundred native troops and forbade him to attack either Rivas or the Legitimist-controlled city of Managua, preferring instead to guard against a possible attack by Guardiola in the north. Furthermore, Muñoz, who resented the presence of the American troops, proposed dissolving Walker's *falange* and reassigning his men to Nicaraguan-led units. About three hundred Nicaraguan troops occupied the barracks across from the Americans, apparently to cow Walker into submission. Despite having a vastly superior force, Castellon and Muñoz withdrew the troops after Walker threatened to attack them.[46]

Having emerged the victor in his battle of wills with Castellon and Muñoz, Walker was now determined to chart his own course of action. Byron Cole, who by now had arrived in Nicaragua, had renegotiated his treaty with Castellon and included a hidden provision allowing Walker to settle all differences between the government of Nicaragua and the Accessory Transit Company, which controlled the transit route that brought travelers from the East Coast, through Nicaragua, and on to California. The route was of critical importance to Walker, who relied on it to supply him with new recruits from the United States. In accordance with that provision, Walker disregarded Castellon's orders to keep his troops in León and moved to take control of the vital route.[47]

To gain more men while he waited for reinforcements from America, Walker joined forces with José Maria Valle, a veteran Nicaraguan officer who was a fierce enemy of Muñoz. Walker wanted a reliable native officer, while Valle wanted revenge against the Legitimists, who had killed his brother at Granada. With Castellon's grudging acceptance, Valle augmented Walker's meager force with about 170 native soldiers. From Realejo, Walker, now with Valle's men at his side, set out on August 23 for San Juan del Sur, the Pacific terminus of the transit road across Nicaragua.[48]

When he first arrived at San Juan del Sur, Walker reconnected with a man who would become a key figure in his Nicaraguan expedition. Walker had first encountered Parker French, a one-armed con artist who had become a California state senator, as he was planning his departure for Nicaragua. French was intrigued by Walker's plans, though unlike Walker, who thirsted for glory, French wanted only the riches that could be gained from the venture. French boasted that could get the support of C. K. Garrison, a partner in Cornelius Vanderbilt's Accessory Transit Company. Walker disregarded and forgot French's claim. But when Walker arrived in San Juan del Sur, French was there.[49]

French had initially gone to Granada in an attempt to secure the support of its Legitimist leaders. Having been rebuffed, he made his way to San Juan del Sur, where he offered his assistance to Walker instead, telling him that he'd gone to Granada to spy on the Legitimists. Walker didn't necessarily trust French, but realized he could be useful. He sent French back to San Francisco with instructions to bring back 75 troops. And Walker, with about 43 American soldiers and another 120 natives—a cholera epidemic had wiped out some of Valle's forces—would march to the port of La Virgen, where the transit road met Lake Nicaragua.[50]

At La Virgen, or Virgin Bay, as it's referred to in many accounts, Walker won his first true victory in Nicaragua. Guardiola the Butcher, fresh from his defeat at the hands of Muñoz at El Sauce, had moved south, to Rivas, where he commanded about 1,200 soldiers.* The Butcher had sent about half of his force to La Virgen, where they caught the unsuspecting Walker by surprise.

Two columns of what were supposed to be some of Guardiola's best men advanced on Walker and Valle's forces. But Walker's army, desperately outmanned with only 163 men, was able to quickly gain the upper hand. An ancient cannon that Guardiola had brought with him—using his own soldiers instead of horses to carry it, because the decrepit gun no longer had wheels—malfunctioned and collapsed when he tried to fire it. His useless cannon now lying broken in the

* Muñoz had defeated Guardiola, but the victory cost him his life, most certainly a welcome development to Valle and Walker. Castellon hoped that the death of Walker's nemesis would help to heal the widening rift between them, writing to Walker, "Now, Muñoz being out of the way, all will be well" (Dando-Collins, 82).

dirt, Guardiola decided to charge the Accessory Transit Company warehouse where Walker's men had taken cover. "They went down like grass before a scythe, their bodies and the severity of the fire abruptly checking their advance," wrote C. W. Doubleday, a member of Walker's *falange*.

Walker's forces suffered few casualties in the victory at La Virgen, though the filibuster himself nearly became one. A bullet hit him in the throat, but, having spent most of its momentum, bounced off of him. Another hit him in the chest, where a packet of letters in his breast pocket saved him from a certain death.[51]

Rather than send his outnumbered army to pursue Guardiola as he retreated to Rivas, Walker moved his force back to San Juan del Sur and sent a courier to León to inform Castellon of the great victory at La Virgen. But Castellon was not long for this world. The courier found him bedridden and dying of cholera, which would soon claim the Democratic leader's life. Don Nazario Escoto succeeded Castellon as the country's provisional director.[52] Walker had barely showed any allegiance to Castellon, whom he technically served. He would show less to Escoto.

While Walker pondered his next move in San Juan, he received information that gave rise to his boldest move yet. Through his spies and a captured courier, Walker learned of the sad state of affairs in the Legitimist camp. Corral, disgusted with Guardiola's defeat at La Virgen, sent the Butcher back to Honduras and took personal control of Rivas, which he planned to use as a staging area for a march against Walker's forces. Virtually the entire Legitimist army was in Rivas, leaving Granada almost completely undefended. With the road to the Legitimist capital now wide open, Walker wasted little time in seizing the initiative.[53]

Granada lay north of Virgin Bay, on the coast of Lake Nicaragua. When *La Virgen*, a lake steamer owned by the Accessory Transit Company, arrived in port on October 11 to deposit its California-bound passengers along the transit road, Walker commandeered the vessel over the protests of its captain and of Cortland Cushing, the transit company's agent in La Virgen. The next morning, with his army now numbering about 350 men, thanks to an influx of new recruits, the ship slipped out of the dock and into Lake Nicaragua, past the looming volcanoes of Ometepe and toward Granada.[54]

Under the cover of night, Walker's men disembarked three miles north of the Legitimist capital. With Walker's Americans leading the way, the *falange*, as quietly as possible, made their way toward Granada. As they reached the outskirts of the city under the first sunlight of daybreak, the ringing of church bells from inside Granada shattered the dawn's silence. Walker worried that the Legitimists had spotted his army and that the pealing of the bells was warning their soldiers. But an elderly man who'd been waiting for Walker's troops to pass informed him that the bells rang out in celebration of the Legitimists' recent victory over the Democrats in a battle at the town of Pueblo Nuevo.

The church bells were still pealing when Walker's forces reached Granada. The unsuspecting Legitimists put up little resistance. A detachment of troops under the command of Charles Hornsby plowed through undefended barricades and into the town's central plaza. With only one casualty, a Nicaraguan drummer who'd been killed by the errant ricochet of Legitimist bullet, Walker had taken the capital in just a few minutes of what could only generously be called fighting. "[T]he Legitimist force in the town had been trifling, and the encounter between it and the Democrats could scarcely be dignified with the name of an action," Walker later recorded. For a man as convinced as Walker that he was destined for greatness, the nearly bloodless fall of Granada could have been no clearer sign.[55]

Walker was well-received in Granada. He freed one hundred Democratic political prisoners chained to the walls of the convent basement and forbade his troops from engaging in the looting and marauding that so often accompanied the fall of a city in the bloody civil war. The soft-spoken and diminutive Walker contrasted pleasantly with the locals' stereotype of a filibuster, "a sort of a centaur with far more of the beast than of the man in his nature."[56]

Learning of Granada's fall, Corral, still in Rivas plotting what he'd hoped would be his death stroke against Walker, did not yet believe he was beaten. Corral turned away Walker's emissaries who'd brought offers of peace—John H. Wheeler, the American minister in Granada, was briefly held prisoner by the Legitimists in Rivas after bringing such an offer at Walker's behest—and marched his troops south to La Virgen, now emptied of the filibuster's troops.

The capture of Granada was not the only provocation that spurred Corral to action. After arriving in Granada with sixty new recruits for Walker's army, the duplicitous Parker French had convinced Walker to let him take his fresh troops to seize the fort of San Carlos, which guarded the spot where the San Juan River met Lake Nicaragua in the east.

French took sixty men on *La Virgen*, which already had two hundred passengers aboard for the Accessory Transit Company's journey to California, and ordered the ship to sail to San Carlos. Upon reaching the fort, French sent three men ashore to demand its surrender. The Legitimists took the messengers prisoner and fired on *La Virgen*, killing three passengers. French gave up the fight and turned around, leaving the prisoners to be freed later by the Accessory Transit Company.

Corral rushed his troops to La Virgen, which Walker had abandoned, and in retaliation fired into the Accessory Transit Company warehouse, where the passengers who'd become unintentional participants in French's aborted attack on San Carlos were housed. Three unarmed civilians were killed. Corral's soldiers pillaged the warehouse and took its manager prisoner. In the meantime, back at

San Carlos, another transit company steamer, its captain and passengers ignorant of the recent attack by its sister ship, approached the fort. The Legitimists, prepared this time for an assault by Walker's forces, fired its cannon. A widow from California, along with one of her two children, was killed when a cannonball came crashing through the ship's deckhouse.

Walker's retribution for the Massacre of Virgin Bay was swift and cruel, but was not directed at French, who by any analysis bore all responsibility for the debacle, or the Legitimist soldiers who'd killed the civilians. It was a member of the Legitimists' civil government who would suffer the consequences for French's blunder. In Granada's grand plaza, Walker's troops executed Mateo Mayorga, a Legitimist government minister who'd been taken prisoner in the fall of Granada. And Walker sent a message to Corral, who'd moved his troops to the town of Masaya in preparation for an assault against Walker's forces, informing him that he had sixty more Legitimist hostages whose lives would be forfeited if the Legitimists committed further outrages.[57]

Now Corral knew he was beaten. On October 22, he sent word to Walker that he was ready to make peace.[58]

Walker had turned down an offer to become Nicaragua's president when he took Granada. Under the terms of the peace treaty with Corral, the country's new president would be Patricio Rivas, the former Legitimist port collector for San Juan.* But though Rivas was president in name, he would be no more than a puppet. Walker, who had arrived less than five months earlier with a ragtag army of forty-five men, now ruled Nicaragua. He signed the treaty as "Commander-in-chief of the democratic army that occupies Granada."[59]

Like many a dictator who would follow him in countless nations, Walker created a newspaper to praise his regime. The bilingual *El Nicaraguense* lauded Walker for audiences in both Nicaragua and the United States, attracting enthusiastic recruits from America and constructing the myth of the great filibuster for the nation he now ruled. Borrowing liberally from local Indian folklore that said the natives would be one day be freed by a "gray-eyed man," *El Nicaraguense* gave Walker a new name, one that would be remembered by history and would feed his growing megalomania: the Gray-Eyed Man of Destiny.[60]

The Legitimists had been subdued and Walker was firmly in control of Nicaragua. He also controlled the vital transit route that kept his army supplied with new soldiers from America. But the filibuster now had a new foe to contend with: Cornelius Vanderbilt.

---

* Corral would not survive a month under Walker's regime. Valle provided Walker with evidence that Corral was plotting against him, writing letters to Guardiola and other Honduran Legitimists, urging them to come to his aid. Walker, a fierce disciplinarian who brooked no opposition from his own men, could not tolerate Corral's attempted conspiracy. On November 8, Corral was executed by firing squad in Granada's grand plaza.

Of all the enemies Walker made in between Central America and the United States, one could argue that none were as dangerous, or as detrimental to his cause, as Vanderbilt. Also known as "the Commodore," Vanderbilt was far more willing than the federal government to bring the full force of his substantial resources to bear on Walker, and it would help to bring about Walker's ultimate downfall in Nicaragua.

In terms of fame, prestige, and celebrity status, Vanderbilt, the richest man in America, was perhaps one of the few Americans who loomed larger than the filibusters in the imaginations of their countrymen. In terms of the power he could exercise over his enemies, Walker and his fellow mercenaries couldn't have held a candle to the tycoon had they conquered every inch of land between Mexico and Colombia. Once Walker began interfering with his lucrative business interests in Nicaragua, Vanderbilt put that power to work.

The Commodore had created the Accessory Transit Company in 1850 to ship passengers to California via Nicaragua, where he hoped to build a pan-isthmus canal. The gold rush was in full swing in California, and demand for passage from the East Coast to the West was at its peak. Though he sold his controlling share in his shipping companies in 1853 and stepped down from his positions as director and president, Vanderbilt still owned a large number of shares, and was the company's largest bondholder. He was also the company's New York shipping agent for the Nicaragua route, which earned him 2.5 percent commission on every ticket sold. In addition, a secret arrangement gave Vanderbilt 20 percent of the company's income.

Vanderbilt's conflict with the gray-eyed man of destiny began as an extension of his feud with two associates who'd tried to wrest these prizes away from him. Cornelius Kingsland "C. K." Garrison, the Accessory Transit Company's shipping agent in San Francisco, and Charles Morgan, the company's director, seized control of the company while Vanderbilt was in Europe. At a May 1853 board meeting, Garrison and Morgan convinced the board to name Morgan as the company's new president and as its New York shipping agent, depriving Vanderbilt of his commission from the Nicaragua ticket sales. On top of that, they took away his 20 percent share of the company's income.

Vanderbilt was not a man to take such a coup lightly. Upon his return to America, an incensed Vanderbilt warned Garrison and Morgan, "Gentlemen, you have undertaken to cheat me. I won't sue you, for the law is too slow. I'll ruin you."

The first step in Vanderbilt's war against his backstabbing employees was the creation of a new steamship line, the Independent Opposition Line, in January 1854, which shipped passengers to the West Coast through the longer Panamanian route at a price low enough to undercut the Accessory Transit Company. Next, he dumped five thousand transit company shares onto the market, depressing the price of the company's stock. Despite his insistence that the law was too slow a way to ruin a man, Vanderbilt sued for his lost commissions, though he was rebuffed in court. A second lawsuit from his son-in-law Daniel Allen, the Accessory Transit Company's former vice president, further cut into the still-dropping stock price. With the stock now at $15 per share, Vanderbilt began to buy up shares of the company. All that remained was to seize back the control he had lost to Garrison and Morgan.[61]

It took two years, but Vanderbilt regained control of the Accessory Transit Company. In November 1855, he'd acquired enough shares of his old company to convince the board to elect him director, the position he'd voluntarily ceded in 1853. But by the time he won his battle against Garrison and Morgan, Walker had interfered in his plans.

In December 1855, Walker's old friend Edmund Randolph arrived in Nicaragua with one hundred new recruits for the Immortals' army, along with Garrison's son and Charles McDonald, the elder Garrison's agent. Walker had already become acquainted with McDonald after Parker French, who'd boasted in San Francisco that he could convince Garrison to support the filibuster's war, brought him to meet with Walker during the run-up to the capture of Granada. At the time, McDonald suggested that Garrison might be willing to offer the Accessory Transit Company's services to ferry troops to Nicaragua. After the fall of Granada, McDonald loaned Walker $20,000 worth of gold from Garrison.

Now, Randolph, McDonald, and Garrison the younger brought with them a more intriguing proposition than just gold. Morgan and the elder Garrison wanted Walker to revoke the Accessory Transit Company's charter with the Nicaraguan government and award a new one to them. In exchange, Walker's men would get free passage to Nicaragua on Garrison and Morgan's own shipping line.[62]

Walker believed that the Accessory Transit Company had cheated the Nicaraguan government, a sentiment shared by the Nicaraguan officials. Indeed, through feats of devious bookkeeping, Vanderbilt had underhandedly avoided paying Nicaragua the 10 percent of the shipping route's profits owed under the agreement by claiming that he actually made no profit. After a thorough examination of the company's 1849 charter, Randolph and Walker, both trained lawyers, determined that it was forfeit because the company had failed to build a canal across Nicaragua, as the charter stipulated.[63]

In February 1856, just as the Accessory Transit Company board completed Vanderbilt's takeover by naming him director once again, President Rivas revoked the company's exclusive charter to transport passengers across Nicaragua. At Walker's urging, the new contract was awarded to Randolph on behalf of Garrison and Morgan's new shipping line. Walker had rendered Vanderbilt's great victory quite hollow. The filibuster did not know it yet, but in snatching Vanderbilt's prize from his hands, Walker had helped to ensure his own downfall.[64]

Vanderbilt was not the only problem Walker was bringing upon himself. As Walker plotted through December 1855, his adventures in Nicaragua had finally raised enough ire in Washington to force President Franklin Pierce to take action.

Buoyed by the official recognition bestowed on the Rivas regime by John Wheeler, the American minister in Nicaragua, who was a devout believer in Manifest Destiny, Walker sent Parker French as his ambassador to the United States. Despite French's baffling recklessness in the San Carlos fiasco, Walker for some reason trusted him, at least enough to represent his regime in America.

Walker's seizure of power put Pierce in an awkward position politically. Filibustering in general and Walker in particular were popular, especially in the South. But Walker was also breaking the law, and on top of that he was complicating America's foreign policy. Pierce at the time had been in negotiations with Great Britain over its claim of a protectorate of the Mosquito Coast in Nicaragua's east, and the president didn't need some headstrong mercenary causing problems by making a mockery of America's neutrality laws.

The fact that Walker held the reins of power did not make his government legitimate in the eyes of the White House. Nor was Pierce's administration swayed by Wheeler's formal recognition of the Walker-Rivas government, which Secretary of State William Marcy had swiftly ordered his minister to rescind. Marcy also refused to receive French as Nicaragua's minister to the United States, leaving him waiting in his anteroom for several days before sending his subordinates to turn him away.[65]

Still, Pierce seemed to have little hope of stemming the flow of new soldiers to Walker's army. Barely disguised newspaper advertisements sought fresh recruits for the filibuster's conquests. One, which appeared in the *New York Herald*, claimed to be seeking "Ten or fifteen young men to go a short distance out of the city." In a vain attempt to enforce the Neutrality Act, Pierce issued a proclamation on December 8 warning Americans against joining Walker's army.[66]

Several weeks later, the Pierce administration attempted more drastic measures when it made its first sincere attempt to enforce the Neutrality Act against Walker and his Nicaragua-bound recruits. On orders from the attorney general, John McKeon, the federal district attorney for southern New York, went to the harbor to stop the well-publicized Christmas Eve departure of Walker's recruits, who were scheduled to ship out on the *Northern Light*, an Accessory Transit Company ship that Vanderbilt had built specifically for the Nicaragua line.

With two US marshals at his side, McKeon boarded the *Northern Light* and attempted to read Pierce's proclamation, but was drowned out by the shouts of the ship's passengers and their cheering supporters on the pier. Against McKeon's orders, the ship slid out of the harbor and seemed well on its way until a federal revenue cutter, towed by a steamboat that McKeon had commandeered, fired a warning shot across its bow. The *Northern Light* returned to its pier and McKeon searched the ship for Walker's would-be soldiers.

Finding Walker's recruits among the ship's five hundred passengers proved difficult, in large part because they had tickets just like any other passenger. Each recruit had received a black button several days earlier as an "open sesame," which they were told to exchange with the ship's officers in exchange for a ticket. McKeon arrested forty men he'd identified as bound for Walker's army, including Parker French and Joseph Male, the editor of *El Nicaraguense*, who'd come to New York to purchase printing supplies.[67]

McKeon accomplished little besides temporarily delaying the *Northern Light*. The *New York Atlas* highlighted the pointlessness of Pierce's efforts to stymie the filibustering crusaders: "When will this child's play cease? Like India rubber, North American filibusters jump higher every time they are stricken down; and all such opposition recently made to their movements, by the instructions of the President and his cabinet, only increases their numbers and emboldens them to cling more tenaciously to their enterprise."[68]

Still unaware that Garrison, Morgan, and Walker had snatched his charter out from under him, Vanderbilt protested to McKeon about the government's treatment of the *Northern Light*. In language that could be interpreted as an attempt to bribe the district attorney, Vanderbilt wrote, "I am desirous to have no difficulty with the ships. Any mode you may point out to save trouble that may arise I will most cheerfully join you in. Therefore, if at any time you see or hear of anything wrong, you will always find me ready to make it right so far as it is in my power."[69]

Vanderbilt had previously viewed Walker as a civilizing influence amid the anarchy that had engulfed Nicaragua, and even continued Garrison's agreement to ship filibusters to the country for free. He would be far less enamored with Walker when he learned that the Accessory Transit Company's charter had been revoked. Vanderbilt now boiled over with rage as he hurried to Washington to confront Marcy. "One William Walker has interfered with my American property, Marcy!" he bellowed at the secretary of state. Marcy was eager to see Walker dislodged from Nicaragua, but there was little he could do for the Commodore. For good measure, he reminded Vanderbilt of his hypocrisy for demanding the government help him against Walker after intervening on the filibusters' behalf during the *Northern Light* incident. Vanderbilt left with only a weak assurance from Marcy that the State Department would examine the situation. Vanderbilt would have to take matters into his own hands.[70]

Fortunately for Vanderbilt, the federal government was not the only lever he could use to exert pressure on Walker. The day after his unproductive meeting with Marcy, Vanderbilt called upon John Crampton, Great Britain's ambassador to the United States. The two had a common interest in clipping Walker's wings, as Britain had grown concerned that the filibuster would seize the Mosquito Coast port of Greytown, its economic lifeline to Nicaragua. The town on Nicaragua's Atlantic coast was also critical to Walker, for whom the port served as a gateway for his recruits departing from the East Coast and New Orleans. Crampton agreed to ask his government to station a British warship in the Greytown harbor to block Walker's troops from landing there, and informed the Commodore that the ship would be at his disposal should he need it.[71]

Next, Vanderbilt met with the ambassadors of Nicaragua's Central American neighbors and urged them to take action against Walker, for which, of course, he would be happy to provide assistance. They needed no prodding to recognize the threat that the filibuster posed to them. Walker had proposed a union of the five Central American nations, sending a delegation to Costa Rica to pitch the idea. The delegation, headed by Louis Schlessinger, a Hungarian revolutionary who'd participated in the last filibustering expedition of Narciso López in Cuba, was not well received in San José. Costa Rica was not alone in viewing Walker's overture as the first step in his next war of conquest. As if Costa Rica, El Salvador, Guatemala, and Honduras weren't already suspicious enough, Vanderbilt informed the ambassadors that Walker had recently unveiled a new Nicaraguan flag that showed the designs he had for Nicaragua's neighbors: five blue stripes with one white star in the center.[72]

Schlessinger's peace overtures had the opposite effect of that intended by Walker. Juan Rafael Mora, Costa Rica's president, had been wary of Walker from the moment he had set foot in Nicaragua. And Great Britain, no friend to Walker, had been arming Mora's government and urging it to action against the filibuster. When Lord Clarendon, the British foreign minister, learned that Mora had massed eight hundred men on the border with Nicaragua, he told the Costa Rican consul in London that "[this] was the right step."[73]

With Great Britain and Vanderbilt at his back, Nicaragua's neighbors at his side, and nine thousand soldiers at his disposal, the time was ripe for Mora to act. On March 1, 1856, Mora convinced Costa Rica's parliament to declare war on Rivas and Walker's regime. "To arms!" Mora shouted to the national assembly members. "The moment has arrived. We march into Nicaragua to destroy this impious *falange* which has reduced the people to oppressive slavery. We march to fight for the liberty of every man!"[74]

Just as Walker's need for new filibusters was greatest, Vanderbilt struck a devastating blow. The Commodore sidelined all eight of the steamers on his Nicaraguan route, letting them lay idle at their wharves. Until Vanderbilt decided otherwise, the flow of new recruits to Walker's army would slow to a trickle. "The Nicaragua Line is withdrawn for the present, in consequence of the difficulties in that country growing out of the extraordinary conduct of General Walker, in seizing or taking by force the property of American citizens. I deem it a duty I owe the public, to the country, and to the Transit Company, to remain quiet, by letting the ships of the company lay at their wharves, until our government has sufficient time to examine and look into the outrage committed upon their property," Vanderbilt announced.

Walker was faced with a difficult choice: Holding the transit road had long been his chief concern, but with the pipeline that supplied him with troops from the United States largely severed by Vanderbilt, there was little reason to expend the increasingly scarce resources needed to maintain control of the precious route. A filibuster army commanded by Schlessinger had already been routed at Santa Rosa, near the Costa Rican border, and Walker warily watched the north, where he expected the Guatemalans and Hondurans to attack. With the next shipment of soldiers from California six weeks away, Walker ordered the Immortals to abandon the city of Rivas and the transit road. Mora's Costa Rican army occupied Rivas, La Virgen, and San Juan del Sur.[75]

Fortunately for Walker, 250 new recruits under the command of the Cuban filibuster Domingo de Goicouria, a veteran of Narciso López's expeditions, had slipped out of the United States before Vanderbilt had halted traffic on the Nicaragua route. Walker retreated with his army to Granada, while President Rivas's government relocated to León.[76]

In Granada, Walker, having just recovered from a bout of dengue fever, decided to double back to Rivas. At full health and with 650 troops at his command, he marched south to the city he'd abandoned just five days earlier, where he hoped to dislodge the Costa Ricans and capture Mora, which he believed would bring the war to an end. Walker's troops caught the Costa Ricans by surprise and were able to seize the city's plaza. But the victory was short-lived. The Costa Ricans regained their composure and forced Walker's *falange*, which lacked artillery, out of the city. Walker retreated again to Granada, with 58 of his soldiers killed, 62 wounded, and 13 more missing.* The second battle of Rivas, like the first, was a failure for Walker. The victory would be only temporary for Mora, however. Within three weeks of the battle, as a cholera epidemic decimated his troops, Mora was forced to withdraw from Rivas to squelch a plot against him in San Jose. For the time being, at least, Costa Rica was out of the war.[77]

While Walker fended off Mora's invasion, allies in the United States, stirred by his filibustering crusade and angered by the intervention of Britain, were

* Every April 11, Costa Rica celebrates the national holiday of Juan Santamaria Day, so named for the drummer boy who was killed while setting fire to an inn where Walker's soldiers had been holed up during the Battle of Rivas.

taking up his cause. As was promised to Vanderbilt, the British had blocked Garrison and Morgan's ship Orizaba from depositing its troops at Greytown. In New Orleans, a pro-Walker rally invoked the sacred name of the Monroe Doctrine in demanding that the United States curb British activities in Nicaragua. Support for Walker was gaining momentum in Washington as well.

Walker had written to US Senator John B. Weller of California, urging American support. "I may not live to see the end, but I feel that my countrymen will not permit the result to be doubtful. I know that the honor and the interests of the great country which, despite the foreign service I am engaged in, I still love to call my own, are involved in the present struggle," he wrote. Weller defended Walker in the Senate, where he introduced a resolution calling for the Pierce administration to make public Walker's correspondence with the American minister in Granada. Senator Stephen Douglas entered the fray as well, demanding that the United States recognize Walker's regime. "I hold that the government is as legitimate as any which ever existed in Central America," Douglas proclaimed.[78]

Even Pierce was contemplating granting official diplomatic recognition to the Walker regime, which had sent Father Augustin Vigil, a Granada priest who was less offensive to the White House's sensibilities than Parker French, as his new minister to Washington. Marcy sent word to John Wheeler to resume diplomatic relations with the Walker-Rivas regime. By the time Wheeler received his orders, the regime would belong to Walker alone.[79]

The gray-eyed man of destiny's final ascendance to power in Nicaragua began on May 30, when Walker, after learning of troubling developments in León, rode with two hundred of his men to the temporary capital. He arrived on June 4 to the cheers of the city's exuberant residents. His ostensible puppet rulers were less joyful. When Walker met with Rivas and members of the president's cabinet, he learned what troubled lurked. The president had repeatedly warned of an attack from the north by El Salvador and Guatemala. The Salvadoran government had issued a proclamation saying that Walker's American troops were a threat to the independence of the Central American nation. In response, Rivas and his Salvadoran counterpart had agreed to reduce the number of American troops in Nicaragua to just two hundred.

Walker saw the move for the attempted coup it was. He proposed to Rivas that an election be held at once. Rivas and his cabinet rejected the proposal, but were cowed into submission after Walker arrested one of his generals for selling to the government, at an inflated price, some brazilwood he'd illegally smuggled into the country. With the election set, Walker put his name on the ballot.[80]

In anticipation of a move against him by Rivas and Maximo Jerez, one of the president's cabinet ministers, Walker withdrew his army from León and marched south to Granada, where he issued a decree dissolving the Rivas government.

Three days before the June 29 election began, Rivas issued a decree of his own, branding Walker and his Americans as traitors and enemies of Nicaragua. The southern provinces that Walker's men now controlled were the only places where the election would take place. Rivas canceled the election in the northern provinces.

Under those circumstances, the results of the three-day election could not be in doubt. According to *El Nicaraguense*, Walker received 15,835 votes, which no doubt included the ballots of his soldiers, who had been granted voting privileges as nominal citizens of Nicaragua. Coming in second was the provisional president Walker had installed after dissolving Rivas's government, with 4,447 votes, followed by Mariano Salazar, the general whom Walker had punished for selling the smuggled wood. Rivas received only a paltry 867 votes, according to Walker's propagandistic newspaper.[81]

There would be no more puppet presidents. There would be no more charades that Walker served only the regime that had hired him. On July 12, fourteen months after arriving in Nicaragua, Walker would be inaugurated as Nicaragua's president. "The Republic has reached an era in its history not second in importance to the day of her independence from the Spanish monarchy," a triumphant Walker declared in his victory speech.[82]

Walker should have paid heed to Rivas's warnings about an invasion from the north. Six days after Walker was sworn in as Nicaragua's president, Guatemalan soldiers under the command of General Mariano Paredes marched into León in defense of the ousted president. Generals from El Salvador and Honduras joined them. They were now united in one overriding mission: to rid Nicaragua of William Walker.[83]

Marcy was livid that Wheeler, who had been instructed to recognize a regime that no longer existed, now extended that diplomatic recognition to Walker. The secretary of state withdrew recognition and ordered Wheeler, whose quasi-freelance diplomacy had caused so much discord, back to Washington.[84] But Walker, already a popular hero in much of the United States, was about to catapult himself to new heights of fame and adulation in the South by hitching his cause to its holiest of institutions.

On September 22, Walker issued a decree legalizing slavery, which Nicaragua had abolished in 1824. Proponents of slavery had for decades pined for the institution's expansion in Central America, which was a driving force behind the filibuster movement and America's enthusiasm for it. Those calls grew louder as Walker rose to power in Nicaragua. In February 1856, one newspaper bemoaned that Nicaragua's only drawback for Americans was its "want of slaves." Pierre Soulé, a former US senator from Louisiana, publicly postulated that the extension of slavery into Nicaragua would bring about a sea change in the balance of power between North and South. "If, by any chance, Nicaragua should become a part of this republic, the preponderance of the North is gone," Soulé had announced. Historian Stephen Dando-Collins ascribed Walker's decision to reintroduce slavery to Soulé's suggestion, while visiting the filibuster in Granada, that Southerners would be more willing to invest in his Nicaragua if they could use slave labor. Shortly before Walker issued his infamous decree, Soulé spent $40,000 on a cacao farm in anticipation of the reintroduction of slavery to the country.[85]

The slavery decree was just one of a series of proclamations that Walker, now firmly in control as the regime's president, began issuing within days of his inauguration, with the purpose of remaking the country and attracting American emigrants to his republic. On July 14, Walker decreed that all laws would be published in both English and Spanish, and that legal documents in either language would be viewed as equal by the state. Walker, who had learned a great deal of Spanish since arriving in Nicaragua, wanted to make it easier for Americans to acquire property in the country, and knew "the decree concerning the use of the two languages tended to make ownership of the lands of the State fall into the hands of those speaking English."[86] To ensure that there was plenty of land to go around, Walker decreed two days later that property of "enemies of the state" would be confiscated and sold to the highest bidder. A third decree created a state registry of all property in Nicaragua.[87] The decrees all shared one overarching goal of Walker's: "They were intended to place a large proportion of the land of the country in the hands of the white race."[88]

But it was the slavery decree that would be the capstone of Walker's plan to attract a flood of American colonists to bolster his rule. Walker called it "the act around which the whole policy of the administration revolved." He credited slavery with the prosperity of the Spanish colonial government in Cuba, and believed that the "permanent presence of the white race" in Nicaragua depended on the reestablishment of slavery there as well. "Without such labor as the new decree gave, the Americans could have played no part in Central America than that of the pretorian [*sic*] guard at Rome or of the Janizaries of the East," Walker later wrote in justification. With their African slaves as their "companions," Walker wrote, "the white man would become fixed to the soil."[89]

For the South, Walker's reinstatement of slavery in Nicaragua was a potential godsend. The slavocracy, fighting for its life in Bleeding Kansas, now had new lands in which to expand as civil war loomed. "The institution of slavery is, therefore, in effect, now recognized and authorized in Nicaragua," wrote the pro-Walker *New York Herald*. "Thus it will be perceived that the late decree of President Walker is highly important to planters and others in the southern portion of the United States, who desire to emigrate with their property to this 'garden of the world.'"[90]

But Walker had no interest in having Nicaragua annexed to the United States. He intended the decree to "bind the Southern states to Nicaragua" as an ally, not as a future state itself. It was "important, in every respect, to make it appear that the American movement in Nicaragua did not contemplate annexation," Walker later wrote.[91]

To the newly cemented alliance between El Salvador, Guatemala, Honduras, and the remnants of the Rivas government, the slavery decree only confirmed their worst fears about Walker. The allies, who were by now receiving considerable assistance from Vanderbilt, marshaled their forces at León in preparation for a final assault on the American adventurers. With only about 800 troops at his disposal, Walker did not believes his forces were strong enough to take the Legitimist stronghold, which was held by an army of about 1,200, until he received more recruits.[92]

By October 11, with new soldiers swelling his ranks, Walker decided it was time to engage the enemy, though not at León. Walker had abandoned Masaya and Managua at the start of the war against the Central American allies. Now he decided a show of strength was needed, and he chose Masaya, about fifteen miles inland from Granada, as the site of the showdown.

The decision was a disaster for Walker. Not only was the *falange* forced back at Masaya, but by bringing his eight hundred troops out of Granada, he had left his capital defenseless. Guatemalan general Victor Zavala split about seven hundred troops off from the main force in Masaya and took Granada effortlessly, looting and killing foreigners until the approach of Walker's forces led the general to evacuate the city.

Walker's troubles were mounting. In Costa Rica, President Mora, who, unbeknownst to Walker, was being aided by Vanderbilt, took the opportunity to renew his war against the "immigrant usurpers" on November 1, and aimed his forces for the filibusters' precious transit road. His army promptly occupied San Juan del Sur, which Walker had left undefended, severing a vital link in the "highway of filibusterism."[93]

The transit road was critical to the continued existence of Walker's regime, and he was determined to take back San Juan del Sur in defense of it. Walker sailed for Virgin Bay, from which he hoped to launch an assault that would drive Mora's army from San Juan del Sur and send it back into Costa Rica. With the English mercenary Charles Frederick Henningsen as his second-in-command, Walker liberated the crucial Pacific port.[94]

With his 250 demoralized and poorly fed soldiers, Walker again tried and again failed to take Masaya from the allies. The filibuster, always convinced of his great destiny, had remained confident that he could defeat the allied armies. But following his second debacle at Masaya, the desperate president came to a grim realization: After arriving back in Granada on November 18, Walker concluded that he would be unable to hold the city. He set his sights instead on Rivas, and marched his army south to pry the city from the allies' hands.[95]

Had Walker not already made the decision to abandon Granada, its necessity would have become quickly apparent several days later when the allies began their final assault on the city on November 24. But Walker was unwilling to leave the city in peace. He ordered Henningsen to destroy Granada as he abandoned it to the allies.

The battle raged for days as Henningsen and his troops in Granada, which had been attacked from three directions on land by the allies, fought their way to the shore of Lake Nicaragua, from which they could make their escape. For many nights, Walker watched offshore from aboard a lake steamer as smoke billowed out of the city, waiting for Henningsen to make his final escape. Surrounded by burning buildings, blown-up churches, and corpse-strewn streets, Henningsen added a final touch to his decimation of the historic city as he stood on the wharf, where he would board *La Virgen* for his escape from Granada. Using a charred piece of wood as a pencil, he wrote a departing message to the allies on a piece of leather, attached it to a lance, drove it into the ground, and boarded the ship, leaving behind his vindictive epitaph for the city: *Aquí fue Granada*. In Spanish, the crude message cruelly boasted, "Here was Granada."[96]

In Walker's warped mind, there was justice in his cruelty. The people of Granada owed their "life and property" to the Americans who'd come to Nicaragua. And after all he'd done for them—or at least all he'd convinced himself that he'd done for them—they had stabbed him in the back. In his recounting of the war, Walker accused Granada's residents of acting as spies for the Legitimist armies, passing information to the enemy on the filibuster army's movements. "By the laws of war, the town had forfeited its existence," Walker wrote. He also intended the destruction as a blow to the morale of the Legitimists, who "had for their chief city a love like that of woman."[97]

The allies were not the only enemies Walker had to contend with. As the war in the north had ramped up, Vanderbilt had made his most audacious move yet.

On October 21, Sylvanus H. Spencer and William R. C. Webster came to Vanderbilt's New York office with a daring plan: If Vanderbilt could convince the Costa Ricans to rejoin the war against Walker and supply the country with the money and weapons they'd need to be successful, Spencer, a former Accessory Transit Company ship captain who had for years worked the Nicaraguan line, would lead Mora's army to seize the transit route and recover the ships that Walker's regime had stolen. Webster, an Englishman, promised to provide a seasoned British officer who would help lead the incursion.

The Commodore was intrigued. He told Spencer and Webster that he would provide the money and arms they and the Costa Ricans needed. If they succeeded in recovering his property and removing Walker from power, they would each receive $50,000 (the equivalent of more than $1.3 million today). A handshake sealed the deal.[98]

Spencer and the two hundred men under his command reached Hipp's Point, overlooking the filibuster outpost at San Juan Bay, on December 23. With a three-to-one manpower advantage, Spencer overtook Walker's men. From the bay, they floated on rafts down the river to Punta de Castillo, where Captain Joseph N. Scott, who managed Garrison and Morgan's business affairs in Nicaragua, had established a depot for the transit company's ships. With forty-five Costa Rican soldiers at his back, Spencer surprised Scott in bed and informed him that he was taking possession of four purloined steamers that rightfully belonged to Vanderbilt. Spencer sent three of the boats back to Costa Rica and captained the fourth, *Machuca*, which he used to command, up the San Juan River toward the bay.[99]

Near El Castillo, on the San Juan River, Spencer found another of Walker's ships, *La Virgen*. He boarded the ship and sailed up the river toward the filibuster fort at San Carlos, where the San Juan emptied into the Pacific. After luring the fort's commander out to greet the ship, which he still believed to be controlled by Walker's army, Spencer put a gun to the commander's head and threatened to kill him unless he surrendered the fort. Spencer won one more prize after the surrender of the fort when another steamer, the *San Carlos*, bound for Greytown and New York, entered the river.[100]

Spencer had landed a crippling blow. He'd seized six of Walker's ships and a key port on the transit route. The American press declared it a great victory for the Commodore.* Mora was ecstatic when he learned of Spencer's success. "The main artery of filibusterism has been cut forever. The sword of Costa Rica has severed it," he declared.[101] Walker, upon learning of the capture from American newspapers a month later, couldn't help but admire Spencer, whose boldness mirrored his own. "The fortune which proverbially favors the brave certainly aided Spencer much in his operations," Walker mused.[102]

The allies continued their push from the north while the Costa Ricans hemmed in Walker from the south. The combined armies of El Salvador, Guatemala, and Honduras crept continually closer to Rivas and La Virgen. Despondent and growing weary of his haughty attitude, Walker's troops began to desert from Rivas, enticed by Mora's promise of safe passage for those who abandoned the filibuster's army. On March 25, 1857, the allies began their final siege of Rivas, Walker's last stronghold.[103]

There was no hope for Walker to break the siege, but he could still escape with his life. The United States Navy had sent Captain Charles Henry Davis to Nicaragua with the official mission of protecting American citizens. His real mission, ordered by the US Navy secretary, at Vanderbilt's behest, was to see to

---

* Vanderbilt would not regain final control of the Nicaraguan transit line until 1858, when he finalized a deal with the post-Walker government.

Walker's final removal from the country. Mora, eager to bring the war to a close, had agreed to allow Davis to travel through Costa Rican–held territory to meet with Walker in Rivas. To facilitate Walker's exit from the Nicaraguan stage, Mora had also agreed to allow Walker free passage back to the United States if he would leave the country.[104]

Walker resisted Davis's overtures at first. But when his final gambit—the attempted recapture of the San Juan River—fell flat, the filibuster reconsidered his options. His position had become untenable. He was surrounded in his redoubt of Rivas, and had only enough food to last for several more days. Davis persuaded two of Walker's officers to acknowledge the desperate reality of the situation. They were convinced, and now Walker was as well.

On May 1, Walker boarded the *St. Mary*, the warship Davis had brought to Nicaragua, and began his journey home from San Juan del Sur. It had been two years since he'd arrived in Nicaragua. He'd risen from mercenary to de facto president to outright ruler of the nation. Now, he was once again just a private citizen of the United States. At New Orleans, Walker disembarked to a cheering throng of supporters who carried him on their shoulders across the wharf.[105]

Walker was far from gracious in his defeat. He wanted the world to know that he had surrendered not to allied forces of his Central American foes but to the United States, which was affirmed in the agreement he signed with Davis.[106]

In his final general order, issued from Rivas, the vanquished general declared, "Reduced to our present position by the cowardice of some, the incapacity of others, and the treachery of many, the army has yet written a page of American history which it is impossible to forget or erase. From the future, if not from the present, we may expect just judgment."[107]

The *New York Herald* opined that Walker's ouster from Nicaragua presaged the end of the filibustering era. "We have had successive forays into Cuba and into Mexico, and with the same termination to this last and most desperate, complicated and expensive Nicaragua experiment . . . conclude that filibustering in behalf of 'manifest destiny' is used up," the paper, which had formerly cheered Walker's exploits, now wrote.[108]

Walker didn't believe that. To him, his removal from power was only a temporary setback. He immediately set about planning his return.

In his life before filibustering, Walker was certainly no promoter of slavery. His editorials in the *Crescent* and even his political activities in California, where he'd backed an antislavery candidate for the US Senate at a Democratic convention following his return from Mexico, lend credence to that thesis. But slavery provided the foundation for much of his support in America. After his return to his native country, Walker played up his pro-slavery credentials masterfully as he whipped up Southern support for his return to Nicaragua.

Walker blamed his ouster on abolitionists, along with Marcy, Vanderbilt, and the British, claiming that the United States and Great Britain had assisted them in preventing the spread of slavery. He told a crowd in New Orleans that, having been born in a Southern state, he could not "consider slavery a moral or political wrong." To a crowd in Richmond, Walker avowed that his return to power in Nicaragua would be "of great importance to the South."[109] The South cheered him. That he had no intention of allowing the United States to annex Nicaragua seems to have had no bearing on its admiration for the filibuster.

Franklin Pierce was now gone from the White House, replaced by President James Buchanan, whom Walker hoped would be more amenable to his plans. He had, after all, been elected on the Democratic platform, which, at the insistence of Pierre Soulé, included a pro-filibuster and pro-Walker plank. Walker traveled to Washington to meet with Buchanan with the hope of securing a promise to not prosecute him under the Neutrality Act as he plotted his comeback. Walker claimed that the president had looked favorably upon his plans, though Buchanan recorded nothing about the meeting to verify it. If nothing else, certainly Walker could have confidence that Lewis Cass, Marcy's replacement as secretary of state, who had actually spoken at pro-Walker rallies, would view filibustering more warmly than his predecessor.[110]

Unfortunately for Walker, Cass's previous support wasn't a good predictor of future actions. The secretary of state, having fielded a number of complaints from the ambassadors of Nicaragua's neighbors, ordered port officials to block a filibustering expedition that attempted to set sail. Walker was actually arrested as he prepared to depart from New Orleans with two hundred men. After being released on bond, Walker, with the assistance of sympathetic officials in New Orleans, departed the United States to reclaim his presidency.[111]

Napoleon's Hundred Days it was not. Walker eluded a US warship at Greytown—the commander mistakenly believed the ship belonged to Vanderbilt—and traveled down the San Juan River, taking El Castillo, which the Costa Ricans had abandoned. That, however, was as far as Walker would get. Captain Hiram Paulding had come to assist the *Saratoga*, the ship that had allowed Walker to disembark, and sent 350 marines and sailors inland to capture the filibuster. Walker promptly surrendered.[112]

Few events so clearly illustrated the divide that Walker had caused in Washington than the Paulding affair. Paulding, who viewed Walker and his men as "outlaws who had escaped from the vigilance of the officers of the government," unleashed a firestorm of controversy by interfering with Walker's plans.[113] Walker's partisans in Congress denounced Paulding and sought to discipline him, ostensibly on the grounds that he was not permitted to enforce neutrality laws outside of American soil or waters, a position that even the unsympathetic Marcy had held. Buchanan acknowledged to Congress that Paulding had committed a "grave error" in seizing Walker, but that he was a "gallant officer" whose actions were driven by "patriotic motives." He noted that the government of Nicaragua, the only party that truly had any right to complain about a violation of its sovereign territory, had not protested Paulding's actions.[114]

Southerners accused Buchanan of betraying the South. William T. Avery, from Walker's home state of Tennessee, admonished both Buchanan and Paulding, declaring, "In my judgment, a heavier blow was never struck at southern rights, southern interests, the advancement, the fulfillment of our great American destiny, than when Commodore Paulding perpetrated upon our people his high-handed outrage under the pretext of these same forms of law."[115]

On the other side of the debate, antislavery men railed against Walker and praised Paulding for halting his attempted return to power. "There is a party in this country who go for the extension of slavery; and these predatory incursions against our neighbors are the means by which territory is to be seized, planted with slavery, annexed to the Union, and, in combination with the present slave-holding States, made to dominate this government, and the entire continent; or, failing in the policy of annexation, to unite with the slave States in a southern slave-holding Republic," said Congressman Francis Preston Blair Jr., a Missouri Republican and former Free Soil man.[116]

Walker escaped prosecution for his second expedition, and plotted yet another return to reclaim his presidency in Nicaragua. As he prepared for his final filibustering voyage, Walker officially converted to Catholicism, the faith of his adopted homeland and his departed fiancée. Perhaps still wearing the gold crucifix that Helen had given him upon their engagement in 1848, Walker converted at a cathedral in Mobile, Alabama, on December 31, 1858.[117]

The launch of Walker's third and final expedition faced repeated delays as he sought funding and men while trying to keep Buchanan, who was adamant about preventing his departure, in the dark about his plans. His allies spread disinformation about where he would embark from and where he would land. For a while, Buchanan was able to thwart Walker, at one point arresting three of his officers as they prepared to depart from New Orleans.[118]

It was while he tried to get his final expedition off the ground that Walker published *The War in Nicaragua*, an extensive and self-serving account of the expedition that had made him famous. Walker dedicated the book to the men who served under him in Nicaragua. "To the living, with the hope that we may soon meet again on the soil for which we have suffered more than the pangs of death," Walker avowed in the dedication. "To the memory of those who perished in the struggle, with the vow that as long as life lasts no peace shall remain with the foes who libel their names and strive to tear away the laurel which hangs over their graves."[119]

As Walker struggled to assemble his next mission to Nicaragua, a new opportunity presented itself. Residents of the island of Roatán, a part of the British colony of Belize, came pleading to Walker for help in preventing their home country from restoring the island to Honduras. In exchange, they would help Walker in his return to Nicaragua after he'd liberated them from Honduran rule. Walker decided to answer their call.

Leaving his trusted officer Callender Fayssoux in New Orleans to collect reinforcements, Walker set sail for Roatán with 130 men. After the first of the two ships he brought was intercepted by the British, Walker took the bulk of his expeditionary force, which, as had so often been the case in Nicaragua, was fast running out of food, from Roatán to the Honduran mainland. They landed at the village of Trujillo.[120]

Walker's plan was to use the Roatán expedition as a stepping-stone to Nicaragua. Diverting his force to the mainland could only delay his glorious return. But Walker, gripped by dreams of his preordained destiny, had grand visions of what could be accomplished in Honduras. He believed he could rally the support of both the fearful English residents of Roatán and the Honduran supporters of José Trinidad Cabañas, the country's exiled Democratic president. Walker wrote to Fayssoux in New Orleans, "If we get more men and the supplies they require we will guide the destiny of Central America."[121]

The British found Walker long before Fayssoux ever could have. A dragnet of fifteen British warships patrolled the region for Walker—historian Stephen Dando-Collins speculates that the entire Roatán expedition may have been a setup from the beginning—and two frigates found him at Trujillo. While Norvell Salmon, commander of the *Icarus*, waited for Walker to decide whether to surrender, the filibuster packed up his army, destroyed what supplies his troops couldn't carry themselves, and marched into the jungle with about eighty of his men.[122]

After several days in the jungle, Salmon's marines caught up with Walker. Salmon sent word to Walker that he demanded the filibuster's surrender. His demand was backed up by 250 Honduran troops under the command of General Mariano Alvarez, Salmon informed him. With an assurance from Salmon that he would be surrendering to the British and not the Hondurans, Walker agreed to abort his mission and turn himself in.

The British led Walker in chains onto the *Icarus*. But he would not remain in British custody for long. They had decided to turn Walker, for years an irritant in Central America, over to Alvarez. His fate was now in the hands of the Hondurans. And that meant his fate was sealed.

William Walker met his final end in Trujillo on September 12, 1860. One of the defining features of Walker's personality throughout his filibustering career was his ability to stay calm under the greatest duress of pitched battles. He exhibited that cool composure one final time as he walked, upright and dignified, to the old garrison where he was to be shot, as a throng of Hondurans trailed along to see the fearsome American conqueror's demise.

The priests who had escorted Walker administered his last rites. Then he stood against the wall as three rows of soldiers lined up around him. When the command was given, the first row opened fire. A second squad fired a volley into Walker's lifeless body, mutilating his face. As if to be sure that they would finally be rid of Walker, a lone soldier approached his corpse and fired one last bullet into his head.[123]

News of Walker's death was met with mixed emotions in the United States. As he'd learned years before when he prematurely declared himself the president of the unconquered land of Sonora, the public respected victory. By the time of his death, years past the apex of his career, the public's adulation had run out. The New Orleans *Commercial Bulletin* reported that the "mad and unwarrantable enterprise of the great filibuster has ended in disaster and defeat." The *Republican Banner*, a newspaper in Walker's hometown of Nashville, wrote, "There are thousands in this country who will hear of his death with regret—as that of a man who had qualities and capacities entitling him to a better fate. Throughout his career he has shown a degree of steady courage, of unflinching tenacity of purpose under the most disheartening reverses, which would have earned for him a high position if they had been used in subordination to law and in harmony with the public good."[124]

President Buchanan, who'd spoken out against filibustering in his first annual message to Congress in 1857, did not hide his joy at Walker's death in his December 1860 address. In his final message to Congress, filled as it was with the forebodings of a man who was about to bequeath secession and civil war to his successor, Buchanan found at least some solace in the downfall of a man who had brought him so much grief. "I congratulate you upon the public sentiment which now exists against the crime of setting on foot military expeditions within the limits of the United States, to proceed from thence and make war upon the people of unoffending states with whom we are at peace," the president said. "In this respect a happy change has been effected since the commencement of my administration. It surely ought to be the prayer of every Christian and patriot that such expeditions may never again receive countenance or depart from our shores."[125]

Some weren't quite ready to abandon the cause. In a letter that was reprinted in newspapers across the country under the headline, "Filibusterism Not Dead," Henningsen predicted that the spirit of Walker would live on, and that he was prepared to carry the torch for his fallen commander. "I have been overwhelmed by communications from men impatient for immediate action, and most eager, personally, forthwith at all hazzards [*sic*], to depart for the scene of the late tragedy, or from others anxious to countenance and support them. To these all I reply here, to bide their time. When that time comes, their cause will not want either followers or leaders," Henningsen wrote.[126]

Henningsen's prediction would prove overly optimistic. Filibusterism was, in fact, dead. If Walker's death wasn't enough to drive the final nail into the coffin, the advent of the Civil War was.

In retrospect, it seems only fitting that Walker's death came on the eve of Abraham Lincoln's election and the war between North and South that followed. While Walker's motivations transcended domestic political disputes over slavery or Southern power, his battles became a proxy war for them during the tense years bookended by the Compromise of 1850 and the secession of South Carolina. Though the two were unrelated, Walker's death and the start of the Civil War marked the end of one era and the beginning of another, where the slavery question that the gray-eyed man of destiny had helped to inflame would finally be settled.

To call Walker disloyal to his country would be a stretch. Frankly, Walker was so absorbed in his own mission that the notion may have never crossed his mind, though other Americans certainly believed he had done his country great harm. It is doubtful that he ever considered his actions in any other context than the destiny that he believed awaited him, if only he were bold enough to seize it. But Walker's actions were no doubt damaging to the government of the United States, which, like most other nations, did not look favorably upon its citizens interfering with its foreign policy.

Walker's legacy endures more prominently in his adopted country than in his native one, though in quite an unflattering way. Nicaragua remembers him as part of a long line of imperialistic Americans who have meddled in their country's affairs. In the 1980s, as President Ronald Reagan backed the Contras against the communist Sandinista regime, Nicaraguan president Daniel Ortega decried America's long history of imperialism in Nicaragua that began with "William Walker and his mercenaries" invading the country, and credited Walker's ouster as the beginning of the long battle against the United States that culminated in the Sandinistas' seizure of power.[127] More than 120 years after he was forced from Nicaragua, Walker's legacy was still a complicating factor in America's foreign policy.

After his forced return to the United States, Walker longed with all his being to return to the country he once ruled. In his plea to his former comrades to keep the dream alive, Walker may well have been imploring himself to never lose sight of his ultimate goal. "Let it be your waking and your sleeping thought to devise means for a return to the land whence we were unjustly brought. And, if we be but true to ourselves, all will yet end well," he wrote at the end of his book.

All did not end well for Walker. He never returned to Nicaragua, not even to die. In Trujillo, a simple headstone marks the grave where the priests brought his bullet-riddled body. In Nashville, a plaque marks the spot where Walker lived in the days before the grief from his fiancée's death led him to his destiny. But the most fitting epitaph to Walker's life may have been written by the great filibusterer himself in the *Crescent*, long before he'd conceived of his own great destiny: "Unless a man believes that there is something great for him to do, he can do nothing great. Hence so many of the captains and reformers of the world have relied on fate and the stars. A great idea springs up from a man's soul; it agitates his whole being, transports him from the ignorant present and makes him feel the future in a moment. It is natural for a man so possessed to conceive that he is a special agent for working out into practice the thought that has been revealed to him."[128]

Chapter 6

Striking the Copperhead

If it be really the design of the Administration to force this issue, then come arrest, come imprisonment, come exile, come death itself. I am ready here to-night to meet it.

—Clement Vallandigham

There is no question that Clement Vallandigham considered himself a patriot. He loved his country and he cherished its Constitution, whose virtues he spent his career extolling. The way he went about demonstrating his patriotism, however, would leave modern audiences dismayed. No less a critic was Abraham Lincoln, for whom Vallandigham was a particularly vexatious opponent as he struggled to subdue the rebellious Confederacy during the Civil War.

To Vallandigham, loyalty to the Union did not mean fealty to Lincoln. He rejected what he considered Lincoln and the Republicans' attempt to "impose their definition of loyalty upon the country."[1] Unfortunately for him, Lincoln did not necessarily see things his way.

Antiwar Democrats came to be known as "Copperheads," a serpentine epithet that caught on with Republicans after an anonymous writer to a Republican newspaper in 1861 castigated the Peace Democrats with a passage from Genesis 3:14: "Upon thy belly shalt thou go, and dust shalt thou eat all the days of thy life."[2] As a leader of the Copperheads in Congress, Vallandigham was one of the greatest thorns in Lincoln's side, at least among those who remained in the Union. Even after Lincoln helped to engineer Vallandigham's defeat in the 1862 election, the fiery Ohioan continued to agitate against his administration with calls for peace with the Confederacy, the preservation of slavery, and an end to the president's wartime repression of his opponents. As a result, he would find himself arrested in the dead of night, tried before a military commission, and banished from the United States.

Vallandigham was no supporter of secession or the Southern states that had split the Union. Whether he viewed Lincoln as any better is debatable. To

Former Ohio Congressman Clement Vallandigham was a leading figure in the Copperhead movement that challenged Lincoln during the Civil War, and found himself exiled to the Confederacy for his troubles.
LIBRARY OF CONGRESS

Vallandigham, it was Lincoln, not the Confederacy, who bore the ultimate responsibility for tearing the United States apart. Vallandigham considered Lincoln's decision to fight the South as folly. Lincoln's commitment to freeing slaves from their chains he viewed as treachery. And the heavy-handed methods Lincoln used to stifle dissent were nothing less than a betrayal of country and Constitution.

Civil liberties took a backseat to the immediate and more pressing needs of defeating the Confederacy and restoring the Union. Lincoln declared martial law in some states. He suspended *habeas corpus*, the right to challenge unlawful imprisonment, first by presidential decree and later with the blessings of Congress. And military trials of civilian provocateurs became commonplace.

Lincoln compared the suppression of constitutional rights in that time of crisis to the amputation of a limb in order to save a patient's life. With the fate of the nation on the line, the ends justified the means. "Measures, however unconstitutional, might become lawful by becoming indispensable to the preservation of the Constitution, through the preservation of the nation," Lincoln said.[3] In response to Chief Justice Roger Taney's ruling that Lincoln's suspension of *habeas corpus* was unconstitutional because only the legislative branch could take that drastic action, the president famously told Congress, "Are all the laws, but one, to go unexecuted, and the government itself go to pieces, lest that one be violated?"[4]

Shelby Foote, widely regarded as the most preeminent Civil War historian in American history, determined that 13,535 US citizens were confined in military prison between 1862, when newly appointed Secretary of War Edwin Stanton became responsible for internal security, and the end of the war. The total number for the entire war could have been as high as 38,000, though Foote questioned the validity of that number.[5] Of the tens of thousands of civilians who faced military justice, none would cause a greater uproar than Vallandigham.

The Vallandigham family hailed from Virginia, where his ancestors, of Scotch-Irish and French Huguenot descent, had settled. His newlywed parents moved in 1807 to New Lisbon, Ohio, where his father, also named Clement, was appointed as the pastor at a local Presbyterian church. Vallandigham was born in 1820, the fifth of seven children.[6]

Vallandigham's first taste of politics came at the age of twenty-one, when he represented the Maryland township where he'd been working as a schoolteacher at a county Democratic convention. In 1842 he moved back to New Lisbon, was admitted to the state bar, and joined his brother's practice. He quickly made a name for himself as one of the town's best lawyers. Three years later, in 1845, Vallandigham decided to put his talents to work in the world of politics. The Columbiana County Democrats nominated him for a seat in Ohio's House of Representatives, and in December of that year he took his seat as the youngest member of the state's legislature.[7]

As a member of the legislature, Vallandigham was a staunch opponent of banking interests, voted to bar free blacks from moving to Ohio, and was an enthusiastic supporter of the Mexican War. In a statement that would belie his own dissent in the next war, Vallandigham showed little tolerance of those who opposed President James K. Polk's war in Mexico.* Responding to a Whig colleague who decried the war as an "unholy crusade against our Mexican brethren," Vallandigham said, "Palo Alto is ours; Resaca de la Palma is ours; Monterey is ours; the living glories which encircle the brow of a Taylor are ours; the sepulchral honors which adorn the tomb of a Ringgold are ours. Ours, too, is the bright history of this period. To us belong the admiration of other nations, the gratitude of the present generation, and the applause of posterity in coming time. We consent to share it with none of the revilers of this war. We claim it all, all for ourselves and our children. Sir, if you will howl over its calamities, then in the name of the living, by the blood of the slain, you shall have no part or lot in its glories."[8]

Vallandigham ended his speech with a declaration: "The laws of the Federal Government extend over us; we are bound by them; and must bear our part of the burdens thus imposed, and shed our blood and expend our treasure in the conflicts which that government may bring upon us. As a friend to our peculiar system in its true spirit, and as a State-Rights man, I would be sorry to see the day when the individual States shall cease to feel the deepest solicitude in the acts of the Government of the Union."[9] When that day came, Vallandigham would espouse far different views on the necessity of suffering the wartime burdens imposed by the federal government, and would become one of the "revilers

---

* In an ironic reversal of their roles during the Civil War, Lincoln, who entered the US House of Representatives as a Whig in 1847, fiercely denounced the war in Mexico. After Vallandigham's arrest, his allies were quick to accuse Lincoln of hypocrisy, reminding him that he too had vilified a sitting president over the conduct of a war.

of this war" that he'd denounced in the legislature. One must wonder whether Vallandigham ever pondered those words as he whiled away his exile in Canada, awaiting the day when he could safely set foot on Union soil again.

In 1847, Vallandigham was persuaded by friends to move to Dayton, in the western part of the state, to take over a newspaper, the *Dayton Western Empire*, which he and his wife, Louisa, had purchased for $150. It was a short-lived career change. After two years, they sold the newspaper and Vallandigham returned to the practice of law. He also sought a return to elected office, losing a race for county judge and losing a nomination for lieutenant governor before setting his sights on Ohio's Third Congressional District, recently redrawn by the Democratic legislature. He lost his first congressional race in 1852 to the Whig incumbent Lewis Campbell, and was felled again by Campbell two years later. In 1856, it looked again as if Campbell had won by just nineteen votes. But there were allegations of rampant fraud, and Vallandigham contested the election results. In May 1858, Congress awarded Vallandigham the seat he'd won nearly two years earlier.[10]

Vallandigham took his seat as disputes over slavery that had raged for decades threatened to finally rupture the Union. The Compromise of 1850, which Vallandigham had wholeheartedly supported, promised to create a new equilibrium that would stave off civil war. But the Kansas-Nebraska Act of 1856 upset that balance, and the shooting war that erupted in Bleeding Kansas between pro- and antislavery men gave the nation a glimpse of the war to come. The following year, the Supreme Court's ruling in the case of Dred Scott, a Virginia slave who'd sued for his freedom after his owner brought him to a free state, dictated that the federal government had no authority to regulate slavery in its territories and that blacks, whether free or slave, had no citizenship rights, setting the stage for the secession crisis to come.

Despite being branded as the candidate of slave owners and slave catchers in his congressional campaigns, Vallandigham claimed to oppose the institution, which he said he "deplored" as "a moral, social & political evil." But Vallandigham believed slavery was permitted by the Constitution and, as a passionate advocate for states' rights, was adamant that it was an issue for the states to decide for themselves. The federal government, he believed, was accorded no say in the matter by the Constitution, and for the good of the Union should refrain from interfering in it.[11]

Vallandigham didn't believe that war over slavery was inevitable. "In my considerate judgment, a confederacy made up of the slaveholding and non-slaveholding states is, in the nature of things, the strongest of all popular governments," he declared on the House floor in January 1863, reiterating his long-held view.[12] If slavery split apart the United States, it was the radical abolitionists who would be responsible, Vallandigham long believed. In an 1855 speech decrying the perils of abolitionism, Vallandigham declared, "The true and only question now before you is: Whether you will have a Union, with all its numberless blessings in the past, present, or Disunion and civil war, with all the multiplied crimes, miseries, and atrocities which human imagination never conceived, and human pen never can portray?"[13]

Vallandigham's worst fears, and those of the slaveholding South, of meddling by the federal government in the institution of slavery came to a head in 1860. The congressman supported Senator Stephen Douglas for the Democratic nomination for president. Much to his chagrin, Douglas lost to Abraham Lincoln, whose election was the final blow to the precarious balance between free and slave states that had been unraveling throughout the previous decade.

When Congress came back into session on December 3, 1860, the impending secession of South Carolina was in the air. Vallandigham wrote to his wife that he'd "just witnessed the assembling of the last Congress of the *United States*." Most of the Republican congressmen "looked upon it as the beasts look upon the starry heavens," while the members of the South Carolina delegation "seemed full of sorrow, yet accepting their destiny as one who leaves his father's house never to return." Vallandigham explained to his wife the position he would take. "When the secession has taken place, I shall do all in my power to *restore* the Union, if it be possible; and failing in that, then to mitigate the evils of disruption."[14]

Vallandigham pinned his hopes on the Crittenden Compromise, so named for its author, Kentucky senator John Crittenden. The plan would have used the Missouri Compromise's dividing line to determine whether slavery would be permitted in any new territories. Furthermore, it would have severely curtailed the federal government's ability to interfere with slavery or the slave trade, and incentivized enforcement of the Fugitive Slave Act by forcing Congress to pay for any slaves who were rescued from their bondage.

When the Crittenden Compromise fell through, Vallandigham authored a plan of his own, a series of constitutional amendments that he hoped would bring the rebelling states back into the Union fold and keep the Union whole. His proposed thirteenth, fourteenth, and fifteenth amendments to the Constitution were far removed from the amendments that would later bear those numbers. His thirteenth amendment would have divided the United States into four geographic regions—North, South, West, and Pacific—with a majority of electors in all four required for a candidate to be elected president. The proposal would have also lengthened presidents' terms to six years, required a two-thirds supermajority in each geographic section for them to be reelected, and required two-thirds of the senators from each section to approve some controversial congressional actions. Vallandigham's proposed fourteenth amendment would have allowed states to secede, but only with the approval of each of the other states that comprised their section. Finally, the new fifteenth amendment would have ensured that all territories could determine for themselves whether they would permit slavery. Needless to say, Vallandigham's solution did not gain any traction.[15]

Vallandigham, who had declared after Lincoln's election that he would not "vote one dollar of money whereby one drop of blood should be shed in a civil war" that he believed the abolitionists had caused, would be a constant source of criticism in Congress for the administration and the war effort.[16] He excoriated the Republicans for refusing to compromise with the South. He decried Lincoln's suspension of *habeas corpus* and the trials of civilians before military tribunals as overreaches of executive authority. And he warned against the evils of conscription and emancipation.

To rid themselves of the troublesome Vallandigham, Lincoln and Treasury Secretary Salmon P. Chase, the former Republican governor of Ohio, recruited Robert Schenck to run against him in 1862. Schenck, a former state legislator and brigadier general who'd been wounded in the Second Battle of Bull Run, had rebuffed efforts by others to recruit him into the race. Chase and Secretary of War Edwin Stanton, visiting Schenck at the Willard Hotel while he recovered from the wound to his right hand, were able to talk him into it. "You are the only man who can beat that traitor Vallandigham," Chase told him.[17]

The 1862 election was a bonanza for Ohio Democrats, who won fourteen of the state's nineteen congressional districts. The one major exception to their victorious election year was Vallandigham, who lost by more than six hundred votes. Though the Republicans were facing a groundswell of unpopularity fueled by recession and military setbacks, Schenck was aided by a vicious smear campaign in the press, which falsely alleged that Vallandigham had been arrested for treason and was a member of seditious organizations, and by the gerrymandering of his district to include an additional Republican county. Lincoln helped boost Schenck's prospects by promoting him to major general.[18]

The lack of a congressional stage didn't dampen Vallandigham's scathing criticism of the war. Back in Ohio, he decried the Emancipation Proclamation, which he believed vindicated his worst fears about Lincoln's intentions. It wasn't long before he sought a return to the political arena, deciding this time to run for governor. The Democratic Party of Ohio had other thoughts. The party elders wanted the nomination to go to Hugh Jewett, who had carried the Democrats' banner in the 1861 gubernatorial race. Jewett had lost to Republican David Tod, but ran a strong-enough campaign that party leaders believed he deserved another shot. And as a War Democrat, Jewett was far less inflammatory a choice than Vallandigham. But events were unfolding that would yet propel Vallandigham to the nomination.

Around the same time that Vallandigham returned to Ohio, General Ambrose Burnside arrived in the state. Burnside had replaced the inadequate general George McClellan as commander of the Army of the Potomac, but proven himself no more up to the task than his predecessor. Following his disastrous defeat at the Battle of Fredericksburg, Lincoln removed Burnside from his command and replaced him with General Joseph Hooker. Burnside's new posting would be as commander of the Department of the Ohio, covering the greater Midwest.

Ohio was seething with antiwar sentiment when Burnside arrived on the scene, and the general decided drastic action was needed to combat it. On April 13, he issued General Order No. 38, which stated that "all persons found within our lines who commit acts for the benefit of the enemies of our country will be tried as spies or traitors, and, if convicted, will suffer death." Among the undesirables targeted by the order were writers or carriers of "secret mails," people intending to join the Confederate army, and anyone who was found to be aiding the enemy. Furthermore, in a provision that would be of great consequence to Vallandigham, the order said, "The habit of declaring sympathies for the enemy will not be allowed in this Department. Persons committing such offenses will be at once arrested, with a view to being tried as above stated, or sent beyond our lines into the lines of their friends."[19]

Vallandigham, who had spent the duration of the war accusing Lincoln and the Republicans of tyranny, would not accept Burnside's order in silence. After he and his compatriots determined that the order must be challenged, he set out to test Burnside's resolve in enforcing it. On April 30, at a rally in front of the State House in Columbus, Vallandigham announced his intentions to defy Burnside's order. "If it be really the design of the Administration to force this issue, then come arrest, come imprisonment, come exile, come death itself! I am ready here to-night to meet it."[20]

The Columbus speech apparently escaped Burnside's attention. Vallandigham's next would not. Burnside learned that Vallandigham planned to speak at a Democratic rally in Mount Vernon on May 1, and sent two of his men to take notes.[21] Vallandigham was aware that the general would be keeping an eye on him, but didn't let that dissuade him from unleashing a torrent of abuse aimed at Lincoln, Burnside, and the Republicans' war effort.

Below a banner declaring, "The Constitution as it is, and the Union as it was," Vallandigham addressed a crowd of hundreds of proud Copperheads wearing "butternut" badges as symbols of their political allegiances. Vallandigham railed against the "wicked, cruel, and unnecessary war," which the Emancipation Proclamation proved was being waged by "King Lincoln," not for the preservation of the Union, but as "a war for the purpose of crushing out liberty and erecting despotism" and "for the liberation of the blacks and the enslavement of the whites." Had Lincoln wanted to end the war, he could have done so long ago, Vallandigham claimed, but the administration had rejected the Crittenden Compromise that would have guaranteed the South its rights under the Constitution, and more recently rebuffed an attempt by France to mediate the conflict.

He insisted that the "men in power are attempting to establish a despotism in this country" and seeking "to build up a monarchy upon the ruins of our free government." "The sooner the people inform the minions of usurped power that they will not submit to such restrictions upon their liberties, the better," he declared to the crowd.[22]

A number of Vallandigham's barbs were reserved more personally for Burnside, whose two agents, clad in civilian garb, he could see taking notes during the speech. He branded General Order No. 38 "a bane usurpation of arbitrary authority" and "the order of a military dictator." Vallandigham said he was "a freeman," and insisted that his right to criticize the administration was protected by the Constitution, "General Orders No. 1." He warned that Lincoln planned to install military marshals in all districts who would "act for the purpose of restricting the liberties of the people." "Should we cringe and cower before such authority?" asked Vallandigham, who avowed Americans' "right to criticise [*sic*] the acts of our military servants in power."[23]

When Burnside's agents returned with news of the speech, the general ordered Vallandigham's arrest under General Order No. 38. Burnside commandeered a special train to send about a hundred soldiers to Dayton, who arrived at Vallandigham's house shortly after midnight on May 5. Vallandigham refused to come downstairs to open the door for his pursuers, yelling out the window at Captain Charles G. Hutton, Burnside's aide-de-camp, "If Burnside wants me, let him come up and take me." He agreed to come down after the captain threatened to break in the door, but instead shouted out the window for help, then dressed and waited in an upstairs bedroom for the imminent arrival of Hutton's troops. The soldiers smashed Vallandigham's back door with axes and bars, and then broke down the door to the bedroom where he waited with a revolver in his pocket. Vallandigham declined to use the pistol—he'd already used it to fire several shots into the air to alert his friends—and finally agreed to submit. "You have now broken open my house and overpowered me by superior force, and I am obliged to surrender," he said.[24]

The *Dayton Daily Empire*, Vallandigham's former newspaper, greeted the city's Democrats that morning with a headline blaring, "Vallandigham Kidnapped; A Dastardly Outrage!!! Will Free Men Submit? The Hour for Action Has Arrived." Vallandigham may not have been able to alert his supporters from their slumber in time to stop his arrest, but once they learned what had happened during the night, they rallied to his cause the next day in the most violent of manners. An angry mob attacked the office of a local Republican newspaper, the *Dayton Daily Journal*, burning it to the ground and igniting several neighboring buildings.* Burnside's troops arrived to quell the mob and protect the firefighters

* A Republican mob had recently done the same to *The Crisis*, a Democratic newspaper in Columbus.

whom the rioters had tried to inhibit. The mob scattered after a soldier shot dead a rioter who was trying to cut a firefighter's hose. Burnside responded by shutting down the *Empire* and putting Montgomery County under martial law.[25]

From his military prison at the Kemper Barracks in Cincinnati, Vallandigham composed an address, "To the Democracy of Ohio," which he smuggled to the press through a visitor who came to see him after Burnside transferred him to the Burnet House, a luxurious hotel in the city. "I am here in a military bastille for no other offence than my political opinions, and the defence of them and of the rights of the people, and of your constitutional liberties." His only crimes, he said, were that he was a Democrat who was loyal to the Union, the Constitution, and the law. "For no disobedience to the Constitution; for no violation of the law; for no word, sign, or gesture of sympathy with the men of the South, who are for disunion and Southern independence, but in obedience to *their* demand, as well as the demand of Northern Abolition disunionists and traitors, I am here in bonds to-day; but 'Time, at last, sets all things even.'"[26]

Justice, or at least what passed for it in Burnside's eyes, was swift. Just two days after his arrest, Vallandigham's trial began before a military commission that Burnside had formed a week after issuing General Order No. 38, "for the trial of such prisoners as may be brought before it."

At his trial, Vallandigham denied the commission's jurisdiction over him and refused to enter a plea. The military court entered a "not guilty" plea on his behalf. Captains Harrington R. Hill and John A. Means, whom Burnside had sent to the Mount Vernon rally to observe Vallandigham, testified about Vallandigham's alleged violations of Burnside's order. Cross-examining the witnesses personally—he did not avail himself of the services of his three defense attorneys, who spent the duration of the trial in an adjoining room—Vallandigham forced his accusers to concede that he'd insisted on the restoration of the Union and rejected calls to bring peace by allowing the Confederacy its independence. Means acknowledged that Vallandigham had said "something to that effect," and that he'd declared that he and other Peace Democrats were the only ones truly trying to save the Union. The witnesses was less accommodating when Vallandigham asked, "Did I not expressly counsel the people to obey the Constitution, and all laws, and to pay proper respect to men in authority, but to maintain their political rights through the ballot-box?" Means replied that Vallandigham had implored his listeners at the end of his speech "to come up united at the ballot-box and hurl the tyrant from his throne," but, "I did not understand him to counsel the people to submit to the authorities at all times."[27]

More favorable to Vallandigham was the testimony of his own witnesses. Samuel S. Cox, who also spoke at the Mount Vernon rally, affirmed, "He counseled no resistance except such as might be had at the ballot-box. . . . He stated the sole remedy to be in the ballot-box, and in the courts. I remember this distinctly." Cox testified that Vallandigham had shouted down someone who had applauded Jefferson Davis's name, and that his condemnation of the war was "launched at its perversion from its original purpose." At the end of his speech, Cox testified, Vallandigham "invoked the people under no circumstances to surrender the Union."[28]

Once the witnesses were finished testifying, Vallandigham lodged an official protest at having been arrested without due process of law or a warrant from a civil judge. He argued that, not being a member of the army or navy, he could not constitutionally be subjected to military law. "[T]he alleged 'offense' is not known to the Constitution of the United States, nor to any law thereof. It is words spoken to the people of Ohio in an open and public political meeting, lawfully and peaceably assembled, under the Constitution and upon full notice. It is words of criticism of the public policy of the public servants of the people, by which policy it is alleged that the welfare of the country was not promoted. It was an appeal to the people to change that policy, not by force, but by free elections and the ballot-box. It is not pretended that I counseled disobedience to the Constitution, or resistance to the laws and lawful authority. I never have. Beyond this protest I have nothing further to submit."[29]

Given the backdrop of the military commission, composed as it was of Burnside's loyal officers, there could be little doubt as to the final verdict. After only two days of testimony, the eight-person commission found Vallandigham guilty of the charge of "publicly expressing . . . sympathy for those in arms against the Government of the United States, and declaring disloyal sentiments and opinions, with the object and purpose of weakening the power of Government in its efforts to suppress an unlawful rebellion." The officers who formed the commission sentenced him to be imprisoned at Fort Warren, in Boston, until the end of the war, whenever that might be.[30]

Within two days of the conclusion of testimony before the military commission, as Vallandigham awaited his sentence, he and his attorneys applied for a writ of *habeas corpus* with the civilian courts, where they believed his case belonged, demanding that he be released from his illegal imprisonment. His attorney, fellow Democratic politico George Pugh, noted that, though Congress had granted Lincoln the power to suspend citizens' *habeas* rights with its infamous 1863 act, the president had not done so in Vallandigham's case. Secretary of War Stanton had drafted a writ suspending *habeas corpus* for Vallandigham, but Secretary of State William Seward and Ohioan Salmon Chase warned Lincoln that he would pay dearly for it in the court of public opinion. If Lincoln wanted to suspend those rights for Vallandigham, he had full authority to do so, Pugh noted. "Why, then, does General Burnside attempt without law what the President has not seen fit to do by law? Is it for the purpose of treating the Congress of the United States with as much indignity as he has inflicted upon my distinguished client?"[31]

Pugh argued that there was no necessity for martial law in Ohio, which had not been invaded and suffered no threat of incursion by Rebel soldiers. And as a civilian, Vallandigham was not subject to trial by military commission. As such, the only proper place for a trial against Vallandigham would be in a civilian court. And the only proper course of action would be to grant Vallandigham a writ of *habeas corpus* that would free him from his illegal imprisonment. "I insist on his being brought into Court for accusation. If then accused, let him be heard in defense," Pugh said in his closing arguments before the court. "He does not shrink from such an ordeal; he demands it by his petition; he challenges it in the confidence of a triumphant acquittal. But if, when brought hither, no cause of accusation is found against him, your Honor must say, and I hope will take pleasure in saying: "WHY SHOULDST THOU DEFEND THYSELF? GO IN PEACE!"[32]

Burnside defended his actions to the court. If an agent of the Confederacy were found distributing speeches from its leaders that sought to demoralize the Union's soldiers or undermine their confidence in the government, the general declared he would have them tried and hanged, "and all the rules of modern warfare would sustain me." Why, then, should he allow the same sentiments to be spread by the Union's own public men? "The press and public men, in a great emergency like the present, should avoid the use of party epithets and bitter invectives," Burnside wrote in his statement to the court. "The simple names 'Patriot' and 'Traitor' are comprehensive enough."[33]

The federal district attorney, who bore the memorable name of Flamen Ball, stood by Burnside's rationale. While he expressed a great reverence for "that great guarantee of personal liberty, the writ of HABEAS CORPUS," Ball also emphasized that "by reason of this rebellion, the very existence of our whole country, as a nation, is in jeopardy." And the nation's right to self-preservation, he said, was paramount. When the nation is faced with its extinction, Ball argued that individual rights must be subordinated to that national right. Though Ohio itself had not been invaded, the military district of the Department of the Ohio, which included Kentucky, had been. And though Ohio itself was not under martial law, by virtue of being part of the United States, "is not Ohio at war?" Ball asked. "It is true that the foot of no hostile foe in arms has ever trodden our soil, or invaded our peaceful homes; but thousands of those homes have already yielded their fathers and sons to the service of their country." And as part of a military department of the United States, the citizens of Ohio are subject to the laws of war as administered by courts-martial or military commissions, he argued.[34]

For Judge Humphrey Leavitt, the case was clearly about more than matters of law. Leavitt made plain that he had no tolerance of dissension during the emergency of civil war, and his insistence that "there is too much of the pestilential leaven of disloyalty in the community," no doubt contributed greatly to his ruling against Vallandigham, whom he insinuated was guilty of a sort of moral treason, if not treason by law. "Men should know, and lay the truth to heart, that there is a course of conduct not involving overt treason, or any offense technically defined by statute, and not, therefore, subject to punishment as such, which, nevertheless, implies moral guilt and a gross offense against their country," he said. "Those who live under the protection and enjoy the blessings of our benignant government, must learn that they cannot stab its vitals with impunity."[35]

In most circumstances, Leavitt acknowledged that Vallandigham's case would have merit. But, he asked, is the court not bound to consider the state of emergency in which the country now found itself? "The Court cannot shut its eyes to the grave fact that war exists, involving the most imminent danger, and threatening the subversion and destruction of the Constitution itself," Leavitt wrote. Echoing Burnside's defense of the arrest, Leavitt wrote, "Self-preservation is a paramount law, which a nation, as well as an individual, may find it necessary to invoke." If the necessity to do so exists, Leavitt wrote, the president undoubtedly has the right to arrest people who, "by their mischievous acts of disloyalty, impeded or endanger military operations of the government." And if the president deems such actions necessary, the judge ruled, there is no reason why he can't empower his military officers to execute them.

Most importantly, Leavitt said that his court had no authority to interfere with the proceedings of the military commission that tried Vallandigham. The only question at hand was whether the arrest was proper. And as far as Leavitt was concerned, it was.[36]

For much of the proceedings, Lincoln was completely in the dark. Lincoln learned of the arrest from the newspapers while Vallandigham's case played out before the military commission and civil court. Burnside had not cleared the action with the administration, or even informed it of his plans. The president was in an awkward position. The public, even many Republicans, condemned Burnside's actions. Lincoln's cabinet almost unanimously agreed that Burnside had erred by arresting Vallandigham. Had Burnside forewarned his president, it seems almost certain that Lincoln would've ordered him not to arrest Vallandigham. Weeks later, Lincoln would publicly admit, "I do not know whether I would have ordered the arrest of Mr. Vallandigham." But the arrest couldn't be undone, and the only options left to Lincoln were unpalatable. If he set Vallandigham free, it would be viewed as a public repudiation of his general. Let the arrest and conviction stand, and he faced the wrath of the public.[37]

The arrest triggered an avalanche of criticism, the ferocity of which easily matched anything Vallandigham had said at Mount Vernon. *Tyrant, demagogue, dictator*, and *Caesar* were among the choicer words applied to Lincoln by outraged newspapers and politicians. In their biography of Lincoln, John Hay, and John Nicolay, who served as secretaries and assistants to the president, wrote that the Vallandigham affair aroused a greater outpouring of condemnation than any of Lincoln's actions during the war, "and none having relation to the rights of an individual created a feeling so deep and so widespread."[38]

The *Dubuque Herald* opined that "a crime has been committed" against the "right to think, to speak, to live," while Columbus's *The Crisis* declared, "Every reader of every nation and tongue will be astounded at the arrest of a private American citizen, in his own country, upon such charges as are developed in this trial, and that by military authority. . . . If the people cannot discuss public measures, hear speeches, read such papers and documents as they desire, then all idea of a republican form of government is at an end."[39] In an Independence Day speech at the New Hampshire capitol, former president Franklin Pierce, a frequent critic of Lincoln's handling of the war, declared, "It is made criminal . . . for that noble martyr of free speech, Mr. Vallandigham, to discuss public affairs in Ohio."[40] Ohio's *Ashland Union* predicted that Lincoln's next move would be to shut down the Democratic press as a precursor to a military dictatorship.[41] Burnside did his part to lend credence to those fears in early June when he shut down the offices of the *Chicago Times* for "repeated expression of disloyalty and incendiary statements." In the middle of the night, Burnside's troops raided the office, stopped the presses, and destroyed all copies of that day's paper that had already been printed. Twenty thousand people gathered to protest the paper's closure that evening, and prominent Chicagoans demanded that Lincoln rescind Burnside's order. This time, at least, Lincoln decided to rein in his headstrong general and reversed Burnside's decision.[42]

"Even some of the most loyal newspapers of the North joined in the general attack," Hay and Nicolay wrote. Republican newspapers called the arrest a "blunder" and a "great mistake." The *New York Sun* chided Lincoln, writing, "The Union can survive the assaults of all the armed and disarmed Vallandighams of the South and North. . . . But it cannot long exist without free speech and free press." Likewise, the *New York Evening Post*, another Republican paper, wrote, "No governments and no authorities are to be held as above criticism." Senator Lyman Trumbull, Lincoln's fellow Illinois Republican, publicly rebuked Burnside for his decision. "We are fighting for the . . . preservation of the Constitution, and all the liberties it guarantees to every citizen," he said.[43]

Not that there was any shortage of praise for Burnside. The *Cleveland Daily Leader* gloated that Vallandigham had gotten his just deserts. "Seriously, we believe no man in the North more deserving of arrest under Burnside's 'Order No. 38' than this arch traitor. He has persistently and deliberately opposed and thwarted the Government in every possible way. He has done more to stir up sedition and rebellion in the North than any other man, and hence, is guiltier than his dupes and followers," the paper wrote.[44]

In order to pacify public opinion without undermining his general, the president settled on what historian Frank Klement, who has written extensively on Vallandigham and the Copperhead movement, referred to as a "classically Lincolnian solution."[45] A provision in General Order No. 38 that threatened to send violators "beyond our lines into the lines of their friends" gave Lincoln the flexibility he needed. Rather than being left to rot in his "Bastille," Vallandigham would be exiled to the Confederate States to live among the Rebels, whose cause he'd sympathized with so greatly.* On May 19, Lincoln sent a telegram to Burnside, informing the general that he'd commuted Vallandigham's sentence, and that Burnside was to deliver the Copperhead to General William Rosecrans, "to be put by him beyond our military lines."

As they faced each other at Murfreesboro on May 25, Rosecrans told Vallandigham, "Why, sir, do you know that unless I protect you with a guard, my soldiers will tear you to pieces in an instant?" Vallandigham responded, "That, sir, is because they are just as ignorant of my character as yourself." Vallandigham then offered Rosecrans what he called a "proposition" for the general: He urged Rosecrans to assemble his soldiers in the morning and tell them that Vallandigham wanted to vindicate himself before them. "I will guarantee that when they have heard me through they will be more willing to tear Lincoln or yourself to pieces than they will Vallandigham," he said.

Rosecrans was not amused, and certainly not willing to allow his soon-to-be-deported prisoner to address his soldiers. "Vallandigham, don't you ever come back here. If you do, Vallandigham . . . I'll be Goddamned if I don't hang you," Rosecrans told him. The general handed Vallandigham over to a Confederate picket and went on his way. Vallandigham told the private, "I am a citizen of Ohio, and of the United States. I am here within your lines by force and against my will. I therefore surrender myself to you as a prisoner of war."[46]

Vallandigham was escorted to Shelbyville, where Confederate general Braxton Bragg welcomed him to "the land of liberty." That welcome would not last long. James Seddon, the Confederate secretary of war, told Bragg that because Vallandigham was a United States citizen, he must be either charged as an enemy alien or paroled. Bragg agreed to let him go to Wilmington, North Carolina.[47]

Robert E. Lee viewed the Copperheads as the Confederacy's allies, and some welcomed Vallandigham as a mutual enemy of Lincoln. But much of the Southern press didn't share that opinion. After all, Vallandigham's overarching goal was to return the Southern states to the Union. Though he wanted that accomplished on terms amenable to the South—most notably, the preservation of slavery—after more than two years of war, the people of the Confederacy weren't eager to give up the independence for which they'd sacrificed so much. One newspaper

---

* Lincoln was not the only president during the Civil War to use such a solution. Confederate president Jefferson Davis exiled the pro-Union journalist, minister, and politician, William Gannaway "Parson" Brownlow, to the North for treasonous activity in eastern Tennessee (Foote, 633).

called Vallandigham a "mortal enemy" to the Confederate States, while another called him an "earnest agent for [the Confederacy's] political annihilation." The Confederate leadership could not allow him to stay.[48]

Too seditious to remain in the Union and too loyal to it to be welcome in the Confederacy, Vallandigham needed to find another place to live out his banishment. He chose Canada for his exile. Twenty-four days after Rosecrans delivered him to the Rebels, Vallandigham took a blockade-runner to Bermuda and from there boarded a ship bound for Halifax, Nova Scotia. His final destination would be Windsor, Ontario, where he would spend the next year. From his "personal Elba," Vallandigham could stare wistfully into Detroit and his native land, on the other side of the Detroit River. He could also see the Union gunboat *Michigan*, which was anchored in the middle of the river with its guns trained on his house.[49]

Vallandigham never hid his intent to get arrested under Burnside's order. He had openly dared Burnside to punish him. But his martyrdom may have been more than just a principled act of defiance. According to at least one account, it was a calculated move to help Vallandigham secure the Democratic nomination for governor of Ohio in 1863, which the party elders had informed him would go to another.

James A. Garfield, then a member of the House of Representatives, recorded in his diary that the subject of Vallandigham came up during a January 1877 dinner with a handful of fellow Ohioans.* In the course of the conversation, Allen G. Thurman, a Democratic senator and friend of Vallandigham's during the war, explained that Vallandigham's arrest was intended to help him win the elusive gubernatorial nomination. "The character of Vallandigham was quite fully discussed and Thurman stated what I had never before heard, that Vallandigham's arrest was procured in order to make him the candidate for Governor, and that this was done by his Democratic friends," Garfield recorded in his diary.[50]

If Vallandigham intended his act of defiance to clinch the nomination for him, it worked perfectly. By the time he arrived in Windsor, the Democratic nomination was his. Seeing the groundswell of support for "Valiant Val" at the June 11 Democratic convention, Jewett withdrew from the race, throwing the nomination to Vallandigham.[51] The exiled Copperhead would run for governor from Canada. If he won, surely Lincoln would not dare to arrest the lawfully elected governor of Ohio.

Back at home, Lincoln struggled to explain his actions amid the continuing criticism. At a May 16 rally in Albany, New York—similar rallies sprang up in protest across the North—Democratic politicians, led by Congressman Erastus

---

* Garfield was Rosecrans's chief of staff at the time of the Vallandigham incident, and wrote the order authorizing his passage through the Union lines on his way to the Confederacy.

Corning, pilloried Lincoln for the Vallandigham affair. The crowd approved a series of ten resolutions, known as the "Albany Resolves," demanding the preservation of civil liberties and an end to military trials of civilians. Corning sent the resolutions to Lincoln on May 19, the same day he commuted Vallandigham's sentence to banishment.

Lincoln had immediately seen the error of Burnside's actions. But having allowed Vallandigham's punishment to go forward, he had to defend himself. In his response to the Albany Resolves, Lincoln, mistakenly led by the newspapers to believe that Vallandigham in his Mount Vernon speech had publicly encouraged soldiers to abandon their duty, mused that in times of war, desertion is traditionally punished by death.[52] But if a deserter is led astray by nefarious influences who convince him to abandon his duty, why should he be executed while the instigator went unpunished? "Must I shoot a simpleminded soldier boy who deserts, while I must not touch a hair of a wily agitator who induces him to desert? This is none less injurious when effected by getting a father, or brother, or friend, into a public meeting, and there working upon his feeling till he is persuaded to write the soldier boy that he is fighting in a bad cause, for a wicked Administration," Lincoln wrote. "I think that in such a case, to silence the agitator, and save the boy, is not only constitutional, but withal a great mercy."[53]

Even in exile, Vallandigham still posed a severe threat to the administration. The Ohio governor's race had become a referendum on the war, and some Republican newspapers were worried that the party's incumbent governor, David Tod, wasn't up to the fight. Just as Chase and Lincoln had recruited Robert Schenck to help purge Vallandigham from Congress, Ohio Republicans now found their unconventional champion in the form of John Brough, a War Democrat who found Vallandigham as distasteful as the Republicans did.[54]

Brough and the Republicans urged their fellow Ohioans not to disgrace themselves by electing a "convicted traitor" to be their governor. The Republican press viciously slandered Vallandigham throughout the race, distorting and inventing events to cast him in the most disloyal and despicable light possible. Newspapers declared that Vallandigham had vowed at the start of the war that Union soldiers would pass through Ohio over his dead body. They published forged letters which were alleged to show Vallandigham, while in the Confederacy, describing himself as a "friend of the South" whose "heart bled for Dixie." They claimed that Vallandigham had urged Jefferson Davis to invade the North.*

---

* The *Cleveland Daily Leader* reported on December 20, 1860, that Vallandigham "had no objection to the coercing force marching through, but they should not make the battleground in his district". And in Richmond, Vallandigham had actually counseled the Confederates against invading Pennsylvania, telling them that it would rally the Union behind Lincoln, whereas if they waited until the 1864 presidential election, the peace movement would simply sweep Lincoln from office (Jones, J. B. 1935. *A Rebel War Clerk's Diary at the Confederate States Capital, Vol. I.* New York: Old Hickory Bookshop, 357).

They even accused him of failing to care for his widowed mother. Brough was buoyed by an oratorical brilliance described as "a sledgehammer style about him that made him powerful." Prominent Republicans such as Salmon Chase stumped for Brough across the state, while Republican editors hosted rallies, where the flames of Vallandigham's burning effigies illuminated banners declaring, "Hurrah for Brough and Abraham, and a rope to hang Vallandigham."[55]

Prevented by his banishment from campaigning in person, Vallandigham wrote frequent letters from Windsor to rally the electorate. Prominent Democrats visited him to hash out their campaign strategy, predictably running against Lincoln's struggles in subduing the South, his quashing of civil liberties, and his emancipation of slaves in the conquered regions of the Confederacy. With a healthy dose of race-baiting, Democratic newspapers urged voters to cast their ballots for Vallandigham, to "[p]rotect us from the Negro equality." The Democrats blamed the Republicans for causing the war, and said only the Democrats could forge a compromise that would bring peace. And, of course, they held up their candidate Vallandigham as a symbol of the oppression that Lincoln had draped over the citizenry of the United States.[56]

The Republicans' message prevailed. Though he won more votes than any winning statewide candidate except Brough, and had in fact gotten more votes than any previous governor of Ohio, Vallandigham lost the election in a landslide, coming one hundred thousand votes short. Vallandigham had counted on the public's war-weariness to help carry the day for him, but recent victories on the battlefields of Gettysburg and Vicksburg had negated much of the public's consternation. Vallandigham also grossly miscalculated the support he would get from Union soldiers, who were not receptive to his calls for peace and his attacks on the war effort. Only one Ohio regiment cast the majority of its votes for the Copperhead candidate. An Ohio corporal wrote after the election, "Copperheadism has brought the soldiers here together more than anything else. Some of the men that yoused [*sic*] to be almost willing to have the war settled any way are now among the strongest Union soldiers we have got."[57]

When she left Ohio to join her husband in Canada just before the election, Louisa Vallandigham had bragged that she would return to Ohio as the wife of the governor. News of Vallandigham's defeat occasioned one of the folksy jokes for which Lincoln was famous. Lincoln said Louisa's boast reminded him of "a pleasant little affair" from back in Illinois. "A gentleman was nominated for Supervisor. On leaving home on the morning of the election, he said: 'Wife, tonight you shall sleep with the Supervisor of this town.' The election passed, and the confident gentleman was defeated. The wife heard the news before her defeated spouse returned home. She immediately dressed for going out, and awaited her husband's return, when she met him at the door. 'Wife, where are you going at this time of night?' he exclaimed. 'Going?' she replied. 'Why, you told me this morning that I should tonight sleep with the Supervisor of this town, and I was going to his house.'"[58]

Joke as he may, Lincoln was immensely relieved. He'd stayed up all night to follow the election returns and, on a more solemn note, sent a telegram to Brough in celebration of his victory after the votes had been counted. "Glory to God in the highest. Ohio has saved the Union."[59]

Vallandigham's loss in the governor's race was followed a few months later by another blow: the Supreme Court's rejection of his *habeas* claim. In February 1864, the high court reached the same conclusion as Judge Leavitt—that it had no authority to reverse the decisions of a military commission. Republicans cheered the ruling as proof of Vallandigham's guilt, while Democrats decried it as a "cowardly evasion of a question which it was the duty of the Court to decide."[60]

His sentence upheld by the Supreme Court, Vallandigham nonetheless decided after a year in exile that it was time to return to his country. He'd been separated from his family for too long, and was losing the clout he'd held in Ohio Democratic politics.[61] The war, and therefore his banishment from the Union, weren't over. And he would not have the protection of being Ohio's duly elected governor to shield him from the military commission's sentence, Lincoln's vow to imprison him, or Rosecrans's threat to hang him. But he'd grown increasingly restive and gambled on the administration's unwillingness to punish him. He'd also hoped that his old congressional district would send him to the upcoming Democratic convention in Chicago as a delegate, and believed his odds would be better if he were there to make his case in person. Escorted by four friends and wearing a disguise of a fake beard and a pillow under his shirt, Vallandigham returned to Ohio on June 14, 1864. Though Brough initially moved to again arrest him, Lincoln and other national Republican leaders concluded that a free Vallandigham could only further their cause and hurt his party.[62]

The 1864 Democratic convention in Chicago, where Vallandigham would be a delegate from his Third Congressional District, would mark his grand return to the national political stage. Vallandigham and the Peace Democrats were opposed to the nomination of General George McClellan as their party's standard-bearer against Lincoln. At the urging of his Ohio comrades, Vallandigham had written a letter from Windsor urging Democrats to reject McClellan in favor of a Peace candidate.[63] But the Peace Democrats had trouble finding a suitable challenger to McClellan, and still had no one able to credibly contest his nomination by the time the delegates arrived in Chicago. Vallandigham cast his initial vote for former Connecticut governor Thomas Seymour, but later switched to McClellan when his nomination became inevitable.

McClellan won the nomination and Vallandigham grudgingly stumped for him. But, largely due to Vallandigham's efforts, Little Mac left the convention on August 31 burdened by a millstone that would weigh him down throughout the campaign. Vallandigham had spearheaded a push for a plank in the party's platform calling for "immediate efforts . . . for a cessation of hostilities, with a view to an ultimate convention of the States." The resolution fell short of more-radical demands for "peace at any price," and did not call for Southern independence, to which Vallandigham continued to maintain opposition.[64] But it still went too far for McClellan, who rejected the resolution in his nomination letter and continued to disown it throughout the campaign. Nonetheless, it was a drag on McClellan's campaign, as were Vallandigham and the Copperhead movement in general. "Was not a vote for McClellan really a vote for Vallandigham, anarchy, and treason?" one Republican newspaper asked.[65]

Lincoln didn't have to rely on the Copperheads' ignominy alone to keep him in the White House. As with the 1863 Ohio governor's race, victory intervened to boost the Republicans' prospects. Two days after the Democratic convention adjourned, General William T. Sherman took Atlanta, a reversal of fortune that immediately brightened Lincoln's prospects. At the time of the Democratic convention, Lincoln had believed he would lose the election. Instead, he soared to victory. McClellan won only twenty-one electoral votes, winning Delaware, his home state of New Jersey, and the border state of Kentucky, which was rife with pro-Confederate sentiments.

Vallandigham continued his role as one of Lincoln's chief critics. But, chastened by the Democrats' electoral defeats and the Republicans' martial victories, his opposition no longer carried the force that it once had. In less than five months after the election, the war would be over. Vallandigham's nation had won, but clearly he was on the losing side. The day after Robert E. Lee's April 12, 1865, surrender at Appomattox, a mob threw stones at Vallandigham's house, dispersing only after Vallandigham waved a pistol at them.[66]

If Windsor was Vallandigham's Elba, his St. Helena would be his political toxicity in the postwar United States. Northern Democrats struggled to rehabilitate their images as Republicans waved the bloody shirt at every election, and there was no room for Vallandigham's tainted legacy. In preparation for the 1866 National Union Convention in Philadelphia, where President Andrew Johnson's allies hoped to rally support for his Reconstruction policies, an Ohio Democrat wrote to Johnson, "We are hurt more by the prominence given Vallandigham than by all other causes. Our people shrink from contact with him; he must be kept down at the Philadelphia Convention, or we shall be badly crippled in Ohio. The fellow's doctrines are not so bad, but his name is damnation."[67] Despite his tarnished name, Vallandigham hoped to return to Congress. He was rebuffed in an effort to win the nomination for the US Senate in 1868, which went to Allen G. Thurman. He decided instead to run for his old congressional seat in that year's election, which he again lost to his old rival, Robert Schenck. The practice of law, not political office, appeared to be Vallandigham's only future. As the

1872 Senate race loomed, Vallandigham again hoped to secure the Democratic nomination.[68]

Vallandigham wouldn't live to see that race, thanks to a bizarre courtroom mishap. While defending a man named Thomas McGehan, who was accused of shooting a man to death in a barroom fight, Vallandigham attempted to prove that the victim, Tom Myers, had actually shot himself by accident while trying to draw his pistol as he stood up to face McGehan. To demonstrate how Myers could have done so, he brought a pistol of his own as a prop. Vallandigham had planned on bringing an unloaded weapon, but accidentally grabbed a similar revolver, with three bullets loaded in the cylinder, that had been sitting next to the empty gun on the bedside bureau in his hotel room. Not realizing he was holding a loaded weapon, Vallandigham assumed the kneeling position which he claimed Myers had been in and told the jury, "There, that's the way Myers held it . . . only he was getting up, not standing erect." The gun fired and Vallandigham shouted, "My God, I've shot myself!" He died about twelve hours later, on June 17, 1871.[69]

One would be hard-pressed to argue that Vallandigham deserved the fate that Burnside and Lincoln chose for him, no matter how disagreeable his views and words might have been. It is a testament to the great reverence most Americans have for Lincoln that his legacy has not suffered for his suppression of civil liberties, as the legacies of other leaders such as John Adams and Woodrow Wilson have. The more drastic actions he took in restoring the shattered Union are often simply shrugged off as a side note to his triumph of restoring the shattered Union and freeing the nation's slaves. Vallandigham received at least some vindication the year after the war ended, when the Supreme Court curbed the military's ability to try civilians. It must have been small comfort to Vallandigham, remembered by history as a villain while Lincoln stands as one of America's greatest heroes.

Chapter 7

The Will of the People Undone

If I am to be punished for having told the truth as I saw it—I ask for no mercy.

—Victor Berger

Eugene Debs has historically been the face of American socialism and the most enduring symbol of the oppression that his party and comrades faced from the Espionage Act of World War I and the Red Scare that followed the Bolshevik takeover of Russia in 1917. Owing to his numerous campaigns for president, Debs is the only Socialist of the era known to the average American. But perhaps that honor—or dishonor, as some would certainly argue—should belong to Victor Luitpold Berger of Milwaukee.

Berger never ran for president, the platform that made Debs a household name at the dawn of the American century, but he earned the distinction of being the first Socialist elected to Congress in the United States. And he faced a prison sentence twice as long as the one given to Debs. Elected while under indictment for alleged violations of the Espionage Act, Berger was unjustly denied his seat by his colleagues in the House of Representatives. When the voters of Wisconsin's Fifth Congressional District thumbed their noses at the powers that be by choosing him again in a special election, the nation's lawmakers once again denied him his rightly elected seat.

If not for his historic achievement of becoming the first Socialist in Congress or for the oppression he faced, Berger should be remembered for the role he played in encouraging Debs along the path to socialism. Lincoln Steffens, the famed muckraking journalist of the Progressive Era, described Berger as "the man who made a Socialist out of Debs." When Debs was imprisoned for his leadership of the 1894 Pullman Strike, he did not yet identify as a socialist. "No sir; I do not call myself a socialist," Debs testified before the US Strike Commission in 1894. Debs had "heard but little of Socialism" and "had yet to learn the workings of the capitalist system." It was during his incarceration that Debs

Victor Berger of Milwaukee, the first Socialist elected to Congress, fell victim to the anti-sedition measures that followed America's entry into World War I and was denied the seat to which he was rightfully elected.
LIBRARY OF CONGRESS

was to be "baptized in Socialism," as he whiled away his days reading socialist and communist literature. Berger did his part in contributing to Debs's radicalization by bringing him a three-volume copy of Karl Marx's seminal work, *Das Kapital*, which Debs later credited as being "the very first to set the 'wires humming in my system.'"[1]

Born in 1860 in Austria's Nieder-Rehbach region in what was then the Austro-Hungarian Empire, Berger immigrated to the United States with his family in 1878. After a brief stay in New York, the family settled in Bridgeport, Connecticut. Rather than completing the degree he'd begun working on at the University of Vienna and the University of Budapest, where he studied history and political economy, Berger did farm work and other odd jobs, and began learning the trade of metal polishing until his English skills were sufficient enough for him to pass a teacher's examination. In 1881, after wandering west, he moved to Milwaukee and became a public school teacher, primarily teaching German, along with history and geography.[2]

Milwaukee at the time had the most foreign-born population in America and was a center of German-American life. Berger became heavily involved in the city's German community, joining his local *Turnverein*, the fraternal organizations that were founded by German émigrés who'd fled to the United States after the revolutions of 1848.[3]

Around the time he arrived in Milwaukee, Berger also joined the burgeoning socialist movement. He became president of the *Turnverein*, which, because of its political leanings, was known as the "Red Verein." With eleven years' worth of savings, he left teaching and started a German-language newspaper, the *Arbeiter Zeitung*, which he later renamed the *Wisconsin Vorwärts*. Years later he founded the *Social-Democratic Herald*, an English-language socialist paper, and, in 1911, the *Milwaukee Leader*, which would ultimately become the source of the espionage charges that threatened to put him behind bars for twenty years. Berger joined the Socialist Labor Party in 1889, and two years later helped to found the Socialist Party as a union of two feuding factions. He and his wife, Meta, a former student he married in 1897, were leaders of Milwaukee's socialist movement. They frequently hosted political meetings at their home and both sought elected office. Berger lost campaigns for mayor and Congress in 1904, while Meta was elected to the local school board as a Socialist in 1907.[4]

Berger's time was the heyday for the Socialist Party in America. At the time that Berger helped to found the Socialist Party, it had only about 10,000 members. By 1912 it had more than 100,000, and Debs received nearly 900,000 votes in that year's presidential election. As the movement grew, it was beset by ideological and philosophical division. Berger's course was one of relative moderation. He rejected the more radical path of many of his comrades, and molded his views to the circumstances of his adopted country. He eschewed violence and advocated the peaceful transition to socialism that the American electoral system allowed for. Though he professed in his editorials a belief that "an armed people is always a free people," he wrote that "we surely want no Russian kind of revolution. Nor do we want a repetition of the French revolution if it can possibly be avoided."[5] *

The middle path espoused by Berger put him into direct conflict with the more radical members of the socialist movement, including Debs, for whom Berger was not doctrinaire enough for their liking. During an interview that journalist Lincoln Steffens conducted with Debs at Berger's home, Berger sat beside Debs, arguing points of socialist ideology. When the conversation turned to the question of whether America's capitalist barons should be compensated for the confiscation of their property, Debs insisted, "Take them," while Berger countered, "we should offer to pay." Socialist and labor leader William English Walling told Debs, "Berger is a frank and outright opponent of everything revolutionary." When Berger won his campaign for the US House of Representatives in 1910, Debs noted with dismay that labor leader Samuel Gompers had rejoiced in Berger's election, which he described as a sign of both men's heresy. "When Gompers and his fakir lieutenants call a revolutionist their friend and rejoice in his election, there is something wrong with that friend that will bear looking into," Debs wrote in a 1910 letter. Berger frequently described his moderate positions as a hedge against the radical Left, the absence of which would leave the bomb-throwers in control of the party, which he argued would have great consequences for the United States. It was an explanation that Berger would frequently employ in later years when facing government persecution.[6]

* Berger wrote this in 1909, referring to the 1905 revolution that forced Czar Nicholas II to establish a new legislative body, the Duma, and a new constitution, not the bloodier and more famous Bolshevik revolution of 1917.

An overt racist and supporter of segregation, Berger also differed from the more radical wing of the movement in his views on race. "There can be no doubt that [N]egroes and mulattos constitute a lower race," he said in 1902. Others, such as Debs, viewed race issues along class lines. Debs wrote in 1903 that the Socialist Party had "nothing in particular to offer the [N]egro," and that it would make no "special appeals" to people of different races, but that "the Socialist party is the party of the working class, regardless of color."[7]

Unlike his movement's left wing, which largely considered public office a means of nothing more than raising class consciousness—the *International Socialist Review* criticized Berger for rejecting that principle—Berger believed elected office was a means by which socialist ideals and policies could be advanced. He sought to provide effective representation and city services to his constituents, which radical critics derisively referred to as "sewer socialism." Berger believed socialists should "aim at higher things than simply not to steal when they are in office," and said, "We want to show our comrades all over the country that our principles will lose nothing of their revolutionary energy by being thus applied to a local situation." He finally got his chance to put that principle into practice in 1910. In April of that year, Berger was part of a slate of seven socialists who were elected Milwaukee aldermen. As a member of the Milwaukee Common Council, Berger advocated, unsuccessfully, for policies such as a minimum wage for municipal employees and public ownership of utilities.[8]

Berger would not remain on the Common Council for long. A grander stage awaited him. On November 8, with 40 percent of the vote, Berger defeated Republican incumbent William Stafford to become the first Socialist ever elected to the US Congress. Debs, singing a different tune than he did in his private correspondence with others, congratulated Berger on the victory he'd won for their movement. "Your election marks the beginning of the end of capitalism and the end of the beginning of Socialism in the United States," Debs wrote him.[9]

As he had on the Milwaukee Common Council, Berger chose the path of respectability, not obstructionism, in Congress. He was there to pass—or at least to advocate—for laws on behalf of the working class, not to throw rhetorical bombs, and he would not conform to the popular perception of socialists as radical agitators. "There were two ways before me," Berger said at the 1912 Socialist Party convention. "I could make a free-speech fight all alone, try to break down all precedent and all barriers, speak about the coming revolution and the cooperative commonwealth, as long as my lung power would hold out, and wind up my short parliamentary career by being suspended from the House, and thus also make an end to political action by this 'direct action.' Or I could pursue the other course, obey all rules and precedents of the House until they are changed—get the respect and the attention of my fellow members, speaking sparingly and only when measures directly concerning the working class are up for discussion, giving, however, close attention to all the business before the House of Representatives."[10]

In Congress, Berger's first action was to vote "present" instead of casting a vote for Speaker of the House. The first resolution he introduced called for the removal of American troops along the border with revolutionary Mexico. Berger considered himself to be "the representative of not only the fifth district, but of the working class of the United States as well." The centerpiece of his legislative agenda was an old-age pension bill that would have provided $4 per week to poor workers over the age of sixty. As a member of the committee that governed the District of Columbia, Berger fought for home rule for the capital city, a cooperative store for Washington's civil servants, and a shorter working day. Berger introduced legislation to nationalize railways and telephones, and, after the 1912 sinking of the *Titanic*, he advocated for the nationalization of America's radio systems, the need for which he said had been proven by the high-profile disaster at sea.

Some of Berger's proposals were far more radical. He proposed a constitutional amendment to abolish both the presidential veto and the United States Senate, which he thought "an obstructive and useless body, a menace to the liberties of the people, and an obstacle to social growth," which included many members who were "representatives neither of a State nor of its people, but solely of certain predatory combinations." The Seventeenth Amendment, which called for the direct election of senators by the people instead of the state legislatures, would not be ratified until 1917. And he sought to eliminate the power of the Supreme Court, which he considered hostile to organized labor, to review acts of government. In a demonstration of the distrust he placed in the nation's highest court, Berger's pension bill included an unusual provision that barred the Supreme Court from reviewing the legislation.[11] *

As the lone Socialist elected to national office, Berger was a celebrity who received an extraordinary amount of press coverage for a freshman congressman. Debs said his presence in Washington showed the value of having even a single Socialist in Congress. However, his presence would not be felt for long. Stafford, now running as the candidate of the "fusion" ticket of Democrats and Republicans, defeated Berger in his 1912 reelection bid. When the new Congress convened in 1913, it would again be without a single Socialist member. The Socialists

---

* Article III, Section 2 of the Constitution permits "judicial stripping" of Supreme Court jurisdiction, and there are some precedents for such an action, one of which in particular inspired Berger to include that provision in his pension bill. In 1868, William McCardle, a Mississippi newspaper publisher, challenged his military imprisonment under the 1867 Military Reconstruction Act for a series of allegedly "incendiary and libelous" articles. The Supreme Court heard his appeal for a writ of *habeas corpus*, but before the court could rule, Congress repealed a provision of the act that granted the court the authority to hear the case (Miller, 82; Ex Parte McCardle. 74 US 506. Supreme Court of the United States. 1868).

would not elect a second congressman until 1914, when New York's Twelfth Congressional District sent Meyer London to the House of Representatives.

Berger was not content with his one term and hoped to regain his old seat. His campaigns in 1914 and 1916 saw him again defeated by Stafford and his fusion ticket. Those campaigns would be complicated by an epochal event in world history: the outbreak of World War I in Europe.

Berger stood with his party in opposition to the war. "This war is the disgrace of the twentieth century. And it is a misfortune that international Socialism has proved itself too weak to prevent it," he declared. The *Leader* called for the United States to halt war exports to the belligerent countries, and that the government seize control of the nation's food distribution to protect workers from soaring prices. The party's national committee offered mediation and a peace plan to end the war, and warned against American participation in it.[12]

In the *Leader*, Berger blamed the war on "the surviving relics of feudalism—by czarism and kaiserism," though he was accused, as were many others in Milwaukee, of having pro-German leanings. Aside from his latent German nationalism, Berger, like most on the American Left, had a deep-seated loathing of Russia's Romanov rulers that left him seemingly rooting for a German victory. "And in case that the czar and his allies should win, humanity would have to endure for some generations barbaric czarism in Europe as a ruling influence," he wrote. And Berger forgave Germany's Socialists for their support of the war, which he viewed as one of self-defense for Germany. "We cannot very well blame the Socialist parties of the various European nations for standing with the rest of their people in this world crisis. And least of all can we blame any Socialists for defending their homes . . . wherever they were face-to-face with invasion," he wrote.[13]

As hostilities between the United States and Germany grew, Berger still hoped for his country to stay out of the war. At a February 1917 rally in Milwaukee, Berger told a crowd of four thousand, "There are many Americans who will protest against the war because America has nothing to gain and a great deal to lose. We are bound to lose lives, civil liberties and money." But it would soon become clear to Berger that America would not remain neutral for much longer. The sinking of the *Lusitania* in 1916, which he blamed on Britain, along with German submarine warfare against American shipping at the beginning of 1917 had pushed the United States to the brink. The *Leader*'s editorial policy shifted from noninterventionism to creating a Socialist policy framework to guide the United States in the coming war with Germany. The paper demanded the nationalization of war-critical industries and a domestic social program that included an eight-hour workday, a 100 percent tax on all incomes over $10,000, and pensions for the elderly, widows, and orphans. He also called for the preservation of civil liberties during wartime.[14]

On April 2, 1917, the war came to America. Five days after Congress declared war against Germany, the Socialist Party gathered in St. Louis for an emergency convention. Speakers pledged "continuous, active, and public opposition to the war," which they decried as being fought "to secure the profits of the ruling class of this country." Berger was appointed to the fifteen-person committee tasked with drafting the party's statement on the war. The report it produced declared: "The Socialist Party of the United States is unalterably opposed to the system of exploitation and class rule which is upheld and strengthened by military power and sham national patriotism. We, therefore, call upon the workers of all countries to refuse support to their governments in their wars. The wars of the contending national groups of capitalists are not the concern of the workers. The only struggle which would justify the workers in taking up arms is the great struggle of the working class of the world to free itself from economic exploitation and political oppression, and we particularly warn the workers against the snare and delusion of defensive warfare."

The sentiments expressed by the proclamation were a far cry from the statements Berger had been making since the war erupted in 1914. His opposition to the war had been more tempered than that of some of the other party faithful. The left wing even sought his ouster from the party's National Executive Committee in 1916 for alleged militarism. But outnumbered and outmaneuvered by the party's radical wing in St. Louis, Berger and his more conservative allies had little ability to shape the proceedings or the report issued by the convention. Against his better judgment, Berger voted in favor of a proclamation that he did not wholeheartedly support. He would later tell the jury at his Espionage Act trial that he "hardly knew the convention," which he said was one of the few conventions where he never made a speech.[15]

Berger's hopes of preserving civil liberties vanished not long afterward. As John Adams did when he faced war with France and Abraham Lincoln did as he fought the Confederacy, President Woodrow Wilson found it expedient to stifle dissent with new laws. Two months after Congress declared war on Germany, it passed the Espionage Act. In addition to creating new laws against actual espionage, which would be punishable by up to thirty years in prison, and possibly death, the act made it illegal to "convey false reports or false statements with intent to interfere with the operation or success of the military or naval forces of the United States or to promote the success of its enemies," to "cause or attempt to cause insubordination, disloyalty, mutiny, refusal of duty, in the military or naval forces of the United States," or to "obstruct the recruiting or enlistment service" in the armed forces. As Berger and other Socialists would learn, the prohibition against encouraging insubordination or resistance to military service would be broadly construed. The following May, Congress amended that law with the Sedition Act of 1918, which threatened even greater restrictions on Americans' civil liberties. It made it a crime to "utter, print, write, or publish any disloyal, profane, scurrilous, or abusive language" about the United States' "form of government," the Constitution, or the army and navy, along with any other language "intended to . . . discourage resistance to the United States, or to promote the cause of its enemies." Violators could be imprisoned for up to twenty years.[16]

Wilson described the Espionage Act as a wartime necessity. In response to a letter from leftist publisher Max Eastman, who complained about the revocation of the mailing privileges of his socialist magazine, *The Masses*, under the Espionage Act, Wilson replied, "I think a time of war must be regarded as wholly exceptional and that it is legitimate to regard such things which would in ordinary circumstances be innocent as very dangerous to the public welfare." The president essentially acknowledged the arbitrariness of the law in telling Eastman, "The line is manifestly exceedingly hard to draw, and I cannot say that I have any confidence that I know how to draw it. I can only say that a line must be drawn, and that we are trying—it may be clumsily, but genuinely—to draw it without fear or favor or prejudice."[17]

Berger's first brush with the Espionage Act would come when his *Milwaukee Leader* fell victim to the crackdown it prompted against allegedly seditious publications. Enforcement of the Espionage Act against seditious materials sent through the mail fell to the previously unassuming personage of the postmaster general. The Espionage Act did not explicitly empower Postmaster General Albert Burleson with the authority to do so, but nonetheless, he held the power of life and death over any publication deemed seditious. And he wielded it with a heavy hand. "He may deny the mails to any one that he doesn't like, for any reason or no reason. No crime is defined; no hearing is allowed; no notice is necessary; there is no appeal," journalist H. L. Mencken wrote. No indictment or trial was needed, only Burleson's decision that a newspaper or magazine was seditious. "The instant you print anything calculated to dishearten the boys in the army or to make them think this is not a just or righteous war—that instant you will be suppressed and no amount of influence will save you," Burleson told an interviewer.[18]

In September 1917, Burleson decided that the *Leader* met those criteria. Berger wrote to Burleson, a former colleague of his from his term in the House of Representatives, to ask for a meeting. He instead received a hearing before the third assistant postmaster general, a man whom Socialist leader Morris Hillquit, responding to the unelected bureaucrat's suppression of the Socialist newspaper the *New York Call*, had called "the sole accuser, judge, and executioner of the people's organs of public expression. He is a prolific accuser, a merciless judge and prompt executioner." Burleson's assistant provided several editorials from the *Leader* that he said were in violation of the Espionage Act and, without bothering to explain exactly how they had broken the new law, revoked the newspaper's second-class mailing privileges.[19]

As a result, the *Leader*'s out-of-town subscribers were forced to pay twice as much for their newspapers. The *Leader*, which had boasted a circulation of 37,000, lost about 85 percent of its out-of-town subscriptions, though its circulation in Milwaukee grew. Berger mailed the *Leader* outside of Milwaukee in bundles as fourth-class mail, and local Socialists delivered the newspapers to the remaining faithful subscribers. In another hit to the *Leader*'s bottom line, businesses began withdrawing advertising from the paper, oftentimes under pressure from the federal government or pro-war civic groups. Berger scrapped its national edition and halved the size of the twelve-page newspaper. Furthermore, the postmaster general stripped the *Leader* of its right to send or receive first-class mail. Employees resorted to dropping off the newspaper's outgoing letters in mailboxes around Milwaukee, while Socialist mayor Daniel Hoan would sometimes receive letters sent to the *Leader* at his office.[20]

Berger continued to publish, but with new self-censoring editorial policies designed to discourage further suppression. There would be no more criticism of the Wilson administration and fewer editorials. Those editorials that the *Leader* still published had to be checked by two staffers to ensure that they contained nothing likely to get the paper into further trouble. "We will say nothing we don't think, although we think a great deal that we can't say," Berger told the newspaper's staff.[21]

Worse was in store for Berger than the suppression of his newspaper. On March 11, 1918, in the midst of Berger's campaign in a special election to replace the deceased senator Paul Husting,* Berger and four other Socialist Party leaders were indicted for conspiracy to violate the Espionage Act. The five defendants—the other four were Adolph Germer, J. Louis Engdahl, William F. Kruse, and Irwin St. John Tucker—had little in common, outside of their positions of leadership in the Socialist Party. Aside from Berger and Germer, none were personal friends, and they represented different wings of the party. The indictment alleged that they had conspired to violate the Espionage Act through speeches and writings, including five *Leader* editorials that were entered as evidence.[22]

Berger, running on a peace platform, lost his Senate race, though he won more votes than a Socialist had ever received in Wisconsin, and while under indictment, no less. He quickly pivoted to a campaign for his old House seat in the November 1918 election. Stafford's fusion ticket had carried the day in

* Berger was defeated in that special election by Irvine Lenroot, the "man who might have been president." Warren Harding wanted Lenroot to be his running mate in 1920, but the delegates to the Republican National Convention chose Massachusetts governor Calvin Coolidge instead. Had Harding succeeded in choosing his vice president, the progressive Lenroot would have become America's thirtieth president upon Harding's death in 1923.

1912, 1914, and 1916. In 1918, it was a three-way race, with Democrat Joseph Carney joining Berger and Stafford in the fight for the fifth district. After three consecutive losses, and despite a second indictment against him and a slew of other Wisconsin Socialist candidates just a week before the election—the indictment on sixteen Espionage Act counts stemming from statements he'd made during his Senate campaign came during jury selection in the trial for his first indictment—Berger finally prevailed in his comeback bid. He would again be a member of the House of Representatives.[23]

Six days after the election came the November 11, 1918, armistice that ended World War I. The United States was no longer at war against its foreign foes. But the armistice brought no relief for the victims of the government's war against perceived domestic enemies at home. Socialists had never been particularly popular among the great mass of the American public. And being associated in the public mind not only with radicalism but also with the Bolsheviks' decision to forge a separate peace with Germany and remove Russia from the war—despite his general abhorrence of violent revolution, Berger nonetheless supported the Bolshevik revolution in Russia—only exacerbated the hostility toward the Socialist Party. "I was not indicted because I had committed any crime—I was indicted because I stood for Socialism," Berger told a crowd of ten thousand supporters in Chicago several days after the armistice.[24]

Rather than his hometown of Milwaukee, Berger would stand trial alongside his comrades in Chicago before US District Court Judge Kenesaw Mountain Landis, who is better known to history in his role as the first Major League Baseball commissioner, and for the lifetime bans he handed down to the participants in the infamous Chicago Black Sox scandal. In a particularly unflattering description, the communist journalist John Reed, in his coverage of the trial, wrote of Landis: "Small on the huge bench sits a wasted man with untidy white hair, an emaciated face in which two burning eyes are set like jewels, parchment skin split by a crack for a mouth; the face of Andrew Jackson three years dead."[25]

Defense attorney Seymour Stedman sought a change of venue on account of Landis's overt prejudice against German-Americans. The defense attorney alleged that Landis, who himself was of Swiss-German extraction, had recently told a German-American defendant, "If anybody has said anything worse about the Germans than I have, I would like to know it so I can use it." When the defendant responded that Germany has no shortage of men and money, and that Landis should "wait and see what she is going to do to the United States," Landis, Stedman alleged, responded, "One must have a very judicial mind, indeed, not to be prejudiced against the German-Americans in this country. Their hearts are reeking with disloyalty. This defendant is the kind of man that spreads this kind of propaganda and it has been spread until it has affected practically all the Germans in this country. This same kind of excuse of the defendant offering to protect the German people is the same kind of excuse offered by pacifists in this country, who are against the United States and have the interest of the enemy at heart by defending that thing they call the Kaiser and his darling people. . . . You are of the same mind that practically all German-Americans are in this country, and you call yourself German-American. Your hearts are reeking with disloyalty. I know a safe blower, he is a friend of mine, who is making a good soldier in France. He was a bank robber for nine years, that was his business in peacetime, and now he is a good soldier, and as between him and this defendant, I prefer the safe blower."

After reviewing the transcript of the previous case, Landis deemed Stedman's affidavit a "perjurious document" and denied the motion for a change of venue. The jury was empaneled on December 9.[26]

Spectators and reporters packed the courtroom for the trial, which Berger likened to the Salem witch trials. The prosecution's case rested largely on more than one hundred pieces of literature and correspondence it had confiscated. Among the evidence against the five defendants were pamphlets with titles such as "The Price We Pay" and "Down with War," antiwar cartoons, posters, speeches, the Socialist Party's St. Louis proclamation, and five editorials from the *Leader*.

Because the five were charged with conspiracy, "Everything said or done by any of them is admissible against everybody else on the ground that they are responsible for each other as fellow conspirators, and the alleged conspiracy is established by combining the individual acts and statements of the different defendants," as Hillquit explained. The defense attorneys insisted that the Socialist Party advocated the breaking of no laws, and pointed to Berger and others' participation in war bond drives as at least tepid support for the war effort.

Berger spent nearly three days on the stand, testifying to an unfriendly jury, which he said might as well have been selected by the pro-war National Security League. He defended his vote for the St. Louis proclamation as an attempt to fend off the more radical proposals floated at the convention. "There were three shades of opinion on the committee: ours, a radical, and a still more radical," Berger testified. Though he only wrote one of the five *Leader* editorials submitted as evidence, along with part of another, he took responsibility for all as the paper's editor in chief. When Berger claimed that he'd never advocated violence, the prosecution countered with the 1909 editorial in the *Social Democratic Herald* in which he'd quoted Friedrich Engels's line: "Give every citizen a good rifle and fifty cartridges and you have the best guarantee for the liberty of the people."[27]

The trial concluded on January 8. The jury was not convinced by the defense's explanations or justifications for their actions, nor by Stedman's insistence in his closing arguments that Congress had no power to abridge the freedom of speech that was enshrined in the First Amendment. After twenty-three days of trial, it took the jury only six hours to reach a "guilty" verdict against all five defendants. Berger claimed that the district attorney declared in triumph to the newspapers, "Bolshevism has received a fatal blow by this verdict."[28]

In a statement to the court, published across the country, Berger decried his conviction as a political show trial. The only "crime" he and his codefendants were guilty of was being Socialists and opposing the war. "Socialism teaches that modern wars are mostly struggles over business and commercial interests. Socialists hold that these struggles do not interest the modern working class in any country," he wrote. "Now if this teaching of Socialism is a crime, then we are criminals." He described himself and his codefendants as political prisoners. "Under acts passed by congress as 'war measures,' however, many men and women have been persecuted in this country for alleged or real opposition to this war. They have been sentenced to terms of imprisonment far exceeding the worst sentences for similar offenses under the rule of the czar or the Kaiser," he said. "Most of these victims are Socialists. They have, without exception, been prosecuted and imprisoned for expressing their political and economic opinions. These victims, nevertheless, were merely exercising rights guaranteed them by the Constitution of the United States."

Berger accused the government and capitalist society of using "war hysteria" and the Bolshevik takeover of Russia as an excuse to "put the Socialist party out of business." "Any opposition to capitalist, commercial, or imperialistic wars is regarded as 'high treason.' And all opposition to profiteering is denounced as disloyalty and 'German propaganda,'" Berger said. He called the League of Nations a "thin screen" for the capitalists in the victor countries to divvy up the spoils of war, and, in his defense, quoted Republican senator Warren Harding, who would be elected president the following year, who said, "[F]rom the very beginning it was a lie to say that this was a war to make the world safe for democracy." "The *Milwaukee Leader* has never said anything stronger about the cause of this war than these senators say just at the present time," Berger said. Though the capitalist class and its subservient press saw no difference between socialism and Bolshevism, Berger warned that by retarding socialism, the capitalists "will surely create anarchism. They will prepare this country for a revolution such as the world has never seen before." He also warned that, if the Socialists took power, the same laws used to deny him his rightful seat in Congress could one day be used to exclude the capitalist class as well.

In closing, Berger said that if he was guilty, then every member of the Socialist Party was guilty, as was every man who voted a Socialist ticket or criticized the war effort. "And if the Socialist party is a conspiracy against capitalism, then the Republican and Democratic parties are conspiracies against human progress and human welfare," he wrote. "If I am to be punished for having told the truth as I saw it—I ask for no mercy."[29]

Germer, Berger's codefendant, had said he preferred the maximum sentence rather than a relatively minor one of two or three years because it would prove Landis's anti-German prejudice. He got his wish. Determining that the court had seen an abundance of evidence that the defendants had violated the Espionage Act and had obstructed the wartime draft, Landis sentenced them each to twenty years at the federal penitentiary at Leavenworth, Kansas. Landis regretted that the Espionage Act only allowed a maximum sentence of twenty years. "I believe the law should have enabled me to have him lined up against the wall and shot," he told a crowd during a speech in Chicago. Landis refused to set bail, but within several hours, an appellate court reversed his decision, releasing the defendants on $100,000 bail. Chicago Socialists quickly raised the money, with much of it coming from wealthy attorney William Bross Lloyd. Berger and his four comrades would remain free while they appealed their conviction.[30]

For Berger, that meant he would be free to take his seat in the House of Representatives while his appeal played out—or so he thought. However, his colleagues were less than accommodating. For the rest of the House, the votes of Wisconsin's fifth district weren't enough to vindicate a Socialist who'd been convicted of espionage. They did not want a convicted traitor in their midst. On the first day of the new session of Congress, Representative Frederick Dallinger, a Massachusetts Republican, said Berger shouldn't be sworn in because he'd been convicted of violating the Espionage Act. A committee was appointed, with Dallinger as the chair, to investigate the matter.[31]

The committee hearing reprised much of the evidence from Berger's recent trial in Chicago, including scores of articles from the *Leader*. Congressman Joe Eagle, a Texas Democrat, said the committee would reach its own conclusions rather than simply accept the jury's verdict. "He gets a new trial here, so far as we are concerned," Eagle said. Amid his lectures to the committee on the tenets of socialism and the sins of the "capitalist class," Berger argued that the Espionage Act was an unjust law and deemed its victims, himself included, as "political prisoners." "The entire affair has not been paralleled in our history since the day Cotton Mather hanged witches in Massachusetts," he said. Berger insisted that he'd been found guilty in Landis's court of exercising his right to free speech, which "should have nothing to do with my being seated in the House of Representatives." The law under which he'd been convicted "is a flat denial of rights guaranteed to every citizen," his conviction "a travesty upon impartial justice," and his sentence "imposed upon me by a sensational and prejudiced judge." He reminded the committee that the sentence was under appeal. Berger told the men who would have been his colleagues in the sixty-sixth Congress that it would be "foolish and criminal" to take from the Socialist Party, which had cast more than one million ballots in the last election, its only representative in Congress. "It may depend upon your decision in this case to a great extent whether the common people are to lose all faith in political elections and representative government," Berger said.

Contrary to the view most congressmen held of him, Berger defended himself as a patriot. "I have proven my love for this my country by a life of labor in it and for it; by striving constantly with all my energy to improve the conditions of my fellow man. And, finally, I have proved my love for America, my faith in America's justice, by risking my liberty in defense of the constitutional right of all American citizens to discuss freely and fully the official acts and policies of their public servants," he said. Henry Cochems, who'd served as one of Berger's defense attorneys during the Espionage Act trial, compared Berger to Lincoln, who, as a young congressman, had opposed America's war against Mexico. "You would not say that Abraham Lincoln in the Mexican War, because he criticized President Polk so bitterly, such as no critic has given from any source in this war, you would not say that he was a traitor . . . nor would you say that Webster and Clay were traitors," Cochems said.[32]

After four months of hearings, the committee voted 8–1 to recommend that Berger not be seated as the representative from Wisconsin's fifth district. Though the end of the war was nearly a year past, the committee determined Berger to be ineligible to serve because of his alleged obstruction in the war effort and attempts to embarrass the federal government. The committee's rejection of Berger was based on a provision in the Fourteenth Amendment, included to bar former Confederates from holding office, that prohibited anyone who had engaged in "insurrection or rebellion" against the United States or "given aid or comfort" to its enemies.*

When the matter went to the full House in November, Berger was castigated as "treacherously disloyal," "one of the most dangerous men in the United States," a Bolshevik, and a traitor. Berger warned the House, "Remember, Gentlemen, you may exclude me once, you may exclude me twice. But the fifth district of Wisconsin cannot permit you to dictate what kind of man is to represent it. If representative government shall survive, you will see me or a man of my kind, let us hope many men of my kind—in the nation's legislature."

It was to no avail. A report compiled by the House declared that, "under the facts and circumstances of this case Victor L. Berger is not entitled to take the oath of office . . . or to hold the seat." Only a single congressman, progressive Republican Edward Voigt of Wisconsin, voted against Berger's exclusion from the House, which some newspapers decreed to be one vote too many.[33]

---

* The provision of the Fourteenth Amendment that the committee cited in denying Berger his seat had already been repealed by the time of his ouster. The amendment allowed for Congress to remove that provision with a two-thirds vote, which it did in 1898.

The governor of Wisconsin called a special election to fill the vacant fifth district seat, and Berger sought to make good on his warning that the district's voters would not allow Congress to dictate who would represent them. In an act of defiance, Milwaukee's Socialists nominated Berger as their candidate. The Democrats and Republicans, learning their lesson from Berger's victory in the three-way race of 1918, reverted back to the fusion ticket that had been successful in thrice defeating him before, choosing Henry Bodenstab as their champion. Bodenstab campaigned on the slogan, "Protect your homes from Bolshevism," while anti-Socialist newspapers portrayed the race as being between "Bergerism" and "Americanism," and a "challenge to loyalty" for the district's voters.

With the eyes of the nation upon them, Milwaukee's voters again chose Bergerism. In the December 19 special election, Berger prevailed, this time by an overwhelming margin of 5,998, an improvement of more than 400 from his November 1918 victory. Socialist voters, incensed by Congress's rejection of their wishes, increased their turnout by 40 percent from the previous year. Berger called the win "the first sign of the reawakening of genuine democracy in this country since the days of the struggle for the emancipation of the black race," and said the reaffirmation of his 1918 victory "vindicated one of the basic principles of modern democracy—representative government."[34]

The voters' repudiation did not sway Congress, which did not appreciate being shown up by Berger. When Berger arrived back at the House on January 10, 1920, the chamber again refused to seat him. The House refused even to allow him to speak on his own behalf. Voigt again stood as Berger's lone defender. "You may laugh and scoff, gentlemen, but I know Victor Berger. No man can devote his whole life and fortune to the great cause of endeavoring to better the conditions of the toiling millions, stand by his principles like a Rock of Gibraltar, regardless of personal consequence, without being morally great," Voigt told his colleagues. "Victor Berger's name will stand in the future as that of a martyr to a great cause—the rights of free speech, free press, and representative government." Voigt would not stand alone in insisting that Berger be seated. Five of his colleagues now joined him in voting to swear in Berger. But the result was the same: Twice chosen by the voters of the fifth district, Berger would again be denied his seat. More than a year after the end of the war, the members of the House would not forgive nor forget Berger's opposition.[35]

Wisconsin's Socialist Party announced that it would keep nominating Berger "until Hades freezes over if that un-American aggregation called Congress continues to exclude him." And Berger threw down the gauntlet with yet another run for the House seat he had been unjustly denied. But the fifth district's Socialists had finally grown weary of testing Congress's resolve to bar Berger from its halls, and they nominated another in 1920. For the first time since 1908, Berger would not be on the ballot in the general election. Stafford, unseated by Berger in 1918, would return to Congress.[36]

Berger still had other battles to fight. He was appealing both Burleson's suppression of the *Leader* and his conviction in Chicago. In January 1921, the Supreme Court ruled on Berger's appeal in the *Leader* case. That ended about as well as his congressional comeback campaign had. Berger had argued that the Espionage Act was unconstitutional because it denied him his right to due process by allowing Burleson to revoke the *Leader*'s second-class mailing privileges without a trial, and that it infringed on his right to free speech.[37]

The Supreme Court had already upheld the constitutionality of the Espionage Act in challenges to several convictions, including those of Debs, who famously ran for president while behind bars, and of Charles Schenck, a Socialist Party national committee member. Schenck's appeal led to the 1919 Supreme Court opinion in which Justice Oliver Wendell Holmes Jr. wrote the immortal words, "The most stringent protection of free speech would not protect a man in falsely shouting fire in a theatre and causing a panic."[38]

An appeal to free speech would not save the *Leader*. Justice John Hessin Clarke cited the Debs and Schenck cases, along with several others, in his affirmation of Burleson's order. Clarke noted that articles in the *Leader* denounced the US government as a "plutocratic republic," while others called the wartime draft "unconstitutional, arbitrary, and oppressive, with the implied counsel that it should not be respected or obeyed." In the court's opinion, Clarke wrote, "The Constitution was adopted to preserve our government, not to serve as a protecting screen for those who, while claiming its privileges, seek to destroy it. Without further discussion of the articles, we cannot doubt that they conveyed to readers of them false reports and false statements, with intent to promote the success of the enemies of the United States, and that they constituted a willful attempt to cause disloyalty and refusal of duty in the military and naval forces, and to obstruct the recruiting and enlistment service of the United States, in violation of the Espionage Law."[39]

Berger would receive much better news less than two weeks later when the court overturned his 1918 conviction. The Supreme Court tossed out the convictions of the five Socialists not because of the rank injustice of the Espionage Act, but because Landis should not have presided over the case after Stedman accused him of prejudice against Berger, Germer, and Kruse, the three German- and Austrian-born defendants. "Judge Landis had no lawful right or power to preside as judge on the trial of defendants upon the indictment," Justice Joseph McKenna wrote. The twenty-year convictions were reversed. Berger's legal ordeal was finally over.[40]

Gradually, as the war faded into history, the hysteria that had gripped the nation receded. Congress repealed the 1918 Sedition Act in 1920, though the

Espionage Act itself would live on. President Warren Harding commuted the sentences of some of the act's victims, including Debs, who had served three years of the ten-year sentence he'd received for his speeches against America's participation in World War I.

In May 1921, just four months after the Supreme Court upheld Burleson's injunction against the *Leader*, new postmaster general William Hays restored the newspaper's second-class mailing privileges. Along with the *Leader*, Hays lifted the wartime restrictions against other radical newspapers like the *New York Call* and the *Liberator*. Hays had determined that Burleson had erred in revoking the newspapers' privileges but still allowing them to be distributed in general. If a newspaper was unmailable, it was all or nothing for Harding's new postmaster general, who found such arbitrary halfway measures as the ones taken by his predecessor to not be "in the public interest."[41]

Free of the legal ordeal he'd endured for nearly four years, Berger finally reclaimed his old House seat in the 1922 election, defeating his perennial opponent Stafford. By the time Berger took his seat as the duly elected congressman from Wisconsin's fifth district, the Socialist movement in America had passed its zenith and was returning to its more humble origins as a fringe political party. Berger would be reelected twice more before falling to Stafford in their final rematch in 1928.

Berger would not live to see another campaign. On August 7, 1929, Berger succumbed to the injuries he'd suffered after being hit by a streetcar in Milwaukee. The city's Socialist faithful mourned their fallen hero. Nearly 100,000 people came to pay their respects as Berger's body lay in state at city hall, where his comrades still served, and throngs of supporters lined the streets in the rain as his casket was carried to the cemetery where his ashes were scattered. The funeral procession was called the longest that the city had ever seen. Thus, Milwaukee, and the Socialist Party of America, bid farewell to Victor Berger, "the man whose life had been a parallel with the growth of socialism in America."[42]

Chapter 8

American Bolshevik

I have always advocated a revolution in the United States. . . . Revolution does not necessarily mean a revolution by force. By revolution I mean a profound social change. I do not know how it is to be attained.

—John Reed

To the leaders of the Bolshevik revolution and its supporters in other countries, Russia was to be only the first step in a worldwide revolution. They wanted the same in Britain, in France, in Germany, and in America, where the workers and peasants would build upon the example set by their brothers and sisters in Russia. In America, one of the most famous apostles of this global revolution was John Reed.

As a radical journalist, Reed made Bolshevism his greatest cause. An unofficial ambassador and historian of the Russian Revolution in America, his firsthand account of the Bolshevik takeover, *Ten Days That Shook the World*, became required reading for leftists in America and abroad. Vladimir Lenin himself gave the book his stamp of approval.

Reed's era was a time in which the American Far Left was under siege. The end of World War I signaled the start of America's first Red Scare, inspired by Americans' fear and hatred of Bolshevism. The Russian Revolution was met with immediate revulsion in the United States because the Bolsheviks had pulled their country out of the war, depriving America, Britain, and France of their critical ally on the war's eastern front. Many Americans considered Bolshevism to be a German plot, and their opinions hardened further after the war. The Bolsheviks' dedication to class war and the destruction of capitalism, and their determination to spread their revolution across the globe, led many Americans to the conclusion that they represented an existential threat to America as they knew it.

Like so many others, Reed fell victim to the frenzy that swept the United States during and following the war as American authorities worried that revolutionary rhetoric would soon become revolutionary action. He faced indictment

John Reed went from idealistic Greenwich Village bohemian to one of America's most visible supporters of the dreaded Bolshevik regime after the Russian Revolution in 1917.
LIBRARY OF CONGRESS

under the Espionage Act. American authorities barred his return to the United States. For a time, they even prevented him writing his magnum opus on the Russian Revolution.

The grandson of a successful frontier businessman and son of a well-off family in Portland, Oregon, Reed seemed an unlikely candidate to grow up to become a champion of worldwide revolution. Jack, as he was known to his family and friends, had a wealthy and privileged upbringing, attending the best schools in Portland before being sent to prep school in Morristown, New Jersey, as a prelude to his college days at Harvard. In school he showed a great propensity for writing, including for school publications at Morristown and Harvard, but little interest in politics.

Despite his privileged upbringing, rebellion and progressivism were in his blood. His father Charles "C. J." Reed had been appointed a US marshal in 1905, and was a devoted Theodore Roosevelt progressive as he fought to break up Oregon's timber and land fraud rings. His betrayal of his class left him ostracized from the Portland social scene, but earned him the attention of the progressive muckraking journalist Lincoln Steffens, who became a friend to the elder Reed, and later, a mentor to Jack.[1]

Dubbed by biographer Robert Rosenstone* as the "romantic revolutionary" and by novelist Upton Sinclair as the "playboy of the revolution," one could be forgiven for wondering if Reed's revolutionary path was driven more by a youthful artist's exuberance than by ideological fervor.[2] One former schoolmaster remembered Reed for the "mischief and disorder" he caused. "He was a difficult and rather disturbing influence in the school," the schoolmaster remembered. "He was free from ordinary restraints, but was amiable and had no serious disciplinary trouble."[3] At Harvard, Reed was a rambunctious and occasionally

* Rosenstone's *Romantic Revolutionary: A Biography of John Reed* was the basis for the epic 1981 film *Reds*, starring Warren Beatty as Reed.

troublesome young man, but certainly no revolutionary. His youthful hijinks were more those of a prankster, not a radical, and he devoted himself to poetry and writing as he mostly eschewed the political activism that blossomed at Harvard during his time there.[4]

Determined to make a living as a journalist, Reed moved to Greenwich Village after graduating from Harvard, an ideal place for a young, carefree artist. Steffens, whom he'd come to know during his Harvard days, helped him land a job writing for *American Magazine*, and he became immersed in the Village's bohemian scene.[5] He also began to come into contact with the Village's more radical elements.

Reed took his first major step on the road to becoming a leftist scribe in January 1913, when he was published for the first time in *The Masses*. The magazine, largely devoted to the arts, had taken a decidedly radical turn when Max Eastman became its editor in 1912 and called for "a carefully thought-out program of class struggle," and Reed wanted to be a part of it.[6] Reed called Eastman and told him that he had a story that his employer, *American Magazine*, wouldn't print. Rather than mail it, as Eastman insisted, Reed, who had found the editor's address, arrived at his apartment with the article in hand.

Eastman was unimpressed with the man who showed up at his home. In fact, the visit was so unpleasant and intrusive that Eastman considered walking away from the magazine afterward. But his thoughts of quitting disappeared after reading the article that Reed had left behind. "Where the Heart Is" told the story of a well-traveled prostitute working in New York. Eastman was impressed with Reed's description of "an important piece of American life that no other magazine would dare to mention unless sanctimoniously." After reading it, Eastman wrote to Reed, asking that he write "a brief study, or comment, humorous or dramatic, on some current matter as often as you can." Soon after, Reed became an editor for *The Masses* as well.[7]

"Where the Heart Is" may have been risqué, but it was not revolutionary. That description held true for Reed as an individual as well. Eastman thought him "a brilliant and audacious art-rebel with no thought of the class struggle."* Reed believed the magazine's true purpose to be social, "to everlastingly attack old systems, old morals, old prejudices—the whole weight of outworn thought that dead men have saddled upon us—and to set up new ones in their places." *The Masses*, Reed declared in bohemian glory, would "be bound by no one creed or theory of social reform, but will express them all, providing they be radical."[8]

For much of his life, Reed favored general radicalism over rigid adherence to dogma. However, his true entrée into the world of class struggle and left-wing

---

* Eastman became conservative and stridently anticommunist later in his life. He was an early contributor to the conservative *National Review* and was a Goldwater Republican in the 1960s.

politics would come soon after joining *The Masses*, when he covered the great silk workers' strike of Paterson, New Jersey, a six-month showdown in which 25,000 workers ultimately walked off the job. It was a watershed moment for both the radical labor movement and for Reed. Even before he became a contributor to *The Masses*, Reed had been a supporter of the Industrial Workers of the World, the radical labor organization that favored "direct action" and advocated for the world's workers to form "one big union." In the summer of 1912, he'd written a friend, saying, "I have become an I.W.W. and am now in favor of dynamiting." The strike would mark what Rosenstone described as Reed's transition from "sympathetic reporter to involved partisan."[9]

Journalist Walter Lippmann wrote that many believed the "central passion" of Reed's life to be "an inordinate desire to get arrested."[10] And Reed made good on that desire almost as soon as he arrived in Paterson. As he toured the picket lines, a heavy rain began to fall, and he took shelter on the front porch of a nearby house. A police officer ordered Reed to move, and when he refused—Reed claimed to have had the homeowner's permission to stand on his porch—the officer yanked him onto the street. The cop's next order was to keep moving. "I won't get off this street or any other street. If I'm breaking the law, you arrest me," Reed fired back at the officer. The officer didn't want to arrest Reed, but changed his mind after Reed wrote down his badge number and asked his name. The next morning, the judge, Recorder Carroll, who had already doled out countless sentences to striking silk workers, sentenced Reed to twenty days in the Passaic County Jail based on a "clever *mélange* of lies" provided by the arresting officer.[11]

The strike may have been on the outside of the jail, but many of its leaders festered with Reed inside its walls. Reed met Carlo Tresca, who kept the reporter at arm's length, fearing he was a spy planted by the police. The next day Big Bill Haywood, national leader of the IWW, arrived in the jail. Haywood already knew Reed and assured Tresca and other jailed Wobblies that he was trustworthy.* "You tell him everything," Haywood urged his comrades. Reed ingratiated himself with the imprisoned strikers, soaking in their tales of picket lines and police beatings. After four days behind bars, an IWW attorney freed Reed, who promptly returned to New York to write of the things he'd seen.[12] At Haywood's suggestion, Reed tried to rally people to the Paterson strikers' cause with a pageant that would reenact the strike on the stage at Madison Square Garden.[13]

It was Reed's coverage of conflict in Mexico, not in Paterson, that made him a celebrity in America. Carl Hovey, the editor of *Metropolitan* magazine, hired Reed as a war correspondent to cover the revolution in Mexico on Steffens's

---

* Aside from their obvious IWW sympathies, Haywood and Reed would later share another common bond as American radicals who lived, and died, in exile in the Soviet Union. Haywood, sentenced to twenty years in prison under the Espionage Act in a 1918 mass trial of IWW members, jumped bail in 1921 and fled to Russia, where he died seven years later.

recommendation. Reed, who was also on assignment for the *New York World*, managed to slip into Mexico, despite a military decree barring Americans from the country. At Christmastime, Reed reached the headquarters of revolutionary leader Pancho Villa, and the two men took an immediate shine to each other. Reed witnessed and wrote about Villa's victories in battle. *Metropolitan* promoted him as an "American Kipling." After his return to New York, Reed compiled his notes and articles in his first book, *Insurgent Mexico*. Reed's experiences with Villa, whom he greatly admired, were part of a spiritual awakening that had begun in Paterson. He later wrote that Mexico helped him "find himself again."[14]

The revolution in Mexico was but one step in Reed's development as a journalist and a radical. Reed's visceral reaction to the outbreak of World War I demonstrated the extent to which his radicalism had taken shape by August 1914. In an article for *The Masses* titled "The Traders' War," Reed, in true Socialist fashion, ascribed the causes of war to rival commercial interests between Germany on one side and Britain and France on the other. The war of commerce and profit between the two sides had been raging for years as Britain and France conspired to check the upstart Germany's ambitions, Reed wrote, and culminated in the shooting war now raging in Europe. "The situation in short is this. German Capitalists want more profits. English and French Capitalists want it all," Reed wrote.[15]

Reed, who had previously hesitated to identify himself as a Socialist, now wrote that "We, who are Socialists" hope that out of the horrors of war great social changes would emerge. But Reed cautioned his readers not to be deceived by those who portrayed the war as a fight against tyranny. "But we must not be duped by this editorial buncombe [bunkum] about Liberalism going forth to Holy War against Tyranny. This is not Our War," Reed wrote in conclusion.[16]

The Masses was a perfect fit for an idealist such as Reed, but it didn't pay the bills. Its editors and contributors were unpaid, and the magazine was distributed for free. For a steady paycheck, Reed joined the staff of *Metropolitan*, which wanted him back in Europe to write about the war.* Reed was persona non grata in France due to a *New York Post* article alleging that he'd taken a German rifle and returned fire against French forces the last time he'd been in Europe, a charge he spent the next several years denying. But there were other fronts in the war, and Reed, joined by illustrator Boardman "Mike" Robinson, departed for the Balkans. The assignment brought him for the first time to the Russian capital Petrograd, the city that would come to define his career. However, at the time, he

---

* As a staffer at the *Metropolitan*, one of Reed's more esteemed colleagues was former president Theodore Roosevelt. Reed did not share his father's affinity for Roosevelt, whose politics and worldview he despised, and the two strong-willed men clashed frequently in the office. During one exchange, Roosevelt criticized Reed's hero Pancho Villa as "a murderer and a bigamist," to which Reed replied, "Well, I believe in bigamy." A delighted Roosevelt grabbed Reed by the arm and told him, "I am glad, John Reed, to find that you believe in something" (Rosenstone, 210).

was unimpressed with the "dilettante revolutionaries" he met in Petrograd, and believed any real revolution must be led by real revolutionaries. "It's not the real thing," he said. Upon his return, Reed wrote his second book, *The War in Eastern Europe.*[17]

After returning to the United States, Reed had some family business to attend to in Portland. It turned out to be a fateful trip. While visiting his mother, Reed met Louise Bryant, a fellow writer and admirer of Reed who was at the time married to a Portland dentist. Reed wrote to Steffens, telling him, "I have fallen in love again." Steffens didn't think much of it, for Reed was a hopeless romantic who fell in love with a new woman with surprising regularity. But Bryant was different. Reed convinced her to move with him to Manhattan. Later, the two married and bought a home in Croton, on the Hudson River north of New York City.[18]

To the chagrin of many of his Socialist comrades, Reed publicly backed Woodrow Wilson's reelection bid in 1916 for his pledge to keep the United States out of war, and "because Wall Street was against him."[19] He signed an appeal to Socialist voters urging them not to waste their ballots on their party's nominee, Allan Benson,* and join him in supporting Wilson instead. Reed's faith in Wilson would soon be shattered. After Germany informed the recently reelected Wilson in February 1917 that it would resume unrestricted submarine warfare, it was only a matter of time before Wilson went back on his campaign pledge.

"By the time this goes to press the United States may be at war," Reed correctly predicted in the April 1917 issue of *The Masses*. The famous war correspondent emphasized to his readers that he knew what war was. He'd seen it with the belligerent armies in Europe, where he'd "seen men die, and go mad, and lie in hospitals suffering hell." But there were worse things to be found in war, he warned. "War means an ugly mob-madness, crucifying truth-tellers, choking the artists, sidetracking reforms, revolutions and the workings of social forces. Already in America those citizens who oppose the entrance of their country into the European melee are called 'traitors,' and those who protest against the curtailing of our meagre rights of free speech are spoken of as 'dangerous lunatics,'" he wrote. "For many years this country is going to be a worse place for free men to live in; less tolerant, less hospitable," Reed predicted, again correctly. Reed chastised the United States for its hypocrisy in turning a blind eye to British transgressions against neutral nations and German civilians while howling with rage over Germany's conduct, a false neutrality for which he blamed Wilson. "The fault is not ours. It is not our war," Reed wrote in conclusion.[20]

---

* Benson won the Socialist nomination after Eugene Debs, the party's perpetual presidential candidate, opted out of a fifth campaign for the White House and decided to run for Congress in 1916 instead. Debs returned to the presidential campaign trail in 1920 (Salvatore, Nick. 1982. *Eugene V. Debs: Citizen and Socialist*. Urbana: University of Illinois Press, 276).

Reed had no need to fear conscription. A November operation to remove one of his kidneys saw to that.[21] But the magazine for which he'd spent the past four years writing and editing would be an early casualty of the war. On July 5, Postmaster General Albert Burleson declared *The Masses* to be unmailable under the Espionage Act, a fate that befell many a publication deemed unpatriotic or insufficiently supportive of the war effort.

To Reed and his fellow radicals, the world seemed to be falling apart. The war was bad enough while the United States remained neutral, and America's entry into the fray brought with it a wave of repression upon the country's radicals. But there was a ray of light in the darkness. In March 1917—February under the calendar then in use in Russia—revolution swept Czar Nicholas II and his Romanov dynasty from power in Russia. And another revolution seemed to be on the horizon. Reed watched from afar with growing intensity. When Bryant returned to America in August after a stint covering the war in Europe for the Wheeler News Syndicate, Reed had already made up his mind. He wanted to go to Russia and see the next revolution for himself.

With press credentials from *The Masses* and the *New York Call*, a Socialist newspaper, along with $2,000 that Eastman and a friend had solicited from a wealthy Socialist—neither paper could afford to finance the trip themselves—Reed and Bryant set off for Russia. The State Department, concerned about what kinds of activities Reed might partake in while abroad, asked him to sign a pledge that he would not participate in an international Socialist peace conference in Stockholm, which he planned on attending. Reed, not a party member or a delegate, had no problem signing the pledge.[22] It was in Russia, not Stockholm, where Reed would do the work of the revolution.

The October 1917 issue of *The Masses* advised its readers that Reed would soon be telling the story of what was happening in Russia. "He will write the first full history of the Russian Revolution."[23] But that history would not grace the pages of *The Masses*. Crushed under the weight of the Espionage Act, the magazine published its final issue a month later.

Bryant and Reed arrived in Petrograd at a unique period in history, the interregnum between the two revolutions. Petrograd, as the Germanic-sounding St. Petersburg had been renamed after the war broke out, was a city on the brink, and was far different from the place Reed had visited in 1915. The city, like the rest of the country in the months since the czar was deposed and Alexander Kerensky's provisional government took charge, was a bleak, dark place. Robberies and burglaries spiked while the food supply dwindled. Petrograd residents' daily bread allowance had dropped from a pound to a half-pound, then gradually down to a quarter-pound, until eventually there was no bread left for anyone. The availability of sugar, milk, and other staples wasn't any better.[24]

The greatest distinguishing feature of Russia under Kerensky was roiling political instability. Workers' and peasants' councils called "soviets" had sprouted up across the country. In the cities, in the factories, even on the front lines, workers, peasants, and soldiers organized into these soviets to wield power for themselves against the factory bosses and commanding officers. Through the soviets and other mechanisms, myriad political parties and organizations, many of them with leftist and revolutionary worldviews, jockeyed for position. The country's entire political structure tottered precariously on the edge. In August, just before Bryant and Reed arrived in Russia, Kerensky had fended off an attempted coup by General Lavr Kornilov with the help of the Bolsheviks and other leftists, whose success in combating Kornilov's march on the capital had propelled the Bolsheviks into the majority in the Petrograd Soviet, then in the soviets of Moscow and other key cities.[25]

When Bryant and Reed arrived in Petrograd in September, there was uncertainty as to who was actually in control. The Kerensky government still stood, but the soviets were centers of power unto themselves, and the conflict between the two power blocs was escalating. "It looks like a showdown soon," Reed wrote.[26] Bryant and Reed connected with Albert Rhys Williams, a minister, journalist, and fellow Bolshevik sympathizer who'd been in the country since June, reporting for the *New York Post*. Reed got to know the movers and shakers of the Bolshevik movement, such as Leon Trotsky and Vladimir Lenin, whom he called, "A strange popular leader—a leader purely by virtue of intellect; colourless, humourless, uncompromising, and detached, without picturesque idiosyncrasies."[27]

The proverbial ten days that shook the world began on November 6, 1917, when the Bolsheviks rose up against the provisional government in Petrograd, and came to an end on November 15, when they seized the Kremlin in Moscow. Reed and Bryant were immediately swept up in the jubilation and quickly became enthusiastic participants in the revolution, while continuing to chronicle the events for the books they would write back in America. After the Bolsheviks stormed the Winter Palace, Bryant, Reed, and Williams rode in the back of a Bolshevik truck, showering the streets with leaflets announcing the end of Kerensky's provisional government.[28]

Pamphleteering from the back of a truck was only the beginning of Reed's direct participation in revolutionary affairs. He and Williams joined the Bolsheviks' new Bureau of International Revolutionary Propaganda, a division of the Foreign Office under Trotsky's leadership. A half-million leaflets, pamphlets, and newspapers created by the two American Bolshevik converts were distributed on the front lines, encouraging German soldiers to embrace socialism. Reed credited his and Williams's work for contributing to Germany's surrender in November 1918, and at least one German general agreed. After the war, General Max Hoffman said Germany's eastern armies were so riddled with Bolshevism that the military refused to transfer some divisions to the Western front out of fear that they would infect the troops there.[29]

Reed claimed for himself the position of commissar of art and amusement in the new Bolshevik government, a position that would put him in charge of festivals and pageants, like the one he organized for the Paterson strikers in New York. Williams was named commissar of education. Armed with a rifle, Reed patrolled in front of the Foreign Office building with the Red Guards. And at the Third All-Russian Congress of Soviets, Reed addressed the crowd, vowing to bring news of the revolution back to America, where he would "call forth an answer from America's oppressed and exploited masses."[30]

Amid the exhilaration of revolution, Reed found that he was broke. The $2,000 that Eastman had procured only lasted so long, and when the money ran out, Reed was forced to find a new source of funds for the continuation of his Russian sojourn. Raymond Robins of the Red Cross, with whom Reed had grown close despite their very different views of Russia and the war, made a proposal that forced Reed to choose between reality and radicalism. Robins had been urging Russia's new Bolshevik leaders to continue fighting the war, and wanted to create a newspaper to advocate against a separate peace with Germany. Despite Reed's political proclivities, Robins asked him if he was up to the task. Reed was no supporter of continued Russian participation, but idealism temporarily took a backseat to his very immediate need for cash. He soothed his conscience by considering the money as a loan to be repaid. "I wouldn't like to be put down by anybody as having served the interests of the United States or any other capitalist government, for I haven't—if I could help it," Reed told Robins. On a sample masthead for *Russische Tageblatt*, as the ultimately unpublished newspaper was to be called, Reed wrote, "This newspaper is financed by American commercial and financial interests, in order to promote American business in Russia, and friendship and understanding between the two peoples."[31]

Soon enough, Reed was ready to return home and write his history of the revolution he'd witnessed. However, he had a justifiable concern that the American government would seize the notes and other documents he'd amassed. He and Trotsky found a novel solution to the problem. Trotsky named Reed as the Soviet government's consul general in New York, which would give him diplomatic cover for his return voyage. Needless to say, this did not sit well with the American diplomatic community in Petrograd. US Ambassador David Francis was alarmed when he received the communiqué from the Soviets' foreign commissar, informing him, "Citizen John Reed has been appointed consul of the Russian people in New York." Francis convinced Alexander Gumberg, a radical who'd returned to Russia from America after the February revolution, to lean on Lenin to rescind the consulship. After Gumberg showed Lenin the newspaper prospectus that Reed had drawn up for Robins, Lenin vetoed Trotsky's decision.[32]

Thanks to the attention he'd attracted from American diplomatic authorities in Russia, Reed's home country was not eager to see him return to America when he departed Petrograd in February 1918. Edgar Sisson, a representative in Russia of the Committee on Public Information, America's World War I propaganda agency, was convinced that the revocation of Reed's appointment as Soviet consul was a ruse designed to allow him back into the United States without having his papers searched. The State Department was suspicious of Reed as well, having been warned of a report from the American embassy in Petrograd, where officials believed he was a naive tool of the Bolsheviks. "He is an anarchist and a Bolshevik sympathizer and is being urged to travel as a Bolshevist Courier by persons in Russia who desire to make trouble with America and believe that in this way an international incident will be created in the case of his arrest."[33] As such, the State Department temporarily blocked Reed's return, and he found himself waylaid in Christiana, Norway.

Upon his arrival in New York, Reed was interrogated about his activities in Russia, his Soviet consulship, and his revolutionary intentions now that he was back in America. Reed told his interrogators, "I am a Socialist and I am going to engage in Socialistic work within the law. If I do anything against the law I will take the consequences. I am in this country to write my book, and I would rather do that than anything else in the world." After a two-hour interrogation, customs officials sent Reed on his way, but the State Department seized his papers so it could determine if they contained "anything contrary to the interests of the American government." Reed was crestfallen, telling Steffens, "I am therefore unable to write a word of the greatest story of my life, and one of the greatest in the world."[34]

During his time in Russia, Reed expressed doubt to Williams about what kind of revolutionaries they'd be when he returned to the United States. "Do you think we'll ever make the grade? Or are we tagged for life—the humanitarians, the dilettantes?" he asked Williams. Reed had immersed himself in the Bolshevik movement while he was on the front lines in Russia. But what counted more is what they would do at home, he said. "It's easy to be fired by things here. We'll wind up thinking we're great revolutionaries. And at home?" Reed contemplated. "Oh, I can always put on another pageant."[35]

There would be no more pageants. Reed returned to America ready to champion the Bolshevik cause in earnest. He also returned to an America caught in the throes of the Red Scare, of a hysteria enforced by the draconian Espionage Act. A collision between those two incompatible forces was inevitable. Friends like Eastman and Steffens urged a course of moderation. "Really, I think it is wrong to try to tell the truth now. We must wait. You must wait," Steffens told him. Reed brushed off their advice and hit the soapbox in defense of the revolution. After all, with most newspapers now unwilling to publish his articles and the federal government holding his precious papers hostage, it was the only way he could make a living.[36] Benjamin Gitlow, a Socialist comrade of Reed's who later became a committed anticommunist, wrote of Reed after his return from Russia, "His words seemed to carry a genuine message from the land of revolution and a challenge to the whole capitalist world. . . . It seemed as if John Reed felt that the revolution was near in America and time must not be lost in preparing for it."[37]

Reed had legal problems awaiting him when he came home. He, along with Eastman and three other editors at *The Masses*, had been indicted under the Espionage Act while Reed and Bryant were in Russia. The other four defendants went on trial during Reed's voyage back to America, dodging a conviction after the jury deadlocked thanks to two jurors who were accused by the other ten of "Socialist and pacifist" tendencies. Two days after his arrival in New York, Reed was arraigned on the indictment he'd received in absentia.[38]

The pro-Bolshevik speaking tour Reed embarked upon compounded his legal issues. When city officials in Philadelphia refused to issue a permit for a Socialist rally on May 31, Reed spoke instead to a thousand people on the street outside the shuttered hall where the rally was to have taken place. He was charged with inciting a riot after the police physically dragged him from his pedestal. On September 13, Reed addressed what may have been the largest demonstration ever held in the United States for the Bolsheviks. At Hunt's Point Palace in the Bronx, Reed railed against the recently announced intervention by America and several of its allies against Red Russia, waged in a vain attempt to reconstitute Russian participation in the war and restore the eastern front. The result was his third arrest since returning from Russia, this time under the dreaded Sedition Act of 1918, for "disloyal, scurrilous, and abusive language about the Military and Naval forces of the United States."[39]

Not long afterward, Reed and his four codefendants went on trial for the first of those arrests, the Espionage Act charge lodged against him while he was in Russia. The charge stemmed from an article Reed penned for the *The Masses*. Headlined, "Knit a Straight-Jacket for Your Soldier Boy," the short blurb, which had been reprinted from another newspaper, claimed a staggering rise in mental illness among soldiers as compared to previous wars.[40] On October 3, Reed took the stand, describing the horrors of war that he'd seen and decrying the "fashionable" attitude of frivolousness that Americans had taken toward the war. In response to a prosecutor who asked if the article was meant to hinder recruiting—such allegations were the source of many Espionage Act cases—Reed said the notion had never occurred to him, and that he only wanted people to "know the truth about the European war." All five were acquitted two days later.[41]

The acquittal wasn't the only good news Reed received that fall. Shortly before the trial began, the State Department agreed to give back the notes and other papers Reed had brought back from Russia after Steffens convinced "Colonel" Edward M. House, an advisor and confidant to Wilson, to intervene. Renting a room on the top floor of a Greenwich Village restaurant, Reed sequestered himself for two months while he wrote his masterpiece.[42] *

Americans' fear over the influence of Russian Bolshevism led to a series of subcommittee hearings in the US Senate. The subcommittee, chaired by Senator Lee Overman, had been convened in 1918 to investigate "Brewing and Liquor Interests and German Propaganda." But with the war over, Americans weren't much concerned about German propaganda. The new threat of Bolshevism now seemed far more real, especially as labor unrest paralyzed the nation after the wartime no-strike pledge followed by many unions ended following the armistice. Bolshevism's adherents were in America and advocating for its spread in the United States. In the wake of a February 2 rally, in which Bryant and Williams defended the Soviet government before a cheering crowd, chanting, "Hurrah for the Bolsheviki," (a commonly used term at the time for Bolsheviks) Senator Charles Thomas, a Colorado Democrat, called their actions "virtual treason," while his Montana colleague, Thomas J. Walsh, urged the Overman Committee to shift its focus to the new menace looming over America.** The refurbished committee convened on February 11. Bryant, Reed, and Williams weren't called to testify, but they insisted that they speak to the subcommittee to clear the air over the misinformation being presented about the state of affairs in Russia.[43]

Even before Bryant and Reed testified, Reed had been a topic of conversation at the committee. Archibald Stevenson, a former agent for the Bureau of Investigation, the forerunner to the modern FBI, warned of Bolsheviks embedded within American society. "The interesting feature of the Bolsheviki movement is that every one of these currents that we have spoken of is now cooperating with the Bolsheviki emissaries. We have several avowed agents of the Bolsheviki government here—avowed propagandists," he told the committee. One, Stevenson said, was Reed, whom he noted, as if to emphasize his all-American roots, was a Harvard graduate and a descendant of Patrick Henry, which Reed himself often mentioned in his speeches. "He is now under indictment, but has not yet been tried, for violation of the espionage act," Stevenson said. He described Williams as the other Bolshevik emissary in the United States. "You think this movement is growing constantly in this country?" Senator Overman asked. Stevenson replied, "I think so. . . . I think it is growing rather rapidly, if we can gauge it by

---

* Reed had to find a new publisher after Macmillan canceled its contract. The book was ultimately published by the Village-based Boni & Liveright.

** In his book, *Reds: McCarthyism in Twentieth-Century America*, historian Ted Morgan describes the Overman Committee as the first congressional investigation into communism, a topic that would occupy seemingly infinite hours of Congress's time in the decades to come.

the amount of literature that is distributed and the number of meetings held. It is a very indefinite sort of thing. It is extremely difficult to state how effective these sheets are."[44]

The senators' disgust with the Bolsheviks was on full display as they obsessed over the idea that, under the new Soviet regime, bigamy and free love were rampant in Russia. And, as a sympathizer of that regime and its perceived wickedness, their hostility toward Bryant was overt from the moment her testimony began. "Miss Bryant, do you believe in God and in the sanctity of an oath?" Overman asked as she prepared to be sworn in. Bryant said she believed in the sanctity of an oath, prompting the committee members to again question her belief in God, which Senator William H. King deemed important, "because a person who has no conception of God does not have any idea of the sanctity of an oath, and an oath would be meaningless." After Bryant conceded that she believed in God, Senator Josiah Wolcott asked if she believed "in a punishment hereafter and a reward for duty." Bryant bristled at the line of questioning. "It seems to me as if I were being tried for witchcraft," she said, noting that none of the other witnesses had faced such inquiries. "I will concede that there is a hell," she said. "Or that there is a life hereafter." With that, Bryant was sworn in.[45]

Having seen the committee's treatment of his wife, Reed came in with an idea of what to expect, not that he would have otherwise expected a friendly reception. After Reed's lengthy explanation of the revolution and the state of affairs in Russia, Wolcott asked if the Bolsheviks' philosophy was "to try to make all the world socialistic, and thus, so to speak, make the world safe for socialism?" Reed said it was. "I may say that they are not going to do it with an invading arm, but by the advertisement of their doctrine," he said.

Major Edwin L. Humes, of the Army's Judge Advocate General's Department, asked Reed, "Have you in any of your public speeches advocated a revolution in the United States similar to the revolution in Russia?" "I have always advocated a revolution in the United States," Reed replied. When Humes pressed Reed on the matter, he elaborated that by "revolution," he didn't necessarily mean the kind of takeover that had occurred in Russia. "Revolution does not necessarily mean a revolution by force. By revolution I mean a profound social change. I do not know how it is to be attained," he said. Reed danced around the committee's questions of whether it is appropriate to overthrow a government by force. He told Humes "that our Declaration of Independence says something about the inalienable right of the people to change the form of government whenever they see fit." But no change in a country's form of government should be made until a majority of the people support it, he said. "If it can be secured by legal means, I do not think there is any justification or excuse for force," he said. Reed assured his questioners, "I do not see any necessity for violence in the United States."[46]

Along with bigamy, Soviet attitudes toward private property, and Reed's thoughts on the subject of revolution in America, the committee took great interest in Reed's activities on behalf of the revolution and Bolshevik government, such as his speech before the Third Congress and his work with the Soviet propaganda bureau. "I was a very small cog in the machine," Reed said of his propaganda work, which he emphasized was directed at the Germans. Reed admitted that Trotsky had appointed him Soviet consul general in New York, but said that he'd never officially represented the Soviet government in the United States.[47]

The press took a dim view of Bryant and Reed's testimony. The *New York Times* called Reed, along with his wife, "an apologist for Bolshevism." Like Bryant, the newspaper wrote, Reed "was not willing to admit that he was in favor of Bolshevism, as it is practiced in Russia, being made the order of things in this country."[48] Another newspaper excoriated Reed under the headline, "One Man Who Needs the Rope."[49]

Nonetheless, the world was going Reed's way. He followed his acquittal in *The Masses* trial by escaping the two other outstanding charges against him. In January, another case against *The Masses* was dismissed. The following month he beat the rioting incitement charge filed against him Philadelphia, and several weeks later the sedition indictment from his anti-intervention speech at Hunt's Point Palace was dismissed.[50]

Even better for Reed, in March 1919, *Ten Days That Shook the World* was finally published. Americans could now read for themselves about the revolution that Reed had witnessed. "No matter what one thinks of Bolshevism, it is undeniable that the Russian Revolution is one of the great events of human history, and the rise of the Bolsheviki phenomenon of world-wide importance," Reed wrote in the preface of the book. "Just as historians search the records for the minutest details of the story of the Paris Commune, so they will want to know what happened in Petrograd in November, 1917, the spirit which animated the people, and how the leaders looked, talked, and acted. It is with this in view that I have written this book."[51]

The book sold five thousand copies in its first three months, and was roundly praised in America's radical publications. Imprisoned Wobblies, rotting in Leavenworth after the mass 1918 trial of IWW members, called it the "minutes of the revolution." Even conservative, mainstream papers lauded *Ten Days That Shook the World* as a well-written and reliable account of the monumental events that had occurred in Russia, despite Reed's open bias in favor of the Bolsheviks.[52]

Reed's conflicts back in America weren't limited to the authorities or the "capitalist class." Some of the fiercest battles were reserved for his foes on the Left. Since its founding in 1901, the Socialist Party of America had been beset by feuds between the left and right wings. Reed was firmly entrenched on the

Left. The party was a far cry from the revolutionary "vanguard party" of Lenin's teachings. Reed thought the party and many of its members were too interested in electing aldermen and assemblymen, "where they turn into time-serving politicians, and in explaining that Socialism does not mean Free Love." Though the Socialist Party could turn out a million votes, "fully a third of the Socialist votes in normal times are . . . cast by middle-class persons who think Karl Marx wrote a good Anti-Trust law."[53] Thus Reed joined the fight to radicalize the party. It would ultimately lead him back to Russia and his beloved revolution.

The "Left Wing" movement, with Reed as one of its leaders, sought to wrest control of the Socialist Party from moderates, men like Victor Berger and Morris Hillquit, who advocated a "gradualist" approach to Socialist politics. Prospects for radicalizing the party looked good. In the Socialist Party's 1919 elections, the Left Wing won twelve of fifteen seats on the party's national committee, one of which was captured by Reed, who defeated the once-and-future Socialist congressman Berger.[54] *

But the Socialist Party's old guard would not cede its power that easily, and the Left Wing's great victory was followed by a purge by the party elders. Soon after the National Executive Committee election, the New York party organization moved to expel local chapters affiliated with the Left Wing. Heeding Hillquit's call to "clear the decks," the national committee, still in the hands of the conservative wing, revoked the charters of the Massachusetts, Michigan, and Ohio party organizations, and booted the radical foreign-language federations from the party as well. The coup de grâce came when the committee nullified the results of the election that gave control of the party to the Left Wing.[55]

Ninety-four outraged Left Wing delegates from twenty states gathered in Manhattan on June 21 to plan their response. Reed, too radical for the leaders of the Socialist Party, found himself urging a course of relative moderation. A faction of the Left Wing led by the party's foreign-language federations—there had long been a deep schism between the native-born and immigrant factions—called for the immediate creation of a new Communist Party. Reed still hoped to seize control of the Socialist Party and drag it to the left. The majority of the delegates backed Reed's call to go to the Socialist Party's August 30 convention in Chicago and try to convince the party to reaffirm the election results that gave the Left Wing an overwhelming majority on the national committee, while the foreign-language wing went its own way.[56]

The dispute between the two factions turned out to be over when—not if—to create a new party. When Reed and about eighty delegates arrived at Chicago's Machinists' Hall, the party's leaders turned them away, calling the police to enforce their edict. Reed gathered his faction in a nearby IWW hall, where they

* See chapter 7 for more on Berger's tumultuous career.

created the Communist Labor Party. In a separate meeting, the largely immigrant faction that split with Reed's group in June formed the Communist Party.[57]

Both new parties wanted Soviet recognition as America's one true communist party and believed that the Bolsheviks would only permit one to join the Communist International. The Communist Labor Party had a secret weapon in its bid for Soviet approval. It decided to send Reed, the famed chronicler of the revolution who was intimately familiar with Soviet leaders, back to Russia to secure the party's place within the Comintern.[58]

Returning to Russia would not be easy. Wracked by civil war and besieged by enemies on nearly all sides, Russia was cut off from the world, and the journey into the country was rife with danger. With forged papers identifying him as a seaman named Jim Gormley, Reed hopped a ship that brought him back to Christiana. After being smuggled into Sweden and then Finland, where he hid out with a local Bolshevik, Reed walked and sleighed to the Russian border and on to Petrograd, where he took a train to the new Soviet capital of Moscow.[59]

Upon reaching Moscow, Reed pleaded his case to the Executive Committee of the Communist International, then spent several months awaiting its decision. When that decision came, Reed learned that he and Louis Fraina, his counterpart from the Communist Party, had succeeded only in convincing the executive committee that their partisan divorce was wholly unnecessary. The committee did not recognize either party. Instead, it dictated that the two feuding left-wing factions unite as one. The disagreements that had so bitterly divided the two groups held little meaning for the committee. Noting that there were no "profound differences of opinion as regards programme," Bolshevik leader Grigory Zinoviev made clear that the prevailing view in Moscow was that it would be counterproductive to have two parties. "The split has rendered a heavy blow to the Communist movement in America. It leads to the dispersion of revolutionary force, to harmful parallelism, an absurd partition of practical work, and senseless discussions and an unjustifiable loss of energy in interfactional quarrels," he wrote to the two parties. Reed and the Communist Party representative in Moscow signed an agreement to merge the parties.[60]

The executive committee had ordered a unity convention between the two parties, and Reed was understandably concerned. Radical organizations were constantly under attack by federal authorities—the notorious Palmer Raids against left-wing radicals occurred in the United States during Reed's absence—and any communist unity convention had a high likelihood of suffering a similar fate. Reed also faced prison time for the outstanding criminal anarchy charge in Illinois, the second time he would leave Russia with criminal charges awaiting him in the United States. Nonetheless, his work done, if not quite as successfully as he'd hoped when he arrived in Russia, Reed could go home.

That is to say, he could at least try. Succeeding in his endeavor was another matter. The same conditions that made entry into Russia so perilous were equally present for anyone trying to leave the beleaguered country. His first attempt to smuggle himself out of Russia by crossing through Latvia was aborted due to heavy fighting between Bolshevik forces and the antirevolutionary Whites, and he made his way back to Petrograd.[61]

In late February, a disguised "Jim Gormley" again left Petrograd, this time bound for Finland, where he snuck onto a freighter preparing to depart from the port of Abo on March 13. Reed hid in the ship's engine room, but was discovered after a customs official found his coat and package. His false identity as the seaman Gormley didn't last long, thanks to the papers, notebooks, manuscripts, and letters he carried, including an introduction Lenin had written for an upcoming edition of *Ten Days That Shook the World*, a copy of which he'd given to the Bolshevik leader.* Reed also carried $1,500 in various currencies and 102 small diamonds, worth about $14,000, which the Comintern had provided to fund the merged communist parties back in America.[62]

Through interrogations and beatings, the Finns hoped to compel Reed to reveal his contacts in Finland, but Reed held strong. His fortitude may have saved his life, as he faced a likely charge of treason if definitively linked to Finland's communist radicals. Instead, the Finns settled on a charge of smuggling on account of the jewels they'd found.[63]

American officials displayed little interest in Reed's fate, and only inquired into his situation after Reed forced their hand by leaking a false story that he'd been executed, which was reported in newspapers across the United States. The ruse, and the flood of demands from Bryant and others to investigate the claim, had its intended effect. The State Department confirmed that Reed was still alive. But it still had no intention of helping him. On April 26, Reed was convicted of smuggling. Technically, his sentence was only a $300 fine and the confiscation of the diamonds he'd been carrying, but the Finns nonetheless left Reed to rot in solitary confinement for three months before setting him free.[64]

While he'd been stuck in Finland during his journey from Russia, Reed had written Bryant, saying he "could go neither forward nor back."[65] Now he could

---

* *Ten Days That Shook the World* was not as well-received by Soviet leadership after Lenin's death. Stalin, who was rarely mentioned in the book, while his nemesis Trotsky featured prominently, later banned Reed's seminal work in the Soviet Union. In *Children of the Arbat*, his novel of the early days of the Soviet Union, Anatoli Rybakov explained Stalin's hostility to Reed's book: "The main task was to build a mighty socialist state. For that mighty power was needed. Stalin was the head of that power, which meant that he stood at its source with Lenin. Together with Lenin he had led the October Revolution. John Reed had presented the history of October differently. That wasn't the John Reed we needed" (Homberger, 1; Reed, John. 1977. *Ten Days That Shook the World*. New York: Penguin. Introduction, xix by A. J. P. Taylor).

go back to Russia, but not forward to the United States. The State Department, hoping that Reed would surrender to American authorities, refused to issue him a new passport. In June, he arrived back in Petrograd, worn bare from his months in captivity and suffering from scurvy as a result of a prison diet almost exclusively consisting of dried fish. His friend Emma Goldman, the Russian-born anarchist who'd recently been deported back to her home country from the United States, nursed him back to health.[66]

Unable to return to America, Reed threw himself into the work of revolution. Reed attended the Second Congress of the Communist International, a gathering of communists from across the globe, as part of a well-stocked American delegation in late July. Reed's solidarity with world communism and the "General Staff of World Revolution"—the perception stuck, though the world revolution that the delegates had believed would be ignited by the Bolshevik takeover was in retreat—quickly evaporated as he found himself dealing with the same kinds of rifts and divisions he'd faced in New York and Chicago.[67]

Reed was appointed to two committees. The first, befitting an American Bolshevik in Russia, was concerned with national minorities and colonial issues. The second dealt with issues of trade unions, the issue that was largely responsible for bringing Reed into the radical leftist fold. And the most contentious issue of the trade union committee was one for which he'd fought passionately for years. Lenin had decried the First Congress's hostility toward "reactionary trade unions" such as the American Federation of Labor, and the leaders of the Congress, namely Zinoviev and Karl Radek, advocated for trying to radicalize the AFL in the interest of furthering world revolution. Reed, certain that the AFL could not be converted, unsuccessfully lobbied against the idea. This was Russia, the vanguard of world revolution, and the Russians were calling the shots. "The revolutionary proletariat considers the position of our American comrades absolutely incorrect," Radek told Reed. Even at the Comintern, Reed somehow found himself on the left wing, fending off attacks from the right. After Reed was appointed as an American representative on the Comintern's executive committee, his battles with Radek and Zinoviev continued, and he began to grow disillusioned with their leadership, though not with the Bolshevik cause.[68] *

In mid-August, Reed learned that Bryant was coming to meet him in Russia. But he wouldn't be in Petrograd to meet her when she arrived. Zinoviev insisted that Reed, as a delegate from an imperialist country, attend a conference in Baku for the "enslaved peoples" of the East, and denied his request to stay behind so he could meet Bryant before he departed. As Bryant embarked on the

---

* Radek and Zinoviev would later find themselves on the wrong side of a far more serious intraparty dispute. Both men met their deaths during Stalin's great purges of the 1930s.

final leg of her journey, Reed rode a train through a countryside ravaged by civil war and typhus into the heart of the Caucasus.[69]

When Reed arrived back in Moscow on September 15, Bryant was there waiting for him, and the reunited couple began planning for their return to the United States. But Reed would never see his homeland again. Ten days after returning from Baku, Reed fell ill. Doctors initially blamed his high temperature, dizziness, and headaches on influenza. Within a few days, however, it was clear that Reed was stricken with something more serious. When his symptoms worsened, the doctors admitted Reed into Mariinsky Hospital and diagnosed him with typhus. With medicine hard to come by thanks to the blockade against Russia, there was little the doctors could do to help him.[70]

On October 17, 1920, just five days before his thirty-third birthday, Reed succumbed to his illness. He was given a martyr's burial. Russian workers carried Reed on their shoulders to the Temple of Labor where a contingent of Red Army soldiers stood guard as mourners paid their respects. A week later, a military funeral procession carried him to the Kremlin wall, where he was buried alongside the heroes of Russian history.[71]

No hero's welcome would have awaited Reed had he returned to New York. But perhaps he, like so many others, would have outlasted the spasm of hysteria-fueled repression against American radicals at home. And had he lived on in the Soviet Union, perhaps he would have fallen victim to the far more vicious terror that felled so many other dissenters who dared speak out against the heirs to the revolution that he had so enthusiastically cheered.

Reed had defended the growing terror he'd seen the Bolsheviks employ against their enemies, both real and perceived, in Russia. When an incredulous Goldman, a lifelong anarchist who harbored deep distrust of all government authority, expressed her increasing skepticism about the Bolsheviks and their tactics, Reed had insisted that it was simply the cost of revolution. "You are a little confused by the Revolution in action because you have dealt with it only in theory," he said.[72] But Goldman and others questioned how dedicated the free-wheeling bohemian artist would have remained to his most cherished cause if he'd not died so early in its history. Biographer Eric Homberger is among those who believe a Reed who'd lived to see the terror and purges would have rejected the ugliness and repression that the Soviet state came to embody. Though Reed was a communist, Homberger wrote, "he was no defender of tyranny, and it is part of his enduring legacy that we can see him as someone who would have been a supporter of Dubček and Gorbachev."[73]

After her deportation, Goldman quickly came to believe that she was "caught in a trap" in Russia. Committed as Reed was to the revolution, Goldman believed that in his dying moments, he too had acknowledged a truth he may never have seen if he'd lived. "I realized that poor Jack had also begun to see beneath the surface. His was the free, unfettered spirit striving for the real values of life. It would be chafed when bound by a dogma which proclaimed itself immutable," Goldman later wrote. "Had Jack lived he would no doubt have clung valiantly to the thing which had caught him in the trap. But in the face of death the mind of a man sometimes becomes luminous: it sees in a flash what in man's normal condition is obscure and hidden from him. It was not at all strange to me that Jack should have felt as I did, as everyone who is not a zealot must feel in Russia—caught in a trap."[74]

But dying when he did, Reed's legacy was set in stone. Not long after his death, Reed's revolutionary epic, *Ten Days That Shook the World*, was republished with the introduction Lenin had written for him. The great Bolshevik leader's words of praise would ensure that Reed lived on as the radical icon he'd been when he died: "Unreservedly do I recommend it to the workers of the world. Here is a book which I should like to see published in millions of copies and translated into all languages. It gives a truthful and most vivid exposition of the events so significant to the comprehension of what really is the Proletarian Revolution and the Dictatorship of the Proletariat. These problems are widely discussed but before one can accept or reject these ideas, he must understand the full significance of his decision. John Reed's book will undoubtedly help to clear this question, which is the fundamental problem of the universal workers' movement."[75]

Chapter 9

The Press Goes to War

Their publication will doubtless be of gratification to our potential enemies and a possible source of impairment and embarrassment to our national defense.

—Henry Stimson

So often in American history, the clash between national security and the First Amendment right to a free press has been portrayed as a contest between patriotism and disloyalty. To reveal classified information, oftentimes of the utmost importance, would be to stab the United States in the back. In times of war, that debate becomes especially contentious.

But those who reveal America's secrets have often done so out of a belief that they are doing what's best for their country. If America, unbeknownst to its citizens, has taken the wrong path, the leakers of classified information believe they must set the record straight. That lesson has played out countless times throughout American history, most recently with the bombshell revelations of former National Security Agency consultant Edward Snowden.

Prior to Snowden, two instances stand out in particular: in 1941, when the *Chicago Tribune* alerted Americans to the war that President Franklin Roosevelt was about to embark upon, and in 1971, when the *New York Times* published the tragic decision-making process that had led the United States into the war in Vietnam. While the latter is a well-known incident in American history, the former has been largely lost in the din of the world war that followed.

Throughout the 1930s, as the storm clouds gathered over Europe, isolationism took root in the United States. Many Americans had a disinterested view of the conflict then raging in Europe. They saw no benefit from America's entry into World War I, and had no appetite for another foreign war. After Hitler's invasion of Poland again embroiled Europe in conflict, isolationist organizations such as the America First Committee flourished across the country, in an effort to ensure that the United States stayed on the sidelines this time.

Robert McCormick and his *Chicago Tribune* demanded that America keep out of World War II, and enraged members of Franklin Roosevelt's administration by publishing the president's secret war plans shortly before Pearl Harbor.
LIBRARY OF CONGRESS

Antiwar sentiment ran especially strong in the Midwest, the great bastion of American isolationism. In the Midwest, isolationism's newspaper was the *Chicago Tribune*, and its champion was its publisher, Colonel Robert McCormick.

As December 1941 began, America was already on the brink of war with both Japan and Germany. In August, Roosevelt ordered an oil embargo against Japan in response to its rampages across Asia. By the end of November, diplomatic negotiations with the Japanese had completely broken down. On the high seas, the US Navy was already in a de facto state of war with Germany, whose ships it was attacking on sight in some areas. Roosevelt had long believed that the United States must fight the Germans and Japanese, and the war that had been inching closer throughout the year now seemed inevitable. His main obstacles were a public and a Congress that was not as convinced as he that America must fight.

Roosevelt detested the isolationist *Tribune* and its publisher McCormick, and the two sides repeatedly crossed swords over the newspaper's editorial positions and attempts to expose the president's insincere protestations that he wanted America to stay out of the war. Throughout 1941, the *Tribune* had been hard at work exposing the "hidden war plans" of the president who'd told America that "your boys are not going to be sent into foreign wars," and sought to discredit his attempts to rally the American public around his cause. When the *Tribune* in August published details of Roosevelt and British prime minister Winston Churchill's secret plans for an invasion of Germany, the president instructed Senator Alben Barkley, the Senate majority leader, to denounce the article, calling it a "deliberate falsehood" on the Senate floor. When Roosevelt claimed in an October 27 speech that secret maps obtained by the United States showed German plans to invade South America from Dakar in West Africa, the *Tribune* mocked the allegations as absurd. "Anyone familiar with such matters knows that every general staff in the world has studied every conceivable problem of military action," the paper wrote. "If Mr. Roosevelt were to go into the files of the War or Navy Department, he no doubt could find documents which indicate how we would attack and seize and govern Canada."[1]

The isolationists believed staying out of a war raging far from America's shores was in the country's best interests. Isolationists had long accused Roosevelt of talking out of both sides of his mouth when it came to the war. Publicly, he stressed the desire to avoid getting sucked into Europe's war, but his critics didn't buy it, nor should they have. Indeed, Roosevelt had been steadily nudging the American public toward acceptance of intervention. King George VI wrote to Roosevelt from England in June 1941, "I have been so struck by the way you have led public opinion by allowing it to get ahead of you." Roosevelt professed his desire to stay neutral while quietly planning for the day when war would eventually come.[2]

A major step in Roosevelt's plans came on June 9, 1941, when he requested a report that became known as the Victory Program, or Rainbow Five, as the fifth installment of a series of war contingency plans that began in 1939 to prepare for the possibility of war against Japan, Germany, and Italy, which sought "the overall production requirements required to defeat our potential enemies." The plan, delivered to him in September, was a comprehensive blueprint for a potential war against Germany.

Rainbow Five was highly classified. But for weeks word had been leaking to the press, which reported various aspects of the Victory Program. In late October, the *Wall Street Journal* described the Victory Program as a "newly evolved munitions schedule which Washington and London expect will beat Hitler." The article revealed that the program could see up to one-third of American men between the ages of eighteen and forty-five in military service to defeat Germany. The *Tribune* reported on October 1 that congressional appropriations would be sufficient to equip a military force of ten million, and on November 26 informed its readers that Roosevelt had a victory plan calling for five million to eight million men at a cost of $40 billion, including $20 billion for Lend-Lease Act aid to Britain and other countries that were fighting the Germans. But the Victory Program report as a whole had been successfully kept under wraps.[3]

The cat was let very much out of the bag on December 4, 1941, when the *Chicago Tribune* and its sister newspaper, the *Washington Times-Herald*, published what McCormick described as "perhaps the greatest scoop in the history of journalism."[4]

The towering headline jumped off the page:

F.D.R.'s WAR PLANS!
GOAL IS 10 MILLION ARMED MEN; HALF TO FIGHT IN AEF
Proposes Land Drive by July 1, 1943, to Smash Nazis; President Told of Equipment Shortage

Reporter Chesly Manly laid out the Victory Program in explicit detail, including manpower projections, logistical problems, equipment needs and shortages, and overall strategy. He wrote that Roosevelt planned a ten-million-man military force, half of which would make up the American Expeditionary Force that would be sent to Europe to invade Germany because, in the plan's words, "Germany and her European satellites cannot be defeated by the European powers now fighting against her." Manly described the "astounding document" created jointly by the Army and Navy as "a blueprint for total war on a scale unprecedented in at least two oceans and three continents, Europe, Africa, and Asia. . . . [I]f our European enemies are to be defeated it will be necessary for the United States to enter the war." He explained America's plan for the "gradual encirclement" of Germany with bases in Britain, North Africa, and the Middle East. The target date for the invasion of Germany was set as July 1943.[5]

Manly wrote that the report backed up the claims of famed aviator Charles Lindbergh, one of the nation's most prominent isolationists, that Britain alone could not defeat the Germans, and "explodes some of the other popular myths that have been most sedulously fostered by administration spokesmen and war propagandists generally," such as the notion that a war against Germany would be waged against Hitler and his Nazi regime, not the German people themselves. "It is believed the overthrow of the Nazi regime by action of the German people is unlikely in the near future, and will not occur until Germany is upon the point of military defeat," the *Tribune* quoted the report as saying.[6]

In Asia, Manly wrote, the report recommended "strategic methods" to contain the Japanese, including the defense of Malaysia, blockades, air strikes, and support for a Chinese offensive. The report assumed that Germany, Italy, Japan, their puppets under occupation, and Vichy France would be potential enemies in the coming war, as well as possibly Portugal and Spain, Manly informed the *Tribune*'s readers. And the war effort against all enemies was to continue even if Britain and the Soviet Union were defeated, read the report, which predicted that Russia would be "militarily impotent" by the beginning of July 1942.[7]

Manly's article included a verbatim copy of the July 9 letter that Roosevelt had written to Secretary of War Henry Stimson asking for the report. "I realize that this report involves the making of appropriate assumptions as to our probable friends and enemies and the conceivable theaters of operation which will be required," Roosevelt wrote his secretary of war.

The front-page story was accompanied by a cartoon depicting a group of American soldiers representing Midwestern states—the Illinois soldier looks suspiciously like Abraham Lincoln—in a trench while warplanes fly overheard, dropping flyers emblazoned with the word *war*. To their backs is a fortress labeled *The Middle West*, and in front are the words *war propaganda* hovering above antiaircraft guns in front of the Capitol. Below the cartoon, a small box with the headline, "You Know Better," featured a comment Roosevelt had made in April 1940: "The Republicans are seeking to frighten the country by telling the people the present administration is trying to put this nation into war or that it inevitably is drifting into war. You know better than that."[8]

For McCormick, the blockbuster scoop on Roosevelt's war plans achieved two goals: Most obviously, it stabbed at the heart of Roosevelt's feigned dedication to keeping America at peace. "[W]e saw it as simple truth that Mr. Roosevelt was out to lie the United States into war with Germany," former *Times-Herald* editor Frank Waldrop wrote years later.[9]

Secondarily, McCormick had been itching to spoil the debut of a rival newspaper in Chicago, Marshall Field's *Chicago Sun*, and had instructed his reporters to find scoops that would deflect attention away from the *Tribune*'s new competitor. The result could not have been better for McCormick if he had invented a story himself. As *Tribune* readers were treated to one of the scoops of the century, an article about a conflict in the Balkans was the feature story in the *Sun*'s inaugural edition.[10]

The disclosure of Rainbow Five ignited a firestorm in Washington. The rest of the press wanted answers, and White House press secretary Stephen Early wasn't eager to provide any. Early refused to officially confirm or deny whether the plan published by the *Tribune* was authentic, though he gave at least unofficial confirmation when he told reporters that Roosevelt and Stimson were likely to investigate the source of the *Tribune*'s information. The press secretary actively tried to discourage other newspapers from reprinting the information. The newspapers were "operating as a free press" and had the right to do so, he said. But, "It depends entirely on the decision of the publisher or the editor or the reporter whether in printing it, it is patriotic or treason."[11]

At a press conference the next day, Roosevelt wouldn't address the issue. He told the press to instead take it up with Stimson at another press conference right afterward. Speaking to two hundred reporters, Stimson stuck to a prepared statement and refused to comment on the war plan itself. Stimson downplayed the significance of the report, which he presented as a contingency plan like so many others the United States and other governments prepare for all conceivable scenarios. He asked rhetorically what the press would think of a general staff "which in the present condition of the world" *didn't* plan for every potential emergency the country might face. He described the plan published by the *Tribune* as "unfinished studies of our production requirements for national defense." "They have never constituted an authorized program of the government," he said.[12]

Like Early, Stimson played the patriotism card for all it was worth. This was not an issue of freedom of the press. It was about national security. Stimson didn't deny that newspapers had the right to publish something like Rainbow

Five—but he tried to shame them for doing so. "While their publication will doubtless be of gratification to our potential enemies and a possible source of impairment and embarrassment to our national defense, the chief evil of their publication is the revelation that there should be among us any group of persons so lacking in appreciation of the danger that confronts the country so wanting in loyalty and patriotism to their government that they would be willing to take and publish such papers," Stimson said in his statement to the press.[13]

The Roosevelt administration needed answers as well. Navy Secretary Frank Knox, who happened to be the publisher of the *Chicago Daily News*, a competitor to the *Tribune*, told the president, "We would be derelict in our duty if we let this flagrant case go by without at least an official attempt to uncover by a grand jury how much secret material got into the heads of newspaper reporters employed by newspaper publishers who were unscrupulous enough to publish it on the very eve of war."[14]

Some members of Roosevelt's cabinet, including Attorney General Francis Biddle and Interior Secretary Harold Ickes, advocated at a December 6 meeting that criminal charges be brought against the *Tribune*. Biddle proposed that the Justice Department charge the *Tribune* with conspiracy to violate the 1917 Espionage Act, and Ickes suggested that the president appoint an "outstanding Republican" with "no New Deal taint" to serve as a special prosecutor. Ickes also questioned whether McCormick was still a reserve officer in the army and, if so, whether he could be court-martialed, though Stimson said he couldn't be court-martialed, even if he were still a reservist.

Strangely enough, other members, as well as Roosevelt himself, seemed uninterested in punishing McCormick, though they were angry that the *Tribune* had revealed the president's war plans to the world. Roosevelt agreed to hand the matter over to his attorney general and the secretaries of the army and navy. Ickes, who noted in his diary that the *Tribune* would have been guilty of treason if it had published the war plan during a time of actual war, thought McCormick should have been punished in the harshest way possible. "I thought that an example ought to be made. As a matter of fact, I believe that the charge of treason should have been thrown at McCormick immediately after his newspaper was off the press. We could have followed this with an explanation to the people that the preparation of war plans to meet any possible contingency was not only not unusual, it was the normal and expected procedure," Ickes wrote in his diary the next day.[15] *

Even many of the *Tribune*'s loyal readers believed McCormick had gone too far. Thousands canceled their subscriptions in protest and adopted the rallying cry, "Millions for defense, but not two cents for the *Tribune*."[16]

---

* Ironically, Ickes had served as editor earlier in 1941 of a book entitled *Freedom of the Press Today*.

The article produced shock waves on the other side of the Atlantic. The British, desperate for their American cousins to join them in the fight against Nazism, saw it as a ray of hope. The Roosevelt administration was all too happy to promote the article for the war-weary countries who were begging for American help. The Office of War Information actually broadcast the story to Europe via shortwave radio as a sign that American help was on the way. British newspapers dutifully reported the morale-boosting revelations.[17]

"The Roosevelt War Plan" was received with great interest in Germany. The German embassy in Washington had cabled a full transcript of Manly's article to Berlin the day after it ran, which the high command deemed "a fantastic intelligence coup." The Japanese put the article to good propaganda use, proclaiming in their newspapers that the article exposed the "secret United States plans against Japan and Germany" and America's unpreparedness for its "gigantic dream plan for war."[18]

Isolationism, of course, came to a sudden end on December 7 when the Japanese attacked Pearl Harbor. The question of whether Roosevelt was pushing America into war became irrelevant when the Japanese brought the war to America. After hearing news of the attack on the radio, isolationist senator Burton K. Wheeler issued a statement to the press: "Let's lick hell out of them." So far, "them" referred only to the Japanese. For the time being, America and Germany were still at peace. And a nation that had just been jarred awake from its isolationist slumber was unlikely to support the war that Roosevelt wanted to wage against Nazi Germany. Hitler would solve Roosevelt's problem for him when he declared war against the United States on December 11.[19]

In publishing the Victory Program, the *Tribune* may have inadvertently done Roosevelt a great service by provoking Hitler into declaring war on the United States. A plan for America's war against Germany would be most irrelevant unless and until the two countries were in fact at war. And on December 8, 1941, America was only at war with Japan. The United States had been roused to action in Asia. But unlike Japan, Germany had not attacked America, and many Americans still saw no reason why the United States should divert its attention away from the real enemy in Asia so it could fight the Nazis in Europe. Hitler's declaration of war made it a moot point, though many former isolationists would spend the war criticizing the "Germany first" policy that Roosevelt and Churchill had agreed upon.

Hitler's declaration of war against the United States four days after Pearl Harbor leaves little doubt as to the role the *Tribune* article played in his disastrous decision. In the speech to the Reichstag in which he announced that Germany would go to war with America, Hitler recited a litany of grievances against Roosevelt, and directly referenced the article that had appeared the week before. "With no attempt at an official denial there has now been revealed in America

President Roosevelt's plan by which, at the latest in 1943, Germany and Italy were to be attacked in Europe by military means," Hitler said. In light of those revelations, Hitler announced that Italy and Germany had been "finally compelled" to join Japan in its war with the United States.[20]

Under the terms of its treaty with Japan, Germany didn't have to declare war on the United States. The alliance only required a declaration of war if America was the aggressor, not if a member of the Axis struck first. And the United States had only declared war on Japan. Roosevelt had not breathed a word about Germany in his December 8 speech to Congress.

Nonetheless, Hitler, who had thus far taken precautions to keep Germany out of war with the United States, which was already attacking German ships, welcomed the opportunity that the Pearl Harbor attack brought about. Joachim von Ribbentrop, Hitler's foreign minister, testified at the Nuremberg trials, "The Fuehrer was of the opinion at that moment that it was quite evident that the United States would now make war against Germany." In Hitler's words, the German people had been "oppressed by the certainty" that the Reich would eventually find itself at war with America, and, "Japanese intervention therefore was, from our point of view, most opportune."[21]

Like most of the rest of the isolationist camp, McCormick's alarmism over Roosevelt's war plans evaporated when the Japanese attacked Pearl Harbor. A cartoon on the front page of the next day's *Tribune* showed a man saluting an American flag. Next to him fluttered a banner that read, "Every American." While visiting the *Tribune*'s Washington bureau a few days later, McCormick claimed to have never even read the article that just a week earlier he'd called the greatest scoop in American history. But Roosevelt hadn't forgotten.[22]

As America went to war against Germany and Japan, the FBI launched its investigation into the Rainbow Five leak. No charges would be brought against the *Tribune* or McCormick, but trouble loomed for whoever had leaked the information, and the Roosevelt administration set out to find out how Manly had obtained the highly classified plan.

Manly's source was Senator Burton Wheeler, a Montana Democrat who had stood with Roosevelt through the New Deal but was bitterly opposed to his efforts to push the United States into war. Wheeler had received a number of visits from a "worried Army captain" in the Army Air Corps who told him in September 1941 that Roosevelt had ordered a master plan for an American Expeditionary Force that proved how deceitful the president had been when he told the American public that his goal was to keep the United States out of the war. Wheeler asked to see it. "I was eager to see how far the President was actually going in facing both ways at the same time," he said. On December 3, Wheeler got his wish when the captain came to his house with "a document as thick as an average novel," wrapped in plain brown paper, labeled "Victory Program."[23]

As Wheeler read the Victory Program, his blood pressure rose. In black and white, it clearly contradicted everything Roosevelt and his allies had been saying about the possibility of American entry into the European war. Wheeler quickly concluded that the information he'd received must be made public.

Initially, Wheeler considered taking the document to the Senate Foreign Relations Committee, but nixed the idea due to the committee's "record of subservience" to Roosevelt. Instead, he turned to Manly, whom he'd known for several months. "I liked Manly and knew his paper would give the plan the kind of attention it deserved," Wheeler said in his 1962 memoir, *Yankee from the West*. Manly came to Wheeler's house that night. They would only have the one night to copy all of the information they needed because the report had to be back at the War Department the next morning. Manly and Wheeler spent the night selecting key passages for one of the senator's secretaries to copy in shorthand.[24]

But that didn't answer the most important question of how Rainbow Five ended up in Wheeler's hands—not that investigators at the time were aware of the senator's involvement anyway. The captain who delivered the document to Wheeler had told him, "I'm only the messenger." Someone above him was calling the shots. At least 109 people in the War Department, and a similar number in the Navy Department, had access to the Victory Program.[25]

The investigation started with the army officer in charge of compiling Rainbow Five, Albert Wedemeyer. Wedemeyer, then a major serving in the department's War Plans Division, was horrified at the disclosure as "an obvious breakdown of rigid security measures."[26] But he had both access to the plan and a potential motive to leak it. The debate between isolationism and interventionism that split the public was as prevalent in the War Department as it was anywhere else in America, and Wedemeyer was on the wrong side. Though not a member of America First, Wedemeyer was "in accord with some of its objectives," and frequently attended the group's meetings in his civilian clothes.* Adding to the investigators' suspicions were Wedemeyer's German ancestry and the years he spent in the 1930s at the German War College, where the United States had sent him to study German military tactics. At the outset of the investigation, he was the chief suspect.[27]

Wedemeyer fell under immediate suspicion within the War Department. Groups of officers speaking in hushed tones scattered as he walked into the office. He learned why when his weeping secretary handed him a copy of that day's *Times-Herald*. Assistant Secretary of War John McCloy called Wedemeyer into his office to make a veiled accusation. "Wedemeyer, there's blood on the

* Wedemeyer was nonetheless strongly committed to the war effort. He played a major role in planning the cross-channel invasion of France on D-Day. He retired in 1951 as a three-star general.

fingers of the man who leaked the information about our war plans." Colleagues, some anonymously, pointed the finger at him during the investigation.[28]

Of the original five numbered copies of the Victory Program that had been typed up—another thirty-five would be distributed by the time it was splashed across the front page of the *Tribune* and the *Times-Herald*—most resided with people whose commitment to Roosevelt's interventionist agenda were beyond reproach. One sat in the safe in Wedemeyer's office. FBI agents found his copy with the portions that had been printed in Manly's story underlined. He told the investigators that he'd highlighted the information that the *Tribune* had published in order to get a better idea of how much of the plan had been revealed.[29]

The FBI repeatedly interviewed Wedemeyer. Agents questioned him about his work on the Victory Program report, the security procedures implemented to keep it secret, his ties to America First, and his time in Germany. FBI agents even traveled to Nebraska to interview Wedemeyer's mother as they delved into his German ancestry. His understandably frightened mother called him in Washington to ask what he'd done. She was concerned that he'd be shot as a traitor.[30]

Wedemeyer was far from the only suspect. FBI director J. Edgar Hoover personally interrogated Admiral Harold R. Stark, the chief of naval operations, and Rear Admiral Richmond Kelly Turner, Wedemeyer's counterpart in the Navy Department who had been responsible for preparing his branch's portion of the report. FBI agents and military intelligence officers both appealed to Manly's patriotism and threatened him with espionage charges. But the reporter refused to name his source. "I don't consider this has anything to do with patriotism," he told his interrogators. Investigators tailed *Tribune* reporter Walter Trohan, as well.[31]

On June 17, 1942, the FBI investigation ended inconclusively. The 1,200-page report to Biddle concluded that, because thirty-five copies of Rainbow Five had been distributed, which hundreds of military and civilian personnel at the War and Navy Departments had access to, "it has not been possible to determine the source" of the leak.

Wheeler's son says his father believed he knew the identity of the "messenger" who brought Rainbow Five: General Henry "Hap" Arnold, the head of the Army Air Corps.[32]

More than twenty years after the fact, former *Times-Herald* editor Frank Waldrop alleged that the FBI knew far more than it let on in its investigation. In a January 1963 article for the *Washington Post* and in a later interview with historian Thomas Fleming, Waldrop said he had lunch years after the investigation with FBI Assistant Director Louis Nichols, who'd interviewed Waldrop during the Rainbow Five probe. "Did you ever find out who gave us that war plan?" Waldrop asked him. "You know it. We had the whole thing inside ten days," Nichols replied.

According to Fleming, Nichols named Arnold as the culprit. He claimed the Army Air Corps chief had leaked the report to draw attention to deficiencies in American air power. Waldrop pressed Nichols as to why the FBI didn't go after the *Tribune* and the *Times-Herald*. People at both newspapers had actually hoped that the Justice Department would prosecute them because they believed it would expose informants and wiretaps placed by Roosevelt. "When we got to Arnold, we quit," Nichols told him.[33]

Fleming raised doubts as to whether Arnold was the true source of the leak. Had the FBI uncovered evidence that Arnold was responsible, word likely would have traveled quickly to General George C. Marshall, the army chief of staff. Marshall put a premium on loyalty, Fleming wrote, and it's unlikely that his close relationship with Arnold—or Wedemeyer, for that matter, had any substantive evidence pointed to him—would have continued after such a betrayal. Arnold and Marshall's biographers reached the same conclusion, the historian wrote in a 1987 article in *American Heritage*.[34]

Some speculated that Roosevelt may have authorized the leak himself to revive the flagging spirits of America's would-be allies or to goad Hitler into declaring war against the United States. Wheeler indicates that he believed the former. "There were those in Washington who speculated that FDR himself might have leaked the report—as a morale booster to the allies who were anxious for reassurance that 'the Yanks are coming' once again," Wheeler wrote. Wedemeyer told Fleming in 1986 that he believed Roosevelt authorized the disclosure. "I can't conceive of anyone else, including General Arnold, having the nerve to release that document," Wedemeyer said. Fleming wrote that Nichols's assertion that the FBI stopped digging when it got to Arnold could imply that it was shielding someone above him, which could implicate Roosevelt himself, as well as explain why the president showed so little enthusiasm for punishing the *Tribune*.[35]

Writer William Stevenson posited in his 1976 book *A Man Called Intrepid* that British intelligence orchestrated the leak to push the United States into war with Germany. The writer alleged that British spy William Stephenson, code-named "Intrepid," who was stationed in New York after Britain went to war with Hitler, "concocted the *Victory Program* out of material already known to have reached the enemy in dribs and drabs, and added some misleading information." Stevenson, who is of no relation to the spy Stephenson, also provided evidence that Intrepid had forged the maps Roosevelt waved before the public to show that the Nazis were planning to invade South America, which helped to bolster the writer's credibility when he first made the fantastic claim.[36]

The claim is highly questionable. By the time the mysterious army captain brought the Victory Program to Wheeler, Roosevelt was well aware that war with Japan was likely to break out any day. And Roosevelt's son, James, had told

Stephenson as much on November 26. But there is no question that Rainbow Five was authentic, which casts serious doubts on Stevenson's claims.[37]

Nonetheless, Fleming leans toward the possibility that Roosevelt orchestrated the leak as a way to prod Germany into the declaration of war that the president couldn't make himself. "No other explanation fills all the holes in the puzzle as completely as FDR's complicity," he wrote in his 1987 *American Heritage* article, a stance he reiterated in his 2001 book, *The New Dealers' War*. While Intrepid's claim was "preposterous," Fleming asks, "Would a President who had already used fake maps and concealed from Congress the truth about the naval war in the North Atlantic hesitate at one more deception—especially if he believed that war with Japan was imminent?" He notes that Roosevelt took great pride in his ability to outfox his enemies. "You know I am a juggler, and I never let my right hand know what my left hand does . . . and furthermore I am perfectly willing to mislead and tell untruths if it will help win the war," the president told Treasury Secretary Henry Morgenthau Jr. in 1942. Walter Trohan of the *Tribune* had described Arnold's skills as a leaker as "second only to Roosevelt."[38]

One argument against the thesis that Roosevelt masterminded the leak, aside from the obvious political ramifications, is that it provided Germany with a cornucopia of military intelligence. Wheeler said he would never have leaked the report if he believed it would have provided the Axis powers with valuable information. "It was not an operational war plan, but it bore out my charges against Roosevelt," he wrote in his memoir, echoing the excuses provided in December 1941 by Steve Early and Henry Stimson. The fact that the Office of War Information "blared Manly's story" across the Atlantic confirmed Wheeler's belief that the information wouldn't be useful to the Germans.[39]

That Germany didn't make good use of the Victory Program may have had more to do with Hitler than with the value of the information it contained. German military leadership at the time had precious little intelligence about American military planning. But thanks to the *Tribune*, the Nazis obtained a blueprint of Roosevelt's plans to make war on Germany. The German high command immediately began making preparations for America's entry into the war. In light of the information from Manly's article, Germany's top brass proposed to Hitler that he remove up to one hundred divisions from the eastern front and halt new advances against the Russians for the winter so that the troops could transferred to the Mediterranean theater, to drive out the British before the Americans could come to their aid. Hitler signed off on the plan, but reversed the decision shortly afterward in response to Soviet counterattacks in the east.

Manly's article could have had grave consequences for the American war effort in Europe and North Africa, as well as the postwar balance of power, had Hitler not changed his mind about diverting manpower and resources away from the eastern front. Military historians have argued that had Hitler succeeded in pushing the British out of the Mediterranean, preventing the landing of American troops in North Africa, it would have seriously impaired the United States' ability to invade continental Europe across the English Channel in 1944. And if he'd followed through on his decision to hold the line on the eastern front to protect his "Fortress Europe" rather than continue his advance deeper into Russia, he may never have suffered his defeat at Stalingrad, the great turning point of the war in Europe that marked the end of the Wehrmacht's eastern advance, ultimately leading the Red Army to the streets of Berlin.[40]

The *Tribune* would eventually be threatened with criminal charges for its reporting on the war, though not for the transgression of December 4, 1941. Roosevelt decided to take action against the newspaper the following year after reporter Stanley Johnston's account of the Battle of Midway indicated that the United States had cracked the Japanese navy's secret codes, a revelation that the US Navy had very much wanted to keep classified. At the request of Navy Secretary Knox, Attorney General Biddle reluctantly empaneled a grand jury in August 1942 to investigate the matter as a potential violation of the Espionage Act. As part of the investigation, the FBI provided more than one thousand pages on its investigation into the Victory Program leak. "We have said and proved that we cannot be intimidated and now, once again, we are going to prove it," the *Tribune* said in response to the threat of a grand jury. However, the case fell apart, not as a result of any defense mounted by the *Tribune*, but because the navy, wary of revealing classified information, unexpectedly refused to provide key evidence against Johnston and his paper. The case had been weak from the start, and, as *Newsweek* observed, "Knox pushed Biddle out on a limb, followed him there, then sawed them both off. Biddle later admitted, 'I felt like a fool.'"[41]

Roosevelt would, at times, continue to harass McCormick during the war.* Treasury Department agents swarmed the Tribune Tower after the newspaper published copies of government checks as part of a story about a payroll scandal at the University of Illinois. For six months after Pearl Harbor, Roosevelt, convinced that McCormick's papers, as well as those of newspaper mogul William Randolph Hearst, were printing pro-German and pro-fascist sentiment, ordered the Justice Department to analyze the content of their editorials and news articles. The Justice Department found criticism of Roosevelt, but no propaganda. Ickes suggested in late 1942 that Roosevelt lean on the Canadian government—which, as a part of the British Commonwealth's war effort, was hostile to the *Tribune*'s antiwar stance—to shut off their supply of newsprint paper. And the

* Roosevelt used a more heavy-handed approach with other papers, whose alleged sins were more egregious than McCormick's. For example, in a move reminiscent of the government's suppression of seditious newspapers during World War I, he used the 1917 Espionage Act to halt distribution of Father Charles Coughlin's *Social Justice* after it wrote that Jews and communists had tricked the United States into war (Winfield, 179).

Justice Department threatened antitrust action over McCormick's blocking of rivals from the Associated Press board, which led to revisions of AP rules that the Colonel had fought strenuously against. One critic during the long-running AP fight, which predated the Victory Program disclosure, expressed his astonishment before a meeting of editors that "a powerful publisher can publish without criticism from his colleagues a secret document of vital importance to the security of his country." Roosevelt had little use for anyone in the extended *Tribune* family. The president ordered surveillance on Joseph Patterson, McCormick's cousin and publisher of the Tribune Company's *New York Daily News*. Patterson's sister, *Times-Herald* publisher Cissy Patterson, had a "subversive mind," according to Roosevelt.[42]

The case of the *Tribune* and its revelations about the Victory Program brings to mind another famous incident in which the press revealed classified war information that had been leaked by opponents of war: the Pentagon Papers case.

The report that came to be known as the Pentagon Papers was commissioned not to prepare for America's entry into a war, but to analyze how it had gotten into one that the country had fought for years. Though far more well-known, the Pentagon Papers had far less potential to damage America's national security. By the time the *New York Times* and *Washington Post* published the report, most of the Vietnam War's damage had already been done. In the case of the *Tribune*, the classified information that was revealed to the public could have had catastrophic consequences for the war effort against Germany, not to mention the political consequences Roosevelt could have faced had Japan not forced America's hand and rendered the debate between isolationists and interventionists moot.

Secretary of Defense Robert McNamara had been the architect of much of President Lyndon Johnson's Vietnam War strategy. But by 1967, he was wracked with doubt about America's ability to attain a military victory. In June of that year, without informing the president, he ordered the Department of Defense to begin compiling a history of American involvement in Vietnam, from the first tentative steps the United States took in 1945 to the bloody stalemate of 1967. McNamara has said he ordered it to document for posterity the decision-making process that led America into the quagmire that the war had become.[43]

Work continued on the project for nearly two years. The 7,000-page study, known officially as *United States–Vietnam Relations 1945–1967*, was completed in early 1969, a year after McNamara's resignation from the Johnson administration, and just as Richard Nixon took up residence in the White House. One of its contributors was a former Defense Department employee named Daniel Ellsberg.[44]

Ellsberg joined the Defense Department in 1964 and traveled to South Vietnam to witness the war firsthand. He spent two years there, returning in 1967. After coming back to the United States, Ellsberg, growing increasingly disillusioned with the war, left the Defense Department and returned to the RAND Corporation, where he was working when he was asked to assist with McNamara's study. Ellsberg spent four months researching and documenting John F. Kennedy's early Vietnam policy, culminating in a 350-page draft report.[45]

By the time Ellsberg left the Defense Department, he had come to see the war in Vietnam as "a moral and political disaster, a crime." After attending an April 1968 conference at Princeton titled "America in a Revolutionary World," he became heavily involved in the antiwar movement, though he was still doing Defense Department work at RAND. Around the time Nixon took office, Ellsberg decided he wanted to read the study. The theme that emerged in the study was that Nixon's four predecessors had all faced the same alternatives when confronting tough decisions, and none had had "the courage to turn down or stay out of" a war in Vietnam. Ellsberg concluded that Nixon was no more likely than Johnson to extract the United States from Vietnam, and, despite the possibility that he could be convicted of espionage for doing so, began considering the possibility of leaking the report in the hope that the revelations it contained would help to finally bring the war to an end. "Once I began to really think about it, I started to see that it might actually be useful to make this history public—if it could be done fast, before the president made it Nixon's war," he wrote. In September 1969, after the army decided not to prosecute six Special Forces members accused of assassinating a South Vietnamese double agent, he made his decision. From 1969 to 1970, he secretly photocopied all forty-seven volumes of the study.[46]

"When I saw the conflict as a problem, I tried to help solve it; when I saw it as a stalemate, to help us extricate ourselves, without harm to other national interests; when I saw it as a crime, to expose and resist it, and to try to end it immediately," he wrote in his memoir, *Secrets*. But who would be the recipient?[47]

Ellsberg started with Senator William J. Fulbright, chairman of the Senate Foreign Relations Committee and a leading congressional opponent of the war. He gave the senator some of the documents from the study, along with a summary of the report, which Fulbright said he would make public at an upcoming committee hearing. But Fulbright backed down, telling Ellsberg that he was giving Nixon, who said he was trying to bring the war to an end, the benefit of the doubt. Other members of Congress, including Senator George McGovern, who would be Nixon's opponent in the 1972 election, refused to publicize the stolen study as well.[48]

The solution to Ellsberg's quandary lay with the *New York Times*. Ellsberg gave reporter Neil Sheehan, whom he'd first met during his two-year stint in South Vietnam, access to the study and the classified documents it contained. The newspaper's editors and its publisher, Arthur Ochs Sulzberger, had their share of misgivings over whether it was right to publish the classified documents or whether they could be found criminally liable. But after several months of internal deliberations, in which they concluded that they wouldn't be subject to espionage laws or endanger national security, they decided to move forward. The first installment of the *Times*'s Pentagon Papers series rolled off the presses on June 13, 1971.[49]

On June 30 in Los Angeles, a federal grand jury indicted Ellsberg for espionage and theft of government property. He faced the possibility of up to 115 years in prison for his efforts to end a war that he believed was a blight upon America. "But I was not wrong," he wrote, "either, to hope that exposing secrets five presidents had withheld and the lies they told might have benefits for our democracy that were worthy of the risks." After he was indicted, Ellsberg told a crowd of reporters outside the courthouse in Los Angeles, "I think I've done a good job as a citizen."[50]

Nixon took a far different view. While Ellsberg, like the *Tribune*, believed he was doing what was best for his country, Nixon's opinion was more reminiscent of Biddle and Ickes. "Whatever others may have thought, I considered what Ellsberg had done to be despicable and contemptible—he had revealed government foreign policy secrets during wartime," he wrote in his memoir.[51]

There were compelling arguments for Nixon to stand aside while the newspapers published the Pentagon Papers, and he initially decided to do just that. The information contained in the Pentagon Papers related exclusively to actions taken under his predecessors, and actually could have been a boon to Nixon as he came under withering criticism from members of the Kennedy and Johnson administrations.

But for Nixon there were far greater considerations than embarrassing his predecessors and critics. The disclosure of the Pentagon Papers threatened to undermine the entire war effort and reveal confidential intelligence assets. More importantly for Nixon, it would hinder the government's ability to withhold classified information whose secrecy was necessary for national security. One could almost hear Biddle and Ickes saying the exact words about the *Chicago Tribune* in December 1941 that Nixon wrote about his 1971 decision to try to block the publication of the Pentagon Papers. "An important principle was at stake in this case," Nixon wrote in his memoir. "It is the role of government, not the *New York Times*, to judge the impact of a top secret document."[52]

After the *Times* refused Attorney General John Mitchell's request to voluntarily cease publication of the Pentagon Papers, Nixon took a step unprecedented in American history. He asked a federal judge to enjoin the newspaper from publishing any more of the classified study. Judge Murray Gurfein issued a temporary restraining order against the *Times* that prohibited the newspaper from continuing publication of the study. Several days later, the *Washington Post* began publishing its own Pentagon Papers series. When editor Ben Bradlee rejected a direct request from Supreme Court Justice William Rehnquist to halt publication, the Justice Department sought an injunction against the *Post* as well.[53]

The Nixon administration's luck would not hold up after Gurfein heard arguments in the case. Despite his criticism of the *Times* and the *Post*, in which he'd said the newspapers, "as a matter of simple patriotism," should be willing to sit down with the Justice Department to ensure that publication of classified information wouldn't jeopardize national security, the judge denied Mitchell and Nixon the prior restraint they'd sought against the *Times*. Gurfein ruled that the publication of the documents would not constitute a vital national security breach. "The security of the Nation is not at the ramparts alone," Gurfein wrote in his ruling. "Security also lies in the value of our free institutions. A cantankerous press, an obstinate press, a ubiquitous press must be suffered by those in authority in order to preserve the even greater values of freedom of expression and the right of the people to know." However, the judge kept the temporary restraining order in place while the Justice Department appealed his ruling to the Supreme Court.[54]

At the Supreme Court, the *Times* prevailed in a 6–3 ruling. Justice Hugo Black, writing for the majority, expressed his disappointment that any of his fellow judges would be willing to enforce prior restraint against a newspaper's right to print the news under any circumstances, which would "make a shambles of the First Amendment." By seeking an injunction in the case, Black opined that the Nixon administration "seems to have forgotten the essential purpose and history of the First Amendment." The Founding Fathers, Black wrote, included freedom of the press in the Constitution for a reason. "The press was protected so that it could bare the secrets of government and inform the people. Only a free and unrestrained press can effectively expose deception in government. And paramount among the responsibilities of a free press is the duty to prevent any part of the government from deceiving the people and sending them off to distant lands to die of foreign fevers and foreign shot and shell," he wrote. In Black's opinion, the *Times*, the *Post*, and the numerous other papers that had published portions of the Pentagon Papers since the case began—the list includes the *Boston Globe, St. Louis Post-Dispatch*, and others—were deserving not of condemnation, but of praise. "In revealing the workings of government that led to the Vietnam War, the newspapers nobly did precisely that which the Founders hoped and trusted they would do."[55]

Nixon's attempts to prevent the publication of the Pentagon Papers had failed. And the Justice Department's prosecution of Ellsberg would fall apart as well. Nixon's desire to discredit Ellsberg would lead to the president's infamous "plumbers" burglarizing Ellsberg's psychiatrist's office to find dirt on him. Defense attorneys sought dismissal of the charges based on a number of questionable actions taken by the Nixon administration, including the recently discovered break-in and Nixon counsel John Ehrlichman's offer of the FBI directorship to Judge William M. Byrne. The judge ultimately declared a mistrial, letting Ellsberg and coconspirator Anthony Russo off the hook, after a prosecutor disclosed that the government had overheard Ellsberg on wiretaps as far back as 1969, and that the records of the potentially illegal wiretaps had disappeared.[56]

The outcome of the case rankled Nixon, who would go on to see some of his own aides suffer the fate that he'd wanted for Ellsberg. "Today the break-in at Ellsberg's psychiatrist's office seems wrong and excessive. But I do not accept that it was as wrong or excessive as what Daniel Ellsberg did, and I still believe it is a tragedy of circumstances that Bud Krogh and John Ehrlichman went to jail"—both were convicted for their roles in the Watergate scandal—"and Daniel Ellsberg went free."[57]

For Francis Biddle, Harold Ickes, Richard Nixon, and others, leaking classified information to the press was an unforgivable betrayal of the country. But for Burton Wheeler and Daniel Ellsberg, patriotism meant doing what they thought was best for their country. And that meant revealing some unpleasant truths. As Ellsberg said in celebration of Edward Snowden, the most famous American whistle-blower of the modern day, "Leaks are the lifeblood of the republic."[58]

Chapter 10

The Road to McCarthyism

If we twelve are convicted, the Communist Party will be officially outlawed in the United States.

—Eugene Dennis

In his historic televised denunciation of Joseph McCarthy in 1954, famed journalist Edward R. Murrow opined that the fault for the creation of the phenomenon known as McCarthyism did not in fact lay with the Red-baiting US senator. "He didn't create this situation of fear; he merely exploited it—and rather successfully. Cassius was right. The fault, dear Brutus, is not in our stars, but in ourselves."[1] While McCarthy bears a unique responsibility for fanning the flames of anticommunist hysteria in the early years of the Cold War, Murrow was no doubt correct in his assessment. And the blockbuster trial of eleven Communist Party members just a few years earlier goes a long way toward proving Murrow's point.

The seeds of McCarthyism had been well planted by the time Tail Gunner Joe stood in front of the Republican Women's Club of Wheeling, West Virginia, in February 1950 and waved an alleged list of 205 Communist Party members working in the State Department, ushering in a new era of fear, persecution, and suppression of free-speech rights in America. Less than one year before McCarthy's infamous speech, eleven members of the Communist Party of the United States of America had been sentenced to prison for essentially nothing more than belonging to their hated party.

The Smith Act trial, named so for the anti-sedition law under which the charges were brought, deserves a place of prominence in Americans' collective memory of the Red Scare of the early Cold War years that has been denied it. The Hollywood Ten, blacklists, loyalty oaths, the hearings of the House Un-American Activities Committee, and McCarthy's infamous witch hunts are the incidents that most readily come to mind when one contemplates the suppression of civil liberties that embodied those dark years. But one could argue that the conviction of the Smith Act Eleven eclipsed them all in significance.

Communist Party USA general secretary Eugene Dennis, left, being served with a subpoena during a 1947 hearing of the House Un-American Activities Committee.
LIBRARY OF CONGRESS

Technically, the eleven communists were convicted of conspiracy to violently overthrow the American government. That weighty charge was demonstrated by virtue of their membership in and leadership of a party that prosecutors said adhered to such beliefs. In other words, belonging to the Communist Party of the United States (CPUSA) was evidence enough that one sought to overturn the government of the United States by force. In reality, those eleven people were sent to federal prison for no other crime than belonging to the wildly unpopular Communist Party of the United States.

However, the reverberations of that trial were felt far beyond the upper echelon of the CPUSA. When the US Supreme Court in 1951 upheld the conviction of the eleven defendants and decreed the Smith Act to be constitutional, it sounded a starter's pistol that inaugurated a wave of repression against Communists. Newspapers confidently declared that the ruling would bring about the conviction of "thousands of rank-and-file communists."[2] That number proved too optimistic for those hoping to eradicate the scourge of communism in America. But the floodgates were opened nonetheless.

One of the government's chief weapons against American communists was a 1940 law known as the Smith Act, named for Congressman Howard Smith, a Virginia Democrat. The act, a culmination of five years' worth of failed attempts to pass anticommunist legislation, made it a federal crime "to knowingly or willfully advocate, abet, advise, or teach the duty, necessity, desirability, or propriety of overthrowing or destroying any government in the United States by force or violence," and to "print, publish, edit, issue, circulate, sell, distribute, or publicly display any written or printed matter advocating" such a violent overthrow. Furthermore, the Smith Act made it unlawful for anyone to "conspire to commit" those crimes.[3] The conspiracy provision would ultimately become the net with which federal authorities caught scores of American communists.

During the United States' uneasy alliance with the Soviet Union during World War II, when both set aside their acrimony toward the other to defeat a greater enemy, the Smith Act posed little to no threat to communists in America. The first prosecution brought under the act, which occurred in 1941, was indeed against communists, specifically Teamsters in Minneapolis who were members of the Socialist Workers Party. The case, in which eighteen of twenty-nine defendants were convicted, helped to settle a dispute between the Communist Party and what it viewed as a heretical Trotskyite faction, and was cheered by the *Daily Worker*, the party's primary news organ.[4]

But the more appealing wartime targets were American Nazis and their sympathizers, who were the subject of the most significant Smith Act prosecution brought during World War II. Thirty-one American Nazis went to trial on Smith Act charges in June 1942. And in April 1944, several high-profile Nazis went to court in one of the strangest trials in American history. The defendants and their attorneys engaged in unruly conduct, bickered constantly with each other in court, openly disrespected the judge, and engaged in myriad disruptive tactics. The defense team tried to disqualify Judge Edward C. Escher for bias, and one defense attorney tried to have him impeached during the trial. The defendants' strategy was to cause enough havoc to force a mistrial, and their efforts were successful beyond their wildest dreams. On November 30, Escher, under constant stress from the circus that had played out in his courtroom, died, and a mistrial was declared. With the war winding down in Europe, the Department of Justice had little appetite for a retrial, and the Nazi defendants got their charges dismissed.[5] The lesson of poor Escher was not lost on Judge Harold Medina when eleven communist defendants, also intent on being as disruptive as possible to the judicial process, walked into his courtroom five years later.

During the war, American communists found common cause with mainstream America in their fight to the death against fascism. Earl Browder, the longtime head of the American Communist Party, which he had rechristened as the Communist Political Association, had become the face of American communism during the wartime détente between the party and the federal government. The hostility of American communists toward Franklin Roosevelt that was engendered by the Molotov-Ribbentrop pact of 1939, which declared nonaggression between Nazi Germany and Soviet Russia, melted away following the German invasion of the USSR and America's subsequent entry into the war against Hitler at the end of 1941. Browder now sought accommodation with American government and society. And the "popular front" between the communist and capitalist worlds brought an air of legitimacy to Browder and the American Communist Party. Browder met with State Department officials and his face beamed from the cover of *Time*, which declared him the emissary of American communism. He even declared that he would be willing to shake hands with J. P. Morgan, the epitome of the capitalist class the communists yearned to destroy, in the interest of unity. Browder confidently asserted that the Russo-American alliance would continue once the war was over.[6]

Needless to say, Browder's optimism was misplaced. The defeat of Nazi Germany quickly altered the relationship between the wartime allies. Tensions spiked as Soviet leader Joseph Stalin flexed his muscles in Eastern Europe, Berlin, Iran, and elsewhere. And as Stalin forged a new path in Europe, American communists did the same at home.

In the Soviets' view, there was no room for Browder's accommodation in the postwar United States, and many American communists agreed. "Having rejected the Browder dream of class peace and revisionism, and confronted now with the first indications of what was rapidly to become the Truman nightmare, our Party emerged with sharp, more realistic perspectives," wrote Peggy Dennis, the wife of Eugene Dennis, who would supplant Browder as the leader of communism in America. The mounting pressure for American communists to change direction peaked with a 1945 article by Jacques Duclos in a French communist journal that castigated Browder for his "notorious revision of Marxism" and blasphemy against the international party line.[7] * The signal was clear: Moscow wanted Browder out. His place at the top of the party hierarchy was taken by Eugene Dennis and William Z. Foster, who would be the more confrontational communist leaders that the Soviet Union desired. Dennis and Foster dissolved Browder's Communist Political Association and reorganized it as the Communist Party of the United States (CPUSA).

Conflict with communists abroad fueled persecution at home. America's attitude toward communism had never been anything but hostile, despite the easing of tensions during the war. After all, the communist philosophy contrasted so vividly with what are often considered the deepest ideological foundations of American society. But in the immediate postwar years, communism came to be viewed as an existential threat to the United States and the American way of life. The authorities responded accordingly, and in some of the harshest terms possible.

President Harry Truman found himself under increasing pressure to eradicate the communist menace at home and was eager to fend off Republican attacks that he and the Democrats were soft on communism. Though Truman rejected some of the greater excesses of the anticommunist hysteria that had gripped the nation—he vetoed the Internal Security Act of 1950, though Congress was able to override the veto—something had to be done. For many Americans, loyalty

---

* The Duclos letter would go on to serve as a key piece of evidence for the Justice Department, FBI, HUAC, and others who sought to portray the CPUSA as a tool of the Soviet Union that took its direction from Moscow. During the first fifteen years of HUAC hearings, Duclos's name came up more than Browder's, despite the latter's many years of leadership of the Communist Party (Schrecker, Ellen. 1998. *Many Are the Crimes: McCarthyism in America*. Boston: Little, Brown, 132).

oaths and even some of the more-severe measures taken by the Truman administration just wouldn't cut it. In 1948, Attorney General Tom Clark asked the FBI to help him build a case against the CPUSA. Fortunately for him, the FBI's fiercely anticommunist director, J. Edgar Hoover, had been doing so for years. Hoover initiated an investigation in 1945, shortly before the war ended, into the "the illegal status and activities" of American communists. By the time he turned over the fruits of that investigation to the Department of Justice in 1948, the file totaled 1,850 pages.[8]

Intent on prosecuting the communist leaders but struggling with the question of what law they could use as the basis of their case, the Justice Department considered using a number of other anticommunist laws, but none provided the framework they needed. The lack of evidence that the defendants were under the direct control of the Soviet Union or that they engaged in military activities ruled out the Voorhis Act or the Foreign Agents Registration Act. Despite a lack of evidence that the defendants had actually plotted to overthrow the government, the Justice Department, at the FBI's urging, settled on the Smith Act as its weapon of choice. Though they couldn't demonstrate that the defendants were actively plotting against the government, the prosecutors didn't actually need to. Thanks to the Smith Act's conspiracy provision, they needed only to convince a jury that the defendants conspired to do so at some undetermined point in the future.[9] On July 20, 1948, a federal grand jury in New York issued its indictments against the twelve top leaders of the CPUSA.*

The defendants represented the upper echelon of the CPUSA. Eugene Dennis had served as the party's general secretary since Browder's ouster in 1945. Benjamin Davis, the lone communist on the New York City Council, ran the party's legislative committee. John Gates served as editor of the *Daily Worker*. Gilbert Green, Gus Hall, John Thompson, and John Winter chaired the communist parties of Illinois, Ohio, New York, and Michigan, respectively. Jacob Stachel was the CPUSA's national education secretary, John Williamson served as the party's trade union secretary, and Henry Winston as its national organizational secretary. Irving Potash ran the CIO-Furriers Joint Council, a fur industry trade union, in New York. All eleven defendants were members of the party's National Committee. Foster, Dennis, Thompson, Williamson, and Winston served as part of the CPUSA's secretariat, which directed the party's activities nationwide.[10]

Though it was the defendants who would be in the dock, it was their party that was really on trial. Prosecutors devoted the overwhelming majority of their time to proving that the CPUSA advocated the overthrow of the government.[11] Once that was established, the defendants' guilt could not be in doubt. The FBI's goal

* William Foster, the CPUSA's chairman, was severed from the case before the trial began due to serious health problems (Schrecker, 313).

was made clear in an internal memo in 1948: "Prosecution of Party officials and responsible functionaries," under the Smith Act, "would, in turn, result in a judicial precedent being set that the Communist Party as an organization is illegal."[12]

That objective was apparent to the defendants and their supporters. The CPUSA immediately denounced the indictments as a "monstrous frame-up" and alleged that Truman had initiated them to undermine third-party presidential hopeful Henry Wallace, whose Progressive Party candidacy actively courted American leftists and was viewed as popular with communists.[13] Dennis told a cheering crowd at Madison Square Garden that the indictments were an attempt to make the CPUSA illegal and were a sign of creeping fascism in the United States. "If we twelve are convicted, the Communist Party will be officially outlawed in the United States," he said. Dennis denied that the CPUSA had any desire or intention to overthrow the government, declaring that socialism could not be imposed by a minority upon an unwilling country, and that the American people would "inevitably find their own way to socialism." In the eight years since the passage of the "unconstitutional" Smith Act, the Justice Department had not once attempted to use it to charge the CPUSA with seeking to topple the government, Dennis said. And in the twenty-nine years since the party's founding, not one communist had been convicted for advocating such a revolutionary course of action. In the "lynch atmosphere" of the Cold War, Dennis said he and his fellow defendants would face trial only for what the government deemed their "dangerous thoughts."[14]

Throughout the trial, the defendants not only had to contend with the prosecutors, but also with Judge Harold Medina, who was overtly hostile to them and provided a great deal of assistance to the Justice Department's prosecutorial team. Though he at times indulged the defendants and their supporters, at least early in the case, Medina was a far cry from an unbiased jurist. He was openly hostile to the defense and showed blatant favoritism to the prosecution. As a result, the defendants faced a judicial pincer movement, with the Justice Department attacking them from one side and Medina, offering whatever assistance he could to the prosecution, from the other.

In her book, *Many Are the Crimes: McCarthyism in America*, author Ellen Schrecker writes of a chance encounter she had with Medina years after the trial that illustrates perfectly the depths of the judge's paranoia about the communists in his courtroom. During a dinner party in the 1960s, years before she began writing about the witch hunts of the McCarthy era, Schrecker met Medina at a dinner party. During a lengthy recitation of the famous trial, Medina explained that whenever he looked at the spectators in the courtroom, he made a point of keeping his eyes moving and not focusing on any particular person, "so that he wouldn't let himself be placed in a trance by the hypnotists that the party might have placed in the courtroom."[15]

Of course, in many respects, Medina could be forgiven for his hostility to the communist defendants and their attorneys, who pushed him to the brink with their disruptive and obstructionist tactics. The roots of those tactics lay in a bizarre legal strategy that was commonplace to communists of that period. Today, as in 1949, it would seem obvious that Dennis and his cohorts should have wrapped themselves in the First Amendment and defended their actions under their rights to free speech. But this was not the communist way. Through the years of Red Scares and witch hunts, communists had defended themselves in courtrooms across America using what was known in the party's parlance as "labor defense."

To call labor defense a legal strategy would be generous. Rather, it relied on propaganda, appeals to the masses, and direct action both inside and outside the courtroom. Partly inspired by the belief that communists and like-minded radicals could not receive a fair trial in the courts of America's capitalist class, labor defense was essentially an indictment of the system as a whole in which the defendants waged their own self-styled prosecution in a sort of propagandistic show trial inside the courtroom, while mobilizing a protesting proletariat beyond its walls.[16]

Labor defense had the potential to be a double-edged sword. Though free speech would seem a natural defense against the charges the eleven defendants faced, labor defense did have a utilitarian function in the courtroom. By trying to explain in explicit detail the tenets of their philosophy, the defendants could demonstrate that they did not in fact support the violent overthrow of the American government. Or at least they could have, had Medina been willing to entertain such lines of argument. Unfortunately for the defendants, he had no patience for anything he considered "propaganda," which included the pillars of their defense. Had the defendants relied primarily on a free-speech defense, they may have fared better, though that conclusion is highly questionable given the revulsion with which the average American viewed communists and Medina's obvious bias toward the prosecution. John Gates later acknowledged that the defense's strategy had been a mistake.[17]

The trial opened on January 17, 1949, with hundreds of protesters chanting outside in Foley Square, though, thanks to the defense team, the actual arguments would not commence until two months later. Part of the defendants' labor defense strategy was months' worth of legal tactics meant to prolong the trial. They lodged constant objections and filed motion after motion, for mistrials, for Medina's dismissal on grounds of bias, and for the postponement of proceedings, re-filing their motions again and again when they were rejected by the judge. Medina insisted that it "must be almost a world's record of motions." They objected to their indictment by a grand jury that they described as being composed of white, wealthy, capitalist men, and raised myriad objections during jury selection for the trial itself, which dragged on for about a week.[18] *

In the meantime, as part of its labor defense effort, the CPUSA and its allies pursued a letter-writing and publicity campaign aimed at pressuring Truman to dismiss the prosecution.[19] Truman, feeling the heat from allegations that he was coddling communists as he faced a highly uncertain election, was not receptive to protesters' pleas. In an October 28 campaign speech in Boston, Truman avowed his hatred of the "godless creed" of communism and swore to continue the fight against it. "I have fought it at home. I have fought it abroad. I shall continue to fight it with all my strength. I shall never surrender," the president told the crowd at Boston's Mechanics Hall.[20]

In the spirit of labor defense, supporters of the defendants gathered outside the courtroom throughout the trial, oftentimes doing their best to antagonize Medina. Among the throngs of demonstrators who crowded into Foley Square were sign-waving provocateurs whose placards bore unnerving messages aimed at the judge. One declared, "Adolf Hitler never died, he's sitting at Medina's side," while another insisted, "Medina will fall just like Forrestal," a grim reference to US Navy Secretary James Forrestal, who had recently committed suicide by jumping from a window at a navy hospital where he was being treated for depression. The situation became so problematic that the *New York Times* editorialized that Congress should pass a law prohibiting picketing at federal courthouses. In addition to being deluged with hate mail, Medina, who was afraid of heights, would receive harassing phone calls in the middle of night from ill-wishers who would say, "Jump," before hanging up.[21]

Finally, on March 21, Assistant US Attorney John F. X. McGohey made his opening statement to the jury. He would, McGohey said, prove that the defendants, in their reorganization of the CPUSA, sought to establish Marxism-Leninism in America, "by the violent overthrow and destruction of our constitutional form of government through the smashing of the State government and the setting up of the dictatorship of the proletariat by violent and forceful seizure of power under the leadership of the Communist Party." CPUSA members in positions of influence awaited their orders to strike, he said, at which point they planned to wipe out "every vestige of the bourgeois state." And the training they received prepared them for that moment, he said. "They teach that this revolution cannot be without violence," McGohey said, "for to be successful the entire apparatus of the Government must be smashed."[22]

---

* If the defendants were outraged that the grand jury consisted of wealthy white males, they must have at least been pleased by the demographic makeup of the trial jury. The jury consisted of seven women, three of whom were black, including foreman Thelma Dial. Historian Michal Belknap writes that even the communist press could find little to complain about regarding the jury (Belknap, 78).

The five-person defense team added Dennis, who wasn't an attorney, but still directed the labor defense strategy the defendants employed, which was more dependent on ideological zeal than legal training anyway. Dennis already had a record of causing havoc at official proceedings. In 1947, while testifying before HUAC—Dennis did so voluntarily to denounce proposed anticommunist legislation—committee chairman J. Parnell Thomas questioned him on whether he'd ever gone by a different name, which Dennis said was irrelevant, though he had indeed changed his birth name of Frank Waldron. Thomas insisted that Dennis be excused for the day and barred him from entering a twenty-one-page statement he'd brought as testimony, but ordered that a subpoena be issued to him. At that point, Dennis erupted, stating, "Mr. Thomas, on behalf of the American people I hold this committee in contempt." Across the country, Americans were treated to newsreel footage of police dragging Dennis out of the committee hearing room while throwing Thomas's subpoena to the floor. When he didn't appear for a follow-up hearing, in defiance of the subpoena, Congress voted almost unanimously to charge Dennis with contempt.[23]

The Justice Department couldn't have found a defendant who more perfectly personified so many of the negative perceptions and stereotypes that Americans held about communists. Dennis had twice lived in the Soviet Union,* including once after he fled the country to escape a sedition conviction in California, and served the communist cause faithfully. He traveled the world at the party's orders to spread its doctrines in China, the Philippines, and South Africa, and was a graduate of the Communist Party's prestigious Lenin Institute.[24] For prosecutors eager to portray the CPUSA as a tool of the Soviets whose activities were directed from Moscow, Dennis's background made him an ideal test case. He'd even changed his name, a tendency of communists that Red hunters often used as evidence of their perfidy.

The Justice Department's strategy relied heavily on a roster of informants from within the CPUSA infrastructure, some of whom had infiltrated the organization at the FBI's behest, and others who had turned against the party and begun informing on their former comrades. The star among those double agents was Louis Budenz, a former mid-level party functionary and one-time writer and later managing editor for the *Daily Worker* who had since become disenchanted with communism. After breaking with the party, Budenz became an all-purpose witness for government entities seeking testimony against communists, whether it be at HUAC, a courtroom, or elsewhere. During the congressional hearings that set the stage for the Taft-Hartley Act, an anti-union law that contained a

---

*When Eugene and Peggy Dennis left the Soviet Union to return to America in 1935, the communist authorities insisted that they leave their five-year-old son behind. The child spoke only Russian, and party leaders, who were sensitive to the (often-true) perception in the United States that American communists took their instructions from Moscow, said he would be a "liability" (P. Dennis, 86).

provision aimed at shutting communists out of organized labor, Budenz testified that it was the Communist Party that had ordered strikes in 1941 and 1946 at a critical defense plant.[25] Peggy Dennis described Budenz as a contemptible figure, a "professional witness testifying, for a good price, at hearings and trials of Communists around the country."[26] *

On the stand, Budenz described what he claimed to be the philosophical underpinnings of the CPUSA, as evidenced by the party constitution's adherence to the principles of "scientific socialism" and Marxism-Leninism. The scientific socialism of Marx and Engels had been interpreted by Lenin and Stalin, Budenz testified, to mean that socialism can only be attained by the "violent shattering of the capitalist state." "In the United States, this would mean that the Communist Party of the United States is basically committed to the overthrow of the Government of the United States as set up by the Constitution of the United States," Budenz said.[27]

The prosecution bolstered its case and Budenz's assertions by introducing reams of communist literature as evidence. *The Communist Manifesto*, Lenin's *State and Revolution*, Stalin's *Fundamentals of Leninism*, and other classic works found their way into the record.[28] Dennis tried to rebut the prosecution's literature-based arguments by explaining the fluid nature of Marxist-Leninist theory and the nature of the philosophy to which American communists adhered. "You cannot find out what to do in 1949 by reading what Lenin said the Russian workers should do under quite different circumstances in 1917," he said.[29]

When defense attorneys cross-examined Budenz, Medina cut off lines of questioning that threatened to contradict his prior answers to the prosecution's questions, such as when they tried to force him to admit on the stand that he'd never advocated the achievement of scientific socialism with violent means in his own writings for the *Daily Worker*.[30] Medina's interjections against defense attorneys' questions that posed a threat to the prosecution would become a constant feature of the trial.

Unfortunately for the defendants, even in instances where their words and the party's literature didn't align with the Justice Department's allegation that they had plotted to overthrow the government by force, the prosecutors found a way to convince the jury that even evidence of innocence, such as writings and speeches in which the defendants themselves eschewed violent revolution and voiced support for a peaceful transition to socialism in the United States, was

* While Budenz was a well-known turncoat to the defendants, the defendants were stunned by revelations that so many of their own were FBI spies, often learning of their disloyalty for the first time when they took the witness stand. One witness, Angela Calomiris, had gone to such great lengths to continue playing the role of a good communist that she protested against the indictments in Foley Square, and contributed fifty dollars to the defense fund established by the CPUSA shortly before taking the witness stand (Belknap, 89).

intentional misdirection, and therefore proof of their guilt. They were able to do so by way of an archaic term from Lenin's days as an underground revolutionary in Russia known as "Aesopian language." Lenin described the practice as veiled language that allowed revolutionaries to make political observations with "extreme caution" through hints and allegorical language, "to which Czarism compelled all revolutionaries to have recourse whenever they took up their pens to write a 'legal' work."[31]

Many American communists were as unfamiliar with the term as anyone else in the country. When the FBI instructed its field offices to investigate the concept in 1947, its communist informants said they'd never heard of it. One informant was able to get an explanation for the out-of-use term from a longtime communist, but when the informant asked if it was still in use, he was told, "Of course not. We are a legal organization, and it isn't necessary for us to hide what we want to tell the people."[32] Regardless, Budenz described Aesopian language as a core component of communist activities in the United States, which meant that any statements to the contrary were mere "window dressing" to hide the CPUSA's true intentions.[33]

Medina's invocation against propaganda in his courtroom left little room for the defendants to explain why their dedication to Marxism-Leninism did not include advocacy of violent revolt. After Garfield Heron, an FBI informant, recited passages from communist literature that he said demonstrated the CPUSA's true intentions, the defense insisted that the stand-alone sections were being taken out of context, and asked that the entire works be entered as evidence. Medina would have none of it, telling defense attorney Harry Sacher, "I have never heard such propaganda in a trial in my life. I am not going to have this trial carried on for the purpose of pushing out propaganda."[34] Whenever Dennis, acting as his own attorney, told the jury that he would explain what communists actually believed and preached, Medina shut him down, acerbically responding, "That's what you think," according to Peggy Dennis's account of the trial. An exasperated Davis told Medina that he wanted nothing more than to speak the truth. "If you wanted the truth you would let our Party say what it teaches and advocates," he said.[35]

Given the constraints imposed upon them, the defendants did their best. In his opening statement, Dennis informed the jury that the CPUSA's principles did not advocate the duty or necessity for violent revolution. That, he said, was nothing more than a "fantastical conspiracy" peddled by McGohey, and the party was committed to bringing about socialism through a peaceful transition. Foster submitted a statement to the court detailing the changed direction the party took in 1935, when the newly established "popular front" strategy dictated cooperation with capitalist governments against the greater menace of fascism, and explained that much of the old communist literature presented by the prosecution was outdated.[36] "We do have a program, and that program is to elect a democratic coalition government which will have the potentiality of moving in the direction of socialism. I mean legally elected under the existing legislative or election machinery," Foster explained in his deposition.[37]

George Crockett, one of the defense attorneys, said the defendants' strategy was to educate the jury on the tenets of Marxism-Leninism, and to "let the jury conclude whether . . . there is any teaching or advocacy of the overthrow of the Government by force and violence." Medina rejected the strategy, which he said would extend an already-lengthy trial for years. When Green angrily reacted to Medina's refusal to let him introduce an article from a communist publication in his defense, Medina jailed him for the rest of the trial.[38]

Of course, the defendants' reliance on labor defense did them no favors. Numerous witnesses, including the defendants themselves, regaled the jury with tales of how they became communists, lacing their statements with as much propaganda as Medina would allow. One defense witness used the better part of two days on the stand to make political speeches, at which point Medina cut her off.[39] Throughout the proceedings, the defendants and their lawyers repeatedly denounced them as a political trial.

Medina refused to allow testimony from some of the defense's expert witnesses, such as communist historian Herbert Aptheker, who were slated to explain the finer points of Marxism-Leninism. The judge used a clear double standard in prohibiting defense witnesses from answering some of the same questions posed by the prosecution to Budenz and other FBI informants. He even refused the defendants' request to dismiss a juror, Russell Janney, who had given several interviews about the trial to news outlets, and had publicly spoken during the trial of the need for a "fight to the death" against communism.[40]

One of the prosecution's favorite tactics, which the Justice Department would continue in subsequent cases, became asking witnesses, including the defendants, to identify other communists, sometimes leading Medina to cite them for contempt when they refused. The first contempt charge came when Gates took the stand in his own defense. After some hesitation, Gates confirmed the names of his fellow defendants, but refused to identify others on the grounds that exposing them as communists could cost them their jobs. Crockett urged Medina to reconsider an order that Gates answer McGohey's question, with the defense attorney, who was black, telling the judge that "if the abolitionist of another day had not taken the same position as Mr. Gates has taken today, I probably would be a slave instead of a free American citizen." Medina was unpersuaded and promptly sentenced Gates to thirty days in jail for contempt.[41]

The defense table erupted in furor. An outraged Hall shouted at Medina, "It sounds more like a kangaroo court than a court of the United States. I have heard more law and more constitutional rights in kangaroo courts," leading the judge to remand him to jail for the remainder of the trial.[42] Winston, who, like Crockett, was black, and perhaps intending to elaborate on Crockett's comments, yelled, "More than five hundred [N]egroes have been lynched in this country." The outburst earned him thirty days in jail from Medina as well.[43]

On October 12, following months of delays imposed by the defense, Dennis closed the defendants' case with a final appeal to the jury. After attacking the prosecution's tactics and the trial itself, which he again decried as a political witch hunt, along with the allegation that the Justice Department was trying to silence their First Amendment rights, he launched into a defense of communist philosophy and what he averred were its peaceful intents. In the postwar period, he explained, communists still believed scientific socialism to be inevitable, but that it could be achieved through nonviolent means. He said violence would only be necessary if the ruling classes forcefully blocked those peaceable efforts. The prosecution, he said, had tried to prove otherwise with the use of outdated literature that didn't reflect the contemporary beliefs of the CPUSA. McGohey followed, speaking of Marxist-Leninist doctrine and the communists' alleged commitment to the violent overthrow of the nation's government, which, he emphasized, was the crime with which they were charged. For good measure, he reminded the jury of the party's secrecy and refusal to identify fellow communists.[44]

Now it was time for Medina to lay out his instructions to the jury. He acknowledged the defendants' First Amendment rights, telling the jury that it must acquit them if it believed they had no more than engaged in peaceful studies, teaching, and advocacy. But if the jury believed the defendants had in fact conspired to violently topple the government, it must find them guilty. "I charge you that it is not the abstract doctrine of overthrowing or destroying organized government by unlawful means which is denounced by this law, but the teaching and advocacy of action for the accomplishment of that purpose, by language reasonably and ordinarily calculated to incite persons to such action," the judge instructed. The next morning, the jury came back with its verdict: guilty.[45]

The trial, which at nine months had been the longest in American history up to that point, with a whopping record of about 16,000 pages, was over. And with the verdict out of the way, Medina focused his attention on the defense attorneys who had so vexed him throughout the trial. "Now I turn to some unfinished business," he said.[46] Medina recited a litany of offenses by the defense team, including intentionally delaying and prolonging the trial, and, remembering how the Nazi defendants of 1944 had helped to drive Judge Escher to his death, seeking to "impair . . . my health so that the trial could not continue."* Dennis, Richard

* Belknap writes that the trial did seriously strain the health of Medina, who suffered from chronic back pain and became pale and tired throughout the trial, contributing to his hostility toward the defense, which he blamed for his ailments (Belknap, 101).

Gladstein, and Sacher each received six months in jail for their contempt, Crockett and Abraham Isserman received four months apiece, and Louis McCabe was jailed for thirty days.[47]

The verdict was met with popular acclaim. McGohey was rewarded with a federal judgeship shortly after the trial concluded, while Medina was promoted to the appellate court. For winning his "battle to keep order in the court," the Associated Press named Medina as its "Man of the Year" for 1949.[48]

When the defendants appealed to the Second Circuit Court of Appeals, having abandoned labor defense for the First Amendment, their draw of Judge Learned Hand as part of their three-judge panel should have been cause for rejoicing. Hand in 1917 had written a landmark decision against the United States postmaster general for barring circulation of *The Masses*, a socialist magazine, under the Espionage Act, and seemed just the kind of judge that an unpopular defendant should have been able to rely on to defend his civil liberties and free-speech rights. Unfortunately for the defendants, the free-speech icon of *The Masses* took a decidedly different view in the Smith Act case.

The defendants' attorneys spent three hours pleading their case before the appellate court, arguing that the Smith Act was unconstitutional, that the prosecution had not shown that they presented a clear and present danger, and that Medina had made numerous errors and shown flagrant bias. Hand was wary of Cold War hysteria, which he believed "has now reached such a peak that there are few who would dare to acknowledge any Communist inclinations, if they had them,"[49] but was also cognizant of the geopolitical realities of the day, writing in the opinion that upheld the conviction that, "We must not close our eyes to our position in the world at that time," and that the risk of war was very real. Though he had never been a fan of the "clear and present danger" test established by Supreme Court justice Oliver Wendell Holmes as the threshold for restricting free speech, Hand concluded that the danger indeed existed. "We do not understand how one could ask for a more probable danger, unless we must wait till the actual eve of hostilities," Hand wrote. He cited incidents such as the Berlin airlift as sparks that could engulf the country in war at any time.[50]

The fact that North Korea invaded South Korea on the final day of oral arguments was not a good omen. The timing of the defendants' hearing at the Supreme Court, coming as Chinese soldiers flooded across the Yalu River, transforming a seemingly inevitable American victory in the Korean War into a bloody, three-year stalemate, was an even worse sign.

By the time the Smith Act Eleven pleaded their case before the Supreme Court, Truman had had ample opportunity to stack it with his own justices. Along with Tom Clark, the attorney general who had brought the original indictment—Clark recused himself from the case—Truman had appointed Harold

Burton, Sherman Minton, and Chief Justice Fred Vinson, stolid allies all in the president's war against domestic communism.

Setting aside the issue of whether the defendants did in fact advocate the violent overthrow of the government—the justices determined the issue to have been satisfactorily vetted by the appellate court—the Supreme Court's opinion, written by Vinson, sought to determine whether the defendants' actions met the "clear and present danger" test that would extend beyond their free-speech rights into the realm of criminal activity. And to the majority of the justices, it did. In rejecting the defendants' free-speech arguments, Vinson wrote that the violent overthrow of the government is "certainly a substantial enough interest for the Government to limit speech."[51]

Whether a revolution would be attempted at an undetermined date in the distant future, or even whether it had any chance of success, was immaterial. "Obviously, the words cannot mean that, before the Government may act, it must wait until the putsch is about to be executed, the plans have been laid, and the signal is awaited," Vinson wrote. "If Government is aware that a group aiming at its overthrow is attempting to indoctrinate its members and to commit them to a course whereby they will strike when the leaders feel the circumstances permit, action by the Government is required." As Medina told the jury in New York, the defendants are guilty if they planned to overthrow the government "as speedily as circumstances would permit."

Vinson also echoed Hand's comments about the state of world affairs. The fact that the defendants' activities had not actually resulted in an attempt to topple the government was not a suitable defense if they were part of a group that was ready and willing to make that attempt. Their membership in a party of rigidly disciplined adherents who were subject to their leaders' beck and call when they thought the time was right, combined with the "inflammable nature of world conditions" and the "touch-and-go nature" of America's relations with nations to which the defendants were "in the very least ideologically attuned," convinced the court that the convictions were justified.

The Supreme Court reached the same conclusion as Medina's jury, and opined that the defendants had been constitutionally convicted for violating the Smith Act. "Petitioners intended to overthrow the Government of the United States as speedily as the circumstances would permit. Their conspiracy to organize the Communist Party and to teach and advocate the overthrow of the Government of the United States by force and violence created a 'clear and present danger' of an attempt to overthrow the Government by force and violence," Vinson's opinion read.[52]

Only justices Hugo Black and William O. Douglas, the court's liberal stalwarts, dissented from the majority opinion, declaring the Smith Act and its use against the defendants as a violation of the First Amendment right to free speech. While roundly condemning communism as a creed, Douglas questioned how the defendants could be convicted for preaching ideas contained in books that were legally sold in bookstores and available on library shelves across the country. There comes a time, Douglas wrote, when speech loses the protections guaranteed it under the First Amendment. But that determination must be based on more than fear, opposition, or dislike of that speech, he said. The speech for which the defendants were convicted, the justice said, fell short of the "clear and present danger" test.[53]

Douglas excoriated the majority's understanding of what qualified as a "conspiracy" under the Smith Act. "To make lawful speech unlawful because two men conceive it is to raise the law of conspiracy to appalling proportions," he said. Douglas compared the conviction of the Smith Act defendants to the concept of "constructive treason" that once flourished in Britain. "Men were punished not for raising a hand against the king, but for thinking murderous thoughts about him," he wrote. The Framers of the Constitution were well aware of those abuses, Douglas said, and took steps to ensure that repeats would not occur in the United States. "Treason was defined to require overt acts—the evolution of a plot against the country into an actual project. The present case is not one of treason. But the analogy is close when the illegality is made to turn on intent, not on the nature of the act," the justice said.[54]

Black too emphasized the lack of evidence, or even of accusations, that the defendants planned to violently overturn the government. "These petitioners were not charged with an attempt to overthrow the Government. They were not charged with overt acts of any kind designed to overthrow the Government. They were not even charged with saying anything or writing anything designed to overthrow the Government. The charge was that they agreed to assemble and to talk and publish certain ideas at a later date," Black wrote in a separate dissenting opinion. "No matter how it is worded, this is a virulent form of prior censorship of speech and press, which I believe the First Amendment forbids."

Black ended his dissent with words that would prove prophetic. "Public opinion being what it now is, few will protest the conviction of these Communist petitioners. There is hope, however, that in calmer times, when present pressures, passions, and fears subside, this or some later Court will restore the First Amendment liberties to the high preferred place where they belong in a free society," he wrote.[55]

That day would not come in time to save the Smith Act defendants. The Eleven had been out on bail since their initial arrests, but they had exhausted their appeals, and prison awaited. All had been given five-year sentences except for Thompson, whom Medina sentenced to only three years in deference to his service in World War II. Those sentences were to begin after the Supreme Court handed down the final word on their case.

Four of the defendants fled rather than serve their sentences, a decision made collectively by the CPUSA's leadership. Davis, Foster, and Thompson initially advocated that all eleven go on the run due to a belief that the United States was entering a "fascist" period, and they were unlikely to ever emerge from prison, irrespective of the actual length of their sentences. Some argued that they would cause severe problems for the party if they absconded. Davis, whose conviction had already cost him his seat on the City Council, insisted he should serve his sentence because of his political prominence, while Gates worried that he would jeopardize the legal status of the *Daily Worker* if he became a fugitive.[56]

The party's leaders settled on a compromise in which Dennis, Green, Hall, Thompson, and Winston would flee, though Dennis, who wasn't eager for life as a fugitive—he'd already done his time underground—didn't make it out in time due to what Gates described as a "snafu."[57] Hall fled to Mexico, swimming across the Rio Grande to escape his punishment, but lasted only a few months as a fugitive before being arrested and extradited. Thompson was arrested in 1953 in a mountain cabin near Twin Heart, California. Green and Winston hid in Chicago until 1956, when they decided to turn themselves in.[58]

With the Supreme Court's ruling in *Dennis v. United States*, the Justice Department and the FBI had the green light they needed. Indictment after indictment followed as the authorities, with the Supreme Court's blessing, used their newly sanctioned powers to run roughshod over the CPUSA across the country. The second wave of indictments presaged total war against the CPUSA, beginning in June 1951 when sixteen communists were arrested in New York, along with one more in Pittsburgh. The group included several of the top CPUSA leaders who had escaped indictment in the Dennis case, such as Elizabeth Gurley Flynn, a member of the CPUSA's National Committee, and Alexander Trachtenberg, who ran the dummy corporation that published the *Daily Worker*.[59]

Several days later, Oleta Yates, the party's organizational secretary in California, told a crowd of supporters, "The new batch of indictments demonstrate [*sic*] that the government intends to follow up the Supreme Court decision by beheading the Communist Party of its leadership throughout the country." She was arrested on July 26, along with fourteen of her comrades in California. The feds came for leaders of the Maryland communists on August 7, followed shortly by their brethren in Philadelphia. Then came the arrests of seven party functionaries in Hawaii that August, with arrests following in Michigan, Missouri, and Washington a month later.

The end of the Truman presidency, which had used the Smith Act to fend off the soft-on-communism tag, brought no reprieve from what Peggy Dennis dubbed "the Truman nightmare." President Dwight Eisenhower, who, like Truman, was under pressure to appease the insatiable McCarthy, declared, "There is no vacillation nor inaction on the part of this Administration in dealing with those who, by force or violence, would overthrow the government of the United States," and his new attorney general, Herbert Brownell, continued the arrests and indictments, targeting communists in Philadelphia in July 1953 and in Cleveland three months later. Eisenhower's second year, which saw the president sign arguably the most restrictive anticommunist legislation to date,* featured indictments against CPUSA members in Colorado, Connecticut, Puerto Rico, and Utah.[60]

Not even the fall of Senator McCarthy in 1954, punctuated by Joseph Welch's famous rebuke, "Have you no sense of decency, sir, at long last?," brought an end to the Smith Act persecutions of CPUSA members. Ironically, it was Hoover himself who put the brakes on the wave of prosecutions, though not out of any concern for civil liberties of the prosecuted. The FBI had spent years infiltrating the Communist Party, and Hoover had grown concerned over the vast number of confidential informants it had lost as more and more were needed to testify in court.** Hoover urged the Justice Department to reserve its prosecutions only for high-ranking leaders of the CPUSA, not the lower-level members who had become its focus since the Supreme Court handed down its ruling in the Dennis case. The Justice Department obliged, and stopped seeking new indictments not long after the 1954 election. The temporary lull lasted until the 1956 elections, when the Justice Department brought three new indictments. But the conviction of seven members of the Massachusetts communist party marked the last prosecution of party members under the Smith Act.[61]

Final deliverance from the Smith Act came on June 17, 1957, dubbed "Red Monday" by the disapproving press, when the court overturned the conviction of Yates and her fellow California communists, effectively neutering the law while overturning Red Scare–inspired convictions in three other cases as well. The composition of the court had changed significantly since 1951, and the court, now headed by Chief Justice Earl Warren, was more sensitive to questions of civil liberties, whereas the four justices who had since departed had a more "deferential approach" to anticommunist laws. Some of those who remained from 1951 had misgivings as well. Justice Felix Frankfurter, who had concurred with the opinion in *Dennis*, started to grow concerned within months of the ruling, and came to believe that the lower courts "must not treat defendants even under

---

* In his 1954 State of the Union address, Eisenhower asked Congress to pass legislation that would strip CPUSA members of their American citizenship. Congress obliged, sending him the Expatriation Act in August. Just days earlier, he'd signed the Communist Control Act, which expressly outlawed the CPUSA and membership in it.

** The cases required so many witnesses, whom the Justice Department kept as paid, full-time consultants, that they started to become a financial strain. In 1954, the Justice Department instead started paying its witnesses on a per-diem basis to cut costs (Belknap, 164).

the Smith Act prosecutions as though they were an indiscriminate lump, and especially as though their guilt were already assumed."[62] Frankfurter had become so alarmed by the flurry of Smith Act prosecutions he'd helped to unleash that he instructed his clerks to find cases the court could use to curtail the precedent set by *Dennis* without overturning it completely.[63]

The result was an opinion that one scholar referred to, in its complexity and precision, "as sort of [a] *Finnegans Wake* of impossibly nice distinctions."[64] In a 6–1 decision,* the high court effectively gutted the Smith Act with its ruling in *Yates v. United States*, while still leaving intact the holding from *Dennis*.[65] Instead of overturning the 1951 opinion, Justice John Harlan, perhaps influenced by Frankfurter's desire not to embarrass the court by disavowing an earlier ruling—or perhaps his own, as he had previously upheld a different Smith Act conviction[66]—said the trial court had merely misinterpreted the landmark ruling in *Dennis*. The essence of that ruling, Harlan wrote, was that the type of speech prohibited by the Smith Act, the indoctrination and exhortation to violent action, whether in the present or future, "is not constitutionally protected when the group is of sufficient size and cohesiveness, is sufficiently oriented towards action, and other circumstances are such as reasonably to justify apprehension that action will occur." The circumstances were far different in *Yates*, he wrote, in which the "doctrinal justification of forcible overthrow" existed, but that it "is too remote from concrete action to be regarded" as punishable under the Smith Act.[67]

Harlan seems to accept the assertion that the *Dennis* defendants were preparing to take action in a way that would violate the Smith Act. The court in that case was not "concerned with a conspiracy to engage some future time in seditious activity, but rather with a conspiracy to advocate presently the taking of forcible action in the future. It was action, not advocacy, that was to be postponed until 'circumstances' would 'permit,'" the justice wrote.[68]

For Harlan, the difference between *Dennis* and *Yates* was a bright line between the abstract concept of advocating government's overthrow and actually inciting people to do so. Harlan said the Justice Department had failed to show that the defendants' advocacy to overthrow the government included an incitement to illegal activity, rather than simply an abstract concept protected by the First Amendment. He noted that the trial court rejected proposed instructions that would have required the jurors to consider whether the alleged advocacy extended beyond the abstract into "the use of language reasonably and ordinarily calculated to incite persons to such action," on the belief that the Supreme Court's ruling in *Dennis* eliminated whatever need may have existed to do so. (Medina had given such instructions to the jury in 1949.) The question, Harlan

---

*Justices William Brennan and Charles Whittaker didn't vote in the decision, having been appointed too late to take part in all stages of the case (Belknap, 244).

said, was whether the Smith Act outlawed such advocacy if there were no effort to actually instigate action to overthrow the government.

The answer, the court concluded, was no. "The essential distinction is that those to whom the advocacy is addressed must be urged to do something, now or in the future, rather than merely to believe in something," Harlan wrote. The Smith Act targeted advocacy of action, he said, not of ideas. "For all purposes relevant here, the sole evidence as to [the defendants] was that they had long been members, officers, or functionaries of the Communist Party of California," Harlan said. "So far as this record shows, none of them has engaged in or been associated with any but what appear to have been wholly lawful activities." Belief in the inevitability of the violent overthrow of the government, or even support for such an action, did not constitute advocacy as defined in the Smith Act, in the eyes of Harlan, who wrote, "Prediction or prophesy is not advocacy."[69]

Harlan also opined that the trial court in *Yates*, along with the prosecution, had misconstrued the meaning of the word *organize* for purposes of determining whether the defendants had violated the Smith Act's prohibition against organizing a group that teaches, advocates, or encourages the violent overthrow of the government. The defense argued that the Justice Department brought the charges after the three-year statute of limitations because the alleged organization occurred with Dennis and Foster's restructuring of the CPUSA. The court agreed that the statute of limitations negated a 1951 indictment for an event that happened in 1945.[70]

The lone dissent on the Supreme Court was from Tom Clark, who as attorney general had initiated the indictment that led to the fateful decision in *Dennis*. Clark could not divorce the cases and saw no difference between the charges brought against Eugene Dennis and Oleta Yates. Clark argued that the defendants in *Yates* had been engaged in the same conspiracy as Dennis and his codefendants. "The conspiracy includes the same group of defendants as in the *Dennis* case, though petitioners here occupied a lower echelon in the party hierarchy. They nevertheless served in the same army and were engaged in the same mission," Clark wrote in his dissent. "This Court laid down in *Dennis* the principles governing such prosecutions, and they were closely adhered to here." Clark ended his opinion on an ominous note: "We all know that the Communist movement has as its ultimate objective the overthrow of government by force and violence or by any means, legal or illegal, or a combination of both. That testimony was indisputably produced before the special committee of which I was chairman, and came from the lips not of those who gave hearsay testimony, but of the actual official records of the Communist Party of the United States. . . . Therefore, a Communist is one who intends knowingly or willfully to participate in any actions, legal or illegal, or a combination of both, that will bring about the ultimate overthrow of our Government. He is the one we are aiming at."[71]

The court overturned the convictions of five defendants and ruled that nine others, including Yates, could be retried, though the Justice Department declined to do so, acknowledging in a letter to the trial court judge that it could not meet the new evidentiary requirements established by the Supreme Court.[72] * Though the original defendants from *Dennis* and other cases had no recourse left—the court, after all, had been careful to leave the original 1951 opinion on solid legal ground—eighteen pending Smith Act indictments were dropped following the *Yates* ruling, with one judge lamenting that the Supreme Court had left the Smith Act "a virtual shambles."[73] The court had succeeded in preserving its ruling in *Dennis*. But it had signed the death warrant for the Smith Act, at least as far as the Justice Department's ability to prosecute people for the de facto crime of being communists was concerned. The floodgates that the Supreme Court had opened in 1951 were now officially closed.

The communist press, and even some mainstream news outlets, praised the watershed ruling. "Victory is indeed sweet," declared *People's World*, a communist newspaper.[74] The ruling was far less well-received by other publications, as well as by Red hunters in Congress. Outraged by the devastating blow to the federal government's anticommunist efforts, US Senator William Jenner, an Indiana Republican, introduced legislation to strip the Supreme Court of jurisdiction over several types of subversion and loyalty cases. It may have provided some small consolation to Jenner, Hoover, and others that some legal persecution of communists continued in other forms.[75]

For the communists, the *Yates* ruling couldn't have come soon enough. By the arrival of Red Monday, 126 members of the CPUSA had been indicted under the conspiracy provision of the Smith Act since the Supreme Court had upheld the convictions of Eugene Dennis of his fellow communist leaders. Of those indicted communists, 93 were ultimately convicted. Only 10 of the 126 who escaped conviction were actually acquitted. One case ended in a hung jury. Three defendants, like Foster, were severed from their cases for health reasons. One died awaiting trial. The indictments of 18 others were dropped after Red Monday. By the time President John F. Kennedy took office, two of the original Smith Act defendants—Green and Winston, who had both gone on the run before later turning themselves in—remained behind bars. Kennedy commuted their sentences in 1961. The last remaining prisoner from the Smith Act prosecutions, North Carolina communist leader Junius Scales, had his sentence commuted on Christmas Eve, 1962.[76]

---

* Yates was ultimately sentenced to one year in jail for contempt of court after refusing to answer questions posed by the prosecution, though the Supreme Court reduced the sentence after ruling that Yates could only be charged with a single count of contempt, not one for each of the eleven times she refused to answer the same question ("Decisions of Supreme Court Seen Reflecting Freedom of Expression," *The Gazette and Daily* (York, Pennsylvania), July 8, 1958).

Though the reign of terror that began with the Supreme Court's ruling in *Dennis* ended on Red Monday, the Communist Party of the United States never recovered. It would be folly to attribute the party's downfall solely to the Smith Act. Factional infighting, long a feature of communist life, led the party to cannibalize itself in an orgy of ideological strife. Cataclysmic events in 1956, such as Nikita Khrushchev's denunciation of Stalin and the violent suppression of a popular revolt in Hungary, inspired factionalism and internal disputes so severe that even direct intervention by the Soviets in CPUSA affairs failed to heal the rifts.

But the tremendous toll taken by the Smith Act is undeniable, and the judicial repression the party suffered compounded the problems it faced from the discord caused by external events in the communist world. In his book *Cold War Political Justice*, likely the most comprehensive account ever written of the Smith Act trial and its ramifications, Michal Belknap outlined the ways in which the trial and its aftermath brought about the decline of the CPUSA. Of course, the prosecutions left the party's leadership structure in disarray, but the impact went far beyond the convictions of individuals.

The prosecutions were a massive drain on the party's financial resources, costing the CPUSA about $500,000 in the *Dennis* case alone. And by exposing the staggering number of members who were secret FBI informants, the 1949 trial instilled an intense fear among party members, who were unsure about whom they could trust. The result was internal purges of any communist whose loyalties came under suspicion, coupled with paranoia that discouraged the recruitment of new members, as if the possibility of prosecution weren't deterrent enough for potential newcomers. The CPUSA reduced the size of its local clubs and other organizations to limit the damage a lone informant could do, and scaled back its large conventions to protect party leaders from arrest. New security measures, such as prohibitions on using the phone to discuss party business, made it difficult for members to communicate. Many members went underground, and the party as a whole became more isolated, ending many of its most effective propaganda efforts, such as leaflet drives, newspaper and radio advertisements, and testimony before legislative bodies. CPUSA membership, which stood at about 73,000 after a 1946 recruiting drive, dwindled to fewer than 23,000 by 1955. The party had always been able to recover from internal divisions in the past, but the fallout from the Smith Act prosecutions had sapped it of its strength. "As a political force American communism had for all practical purposes ceased to exist" by 1958, Belknap writes.[77]

Though largely unenforceable, at least in the way imagined by Tom Clark, John McGohey, and J. Edgar Hoover, the Smith Act remains on the books today. And the CPUSA still exists as well, though in a severely truncated form that to most Americans probably serves as nothing more than an undesirable historical curiosity. Many—if not most—Americans would no doubt consider that a good thing. The Soviet Union had been the Evil Empire and its communist allies in America an insidious fifth column. The end of the Cold War, when the nations of Eastern Europe finally cast out the oppressive communist regimes that had for decades kept the proverbial boot on their necks in 1989, was the great postwar triumph of the United States, and the fall of the Soviet Union two years later punctuated the end of the era that had emerged from the ashes of World War II. At home and abroad, the war against communism has been won, and few Americans can doubt that the world is a better place because of it.

Given the significance of the conviction of the Smith Act Eleven, one must wonder how such an epochal event could be so largely forgotten by history, especially when so many other shameful moments from the Red Scare have been burned into our national consciousness. While America largely remembers the victims of the McCarthy era as those whose lives were destroyed by unfair accusations, maybe the fact that the Smith Act defendants were convicted in a court of law allowed them to fade from memory while so many others are remembered as martyrs to Cold War hysteria. After all, Murrow reminded his viewers that "accusation is not proof," and that "conviction depends upon evidence and due process of law." However flawed, the eleven defendants of the Smith Act trial got their due process.

But there must be more to it than that. One can only surmise that the victims' membership in a party whose name still evokes loathing among most Americans grants them far less sympathy than other victims of the witch hunts of the 1940s and 1950s. Perhaps even today, learning for the first time of the brutal repression of people who, though reviled, were still as entitled to their civil liberties as any other American, many would greet the revelation with nothing more than a shrug. Perhaps today, many Americans would still say the Justice Department and the FBI did the right thing.

Chapter 11

The Chennault Affair

They oughtn't to be doing this. This is treason.

—Lyndon Johnson

Say Richard Nixon's name to the average American, and most likely the first thing that comes to his or her mind will be the Watergate scandal that forced him from the White House. Far less prominent in the public's consciousness is the Chennault Affair, the scandal that helped get him there in the first place.

As the 1968 election approached, Richard Nixon watched with apprehension as his once-mighty lead over Democrat Hubert Humphrey shrank. Humphrey promised an end to the war in Vietnam, and a weary public was becoming more receptive. Worse yet for Nixon were the rumors that President Lyndon Johnson, desperate to salvage his legacy and at least take the first steps toward ending the war as he departed the White House, would halt the bombing of North Vietnam in a bid to kick-start the peace process.

When Johnson announced a bombing halt—and the impending peace talks it was meant to facilitate—just five days before the election, it contributed to Humphrey's surge in the polls. But that surge dissipated two days later when the South Vietnamese announced they wouldn't come to the peace talks. South Vietnam was wary of Humphrey, and understandably so. The Democratic nominee made no secret of his desire to end the war, and Saigon believed it would get a better deal under the more hawkish Nixon, whose unflinching anticommunism had become his trademark as he rose to the top in American politics.

However, Nixon didn't leave it to chance that Saigon would take the steps needed to scuttle the nascent peace talks that could push Humphrey over the top.

Through Anna Chennault, whom the members of the Johnson administration would come to know as the "Dragon Lady" or "Little Flower," Nixon persuaded South Vietnam to reject Johnson's peace overtures. It was a risky move for Nixon. Succeed, and he would undercut the burgeoning peace movement that

The Watergate scandal ended Richard Nixon's presidency, but the Chennault Affair helped him reach the White House in the first place.
LIBRARY OF CONGRESS

was boosting Humphrey's chances of victory. But if the subterfuge was discovered and made public, the ensuing scandal surely would end Nixon's chances of victory.

The gamble paid off. The president's grand bombing halt came to naught as South Vietnam refused to come to the negotiating table. Peace would not come before the election, and at least partly because of that, Humphrey would not be president. South Vietnam bought itself a few more years of existence and Nixon cemented his victory in the 1968 presidential election. By the time Nixon finally ended America's involvement in the Vietnam War, more than 21,000 American combat troops had died on his watch.

Anna Chennault was the widow of Lieutenant General Claire Chennault. The two had met during World War II when he led the Flying Tigers volunteer air force that helped to defend China from the Japanese. They married after the war and planned to continue living in China, where they would run their new airline, a plan they had to abandon after Mao Zedong's communist army seized control of the country, forcing them to flee to Taiwan along with the remnants of the Nationalist government that Mao had defeated.[1]

As an active member of the China Lobby, the conservative network of anti-communist hard-liners who had spent the past twenty years accusing Harry Truman and the Democrats of "losing China," strove to ensure that other Asian countries wouldn't suffer the same catastrophe that befell Chennault's homeland, Chennault had long crusaded against communism in the Far East. She moved to Washington after her husband's death and became a prominent social figure and GOP operative. Due to her position as a columnist for a Taiwanese newspaper and her work with the air freight company her husband had founded—the Flying Tiger Line, which handled a large amount of Defense Department shipping between the United States and South Vietnam—Chennault traveled to Asia frequently, and had regular access to the upper echelons of leadership among America's Asian Cold War allies.

Chennault first met Nixon in 1955 when the then-vice president visited Taiwan for a banquet hosted by Taiwanese president Chiang Kai-Shek. She and her husband had hosted a reception for him during the trip as well. Chennault and Nixon wouldn't cross paths personally again until a decade after they first met. But after he sent her a condolence card following her husband's 1958 death, the two began exchanging letters, mostly discussing issues of communism in Asia, a shared interest of a woman who'd seen Mao's armies conquer China and a man who'd spent his career as one of America's premier anticommunist leaders. During Nixon's 1960 presidential campaign, Chennault volunteered to help at the urging of the chair of the Republican Women's Federation of Maryland, which was looking for someone to organize minority groups for the vice president's campaign. Nixon and Chennault would meet again five years later, while both were in Taipei on business.[2]

Nixon brought Chennault into the folds of his campaign in the spring of 1967, by which time he knew her as a well-connected expert on Asian geopolitics and a reliable Republican. He sent her a cable while she was on an Asian lecture tour, asking her to meet with him at his Fifth Avenue apartment in New York. When the two sat face-to-face, a "disarmingly conspiratorial" Nixon asked Chennault if she would serve as an advisor to him on Southeast Asia in his upcoming presidential campaign. The war in Vietnam promised to be the dominant campaign issue in 1968, and Nixon said he couldn't trust the State Department or even his allies in Washington for the information he'd need. Chennault agreed, and asked Nixon if he'd be willing to meet with the South Vietnamese ambassador, which he said he would do. Nixon assured her, "I want to end this war with victory."[3]

The goal of ending the war with victory had thus far proven quite elusive for Lyndon Johnson. After sacrificing tens of thousands of American lives and bombing North Vietnam into oblivion, peace seemed no closer than it had when Johnson committed the United States to an escalation of the war in 1964. The Tet Offensive in January 1968 had driven the point home to the American public.

The embattled Johnson stunned the nation two months later when he announced on March 31 that he would not seek reelection that year. In his address, he announced that he would restrict American bombing of North Vietnam, and said even that this limited bombing could come to an end "if our restraint is matched by restraint in Hanoi." He portrayed his decision to not run for another term as a commitment to bringing an end to the war. "With America's sons in the fields far away, with America's future under challenge right here at home, with our hopes and the world's hopes for peace in the balance every day, I do not believe that I should devote an hour or a day of my time to any personal partisan causes or to any duties other than the awesome duties of this office—the presidency of your country," Johnson said. "Let men everywhere know . . . that a strong, a confident, and a vigilant America stands ready tonight to seek an honorable peace—and stands ready tonight to defend an honored cause—whatever the price, whatever the burden, whatever the sacrifice that duty may require."[4]

Johnson would devote the last year of his presidency to ending the war. To do that, he had to convince the recalcitrant North Vietnamese to negotiate at the peace talks he'd convened in Paris. Hanoi demanded an unconditional end to the bombing, which Johnson believed would endanger American lives in Vietnam. Behind the scenes, he secretly laid out three conditions that North Vietnam must meet before he'd stop attacking it. Hanoi must stop shelling South Vietnamese cities, stop smuggling arms and soldiers into the south through the demilitarized zone that separated the two countries, and accept peace talks with the South Vietnamese government. While the US would bring the South Vietnamese, Johnson agreed that the North Vietnamese could bring the National Liberation Front—the South Vietnamese communist rebels better known to Americans as the Vietcong—in a format dubbed, "Our side/your side."[5]

As the campaign heated up and Nixon seemed poised to win the GOP nomination at the Republican National Convention in August, his foreign policy advisor Richard Allen wrote a memo to the candidate, suggesting he touch base with Chennault, who'd proposed that Nixon take a meeting with Bui Diem, South Vietnam's ambassador to the United States. "Mrs. Chennault has apparently asked him if he would talk to [Nixon]. I explained schedule tight, but possible to check on available time," Allen wrote in a July 3 memo. "Meeting would have to be absolute top secret." If Nixon was able to see Diem, Allen said he'd contact Chennault and she'd arrange a sit-down in New York, where Nixon kept his campaign headquarters. "This would be a good opportunity to get filled in on events in Paris and other developments," Allen wrote, referencing the stalled peace talks in the French capital.

In the margins of the memo, next to the words *Top Secret*, Nixon wrote that he didn't see how the meeting could be kept secret, given his Secret Service protection detail. Allen concluded that the meeting would be a mistake, and filed the memo away, believing that it had never taken place.[6]

Unbeknownst to Allen, the meeting did take place nine days later. Chennault's main contact with the Nixon camp was campaign manager John Mitchell, the "commander in chief" of the campaign who would go on to serve as Nixon's attorney general. At the height of the campaign, the two were in contact on a near-daily basis, with Chennault using a private number that Mitchell changed frequently in case of wiretaps. She passed on the word to Diem that Nixon was eager to talk with him, and the meeting was set.[7]

Nixon was not the only one concerned about word of the meeting leaking out. To Diem, the meeting was "an enticing prospect, but also a dangerous one," because of the risk that he'd be viewed as "dealing behind the Democrats' backs" if it became public knowledge. But the stakes were too high in the presidential contest for South Vietnam to not take an interest, especially with the Democrats distancing themselves from Johnson's war. Diem later claimed that he decided to meet with Nixon, but without telling Saigon, so President Nguyen Van Thieu would have plausible deniability if it became public.*

The meeting that may have changed the course of the 1968 election occurred on July 12. According to Diem's account, he spoke with Nixon and Mitchell about the state of the war and South Vietnam's need for M16s and other weaponry. He also mentioned the growing unpopularity of the war with the American public, and said that in anticipation of the eventual withdrawal of US forces, he hoped to see an intensive training program for South Vietnam's soldiers, which Nixon would later do under his Vietnamization policy.[8]

Nixon told Diem that Chennault would be the only point of contact between his campaign and the South Vietnamese government. "Anna is my good friend. . . . She knows all about Asia. I know you also consider her a friend, so please rely on her from now on as the only contact between myself and your government. If you have any message for me, please give it to Anna and she will relay it to me and I will do the same in the future. We know Anna is a good American and a dedicated Republican. We can all rely on her loyalty," Nixon said, according to Chennault's description of the meeting. "If I should be elected the next president, you can rest assured I will have a meeting with your leader and find a solution to winning this war."[9]

As Nixon and Diem were cutting their backroom deal to use Chennault as a conduit between the campaign and Saigon, Johnson's frenzied efforts to find an honorable peace were pushing him ever closer to the announcement that he would halt all bombing of North Vietnam. A bombing halt had been rumored for months, and was feared by Nixon, who knew that peace in Vietnam would be a boon to the Democrats in the presidential race.

To ensure that they wouldn't undermine the secret conditions he'd laid out for North Vietnam, Johnson revealed his plans to the frontrunners in the race to replace him. Several weeks after Nixon's sit-down with Chennault and Diem, Johnson called on the presumptive Republican nominee to confirm the grand bargain he was proposing to Hanoi.[10]

Nixon and the South Vietnamese shared a belief that Johnson's rumored bombing halt was a political ploy intended to boost Humphrey's flagging

---

* According to Johnson aide Clark Clifford, Diem informed State Department official Bill Bundy of the meeting. Clifford said Bundy didn't object, and thought it perfectly appropriate for them to meet. "But Diem neglected to mention to Bundy that, at Nixon's request, he had opened a secret personal channel to John Mitchell and other senior members of the Nixon team through Chennault and [Republican Texas Senator] John Tower," Clifford wrote (Clifford, Clark M., and Richard C. Holbrooke. 1991. *Counsel to the President: A Memoir*. New York: Random House, 581).

campaign. But after Johnson laid out his proposal for the Republican frontrunner on July 26, Nixon was supportive. He didn't really believe North Vietnam would accept Johnson's conditions anyway.[11]

It seemed likely that the Democrats, not the Republicans, would be a bigger problem for Johnson as he tried to wind down the war. After four years of rising body counts, liberals wanted America out of Vietnam, and the Democratic presidential contenders heard those cries loud and clear. Robert Kennedy and Eugene McCarthy had both advocated an end to the bombing of North Vietnam, and Johnson had threatened a public break with Humphrey if he repudiated the administration's policies. "The GOP may be of more help to us than the Democrats in the last few months," Johnson had speculated after his meeting with Nixon.[12]

Under pressure from Johnson, Thieu accepted the proposal for peace talks "with profound inner reservations." Diem said Thieu viewed the proposed bombing pause as an attempt by Johnson to boost the dovish Humphrey, and hoped that Hanoi wouldn't accept the deal. "By accepting the American offer, the North Vietnamese were achieving both a bombing halt and this potentially vital ability to affect the election. In return, they were agreeing merely to begin another round of talks, which would be only as substantial as they themselves desired. In other words, it was costing them nothing," Diem wrote.[13]

The largest obstacle standing in the way of a bombing halt had been North Vietnam's demand that it be unconditional. Johnson had his three conditions that Hanoi wasn't willing to meet, even if those "facts of life," as Johnson called them, as a diplomatic sop to the North Vietnamese, were kept secret to avoid the appearance that it was giving in to American pressure. For months, Hanoi rebuffed Johnson's overtures, just as Nixon had expected.[15]

Johnson finally got a small opening on October 9, when the North Vietnamese conveyed to American negotiators in Paris that they would be willing to discuss South Vietnamese participation in the peace talks one day after a bombing halt. Hanoi had long refused to sit down with the South Vietnamese, whom they considered American puppets. It wasn't quite a breakthrough, but after months of refusal, it was a tentative step in the right direction.

Over the next few days, a flurry of activity followed that would breathe new life into Johnson's stalled peace talks. The Soviet Union, Hanoi's chief backer, informed an American diplomat that it "had good reason to believe" Hanoi would consent to four-way talks between the United States and South Vietnam on one side and North Vietnam and the National Liberation Front on the other "if the U.S. stops unconditionally and completely the bombardments and other acts of war." On October 14, North Vietnamese negotiators agreed to the president's three "facts of life," but there was no deal yet, as Hanoi was balking at Johnson's demand that peace talks begin twenty-four hours after the bombing stopped. But they were getting closer.[16]

Johnson tempered his expectations, as well as the expectations of the three men vying to succeed him. In a conference call on October 16 with Humphrey, Nixon, and George Wallace, the segregationist Alabama governor who was running a third-party campaign for the White House, the president explained that there was still no deal with Hanoi, despite press accounts to the contrary.

In giving his periodic updates to the three candidates, Johnson was placing a tremendous amount of trust in them to not repeat the information or leak it to the press, and he warned that doing so "[would] be injurious to your country." In short, Johnson told them that the American government's position hadn't changed. It still demanded that North Vietnam respect the demilitarized zone, stop shelling South Vietnamese cities, and accept Saigon's participation in the peace talks before the United States stopped bombing. And a bombing halt had to be done in a way that wouldn't endanger American lives. As of that day, North Vietnam hadn't signed on. "We do not have to get a firm contract on all these three things, but I do have to have good reason to believe that it won't be on again, off again," Johnson said.

Nixon's interference would not become apparent until later. For now, Johnson was more concerned about Humphrey and other Democrats. Several days earlier, former National Security advisor McGeorge Bundy had called for the unconditional withdrawal of troops from Vietnam, which followed a Humphrey speech from late September calling for a bombing halt in exchange only for negotiations. Without mentioning Humphrey by name, Johnson made clear that such comments were encouraging Hanoi to hold out for a better deal. "The Bundy speech didn't do us any good and there are other speeches that are not helping at all, because these people when they read one of these speeches and hear them, then they take off for Hanoi or they do something else," Johnson said. The president added, "I know you don't want to play politics with your country."[17]

Throughout the campaign, Nixon had pledged to Johnson that he wouldn't do or say anything that would jeopardize his efforts to bring peace. At least in public, Nixon had stayed true to his word, despite his concerns that Johnson would stop bombing to help Humphrey. But the rules of the game changed on October 22. A memo from campaign aide Bryce Harlow warned that he'd received information from a source in Johnson's inner circle that the president was "pathologically eager" to call a bombing halt, and that "Careful plans are being made to help [Humphrey] exploit whatever happens." Confirming Nixon's fears that Johnson would use a bombing halt to his vice president's advantage, Harlow wrote, "White Housers still think they can pull out the election for HHH with this ploy; that's what is being attempted."

After reading Harlow's memo several times, growing "angrier and more frustrated" with each rereading, Nixon decided that the only way to prevent Johnson from cutting the legs out from under his campaign at the last minute was to tell America that a bombing halt was imminent. "In addition I wanted to plant the impression—which I believed to be true—that his motives and his timing were not dictated by diplomacy alone," he wrote in his memoirs.

To achieve that end, Nixon publicly aired the rumor that Johnson was playing politics with the war, but tried to give himself some political cover by insisting that he didn't believe the president would do such a thing. In a statement to the press in New York on October 25, Nixon said, "In the last thirty-six hours I have been advised of a flurry of meetings in the White House and elsewhere on Vietnam. I am told that officials in the administration have been driving very hard for an agreement on the bombing halt, accompanied possibly by a cease-fire, in the immediate future. I have since learned these reports are true." Getting to the true purpose of his statement, Nixon added, "I am also told that this spurt of activity is a cynical, last-minute attempt by President Johnson to salvage the candidacy of Mr. Humphrey. This I do not believe."[18]

Johnson was outraged. In his characteristically colorful language, the president angrily told Everett Dirksen, the Senate minority leader, "I thought Dick's statement was ugly the other day, that he had been told that I was a thief, and a son of a bitch, and so forth, but he knew my mother and she really wasn't a bitch. I mean you set up a statement like that and then deny it, it's not very good, because he knows better, and that hurt my feelings." As if a bombing halt wouldn't already be viewed as a political machination, Nixon had firmly implanted the idea in the public's mind.[19]

Johnson also worried that a bombing pause right before the election would look like an attempt to help Humphrey. But on Sunday, October 27, the president got the last concession he needed from Hanoi when the North Vietnamese dropped a precondition that secret minutes of the peace talks state that the bombing halt was unconditional. Walt Rostow, Johnson's national security advisor, tried to alleviate the president's concerns. "I understand well the certainty that some will accuse the President of playing politics," he wrote in a memo to Johnson. "But the tragic dilemma is that you will also be accused of playing politics if you let this slide—and politics against the party you lead." Rostow ended his memo with a warning that, if Johnson hesitated, "I am not even sure the deal will be there to pick up after the election." The next day, Saigon informed American ambassador Ellsworth Bunker that Thieu was on board and had accepted that the National Liberation Front would be at the table, though neither South Vietnam or the United States would recognize them as an independent entity under the "our side/your side" formula. Johnson had everything he needed to move forward. The talks would begin on November 6, the day after Americans chose their next president.[20]

Two days before Johnson was to announce the bombing halt, and just one day after Thieu had given his seal of approval to the deal, the South Vietnamese president made a sudden about-face. Only days before, Thieu had agreed that the peace talks would begin three days after America stopped its bombing of the north. Now, he was insisting that three days was not enough. It reeked of a false pretext.

Thieu's change of heart shouldn't have come as a surprise, given the shocking information that Johnson had received just hours earlier.

Eugene Rostow, undersecretary of state for political affairs at the State Department, had spoken with Alexander Sachs, a Wall Street economist and former confidant of Franklin D. Roosevelt. Sachs revealed to Rostow a bit of information he'd gleaned at a lunch the previous day from "a member of the banking community" who was close with Nixon: the prospects for a bombing halt or a cease-fire were bleak because Nixon was actively working to block them. "They would incite Saigon to be difficult, and Hanoi to wait," Rostow reported. "These difficulties would make it easier for Nixon to settle after January. Like Ike in 1953, he would be able to settle on terms which the President could not accept, blaming the deterioration of the situation between now and January or February on his predecessor."[21]

American intelligence agencies, which had been monitoring Thieu, had already taken note of Chennault's communications with Saigon. The White House had discovered that on October 27—Johnson wouldn't receive this information until two days later, when he learned of Thieu's reluctance and Sachs's warning—Chennault had instructed Diem to tell his president to "abort or cripple the [Paris] deal by refusing to participate." In a cable that same day, which was intercepted by the National Security Agency, Diem wrote to Thieu, "I explained discreetly to our partisan friends our firm attitude. . . . The longer the situation continues, the more we are favored, for the elections will take place in a week and President Johnson would probably have difficulties in forcing our hand. I am still in contact with the Nixon entourage, which continues to be the favorite despite the uncertainty provoked by the news of an imminent bombing halt." Diem confirmed in his memoirs that the "Nixon entourage" was Chennault, John Mitchell, and John Tower, a major figure in the Nixon campaign.[22]

In her travels to Saigon, Chennault spoke frequently with Thieu. Whenever they met, Thieu would complain about the pressure that the Johnson administration was putting on him to negotiate with Hanoi and the National Liberation Front. "Why should I go?" he asked Chennault. "Why should I walk into a smoke screen? There is no real agenda, no one is ready." Thieu would bemoan his country's dependence on American aid, saying, "We're at the mercy of your President!" But he suggested that it may be time for South Vietnam to stand up to Johnson. "I would much prefer to have the peace talks after your elections," he said. Chennault would always ask, "Is this a message to my party?" "Yes, if I may ask you to convey this message to your candidate," Thieu would respond.[23]

The intelligence Johnson had received so far left it unclear whether the Nixon campaign itself was involved. Thanks to the information provided by Sachs, the picture suddenly became much clearer. "It all adds up," Johnson said, noting that Thieu had been refusing to see Bunker in Saigon. If people found out that Nixon had persuaded Thieu to boycott the peace talks, "it would rock the world."[24]

According to Johnson aide Clark Clifford, the administration gradually came to realize through its regular intelligence channels "that President Thieu's growing resistance to the agreement in Paris was being encouraged, indeed stimulated, by the Republicans, and especially by Anna Chennault."[25]

After Eugene Rostow passed along Sachs's information, Johnson discussed the revelations with Senator Richard Russell, the legendary Georgia Democrat who'd mentored him in the Senate. "We have found that our friend, the Republican nominee, our California friend, has been playing on the outskirts with our enemies and our friends both, our allies and the other. He's been doing it through rather subterranean sources here," Johnson said. "And he has been saying to the allies that you're going to get sold out" and that, "You better not give away your liberty just a few hours before I can preserve it for you." Johnson told Russell that Chennault had been acting as "go-between" with the South Vietnamese ambassador. "I know it's her. It's Chennault, you know, the flying tiger."[26]

Ignoring the setbacks and the strong possibility that Thieu would dig in his heels and reject the peace talks, Johnson determined to push forward. If he waited until after the election, the South Vietnamese would lose what little incentive they already had to come to the table. The situation was concerning, but not unsalvageable. Bunker still believed there was a fifty-fifty chance that Thieu would send a delegation to the peace talks.[27]

Johnson again convened a conference call with Humphrey, Nixon, and Wallace on October 31 to explain the announcement he was going to make that night. He told them that he would stop bombing North Vietnam—the weather in the north already precluded it, and he would redirect American airpower to the south and to Laos—and that Hanoi had agreed that South Vietnam would be "permitted to attend" the peace talks, while North Vietnam would be able to bring the National Liberation Front. He added that he wouldn't be saying anything about North Vietnam shelling South Vietnamese cities or respecting the demilitarized zone because it would trigger Hanoi's aversion to the idea that the United States was imposing conditions on it. "The talks will be held," Johnson assured them.

Johnson also had another message for the three candidates, though it was really only intended for Nixon. "Some of our folks are—even including some of the old China lobbyists—they are going around and implying to some of the embassies and some others that they might get a better deal out of somebody that was not involved in this. Now that's made it difficult and it's held up things a little bit. And I know that none of you candidates are aware of it or responsible for it," he said.[28]

Lest Nixon not realize who his message was intended for, Johnson reached out before his conference call to Senator Dirksen. Johnson issued a thinly veiled warning for the Senate minority leader to pass on to Nixon. "It's despicable, and if it were made public I think it would rock the nation," the president said. "Now, I rather doubt Nixon has done any of this. But there's no question folks for him are doing it. And quite frankly, we're reading some of the things that are happening." Later in the conversation, Johnson told the senator, "I really think it's a little dirty pool for Dick's people to be messing with the South Vietnamese ambassador and carrying messages around to both of them. And I don't think people would approve of it if it were known. So that's why I'm afraid to talk."[29]

Later that night, Johnson made a follow-up call to Humphrey. It was time to warn the vice president, at least to a certain extent, about what the Nixon camp was up to. Johnson didn't mention Chennault, but told Humphrey, "[T]he China lobby crowd's been in it some, and they've been telling them that Humphrey wouldn't stick with them at all, so they better put off and not let Johnson make any kind of peace because they'll do a much better job, they'll be much tougher." He said Nixon's people were responsible, but that he didn't know whether the candidate himself had anything to do with it. "Don't charge that he did. I can't prove it," Johnson said. But "Nixon's folks" had told the South Vietnamese, "[D]on't . . . let Johnson sell them out here at the conference table," and that "Humphrey's going to get beat and they'll have a bright future."[30]

Johnson wouldn't rely on warnings alone to deter Nixon from continuing to frustrate his efforts. He ordered the FBI to tap Chennault's home phone at the Watergate apartments and Diem's phone at the South Vietnamese embassy. He also ordered physical surveillance on the embassy so he would know who was coming and going. Finally, the White House told the FBI to follow Chennault wherever she went.[31] The next time Nixon, his underlings, or his allies used the Chennault pipeline to pass instructions on to Saigon, the Johnson administration would be ready to catch them in the act.

As scheduled, Johnson announced to the American people that night that he was halting all air, naval, and artillery bombardment of North Vietnam. "I have reached this decision based on the basis of the developments in the Paris talks. And I have reached it in the belief that this action can lead to progress toward a peaceful settlement." He also noted that, while the three presidential candidates had different positions on the war, they had been able throughout the campaign to present a "united voice" in support of American troops in Vietnam. "I hope, and I believe, that this can continue until January 20 of next year when a new president takes office. Because in this critical hour, we just simply cannot afford more than one voice speaking for our nation in the search for peace," Johnson said. "I do not know who will be inaugurated . . . but I do know that I shall do all I can in the next few months to try to lighten his burdens."[32]

The election was only five days away.

John Mitchell contacted Chennault that night. "'Anna, I'm speaking on behalf of Mr. Nixon. It's very important that our Vietnamese friends understand our Republican position and I hope you have that clear to them," Mitchell told her. Chennault later wrote that Mitchell sounded nervous as he asked, "Do you think they really have decided not to go to Paris?" She responded, "I don't think they'll go. Thieu has told me over and over again that going to Paris would be walking into a smoke screen that has nothing to do with reality."[33]

At 7:30 the next morning, the FBI's wiretap picked up a call from an unidentified woman to Diem at the embassy. "I thought you might have some information this morning. What is the situation?" the woman asked. "Just among us, something is cooking," Diem responded. Diem suggested that the woman come to the embassy to talk with him, which she said she would do as soon as she was finished with a "luncheon for Mrs. Agnew," the wife of Nixon's running mate, Maryland governor Spiro Agnew. Later that day, FBI agents watched Chennault walk into the embassy. She stayed for a half-hour.[34]

Thieu's private reluctance became public on November 2, three days before the election and two days after he'd ceased his opposition to Johnson's bombing halt, when he announced in a speech to South Vietnam's National Assembly that Saigon wouldn't participate in the Paris peace talks. His stated reason was that South Vietnam could not accept the National Liberation Front as a separate entity. Of course, the "our side/your side" formula meant he never would have had to. Johnson had actually emphasized this point in his October 31 speech, saying "their attendance in no way involves recognition of the National Liberation Front in any form."[35]

The Nixon camp had no illusions that Johnson would put tremendous pressure on Thieu to reverse his position on the peace talks. Chennault urged the South Vietnamese to stand their ground. The FBI intercepted a call that day from her to Diem in which Chennault said "her boss" had just called from New Mexico and asked her to pass along this message to Thieu: "Hold on, we are gonna win." She reiterated that her unidentified boss had said, "Hold on, he understands all of it."[36] That call represents the most damning piece of evidence against Chennault, if not against Nixon, who remained unidentified in the conversation.

Not long after learning of the New Mexico call that night, Johnson called Dirksen again. He was incensed by both the revelations about Chennault's conversations with Diem and by a Nixon campaign aide who'd anonymously told the press that Johnson had inaccurately assured them "that all the diplomatic ducks were in a row" before he announced the bombing halt, which made it appear that Johnson had intentionally misled Humphrey, Nixon, and Wallace about South Vietnam's willingness to come to Paris. "Now if Nixon keeps the South Vietnamese away from the conference, well, that's going to be his responsibility. Up to this point, that's why they're not there. I had 'em signed on board until this happened," Johnson fumed.

Johnson told Dirksen about the New Mexico call. "Now I'm reading their hand, Everett. I don't want to get this in the campaign. And they oughtn't be doing this. This is treason," he said. He told Dirksen to tell Nixon's camp to "quit playing with it," and Dirksen said he'd pass along the message that night. Johnson also told him to pass on an unmistakable threat. "You just tell them that their people are messing around in this thing and if they don't want it on the front pages, they better quit it," he said.[37]

Dirksen got in touch with Nixon, who followed up with a call to Senator George Smathers, a conservative Florida Democrat who'd served as a liaison between the White House and the Nixon campaign. Smathers called the president and relayed to him that Nixon had heard Johnson was preparing to "blast him with the accusation that he had connived with John Tower and Anna Chennault"—Johnson hadn't mentioned Tower to Dirksen, though Chennault spoke with him frequently regarding Nixon campaign business—to keep Saigon from coming to the conference table. As he had with Dirksen, Johnson explained that the South Vietnamese were told that they could get a better deal if they waited until after Nixon's victory, and restated his gripes about Humphrey giving encouragement to Hanoi by saying "he would stop the bombing, period, not comma, not semicolon, but period." Saigon had repeatedly agreed to Johnson's proposal throughout October, until "this came along."

Johnson said he didn't know how much Nixon knew about what was happening, but told Smathers, "I know what's been said and it's coming from his people, and I know what the [South Vietnamese] president's saying to his prime minister." Whoever was talking to the South Vietnamese on behalf of Nixon, Johnson said, told them that they'd get a better deal from somebody who wasn't involved in the war. "Somebody not involved is what they referred to as their boss. Their boss is the code word for Mr. Nixon," Johnson said.[38]

Not long afterward, Nixon called Johnson personally to discuss the allegations. He first mentioned that he'd just gone on *Meet the Press*, where he said he thought Saigon should come to the negotiating table, and that he'd do whatever Johnson felt was needed, either before the election or after, if he won, to help move the process along. Then he got to the heart of the matter. "Any rumblings around about somebody trying to sabotage the Saigon government's attitude, there's . . . absolutely no credibility, as far as I'm concerned," Nixon said. Johnson responded, "I'm very happy to hear that, Dick, because that is taking place." Later in the conversation, Nixon told Johnson, "I would never do anything to encourage . . . Saigon not to come to the table, because basically that was what you got out of your bombing pause."[39]

Geoffrey Hodgson, who covered the campaign for London's *Sunday Times*, later wrote that as soon as Nixon ended his conversation with the irate president, "Mr. Nixon and his friends collapsed with laughter. . . . It was partly in relief that their victory had not been taken from them at the eleventh hour."[40]

Their relief was justified. On November 5, 1968, Americans went to the polls to elect the thirty-seventh president of the United States. Nixon's lead had narrowed as the campaign came to a close, but Humphrey's momentum petered out after Thieu rejected Johnson's peace talks. Nixon won the day with 301 electoral votes to Humphrey's 191. In Saigon, a South Vietnamese official boasted, "We did it. . . . We helped elect an American president."[41]

The election may have been over, but Johnson wanted Chennault's mystery boss in New Mexico identified. Spiro Agnew had been in Albuquerque that day for a campaign stop, and the White House wanted the records of every phone call made from the campaign's plane. Because the call was placed on a Saturday, it would take a couple of days to get the information in a way that wouldn't draw much attention. Johnson wouldn't receive the information until after the election, and even then, only got it after personally calling Cartha "Deke" DeLoach, the third-ranking official at the FBI behind Hoover and Associate Director Clyde Tolson, and twisting his arm. "I want it only for the security of our country. I'm not going to make any of them public. I'm not going to involve any of them in politics," Johnson told him. "I do think that I've got to protect the security of the country, and I think that this is essential." DeLoach came through with the information Johnson wanted, but it wasn't very useful. Only five calls were made from the plane while it was in New Mexico, and none of those calls were to Chennault.[42]

But there was one possible lead buried among the seemingly irrelevant information. The same aide who was responsible for keeping Agnew informed about Vietnam had made a call while they were in Albuquerque to Robert Hitt, an official with the Republican National Committee, whose wife, Patricia, Chennault had initially suggested to Nixon as someone he could use to pass messages along to her.[43]

Chennault continued acting as an intermediary between Nixon and Saigon. On November 7, she contacted the South Vietnamese embassy to inform Diem that she had "made contact," and told an embassy secretary that she'd spoken to "him." Chennault had lunch with Diem that day, and called him again that evening to tell him, "The person she had mentioned to Diem who might be thinking about 'the trip' went on vacation this afternoon and will be returning Monday morning, at which time she will be in touch again and will have more news for Diem. . . . They are still planning things but are not letting people know too much because they want to be careful to avoid embarrassing you, themselves, or the present US government," according to a report to Johnson.[44]

Nixon's attitude toward South Vietnamese participation in the peace talks changed almost immediately after the election. On November 13, Chennault met with Mitchell, who now asked her to persuade the South Vietnamese to go to Paris. Chennault later wrote that she was "flabbergasted." "You must be joking," she told Mitchell. "Two weeks ago, Nixon and you were worried that they might succumb to pressure to go to Paris. What makes you change your mind all of a sudden?" Mitchell responded, "Anna, you're no newcomer to politics. This, whether you like it or not, is politics." Chennault said she refused and angrily stormed out of the room. Another Nixon aide later called and asked her to send word to Thieu that Nixon wouldn't be able to visit South Vietnam just yet, but that he wanted Saigon to send a delegation to the peace talks.[45]

Nixon's people also repeatedly impressed upon Chennault the importance of keeping their arrangement a secret, and she feared for her safety if she spoke to the press about what they'd done. After Nixon assumed office, he thanked Chennault at a White House event for the help she'd provided him during the campaign. "I've certainly paid dearly for it," she said. "Yes, I appreciate that. . . . I know you're a good soldier," Nixon responded. Chennault would come to loathe Nixon. When he died in 1994, she did not attend the funeral of the man she had helped elect president.[46]

Johnson had a serious decision to make now that the election was over. Nixon's intrusion into the White House's Vietnam diplomacy was a potentially criminal act under the 1799 Logan Act, which prohibits Americans from conducting their own freelance diplomacy with foreign powers.*

But Johnson didn't push for any prosecution of Nixon or Chennault, nor did he make the information public in any way. Johnson feared that if the public learned of Nixon's actions, it would severely undermine Americans' confidence in the incoming administration and would hinder Nixon's ability to negotiate an end to the war. When reporters came sniffing around the story, Johnson ordered his people to say nothing.[47]

Another major problem is that Johnson's evidence came from classified intelligence sources that he couldn't make public. As he'd said to George Smathers, "We know pretty well what goes to Saigon," but, "Obviously, it's so sensitive that

---

* See chapter 1 for more about the Logan Act.

I can't do anything about it except just say 'quit it.' I don't say that he is doing it. I don't know that he is."[48]

The lack of a smoking gun against Nixon was at least partly the handiwork of FBI director J. Edgar Hoover. Hoover, who was rooting for a Nixon victory, was hesitant to bug Chennault's phone due to her political status, and had simply ignored Johnson's order, tapping only Diem at the embassy. Had Hoover complied with the wiretap request on Chennault, it likely would have provided the proof that Johnson needed. Without it, the administration only had a few pieces of the puzzle. And the missing pieces shielded Mitchell's communications to Chennault and Chennault's with Diem.

Hoover, uncertain of his future in the Nixon administration, met with the president-elect on October 10. The FBI director told Nixon everything. In fact, he told him more than everything. Hoover lied to Nixon, telling him that Johnson had bugged his campaign phones and plane, and blamed DeLoach, who wanted the director's job. Hoover's secret files on every power player in Washington were the stuff of legend, and had for decades been a source of his immense power, ensuring his continued employment, no matter who was in the White House. With Nixon about to take power, Hoover's position was now secure. Considering what Nixon must have believed Hoover knew, how could he possibly replace the famed FBI director?[49]

Like Johnson, Humphrey had been concerned about going public without enough evidence. Bill Bundy, an assistant secretary of state for East Asia, had passed on some information to Humphrey at Johnson's request, and the vice president learned more fully after Johnson informed James Rowe, one of his campaign aides. After his accusatory call with Nixon on November 2, Johnson called Rowe, whose law partner, longtime Democratic insider Tommy Corcoran, was a close friend of Chennault. "Nixon picked up that ball right quick and started going into [Thieu] through your China lobby friend.... This damn little old woman, Mrs. Chennault, she's been in on it," he said. Johnson told Rowe not to tell anyone that they'd talked.[50]

Nonetheless, Rowe immediately went to Humphrey, who was infuriated. "By God, when we land I'm going to denounce Thieu. I'll denounce Nixon. I'll tell about the whole thing," he said on his campaign plane. "What kind of a guy could engage in something like this?" But Humphrey never believed he had enough information to go public, though he hoped that Johnson might take the initiative himself, telling the president that he might "want to consider that you have an obligation to disclose this to the American people."[51]

Despite his own reticence to do so, Johnson appears to have held Humphrey's trepidation against him. Journalist Jules Witcover wrote that former Johnson aide Joseph Califano told him, "Johnson thought Hubert had no balls, no spine, no toughness," and that his failure to use the information about Chennault "became an occasion for a lasting rift" between Johnson and his vice president.[52]

Humphrey certainly wondered if the election's outcome would've been different had he gone public with what he knew. In his memoirs, Humphrey described the flurry of thoughts that jostled around in his head after his defeat, one of which was, "I wonder if I should have blown the whistle on Anna Chennault and Nixon. He must have known about her call to Thieu. I wish I could have been sure. Damn Thieu. Dragging his feet this past weekend hurt us. I wonder if that call did it. If Nixon knew. Maybe I should have blasted them, anyway."[53]

The Chennault Affair may have had a far greater legacy, and a far uglier one, than a presidential candidate manipulating peace talks and potentially prolonging the war in Vietnam in order to win an election. It may have contained the seeds of Watergate itself. Author Ken Hughes wrote in his 2014 book *Chasing Shadows* that a 1971 decision by Nixon to burglarize the offices of the Brookings Institution to steal files on Johnson's bombing pause—which he told aides he wanted in order to blackmail Johnson with proof that the halt was intended to help Humphrey politically—was likely intended to eliminate evidence of his misdeeds in the Chennault Affair. Nixon's insistence on breaking into the Brookings Institution contributed to his decision to create his Special Investigations Unit, known to history as the "plumbers." One year later, they would break into the Democratic National Committee's office at the Watergate.[54]

There were no documents on the Chennault Affair to be found at the Brookings Institution. As Johnson prepared to leave the White House, he asked Walt Rostow to see to that. Johnson handed over the evidence that the FBI, CIA, and NSA had obtained over to Rostow. In June 1973, as per the wishes of the now-dead president he'd served, Rostow gave the "X envelope" containing all known evidence of the Chennault Affair to the head of the LBJ Presidential Library with a note that read, "The file concerns the activities of Mrs. Chennault and others before and immediately after the election of 1968. At the time President Johnson decided to handle the matter strictly as a question of national security; and, in retrospect, he felt that decision was correct." The file, Rostow said, was not to be opened for fifty years, in 2023.[55]

Johnson never disclosed what had happened in the waning days of the 1968 election. He wrote in his memoirs that he believed Thieu's refusal to join the peace talks was based on Saigon's belief that Nixon would win the election, and on concerns over Humphrey's September 30 speech. He only hinted at what he really knew and didn't mention Chennault's name. "I had reason to believe they had been urged to delay going to the Paris meetings and promised they would get a better deal from a Nixon administration than from Humphrey," he wrote. "I had no reason to think that Republican candidate Nixon was himself involved in this maneuvering, but a few individuals active in his campaign were."[56]

Accusations began swirling not long after the election, and would continue to do so for years. Clifford lamented in his 1991 memoirs that no "smoking gun" had ever definitively linked Nixon to Chennault's secret messages to Saigon. In the years since then, incriminating evidence has shed more light on the situation.

Rostow decided not to wait fifty years to open the "X envelope," which he did in 1995, the year after Nixon's death. The public wouldn't see the evidence until several years later, with the FBI's 1999 declassification of several key documents, including evidence of the New Mexico call and Chennault's November 7, 1968, call to Diem.[57]

Chennault omitted some key details in her 1980 memoir, *The Education of Anna*. She acknowledged providing the Nixon campaign with information she learned in Asia about South Vietnamese attitudes toward the peace talks, and Thieu's repeated insistences that negotiations would be nothing but a "smoke screen." But her account makes no mention of the New Mexico call or her meeting with Diem on November 11. The narrative jumps from her October 31 conversation with John Mitchell directly to Election Day.

In later years, Chennault was more candid about her involvement with authors and journalists. Jules Witcover writes that before Chennault's memoir came out, she told him that her communications with Saigon were done under instructions from the Nixon campaign. "The only people who knew about the whole operation . . . were Nixon, John Mitchell, and John Tower, and they're all dead. But they knew what I was doing. Anyone who knows about these things knows I was getting orders to do these things. I couldn't do anything without instructions."[58] Anthony Summers, the author of *The Arrogance of Power: The Secret World of Richard Nixon*, wrote in 2000 that Chennault told him that Mitchell and Nixon told her to inform Saigon that if Nixon was elected, South Vietnam would get "a better deal." "They worked out this deal to win the campaign. . . . Power overpowers all reason," Summers quotes Chennault as saying, adding that she described the entire operation as "very, very confidential."[59]

Undoubtedly, South Vietnam's boycott of the talks impacted the election. Humphrey had inched closer to Nixon in the polls as the campaign wore on, and an outbreak of peace, or at least the first concrete signs of it after four years of an increasingly unpopular war, could have made the difference. Though Nixon defeated Humphrey by more than one hundred electoral votes, he won the national popular vote by less than 1 percent. Humphrey would be far from the only person to wonder whether the race would have turned out differently had South Vietnam agreed to come to the table.

Whether the South Vietnamese would have acted any differently without the information they received from the Chennault pipeline is still a matter of debate. But regardless of whether Nixon is responsible for discouraging Thieu from participating in the peace talks, the Chennault Affair provides jarring insight into his character. The episode demonstrated Nixon's willingness to prolong a war at the cost of thousands of American lives for the sake the winning a presidential election.

Had Johnson or Humphrey "blown the whistle" on Nixon and Chennault, Americans would have learned a lot about the true nature of the president whose name is now synonymous with scandal and dirty tricks. That lesson would have to wait until Nixon's second term, when the Watergate scandal entered the annals of American history.

Chapter 12

Arms for Hostages and Money for Freedom Fighters

I don't believe that what we did, even under those circumstances, is wrong or illegal. I've told you I thought it was a good idea to begin with. I still think it was a good idea.

—Oliver North

There was a certain mind-set among the key figures in the scandal known as Iran-Contra that explains how the affair could have ever occurred. Among those who had emerged from the era of Vietnam, a war they viewed as being lost in Congress and the media instead of on the battlefield, there was contempt for those who were constrained by the laws of a Congress that refused to do what was best for America, and no small amount of pride in rising to occasions from which others shrank. According to that attitude, described by Arthur Liman, the US Senate's attorney during the congressional hearings on the scandal, it was "patriotic to lie to Congress, to circumvent checks and balances through covert actions, and to create the Enterprise to do what the CIA was not permitted to do."[1]

Surely, the key American participants in the Iran-Contra affair believed they were truly doing what was best for their country. The plight of the American hostages being held captive in Lebanon consumed President Ronald Reagan. "It just drove him crazy" that he just couldn't do anything to help them, his secretary of state, George Shultz, said.[2] And the fate of the Contras, the anticommunist "freedom fighters" battling Nicaragua's Sandinista regime, was an obsession of Reagan, one of many manifestations of his crusade against the evils of world communism.

Arming the Iranians violated a core principle of the Reagan administration. Federal law prohibited the United States from selling weapons to Iran, and Reagan had made it his mission to ensure that other countries followed America's lead in refusing to arm the terrorist regime. So too was arming the Nicaraguan

President Reagan confers with Caspar Weinberger, George Shultz, Ed Meese, and Don Regan to discuss public comments about the Iran-Contra affair that rocked his presidency. RONALD REAGAN PRESIDENTIAL LIBRARY

Contras who were fighting to overthrow the communist Sandinista regime a violation of federal law. Rather than emanating from Reagan, a champion of the freedom fighters since he took office, that prohibition came from a Congress that did not share the president's commitment to their cause.

But to key figures in the Reagan administration, the stakes were so high that the risks were worth the reward. Something had to be done to save the hostages, who were held captive by Iran's allies in Beirut. And the United States certainly couldn't allow another Cuba to take root on its doorstep. When Congress severely curtailed Reagan's ability to assist the Contras in 1985, the president replied, "The United States has a clear, undeniable moral imperative not to abandon those brave men and women in their fight to establish democracy and respect for human rights in Nicaragua."[3]

What we know as the Iran-Contra scandal was in reality two scandals that became intertwined and eventually uncovered in short succession. The first was the Reagan administration's arms sales to Iran, in violation of Reagan's own policies on providing weapons to terrorist states. The second was the diversion of leftover money from those sales to covertly fund the Contras in Nicaragua, in defiance of a Congress that had forbidden it. At the center of both affairs was Lieutenant Colonel Oliver North. From his staff position at the president's

National Security Council, North became the quarterback for both the Iran and Contra initiatives, which he eventually merged into one volatile operation known to those on the inside as the "Enterprise."

The roots of the scandal were in Nicaragua, borne of Reagan's determination to aid the Contras' fight against communism in the Western hemisphere. After overthrowing the American-backed dictatorship of Anastasio Somoza Debayle in 1979, the Sandinistas became increasingly autocratic and communist. The Sandinista regime embraced the Soviet Union and Cuba, and began aiding the communist insurgency in El Salvador. When Reagan took office, he quickly lent his assistance to the counterrevolutionary, or Contra, forces.

Many in Congress were still haunted by the ghosts of Vietnam, distrustful of the Contras, appalled by their human rights record and suspicious of CIA activities in Nicaragua. Congress responded with a series of laws known as the Boland amendments, named for Congressman Edward Boland, which restricted the Reagan administration's ability to support the freedom fighters. Revelations of CIA activities, such as the placing of magnetic mines in Nicaraguan harbors, which had damaged several ships, and the creation of a manual for the Contras convinced Congress to strengthen those restrictions over time.

The first Boland amendment, passed in December 1982, barred the Department of Defense or the CIA from "using any funds for the purpose of overthrowing the government of Nicaragua" during the 1983 fiscal year, though it included a loophole allowing those agencies to assist the Contras for other purposes. Congress in late 1984 passed the most restrictive version yet of the laws that bore Boland's name, which prohibited the CIA, Department of Defense, or any other "entity engaged in intelligence activities" from spending money to assist the Contras' military operations.

That wasn't Reagan's policy. In 1984, the president told his national security advisor, Robert "Bud" McFarlane, to "keep the body and soul of the Contras together."[4] But as money for the Contras started to run dry that year, Reagan's exhortation to maintain the Nicaraguan resistance as a fighting force became a harder directive to follow. Handcuffed by Congress, Reagan and members of his administration scrambled to find ways to continue aiding the anticommunist insurgency in Nicaragua.

Reagan and his cabinet understood the sensitive nature of the pro-Contra efforts. During a June 1984 meeting, McFarlane expressed his hope that everyone present would keep quiet about what they'd discussed. Reagan put an exclamation point on the need for secrecy, telling his cabinet, "If such a story goes out, we'll all be hanging by our thumbs in front of the White House until we find out who did it."[5]

For the job of keeping the Contras together, "body and soul," McFarlane turned to North. The lieutenant colonel occupied a unique position at the NSC, largely separated from the rest of the staff and answerable only to the national security advisor. And at the suggestion of CIA director William Casey, North in the summer of 1984 turned to Richard Secord. A retired major general from the US Air Force, Secord operated several businesses with Albert Hakim, an Iranian exile who had fled the country shortly before the overthrow of Reza Shah Pahlavi. To carry out North's mission, Hakim and Secord started a new venture called Lake Resources. Using a worldwide network of contacts, Secord could circumvent the Boland amendments that had tied the hands of the CIA and funnel weaponry to Contra leader Adolfo Calero, allowing the freedom fighters to continue their war against the Sandinistas. Hakim and Secord dubbed the system, which was effectively a clandestine arm of the NSC, the "Enterprise."[6]

If the Reagan administration wanted to arm the Contras, it first needed the money to do so. And it needed money that didn't pass through US government hands. The first plan to circumvent the Boland Amendment was to raise money through private individuals. And the most successful of those figures was a Republican operative named Carl "Spitz" Channell, who raised more than $12 million through two tax-exempt organizations he'd created.* The fund-raising effort was far more successful on paper than it turned out to be in reality. Only about $2.7 million of the money Channell raised ended up in the Contras' hands.[7]

Another option was using third-party countries to provide the support that America couldn't. Stanley Sporkin, the CIA's general counsel, concluded that the administration could, in fact, legally get third-party countries to provide money for the Contras, as long as no American funds were involved in the transaction or reimbursement and the United States gave no inducements to the third-party nations. In the spirit of that finding, McFarlane in June 1984 dropped a hint to the Saudi ambassador to the United States that "this impending loss would represent a significant setback for the president." The ambassador, Prince Bandar bin Sultan, responding by pledging $1 million a month to the Contras, funds that would last into 1985.[8]

The flow of money continued after a White House meeting between Reagan and Saudi king Fahd bin Abdulaziz Al Saud in February 1985. Reagan had impressed upon the king that "fellow democracies"—a term unlikely to have ever been used before or since to describe Saudi Arabia's oppressive monarchy—had a common interest in stopping the spread of communism. The king responded by offering $2 million a month for another year. In all, the Saudis contributed $32 million to the Contras' cause.[9]

---

* Channell would later face prosecution for his freelance fund-raising efforts. The congressional committees that investigated the Iran-Contra scandal determined that raising money for the Contras from private donors was permissible, but Channell broke the law by using tax-exempt organizations to do it. He was sentenced to two years of probation after pleading guilty to defrauding the government with the scheme.

But by April 1985, the $34 million that McFarlane and North had raised for the Contras—North managed to secure another $2 million from Taiwan—was perilously close to running out. The Enterprise needed a new source of revenue.[10]

As North developed his pipeline to the Contras, the other half of the operation started to take shape on the other side of the globe.

Reagan took office in the aftermath of the 1979 revolution that saw Iran hold dozens of Americans hostage for 444 days. Since assuming the presidency, Reagan had increasingly clamped down on arms sales to Iran, both from the United States and from other countries. In 1983, Reagan launched a program called Operation Staunch, a diplomatic effort aimed at pressuring other countries not to sell weapons to Iran.

Partly as a result of those efforts, Iran in 1985 was a country badly in need of arms. Since 1980, it had been embroiled in a debilitating war against Saddam Hussein's Iraq, which had invaded Iran in response to the revolution that brought Ayatollah Ruhollah Khomeini's Shiite theocracy to power. Thanks to the American arms embargo, it was sorely lacking the weapons it needed to fight the invading Iraqis.

Reagan's rhetoric toward the Iranians left no doubt as to where he stood on the issue, or at least it appeared so publicly. In June 1985, on the eve of his administration's first arms-for-hostages deal, Reagan described Iran—which had been officially designated as a state sponsor of terrorism in January 1984—as "a new, international version of Murder, Incorporated." Reagan proclaimed, "America will never make concessions to terrorists. To do so would only invite more terrorism. Nor will we ask nor pressure any other government to do so."[11]

But despite the mutual acrimony between the United States and Iran, some American officials had begun contemplating their country's need for friends in Tehran. In the zero-sum game of the Cold War, any gain by the Soviet Union was a loss for America, and the Russians appeared to be in a position to dramatically increase their influence in Iran, which was critically situated between the Soviets' southern border and the Persian Gulf. Khomeini wouldn't be around forever, and when the power struggle to succeed him commenced, US officials wanted friendlier leadership to emerge, pro-American rather than pro-Soviet, with which they could do business.

A May 1985 memo to Casey from Graham Fuller, a CIA intelligence officer for the Near East and South Asia, suggested a new line of thinking toward Iran. "The [United States] faces a grim situation in developing a new policy toward Iran. . . . In bluntest form, the Khomeini regime is faltering and may be moving toward a moment of truth; we will soon see a struggle for succession. The [United States] has almost no cards to play; the USSR has many," the memo read. Fuller endorsed a "bolder—perhaps even riskier—policy" that would give the United States a greater voice in Iran.[12]

Along those lines, McFarlane's staff outlined a proposal for the bold new policy that Casey and the CIA were advocating. On June 17, McFarlane sent Shultz and Defense Secretary Caspar Weinberger a proposal for enhancing America's ties to moderate factions within Iran in order to head off a possible Soviet power play and put the United States in a position to make inroads with any post-Khomeini regime. McFarlane suggested that the United States encourage its allies "to help Iran meet its import requirements" in order to make Soviet trade and assistance less attractive. "This includes provision of selected military equipment as determined on a case-by-case basis," the proposal read.[13]

The two cabinet officers did not share McFarlane's enthusiasm for the plan. Shultz supported the idea of reconsidering America's policies toward Iran, but not in the way McFarlane suggested. He believed the NSC's National Security Decision Directive exaggerated both the amount of anti-regime sentiment among the Iranian populace and the threat the Soviet Union posed in the country. And he certainly didn't want the United States selling weapons to Tehran. Weinberger's initial response was as far from a glowing endorsement as he could get. "This is almost too absurd to comment on," Weinberger wrote in a memo to his assistant Colin Powell after the meeting. "It's like asking Qadhafi to Washington for a cozy chat."[14] Weinberger told McFarlane that he too was interested in curbing Moscow's influence in Iran, but that the United States should under no circumstances lift restrictions on arms sales, which he insisted would be "totally inconsistent" with American policy. Of the top officials who saw McFarlane's proposal, only Casey approved, writing that he "strongly endorsed the thrust" of the proposal.[15]

McFarlane's plans included the potential sale of arms to Iran, but the possibility of receiving hostages in return had not yet come into play. That idea came to McFarlane via, of all people, the Israelis. Though viewed as a pox on the world by the Islamist regime in Tehran, Israel didn't want to see Iran steamrolled by Hussein, and hoped to bring some equilibrium to the war raging between two of its enemies. Furthermore, Israel was enticed by the possibility of rebuilding its relations with Iran, which had been a rare ally in the Middle East during the shah's reign.

Israel's proposal originated with Manucher Ghorbanifar, an Iranian expatriate living in Paris, where he worked in the import-export business.[16] Ghorbanifar, often referred to in NSC correspondence by the more manageable moniker "Gorba," was a living spy-novel stereotype who might well have been conjured up by Tom Clancy or John le Carré. An alleged former operative for SAVAK, the fearsome secret police of the shah's prerevolutionary regime in Iran, Ghorbanifar was a consummate con man and wheeler-dealer who had been a CIA source for years, but had recently been deemed so untrustworthy and disreputable that the agency had issued a rare "burn notice" in 1984, urging its employees and other US intelligence agencies not to do business with him.[17] McFarlane deemed him "one of the most despicable characters I have ever met."[18] But he was well-connected enough to still have access to top officials in Tehran, putting him in the perfect position to make himself the middleman between Iran, Israel, and the United States.

Ghorbanifar had first concocted the idea of trading American arms for Hezbollah hostages in early 1985 with Saudi businessman Adnan Khashoggi. In Khashoggi's retelling of the story—there are multiple versions—the two had originally met in Hamburg, Germany, where they were introduced by Roy Furmark, a businessman with ties to Casey, at an auction for Persian rugs that had belonged to the shah. Afterward, the three went to a restaurant, where they discussed the state of affairs in Iran while Ghorbanifar explained the ongoing struggle between the various factions vying for power in Tehran.

There are several versions of what transpired during that meeting, as well as what occurred afterward. Whichever story is true, Khashoggi used his connections to reach out to two Israeli arms dealers, Yaacov Nimrodi and Adolph "Al" Schwimmer, an advisor to Prime Minister Shimon Peres, and pitched a plan he and Ghorbanifar had hatched to arrange arms sales to the Iranians, using Israel as an intermediary. Iran was in desperate need of TOW antitank missiles—the acronym stands for tube-launched, optically tracked, wire-guided—that would be effective against the upgraded Soviet tanks recently deployed by the Iraqis. The Israelis were intrigued by the possibility of rebuilding their ties to Iran, and brought the proposal to Peres. But there was a problem. TOWs were American equipment, and the prime minister was unwilling to sell them to the Iranians without American approval.[19]

To Ghorbanifar and Khashoggi, the ultimate prize was the profits from the arms sales and the lucrative business they could do with Iran if the United States would lift its sanctions. But they needed a greater incentive than their own personal finances to convince Israel and the United States to go along with the plan. The potential of improving relations with an isolated and hostile Iran by arming "moderates" within the country would not necessarily be enough to convince the Americans. So Ghorbanifar added another incentive: If the United States would sign off on the proposed TOW missile sale, he could use his connections in Iran, which he portrayed as extensive and reaching into the highest echelons of the regime, to secure the release of William Buckley, the CIA station chief in Beirut who had been kidnapped a year earlier.[20]

The final piece that brought the three sides together was Michael Ledeen, a think-tank analyst and former State Department official who served as a consultant to McFarlane. The national security advisor sent Ledeen to Israel in May 1985 to meet with Peres to discuss the possibility of obtaining Israeli intelligence on Iran. During their discussion, in which they agreed to continue exploring intelligence-sharing opportunities, the prime minister raised Ghorbanifar's suggestion that the Israelis sell American arms to allegedly moderate officials in Iran, and asked Ledeen to pass the request along to McFarlane.[21]

Initially, nothing more came of Ledeen and Peres's discussion than McFarlane's June 17 memo to Shultz and Weinberger. The intelligence-sharing plan stalled after Shultz—who hadn't been informed of Ledeen's trip, and had only learned of it from the American ambassador in Tel Aviv—took umbrage with McFarlane for working diplomatic channels behind the State Department's back.[22]

But the Israelis were still interested. Hoping to revive Ghorbanifar's proposal, Israel sent David Kimche, a top-ranking official at the Israeli Foreign Ministry, and former deputy director of the Mossad, Israel's intelligence agency, to Washington to meet with McFarlane. In a July 3, 1985, meeting, Kimche told McFarlane of the proposal from "an Iranian official endorsed by the Government of Israel" who wanted to establish a "dialogue" with the United States. In exchange, they may be able to arrange the release of the seven Americans being held prisoner in Lebanon by Hezbollah. McFarlane, skeptical of the intentions of the Iranians whom the Israelis were dealing with, rejected Kimche's overture.[23]

However, another meeting one week later between Ledeen and Schwimmer convinced McFarlane to reconsider. More appropriately, it was the information Schwimmer provided about a meeting the Israelis had had two days earlier that had persuaded him. For his and Khashoggi's meeting with the three Israelis—Kimche, Nimrodi, and Schwimmer—Ghorbanifar had produced Hassan Karoubi, whom he presented as a well-connected, high-ranking Iranian official, an ayatollah even, who wanted to build relations with the United States as a hedge against the Soviets. The Iranians, Ledeen reported to McFarlane, wanted to establish a dialogue with the West and believed they could bring about the release of the hostages in Lebanon. But to do so, they'd need to show some progress of their own in the form of one hundred TOW missiles. An ebullient Ledeen wrote McFarlane after his meeting with Schwimmer, "The situation has fundamentally changed for the better. . . . This is the real thing and it is just wonderful news."[24]

Based on the information Schwimmer had provided to Ledeen, along with his belief that the Israelis were dealing with influential Iranian leaders—he'd been told that Ghorbanifar was an advisor to the Iranian prime minister—McFarlane was sold. On July 13, McFarlane cabled Shultz, telling the secretary of state that the Iranians with whom the Israelis were dealing wanted to establish better relations with the United States, and believed they could obtain the release of the hostages. "But in exchange they would need to show some gain," he wrote. Specifically, he said, they wanted one hundred TOW missiles.[25] In his response, Shultz urged caution and aired a number of concerns. But he ultimately recommended that "we should make a tentative show of interest without commitment. I do not think we could justify turning our backs on the prospect of gaining the release of the other seven hostages and perhaps developing an ability to renew ties with Iran under a more sensible regime."[26]

McFarlane was far keener on making a commitment than Shultz was. It was time to bring the proposal to the president himself. McFarlane visited Reagan on July 18 at Bethesda Naval Hospital, where the president was recovering from abdominal surgery to remove a cancerous growth. At Reagan's bedside, McFarlane explained the proposition to the president and Don Regan, his chief of staff.[27] Reagan's only mention of the meeting in his diary was a July 18 entry in which he wrote that McFarlane had stopped by and explained that two members of the Iranian government wanted to start talks with the United States. He wrote that he planned to send McFarlane to meet with the Iranians in a neutral country.[28] McFarlane later gave multiple accounts of exactly what he told the president, while Regan recalled that the national security advisor had spoken of an Israeli contact who may be able to bring about "a breakthrough in reaching elements in the Government of Iran," and that it "could lead to some help in the hostage situation."[29] Regan's recollection was that the president told McFarlane, "Go ahead. Open it up."[30]

At an August 6, 1985, meeting of the White House's National Security Planning Group, McFarlane pitched Kimche's plan to Reagan and his inner circle. Shultz and Weinberger continued to voice their opposition, while McFarlane and Regan were more favorably disposed. Like so many incidents from the Iran-Contra affair, contradictory accounts of the meeting are rampant. Many of the participants left with different impressions of what the president had or hadn't approved. Weinberger walked out of the meeting believing that the plan was "finished" and wouldn't be brought to fruition. However, Reagan called McFarlane several days later and gave him the go-ahead.[31]

Before they could arrange a deal with the Iranians, they had to figure out how to finance it. The Israelis didn't want to give up their weapons until they got the money from Iran, and the Iranians didn't want to give Israel any money before they received their weapons. The solution was for Khashoggi to provide Ghorbanifar with a $1 million "bridge loan" that would cover the costs until the money and weapons changed hands.[32] With the financing in place, the first arms deal of the Iran-Contra affair occurred on August 20, 1985, when the Israelis shipped ninety-six TOW missiles to Tehran. One week later, the Iranians paid $1,217,410, and Ghorbanifar paid Khashoggi back for the $1 million loan he'd provided.[33]

After more than a week, the United States hadn't gotten back any hostages, and Ghorbanifar told the Israelis that he was uncertain whether that would change. Iran's Revolutionary Guards, Ghorbanifar claimed, had seized the missiles intended for the moderates. But "with just a few more TOWs this whole unpleasant problem will be solved." At Ghorbanifar's insistence, the Israelis sent 408-plus more TOW missiles to Iran on September 15, for which the Iranians paid another $5 million into Ghorbanifar's Swiss account.[34]

The Americans had expected seven hostages, a group that would include the ever-important Buckley. Instead they got one, and it wasn't the captured CIA station chief.* However, it was progress. Benjamin Weir, a Presbyterian missionary, was released on the same day that Iran received the second shipment of missiles. The plan hadn't worked as well as McFarlane had hoped—but it had worked.[35]

Where the first shipment had gone relatively smoothly, the second attempt to send weapons to Iran was an unqualified fiasco. The plan was for Israel to ship the Iranians eighty HAWK antiaircraft missiles, which they would unload in Lisbon and reload onto a non-Israeli plane for the flight to Iran. To hide the true nature of the lethal cargo, they would claim on the flight manifest that the weapons were oil-drilling equipment.

The "horror story" began unfolding on November 18 when Israeli defense minister Yitzhak Rabin informed McFarlane that there was a problem with landing the plane in Lisbon. Schwimmer hadn't gotten the clearance he needed from the Portuguese to unload the weapons in Lisbon, and they were hesitant to grant such a troubling request at the last minute. North, who had thus far been at the fringes of the Iran operation, was now plunged directly into the affair. His solution to the problem lay with Secord, who already had strong ties to the Portuguese defense manufacturer who'd been providing weapons for the Contras. Secord arrived in Lisbon on November 19 to work out a deal.

Secord's proposal was to use one of his Lake Resources planes that was already in Lisbon preparing for a resupply flight to the Contras in Nicaragua. But there was resistance to the idea coming from multiple corners. North was reluctant to redirect a plane that had already been scheduled to make a direct flight from Lisbon to Nicaragua to deliver weapons to the Contras. The Portuguese too were squeamish about allowing an arms-laden flight to fly from Lisbon to Iran, and wanted American acknowledgment of the plane's cargo to clear them of potential future accusations that they'd violated Operation Staunch. "So help me, I have never seen anything so screwed up in my life," Admiral John Poindexter, the deputy national security advisor, exclaimed after North explained the problem to him.[36]

North and Duane "Dewey" Clarridge, the head of the CIA's Latin America division, found another way that didn't require the acquiescence of the skittish Portuguese. Clarridge contacted a Frankfurt-based proprietary airline run by the CIA, which had been used for the first TOW shipment to Iran in August, and arranged for it to make the flight to Tehran.[37]

---

* Unbeknownst to the United States, Buckley was already dead.

On November 23, a CIA plane arrived in Tel Aviv to pick up the weapons. From there, problems mounted to an almost comedic degree. The Boeing 707—Clarridge had asked for a 747—could only fit eighteen HAWK missiles, far fewer than the eighty the Iranians were expecting. North and Secord planned to land the plane in Turkey en route to Iran, but after the Turks started inquiring about the cargo, they improvised and sent the plane instead to Cyprus, which required it to defuel in Tel Aviv because the fully fueled aircraft was too heavy to land on the designated runway, causing yet another delay. After landing in Cyprus, the pilot was forced to create a phony flight manifest to get back out of the country, and he had to take evasive actions to get the plane through Turkish airspace as it made its way through Iran.[38]

The Iranians were not happy with what arrived in Tehran on November 25. Instead of the eighty HAWK missiles they'd expected, they received only eighteen, and several days late to boot. And they had not even received the correct missiles, according to their own HAWK expert. They'd wanted newer-generation HAWKs capable of shooting down high-altitude aircraft, not the obsolete, low-altitude version they'd received.* To top everything off, the missiles still bore the blue Star of David that identified them as Israeli equipment.[39] An enraged Iranian prime minister Mir-Hossein Mousavi called his emissary in Geneva who had helped to arrange the deal to deliver a blistering rebuke and demand that the money the Iranians had transferred to Ghorbanifar's Swiss bank account be returned.[40]

The Iran deal wasn't a CIA operation, and the arms-for-hostages trades would remain within the NSC's purview until the end. But the CIA had been drawn in too deeply to not look out for its own interests. Clarridge and North hadn't gotten approval from the CIA's higher-ups to use the agency's aircraft, and when word reached Langley, they weren't happy about it. John McMahon, Casey's deputy director at the CIA, learned of the incident on November 25, while Casey was in China, and turned to Sporkin to draft a retroactive presidential finding—in Poindexter's opinion, a CYA, or "cover your ass" move by the agency—to authorize the CIA's prior activities.[41]

By signing the presidential finding, Reagan acknowledged that he had "been briefed on the efforts made by private parties to obtain the release of Americans

---

* Author Malcolm Byrne writes that there was disagreement among the Israelis as to whether the Iranians had in fact received the wrong missiles. According to Byrne's book, *Iran-Contra: Reagan's Scandal and the Unchecked Abuse of Presidential Power*, Nimrodi believed the wrong missiles had been sent, for which he blamed the official who oversaw the loading operation, while Menachem Meron, the director general of the Israeli Ministry of Defense, said the right missiles had been sent, but that the Iranians didn't understand that the updated versions didn't fly any higher than the previous versions. The only difference, Meron said, was that the newer versions had improved software that made them more accurate and easier to control (Byrne, 103).

held hostage in the Middle East," and had authorized the CIA to provide assistance for such endeavors. The finding made no mention of restoring relations between the United States and Iran or of bolstering a "moderate" faction in Tehran. There it was in plain English: arms for hostages. And the finding covered "all prior actions taken by US Government officials in furtherance of this effort."[42] However, that was not the most curious aspect of the finding. Under the Intelligence Oversight Act of 1980, Reagan was required to provide timely notification to Congress of such covert actions. But previous findings on covert actions had leaked from the congressional committees that oversaw them, and Casey wasn't anxious to see the same happen with the Iran finding. Though federal law required congressional notification, in cases where the president didn't do so, it said only that he "shall provide a statement of reasons" for withholding the information.[43] Thus, "because of the extreme sensitivity of these operations," the finding instructed the director of central intelligence "not to brief the Congress of the United States . . . until such time as I may direct otherwise."[44]

Casey approved Sporkin's draft, and on December 5, his first day as McFarlane's replacement as national security advisor, Poindexter brought the presidential finding to Reagan. After the president signed the pivotal document, Poindexter put the only copy in his office safe.[45]

Poindexter ascended to the position of national security advisor following McFarlane's resignation. At the time, Poindexter was not yet well-acquainted with either the Iran or Contra operations. But his assistant North was a critical player in both. And Poindexter's decision to remove Ledeen from the Iran operation made North's role as the only American with a direct connection with the Israelis and Ghorbanifar all the more critical. North and Poindexter already had an easy way to communicate about the operations without other prying eyes at the NSC getting wind of it. In August 1985, while Poindexter was still McFarlane's assistant, he had set up a channel through which he and North could exchange computer messages through Professional Office System, or PROFS, an early e-mail system used by the NSC, while bypassing the other staffers who would normally have access to such communications. They referred to the communication channel with a name that would epitomize North's role in the quasi-rogue operation that was Iran-Contra: Private Blank Check.[46]

At the same meeting where Reagan signed the first presidential finding on the arms-for-hostages transaction, Poindexter informed the president that another deal was in the works. Two days later, Reagan and most of his inner circle, sans Casey and Vice President George H. W. Bush, met in the residential quarters of the White House to discuss it. McMahon, Shultz, and Weinberger aired their objections to the operation, emphasizing the Arms Control Export Act's prohibition against arming terrorist regimes and questioning whether there were really any moderates in Tehran to begin with. Weinberger also worried that the deal would leave the United States open to blackmail by the Iranians, or anyone else who knew the details. But Reagan's mind was on the hostages. The president said he could answer to charges that what they were doing was illegal, but not to accusations that "big strong President Reagan" passed on an opportunity to get America's hostages back because "I wouldn't break the law." "The American people will never forgive me if I fail to get these hostages out over this legal question," he said. He also worried that allowing the hostages to spend another Christmas in captivity would make him look powerless. "They can impeach me if they want," said Reagan, who joked that "visiting hours are Thursday."[47]

Not a single hostage had won his freedom in exchange for the bungled November arms shipment. But that debacle paved the way for perhaps the most important turning point in the operation: the diversion of funds from Iranian arms sales to the Contras. The decision that North later joked would "put the hyphen in Iran-Contra" was made in December 1985, when North told several Israeli officials that he planned to divert the extra money from the overpriced weapons to the Nicaraguan freedom fighters.[48] The Israelis had deposited $1 million in Lake Resources' bank account in Geneva to cover the logistics of what Secord expected to be five flights to deliver the HAWKs to Iran. The botched operation, however, had only cost about $200,000. Rather than return the leftover money, North decided to use it to help the Contras.[49]

The idea of using future proceeds from the Iranian arms sales to assist the Contras made another leap forward in January 1986, as North planned the upcoming arms sales to Iran. That there would be "residuals" from the marked-up weapons sales was a given, and North and Amiram Nir, an advisor to Peres, had already discussed the possibility of using the excess money to replace the 504 TOW missiles that Israel had sent to the Iranians in the fall of 1985.[50] Several weeks later, in late January 1986, Ghorbanifar raised the issue with North during a meeting in London. Ghorbanifar took North into a bathroom and, as North later testified, "suggested several incentives to make [the] February transaction work, and the attractive incentive for me was the one he made that residuals could flow to support the Nicaraguan resistance." Ghorbanifar also broached the subject in front of Nir and Secord during the meeting, which was recorded, laughing as he explained what they could do with the money they would get from the deal. "We do everything. We do hostages free of charge; we do all terrorists free of charge; Central America for you free of charge; American business free of charge," he said. "Everything free." North told Ghorbanifar he was interested in "some future opportunity for Central America."[51]

North thought the diversion of residuals from the arms sales to the Contras a "neat idea," and brought it back to Poindexter.[52] In his February report to Poindexter on the London meeting, North told the national security advisor that he thought he'd found a way to provide funds to the Nicaraguan resistance by using money from the Iranian arms transactions. Poindexter gave his verbal approval, and the diversion was born. From that point onward, the Iranians would be overcharged for their weapons to provide not only for reimbursement costs and Ghorbanifar's profits, but also to sustain the Contras as well.[53]

In the aftermath of the December 7 meeting, Poindexter decided that he wanted a new presidential finding authorizing the Iran operations. Poindexter sent the draft to Reagan, along with a memo describing a plan in which Israel would arrange for the shipment of four thousand TOW missiles to "Western-oriented Iranian factions." Unlike the previous deliveries, which came from the Israelis' own supply, the new plan called only for Israel to arrange the shipment, which the CIA would purchase directly from the Department of Defense and deliver to Iran through an "agent." If no hostages were released after the first one thousand missiles were delivered, the rest of the shipment would be halted. The finding itself stated that the US government would "facilitate efforts by third parties and third countries"—the term "third parties" implicitly referred to Secord and the Enterprise—to provide "moderate elements" in Iran with weapons for the purposes of establishing a friendlier Iranian government, obtaining intelligence, and securing the release of American hostages. Reagan signed the finding on January 17, 1986, again with the stipulation that Casey not report the CIA's activities to Congress until he instructed him to do so.[54]

With the president's authorization on paper, Poindexter and North got to work on the new arms shipment. The first five hundred TOWs were shipped to Iran on February 17, with five hundred more following ten days later. When North returned from a meeting in Frankfurt with Mohsen Kangarlou, a deputy to Iran's prime minister, McFarlane sent him a computer message praising the yeoman's work he'd been doing. "Well done—if the world only knew how many times you have kept a semblance of integrity and gumption to US policy, they would make you Secretary of State. But they can't know and would complain if they did—such is the state of democracy in the late 20th century," he wrote. North, focusing intently on the mission at hand, responded that they were headed in the right direction. "With the grace of the good Lord and a little more hard work we will very soon have five [American citizen hostages] home and be on our way to a much more positive relationship than one which barters TOWs for lives," he replied.[55]

However, those hostages would not be forthcoming, at least not as a result of the one thousand missiles North had shipped to Tehran in February 1986. What North had achieved with the February TOW shipment was another payoff for the Contras. Of the $10 million that Ghorbanifar deposited in Secord's Swiss account to close out the deal, only $3.7 million was needed to pay back the Defense Department. Much of the remainder went directly to the Nicaraguan resistance.[56]

In early April, North wrote a fateful memorandum, presumably for Poindexter, that would later become the "smoking gun" proving that he had funneled money from the Iranian arms sales to the Contras. The infamous "diversion memo" of April 4, 1986, spent several pages describing the upcoming plans to sell four thousand TOW missiles to Iran. Seemingly as an aside, at the end of the memo, North unambiguously explained how the excess funds would be used: $2 million to replace the original TOW missiles that Israel had sent to Iran the previous fall, and $12 million that would "be used to purchase critically needed supplies for the Nicaraguan Democratic Resistance Forces." The weapons, he wrote, would allow the Contras to continue fighting until Congress appropriated new funds.[57]

During North's February meeting with Kangarlou, the Iranian had upped the ante in the arms-for-hostages negotiations by asking not for TOWs or HAWKs, but for Phoenix missiles, a top-of-the-line weapon so new and advanced that the United States wouldn't even sell them to Israel. By the time North and two others had met with Ghorbanifar in Paris on March 7, the middleman had a more-reasonable request. The Iranians wanted spare parts for HAWKs they already owned. They also wanted a meeting with the Americans in Tehran, Ghorbanifar informed them. As an inducement, Ghorbanifar again insisted that the excess funds from the sale could be diverted to the Contras.[58]

Nearly everyone involved was looking to make money from the next arms deal. As demonstrated by the diversion memo, North was now actively eyeing the deal as a moneymaker for the Contras. The cost of the HAWK parts, the TOWs, and shipping costs for the entire delivery was pegged at nearly $5.4 million. But the prices were now being dramatically marked up to ensure profits for Ghorbanifar, money for the Contras, and reimbursement costs for the weapons. The price that was ultimately set for the Iranians by Ghorbanifar, Nir, and North was $15 million.[59]

Now out of the administration, McFarlane stayed involved in the Iran operation, keeping in touch with North and Poindexter through the PROFS system. As part of that continued involvement, it was decided that McFarlane would lead the secret May 1986 mission to Tehran. Reagan personally signed off on McFarlane's participation, as did Shultz, despite the secretary of state's specified concerns that the plan was wrong, illegal, and left the president "way overexposed."[60]

Throughout the series of negotiations that took place in Frankfurt, London, Paris, and Washington, the Americans had been adamant that all remaining hostages must be released, and that they didn't want to turn over the weapons and spare parts to the Iranians until that demand was met. "None of this half shipment before any [hostages] are released crap. It is either all or nothing," Poindexter wrote North. The problem of just how to accomplish that goal would plague the McFarlane delegation once it arrived in Iran.[61]

Using false Irish passports, the delegation of McFarlane, North, Nir, CIA official George Cave, the agency's former Tehran station chief from the days of the shah, and NSC staffer Howard Teicher arrived in Tehran on the morning of May 25. The trip got off to a rocky start as the consequences of their lack of preparation or planning meetings with the Iranians became apparent. McFarlane had brought a pallet of spare HAWK parts with him, whereas the Iranians had expected him to bring half the shipment with him. The delegation received disappointing news as well when the Iranian officials they met with informed them that little had been done yet to secure the release of the hostages in Beirut. When the Iranians explained that they'd told their superiors that half the shipment would arrive with the delegation, McFarlane burst out, "I have come from the USA. You are not dealing with Iraq. I did not have to bring anything. We can leave now!"[62]

McFarlane initially refused to attend a meeting the next day because he would be dealing with the subordinates of the high-ranking Iranian officials he'd expected to sit down with. "As I am a minister, I expect to meet with decision-makers. Otherwise, you can work with my staff," he told one of the Iranians. To placate the disgruntled envoy, McFarlane's Iranian host produced an advisor to Akbar Hashemi Rafsanjani, the speaker of Iran's parliament, for a meeting that evening.[63]

On the third day of the trip, the improved atmosphere of the meetings took another downturn. The Iranians informed the McFarlane delegation that the hostage-takers in Beirut had some conditions for the release of the Americans, and none boded well for the conclusion of any deals. They wanted Israel to withdraw from the Golan Heights and southern Lebanon, Israel's allies in Lebanon to release Shiite prisoners, Kuwait to release terrorist prisoners it held, and for the United States to pay for the cost of keeping its own citizens as hostages. It was a jarring reminder that Iran was only the ally of the hostage-takers, and did not necessarily have as much control as they would have liked, or as Ghorbanifar had insisted they had.[64]

The problem became apparent as the meetings broke down. Ghorbanifar had been telling everyone what they wanted to hear, and now that they were face-to-face, it was clear that nobody was actually getting what they'd been promised. The Iranians had been promised that half the HAWK parts shipment would be delivered up front before any hostages were freed, while the Americans were led to believe they would get the near-immediate release of all remaining hostages. Because the Americans had relied on the fast-talking middleman's assurances and hadn't held any preparatory meetings with the Iranians, neither side seemed to be aware of what the other expected. It seems highly unlikely that the trip ever would have occurred had both sides understood the reality of the situation.[65]

On the evening of May 27, the Iranians informed the delegation that the hostage-takers had withdrawn their demands, with the exception of their insistence that Kuwait release its Shiite prisoners. The Americans responded with a proposal in which the hostages would be released by 4:00 a.m. the next morning, and the entire shipment of spare parts would arrive in Iran six hours later. The Iranians balked at the proposal, saying more time and work were needed before the hostages could be released.[66]

At that point, North sprang into action with a plan to break the impasse. The proposal he crafted called for the United States to dispatch a plane carrying the shipment of spare parts, with the flight slated to arrive in Tehran at 10:00 a.m. on May 28. If the hostages weren't released by 4:00 a.m., the flight would turn around midair without delivering the HAWK parts. "McFarlane is not pleased" with the plan, North reported to the Iranians, but was willing to give it a shot. McFarlane conveyed the plan to Poindexter, who brought it to Reagan. The president gave the order for the plane to take off from Israel.[67]

After several extensions of the 4:00 a.m. deadline, the Iranians still had not procured the hostages by the morning of May 28. McFarlane and the rest of the delegation stood next to their airplane, ready to depart for the United States, as the Iranians pleaded for more time. When McFarlane gave his final deadline of 9:30 a.m., the Iranians told him that it might be possible to secure the release of two hostages immediately, but that two others would take more time. "You are not keeping the agreement. We are leaving," McFarlane said. The delegation boarded the plane and took off at 8:55 a.m.[68]

The failure of the Tehran trip left the future of negotiations with the Iranians in doubt. In his post-trip briefing with Reagan, McFarlane suggested shutting down the initiative entirely. Meanwhile, North and Poindexter started exploring other options for freeing the hostages, including a $10 million ransom and a risky rescue mission of the type that had failed spectacularly when President Jimmy Carter had attempted to rescue the Americans held captive during the Iran hostage crisis.[69]

The Iranians had also grown wary of future deals, especially after they discovered a microfiche listing the 1985 prices for the weapons and parts they were buying and learned that they'd been paying about six times the actual price of the equipment from Ghorbanifar and the Americans. Iran's trust in the United States was perilously low, and the revelations about the overcharging stoked their fears that they were being cheated.[70]

It was Ghorbanifar, who had caused so much chaos during the Tehran trip, who brought the arms-for-hostages negotiations back from the dead. He and Nir had discussed ways to facilitate the release of another hostage in the wake of the disastrous Tehran trip. And on July 26, Ghorbanifar's machinations bore fruit when Hezbollah released Father Lawrence Jenco, a Catholic Relief Services director who'd been held prisoner in Lebanon since January 1985.[71]

For Ghorbanifar, failing to facilitate another arms deal was not an option, perhaps even a matter of life and death, as he'd insisted was the case. He'd borrowed $15 million from Khashoggi, with $8.5 million ending up in Secord's Swiss account, and Ghorbanifar was anxious to cut another deal so he could pay the Saudi businessman. In addition, Ghorbanifar was growing fearful that the Americans were planning to cut him out of future deals. Those concerns were not unfounded, as Casey and others had for months been exploring ways to remove him from the equation.[72]

Despite their mounting concerns, both sides were hopeful that the arms deals would continue, and Jenco's release appeared to be the boost they needed to get past the disappointment of recent events. True to form, Ghorbanifar had secured Jenco's release by promising the Iranians a deal that the Americans had not yet agreed to. His plan called for a sequential exchange of weapons, money, and hostages in which the Iranians would eventually receive the 240 HAWK parts they still needed, 39 electron tubes and 2 radars for the missile system, and 1,000 more TOWs. In exchange, the Americans would receive three hostages.[73]

North urged Poindexter to bring the deal to Reagan for approval on July 29, by which time Ghorbanifar had already received the first $4 million payment from the Iranians that he needed to repay Khashoggi. Included in North's memo was a warning that if Ghorbanifar failed to repay his creditors, who had a $22 million life insurance policy on him, he would probably be killed. North also said that Hezbollah would probably kill an American hostage to demonstrate their displeasure if the deal didn't go through. Reagan signed off on the deal, and several days later, the 240 HAWK parts arrived in Tehran.[74]

Ghorbanifar and North hashed out the remaining details at an August 8 meeting in London. The proposal they agreed on called for the Iranians to pay $15.5 million for two more shipments of 500 TOWs, additional HAWK parts, and two radar systems, for which the Americans would receive three hostages and Buckley's body. It was the last time North and Ghorbanifar would meet.[75] *

Jenco's release had proven Ghorbanifar's usefulness at a time when the Americans were more convinced than ever that he was wholly dispensable. But that didn't stop North and Poindexter from trying to find a new channel of communication that would allow the Americans to deal directly with the Iranians and cut out the problematic Ghorbanifar. In late August, Hakim and Secord met in Brussels with Ali Hashemi Bahramani, a nephew of Rafsanjani. It was the first

* Ghorbanifar would resurface as an American intelligence asset in the aftermath of the September 11, 2001, terrorist attacks. After reaching out to his old contact Ledeen and offering intelligence on Iranian activities in Afghanistan, Ghorbanifar met with Pentagon officials in Rome in December 2001 and June 2002. The meetings ended after the State Department and CIA objected to the involvement of the old Iran-Contra figures ("How a Shady Iranian Deal Maker Kept the Pentagon's Ear," *New York Times*, December 7, 2003).

of several meetings that they, North, and others would hold with Bahramani in their efforts to open a "second channel" with the Iranians.[76]

With the second channel opening up, Ghorbanifar looked to be on his way out. Reagan had approved the second channel, despite North's concerns that the president would terminate the entire operation in response to the September kidnapping of two more Americans in Beirut. North began planning for what would turn out to be the final shipment of arms to Iran.

North, Cave, Hakim, and Secord arrived in Frankfurt on October 6 to work out the details of the next arms shipment. The proposal, a nine-point sequential transaction, called for 1,500 TOWs and additional HAWK parts, in exchange for at least one, and preferably two, hostages. The Americans would do what they could to secure the release of Shiite prisoners in Kuwait and southern Lebanon, while the Iranians pledged to continue their efforts to free the remaining American hostages. On October 28, the first shipment of 500 TOWs arrived in Tehran in one of Secord's planes.[77]

On November 2, David Jacobsen became the third and final American hostage to be freed through the secret Iran operation. It would not remain a secret for much longer. By the time North returned from Beirut with Jacobsen, Casey had a sobering piece of advice for him: "You ought to go out and get a lawyer."[78]

For reasons completely unrelated to each other, the interconnected Iran and Contra initiatives began to unravel almost in tandem in late 1986. On October 5, the Sandinistas shot down a plane from Secord's Corporate Air Services that had been carrying supplies for the Contras. The pilot and copilot were killed, but one crew member, an American named Eugene Hasenfus, survived. Through documents and other information from the plane, the Sandinistas were able to tie Hasenfus to the CIA and Corporate Air Services. The White House denied that Hasenfus's plane had been working for the government in any capacity, despite the evidence uncovered by the Sandinistas.[79] But North was quick to grasp the implications. "This only confirmed what many congressmen and journalists already knew: that while large segments of our government were explicitly prohibited from actively supporting the Contras, several of us, including the President, were quietly involved in a host of other efforts to keep them alive," North later wrote. Once Hasenfus was captured, North realized it was only a matter of time before the entire operation became public knowledge.[80]

The Contra resupply program had been threatening to burst into the public's view for months by the time of the Hasenfus incident. In June 1986, the *Miami Herald* published an article headlined, "US Found to Skirt Ban on Aid to Contras," that detailed the private fund-raising efforts that North had spearheaded, though it didn't mention him by name. That changed in August when the *Washington Post* became the first newspaper to print North's name in conjunction with the behind-the-scenes efforts to assist the Contras. Other articles in other newspapers quickly followed. As a result, North found himself in front of a congressional committee, where he falsely denied the fund-raising efforts or violations of the Boland Amendment.[81] * On September 25, North received another blow when the government of Costa Rica announced the discovery of a covert airstrip that had been used for Contra operations in their southern front against the Sandinistas. The new Costa Rican president, Oscar Arias Sanchez, had discovered the airstrip in June when a resupply plane had gotten stuck in the mud during the rainy season, and ordered that it be shut down.[82]

But Iran would truly be the first shoe to drop. The full extent of the Contra resupply operation would stay hidden until the subsequent investigation brought it into the light. It was not a nervous Ghorbanifar, who'd threatened to go public in response to the second channel, or blackmail from a dissatisfied Iran, as Weinberger had worried would happen, that brought the operation into the open. It was the squabbling between the rival factions in Iran, whose power struggle had seemed so promising to the Americans at the start of the operation. On October 15, radical university students in Tehran, inspired by a cleric who had been arrested on Khomeini's orders, distributed millions of leaflets exposing McFarlane's trip to Iran several months earlier. Not long afterward, a small newspaper in Lebanon wrote about the trip, which was followed by a more-in-depth article on November 3 by another Lebanese paper, *Al-Shiraa.*[83]

The press quickly seized upon the shocking information, and Reagan's first instinct was to deflect. During a November 7 press conference with Jacobsen and his family, the press barraged Reagan with questions about the alleged arms sales to Iran. Reagan refused to answer questions about the allegations, saying he couldn't do so without endangering the lives of other hostages who hadn't yet been released. "Why not dispel the speculation by telling us exactly what happened, sir?" one reporter asked him. "Because it has to happen again and again until we have them all back," the president replied. Jacobsen joined Reagan's pleas to put a lid on the Iran questions for the sake of the hostages. "In the name of God, would you please just be responsible and back off?" Jacobsen exploded at the reporters.[84]

On November 13, ten days after the *Al-Shiraa* story, Reagan spoke out for the first time about the allegations. He believed the media was "trying to create

* Amid the unraveling of the Contra operation, Congress lifted some of the Boland Amendment's restrictions on the United States providing humanitarian aid to the Nicaraguan resistance. The State Department's reengagement in the affairs of the Contras led to perhaps the most bizarre episode of the entire operation. In August 1986, Assistant Secretary of State Elliott Abrams convinced the sultan of Brunei to provide $10 million for the Contras, to be deposited into Secord's account. But either North or his secretary accidentally transposed two numbers in the account number that North gave to Abrams, and the money ended up in the account of a wealthy Swiss businessman. (Report of the Congressional Committees, 352-353.)

another Watergate," and wanted to set the record straight.[85] So Reagan went public, though to the minutest degree he could. In a televised address, the president acknowledged some arms shipments to Iran, but said it was "utterly false" that the United States had sent weapons as ransom for American hostages. Reagan said he'd authorized small amounts of "defensive weapons and spare parts" to Iran in the interest of forging a better relationship with the Islamic Republic, an initiative he compared to Richard Nixon's opening to China in 1971. The size of the deliveries was so modest, he falsely stated, that "taken together, they could easily fit into a single cargo plane." At the same time, Reagan said, his administration had emphasized to the Iranians that it must oppose terrorism, with the most significant step it could take in that direction being the release of the American hostages held by its allies. "We did not—repeat—did not trade weapons or anything else for hostages, nor will we. . . . We have not, nor will we, capitulate to terrorists."[86]

Despite the plethora of evidence that subsequently proved that Reagan knew exactly what he was getting into when he approved the arms sales in 1985, the president was adamant, both in public and in private, that the operation was primarily about cultivating a relationship with Iran and moderate officials within the country. "The president's speech convinced me that Ronald Reagan still truly did not believe that what had happened had, in fact, happened," Shultz later said.[87] Lawrence Walsh, who would soon be appointed as independent counsel to investigate the scandal, said Reagan broke the cardinal rule of covert operations: He started to believe his own cover story. "He had persuaded himself that he had not been trading arms for hostages; he had merely tried to establish a friendly relationship with Iranian moderates," Walsh would write years afterward.[88]

Reagan's own words belied the inaccurate explanation he gave to the American public. In a December 7, 1985, diary entry about a "complex plan which could return our 5 hostages & help some officials in Iran who want to turn that country from its present course & on to a better relationship with us," Reagan described the proposal as calling for Israel to sell weapons from its own stockpile to Iran. "As they are delivered in installments by air our hostages will be released. The weapons will go to moderate leaders in the army who are essential if there's to be a change to a more stable govt. We then sell Israel replacements for the delivered weapons."[89]

A month later, Reagan wrote of the "highly convoluted process" by which Israel would free "some 20 Hizbullahs [*sic*] who aren't really guilty of any bloodletting. At the same time they sell Iran some 'Tow' anti-tank weapons. We in turn sell Israel replacements & the Hisballah [*sic*] free our 5 hostages. Iran also pledges there will be no more kidnappings. We sit quietly by & never reveal how we got them back."[90]

The president's denials would continue, even as he revealed more information about the Iran initiative. At a November 19 press conference, Reagan faced the media and acknowledged that eighteen months earlier, he had authorized limited exceptions to the embargo against Iran in order to achieve the goals of curbing Iranian terrorism, improving the relationship between the two countries, helping to end the Iran-Iraq war, and securing the hostages' release. But Reagan emphatically denied that his administration had traded arms for hostages. The "isolated and limited exceptions" to the arms embargo against Iran were meant only as a "signal of our serious intent." And to avoid "the widespread but mistaken perception that we have been exchanging arms for hostages," Reagan said he was halting all further sales to Iran. Reagan falsely asserted that there had been no Israeli shipments to Iran, and repeated his insistence that the shipments were going to select individuals within Iran, not the Iranian government itself, though preceding events, still unknown to the public, had poked plenty of holes in that rationale as well. And he insisted that the arms sales were well within the law, because the president had the authority to waive provisions of the 1977 National Security Act in the interests of national security.[91]

With the scandal now spinning out of the administration's control, Reagan on November 21 ordered Attorney General Edwin Meese to look into the matter. What Meese found would rock the nation.

Poindexter had promised cooperation, and gathered his relevant documents. As he prepared to hand over his documents to Paul Thompson, the NSC's general counsel, he came across one he found a bit too incriminating. When Poindexter came across the retroactive December 5, 1985, "cover your ass" finding for the CIA in his files, he ripped it up in front of Thompson, saying it wasn't important. Unfortunately for Poindexter, he was unaware that the CIA had a copy as well, and his destruction of evidence was later discovered. "I decided that it would be politically embarrassing to the President at this point because it would substantiate what was being alleged," Poindexter later explained.[92]

Something far more damning awaited Meese's investigators than the presidential finding that Poindexter destroyed. North and an aide had begun shredding and altering incriminating documents after Hasenfus's plane was shot down. Even while Meese's aides sat at North's desk going over paperwork, he brazenly walked past with handfuls of documents destined for the shredder.[93] But an important piece of evidence remained: the infamous "diversion memo" of April 4, 1986. "For all my celebrated shredding skills, I had missed that one," North quipped in his memoir.[94]

Thus far, Meese's inquiry was focused exclusively on Iran. That all changed when Assistant Attorney General William Reynolds and John Richardson, Meese's chief of staff, discovered the diversion memo. Reynolds muttered to himself under his breath as he read North's explanation of the planned diversion for the arms sale of spring 1986. He quietly passed it across the desk to Williamson, then put it into his file. They brought the news to Meese over lunch that day. Meese's response was succinct. "Oh shit," he said.[95]

Reagan's diary entry for November 24 describes a two-hour meeting where Meese and Regan told him of the "smoking gun" that the attorney general had found. The president wrote that on "one of the arms shipments" the Iranians had been charged marked-up prices, with the Israelis putting the difference in a secret bank account. "Then our Col. North (NSC) gave the money to the 'Contras.' This was a violation of the law against giving the Contras money without an authorization by Congress. North didn't tell me about this. Worst of all John Poindexter found out about it & didn't tell me," Reagan wrote. "This may call for resignations."[96]

More accurately, it called for one resignation and one firing. Poindexter submitted his resignation to the president. Shortly before Reagan announced Poindexter's resignation, Secord called him and urged him not to resign, to "force the president to step up to the plate and take responsibility for his actions." Poindexter told him, "It's too late. They're building a wall around him."[97]

North, who'd long accepted the possibility that he may be the fall guy if the affair ever became public, didn't get the opportunity to step down on his own. He learned of his termination when he watched Meese and Reagan's November 25 press conference on television. Meese laid the blame solely at North's feet, telling the world, "The only person in the United States government that knew precisely about this, the only person, was Lieutenant Colonel North."[98]

Meese's declaration was, of course, completely untrue. Poindexter, at least, was well aware of North's activities, which he had sanctioned. But contrary to his later acknowledgments, Poindexter initially told Meese only that he knew North was "up to something," but that he "didn't look into it."[99] He used a similar line on Chief of Staff Regan, whom he told, "I had a feeling that something bad was going on, but I didn't investigate it and I didn't do a thing about it. . . . I really didn't want to know. I was so damned mad at [House Speaker] Tip O'Neill for the way he was dragging the Contras around I didn't want to know what, if anything, was going on. I should have, but I didn't."[100]

Poindexter's later testimony would shed more light on what he knew and when he knew it, as would the discovery of as-yet-undisclosed evidence, including thousands of computer messages he and North had deleted. Poindexter had erased more than 5,000 messages, and North, another 736. However, the White House kept backup tapes going back to November 1985, and those messages would become a key part of the investigative record.[101]

Outside of the national security advisor, questions about who else knew about the diversion—George H. W. Bush, William Casey, deputy CIA director

Robert Gates, and other prominent figures—would be harder to definitively answer, and in some cases remain so to this day.

The big question mark was Reagan. Did the president know that members of his administration were illegally arming the Contras? Had he approved, or at the very least, condoned the diversion?

Meese and Regan, who purportedly informed Reagan after the discovery of the diversion memo, were insistent that the president could not have known. "Nobody who saw the president's reaction that afternoon could believe for a moment that he knew about the diversion of funds before Meese told him about it. He was a picture of a man to whom the inconceivable had happened," Regan later said.[102] Meese testified that Reagan was "shocked" to learn of the diversion, and Regan described the president's reaction as "deep distress." Even a professional actor, Regan said, would have trouble feigning the horror that Reagan displayed. "This guy I know was an actor, and he was nominated at one time for an Academy Award, but I would give him an Academy Award if he knew anything about this when you watched his reaction to express complete surprise at this news on Monday the 24th. He couldn't have known it," Regan testified to the congressional committees.[103]

Poindexter was adamant that he'd never informed the president, telling the congressional committees that the omission was a deliberate decision to give Reagan plausible deniability if the diversion ever went public. The national security advisor said Reagan's policy of support for the Contras was clear, and he believed he "understood the president's thinking on this." Had he brought the diversion plan to Reagan, Poindexter said he believed the president would have approved it. But knowing how controversial it would be, "I made a very deliberate decision not to ask the President so that I could insulate him from the decision and provide some future deniability for the President if it ever leaked out. . . . On this whole issue, the buck stops with me."[104]

Among those who have voiced their skepticism at Reagan's alleged ignorance of the Contra side of the Enterprise were adversaries North and Walsh. "Given President Reagan's policies and directives, I have no doubt that he was told about the use of residuals for the Contras, and that he approved it. Enthusiastically," North wrote. Walsh believed that Reagan must have authorized the operation, if for no other reason than that the Iranian arms sales wouldn't have been worth it without the inducement of raising money for the Contras. "Except for financing the Contras, the policy produced rewards too small and entailed risks too high to justify its continuation," Walsh wrote.[105]

Three separate inquiries quickly began. Congress convened a select committee to investigate the matter. Reagan appointed a commission comprised of former Republican senator John Tower, former Democratic senator Edmund Muskie, who'd served as President Jimmy Carter's last secretary of state, and former National Security Advisor Brent Scowcroft, who'd served under President Gerald Ford. And in response to a request from Meese, a federal appellate court appointed Walsh, a former federal judge and prosecutor, as independent counsel.

Some members of the administration even fretted over the possibility that Reagan could face impeachment. The revelations had shocked both sides of the aisle in Congress, and the Democrats, who already controlled the House of Representatives, had won the Senate in the November 1986 election.

As far as North was concerned, impeachment was an impossibility beyond imagination. "In the fall of 1986, President Reagan was still so popular that he and Nancy could have invited Fidel Castro to a testimonial dinner at the White House for Ayatollah Khomeini without suffering overwhelming political damage. People would have shaken their heads, they would have wondered, but Ronald Reagan would have remained popular," he wrote in his memoir.[106]

Whatever prospect of impeachment may have loomed over Reagan effectively vanished when he was absolved by Poindexter's testimony. Some of the committee's Democrats were skeptical of Poindexter's claims. But whether Reagan knew or not, the "wall" was now around him.

Poindexter's testimony was ultimately more consequential, but it was North who stole the show. The lieutenant colonel was the star witness, and his testimony was a blockbuster television event. He owned up to many of the allegations against him, but insisted that he was far from the rogue, one-man operation he was being portrayed as. "I did a lot of things, and I want to stand up and say that I'm proud of them," North told the committee. But, he added, "I have never carried out a single act, not one, in which I did not have authority from my superiors."[107]

North testified that he didn't realize Reagan was unaware of the diversion—this was prior to his assertion in his 1992 memoir that he believed the president had known—until he asked Poindexter point blank on November 21, in the midst of Meese's inquiry, and the national security advisor told him that the president was unaware. "Did you ask him: Admiral Poindexter, why did you not discuss this with the President?" Liman, the Senate committee's lead counsel, asked North. Playing to his audience, the lieutenant colonel was a good soldier to the end.* "I'm not in the habit of questioning my superiors. If he deemed it not to be necessary to ask the President, I saluted smartly and charged up the hill. That's what lieutenant colonels are supposed to [do]. I have no problem with

* Apparently, even the television coverage inadvertently helped North play to the audience. Steven Spielberg later pointed out to Liman something that had caught his film director's eye during the hearings. The camera shots of the committee members that showed them looking down on North from their elevated positions was known to directors as the "villain's angle," Spielberg explained, while the shots of North, looking up at the interrogators above him, is known as the "hero's angle" (Byrne, 290).

that," North replied. "I have no problem with that. I don't believe that what we did, even under those circumstances, is wrong or illegal. I've told you I thought it was a good idea to begin with. I still think it was a good idea."[108] North insisted that the Boland Amendment's prohibition against US intelligence agencies providing military aid to the Contras did not apply to the NSC.[109]

There was no shortage of Americans who agreed with North, and amid the drama of the congressional hearings, he became their hero as "Olliemania" swept the nation. North had broken the law, and then broke it again during the attempted cover-up. But to many Americans, North was a patriot being crucified by Congress and the media for serving his country with honor. In his memoir, North recounts wearing a hat and sunglasses on a family outing to Disney World in the hope that he wouldn't be recognized. The celebrity NSC staffer was nonetheless spotted while leaving Space Mountain, and the crowd converged on its hero and North spent the next forty-five minutes signing autographs.[110]

The committee majority's final report of November 1987 lambasted the Reagan administration for "secrecy, deception, and disdain for the law" by a small group of senior officials who "believed that they alone knew what was right." It heaped the majority of the blame on North and Poindexter, with some for McFarlane as well. Though the committee determined that the evidence was "inconclusive" as to whether Reagan himself knew of the diversion, it ascribed a great deal of blame to the president as well. Even if Reagan didn't know what his national security advisor was doing, the committee reported, he should have. "The President created or at least tolerated an environment where those who did know of the diversion believed with certainty that they were carrying out the President's policies," the final report read. That environment created a situation in which Fawn Hall, North's secretary who had aided him in his cover-up, believed that "sometimes you have to go above the written law," and NSC officials believed their "rightful cause" justified lying to Congress because "Congress is to blame for passing laws that run counter to Administration policy." "What may aptly be called the 'cabal of the zealots' was in charge," the committee concluded.[111]

As Congress began its hearings, Walsh began his own investigation. Walsh viewed the congressional committees as a "rival operation," and his concerns were well founded.[112] He worried that if Congress allowed figures like North and Poindexter to testify with immunity, it would risk scuttling his own cases later on. That immunized testimony eventually overturned almost every conviction Walsh obtained in the Iran-Contra scandal.

It's a cliché of political scandals that the cover-up is often worse than the crime. And in the case of Iran-Contra, it was the cover-up that landed some of the key figures in court. Walsh would eventually secure indictments against eleven people, many of them for their attempts to hide their involvement in the scandal.

The biggest prizes were North and Poindexter. North had been indicted on twelve counts, and in May 1989, he was convicted of three related to altering or destroying documents related to the Iran and Contra initiatives, as well as using $9,000 in Enterprise funds to put a security gate at his house. To the chagrin of North's critics, Judge Gerhard Gesell sentenced him to only two years' probation, $150,000 in fines, and 1,200 hours of community service, with no prison time.[113]

In April 1990, Walsh secured perhaps an even greater victory when a jury convicted Poindexter on five obstruction charges related to the destruction of documents and lying to Congress. Unlike North, Poindexter received a prison sentence. With his concurrent six-month sentences for each of the charges, Poindexter became the first Iran-Contra defendant, as well as the first high-level White House staffer since Watergate, to be sentenced to prison for crimes committed while in office.[114]

Walsh's fears about the congressional committee came to pass three months later when the US Court of Appeals for the District of Columbia overturned North's conviction. From the beginning, Walsh knew it would be imperative for him to insulate himself and his case from the congressional proceedings, where the witnesses gave immunized testimony that wouldn't be admissible in court. In the end it didn't matter what Walsh had done. A three-judge panel ruled that the trial court judge hadn't done enough to ensure that the prosecution witnesses' statements were not colored by North's congressional testimony. Walsh ultimately dropped the case against North after the Supreme Court declined to hear an appeal.

A similar fate awaited Poindexter. The appellate court overturned his conviction in November 1991, again ruling that witness testimony had been tainted by the congressional hearings. North himself had testified during the trial that he was having trouble differentiating between his own memories and Poindexter's testimony to the committee. Again, the Supreme Court refused to take the case.

The reversal of North and Poindexter's convictions were discouraging, but they weren't the end of the case. Walsh procured indictments against a dozen Iran-Contra figures and won convictions against many of them, including McFarlane, Hakim, and Secord. And just days before the 1992 presidential election, Walsh convinced a grand jury to indict Weinberger, who'd stood with Shultz in opposition to the Iran initiative, for obstruction of justice, perjury, and making false statements.

However, Walsh's investigation would go no further. As he prepared to depart the White House after losing his reelection to Bill Clinton in 1992, Bush used the time-honored practice of issuing the most controversial of a president's pardons on the way out the door. Clarridge and the newly indicted Weinberger would not go to trial, while McFarlane and several others would see their convictions wiped clean. Certainly one must wonder whether Clinton inadvertently struck the final blow against the Office of the Independent Counsel. Presidents generally save their most controversial pardons for their last days in office, and it seems unlikely that a president with a fresh four-year term ahead of him would have been willing to cash in so much political capital on such a controversial slate of pardons.

With the last of the Iran-Contra figures officially off the hook, the six-year investigation was effectively over. A disappointed Walsh didn't mince words. "I think it was the last card in the cover-up."[115]

Epilogue

A Right to Know

I'm neither traitor nor hero. I'm an American.

—Edward Snowden

No modern figure more perfectly exemplifies the theme of this book than Edward Snowden.

Snowden's story is by now familiar to most Americans. On June 5, 2013, the *Guardian*, a British newspaper, announced to the world that the ultra-secretive National Security Agency had convinced a Foreign Intelligence Surveillance Act court to force Verizon to turn over information about millions of customers' phone calls on a daily basis. It was an unheard-of level of government intrusion on the daily lives of ordinary American citizens.

The information in the article was shocking on its own. But it was only the first drop in a torrent of revelations that would follow about the existence and details of the NSA's Orwellian surveillance network that had mutated from an ostensible anti-terror safeguard into an all-encompassing dragnet of random Americans' electronic communications.

It wouldn't be until several days after the *Guardian*'s initial bombshell that the newspaper's whistle-blower source would reveal himself as a twenty-nine-year-old NSA contractor who would instantaneously become the most controversial figure in the United States, reviled as a traitor by many, hailed as a hero by others.

Snowden believes strongly in the righteousness of his cause. Nonetheless, America's most famous whistle-blower rejects both labels. "I'm neither traitor nor hero. I'm an American," he said.[1]

Try as he might, Snowden will likely never shake those descriptions. Whichever way (if either) one views Snowden, his impact on political discourse in the United States has been undeniable. His disclosures to journalist Glenn Greenwald and documentary filmmaker Laura Poitras shook the country to its foundations and became the catalyst for the debate that has raged ever since about how much power the government should have in the name of national security, and how much privacy American citizens are entitled to in the electronic age.

That debate had been simmering since 9/11 and the War on Terror opened the door to a massive expansion of the American surveillance state. But Snowden amplified it in a way that previous revelations hadn't. In doing so, Snowden joined the pantheon of America's great whistle-blowers and leakers, a list that includes Daniel Ellsberg, of Pentagon Papers fame,* and Bradley (now Chelsea) Manning, the soldier who gave hundreds of thousands of military and diplomatic secrets to WikiLeaks.

And, like Ellsberg, Manning, and others before him, Snowden's acts picked at an old scab on Americans' collective psyche by forcing them to confront a question that had not been so prominent in their minds since the Pentagon Papers first graced the pages of the *New York Times*: Is it right to reveal the United States' most closely guarded secrets if you believe the country has lost its way? Are you betraying your country by showing its secrets to the world, or are you a patriot for telling Americans things you believe they have a right to know?

Snowden must have seemed an unlikely candidate to become an exiled whistle-blower and fugitive when, driven by the patriotism that gripped so many Americans after 9/11, he joined the army in 2004 with the intention of fighting in Iraq, a war that he believed at the time to be a virtuous cause. By the time he was discharged following a training accident in which he broke both of his legs, Snowden had soured on the cause he'd enlisted in. "I wanted to fight in the Iraq war because I felt like I had an obligation as a human being to help free people from oppression," Snowden explained to Greenwald and Poitras. "Most of the people training us seemed pumped up about killing Arabs, not [about] helping anyone."[2]

A job as a security guard at a secret NSA facility at the University of Maryland gave Snowden his introduction to the intelligence world. The tech-savvy Snowden parlayed that into a job with the CIA, which in 2007 sent him to Geneva under diplomatic cover as part of America's delegation to the United Nations. It was while working in Geneva that Snowden started entertaining doubts about the things his country was doing.

One incident that Snowden described as particularly significant in contributing to his disenchantment was a CIA agent's attempt to recruit a Swiss banker who could provide information from the country's notoriously secretive banking system. The agent got the banker drunk and encouraged him to drive home. As intended, the banker was arrested for drunk driving, at which point the agent swooped in and offered to help—in exchange, of course, for the information he needed. "Much of what I saw in Geneva really disillusioned me about how my

---

* See chapter 9 for more on Ellsberg and the Pentagon Papers.

government functions and what its impact is in the world," he says. "I realized that I was part of something that was doing far more harm than good."[3]

Snowden said he began to consider the possibility of leaking while in Geneva, but held off for two reasons: He was concerned that the CIA intelligence he had access to would endanger the people it was about, and was hopeful that newly elected President Obama would follow through on his campaign promises of transparency. In the latter, he was grossly disappointed, as Obama continued and even expanded the invasive programs he wanted ended.[4]

But it was his work with Dell as a contractor for the CIA that finally convinced Snowden to take drastic action. In that job, he saw the extent of the NSA's surveillance network and the way it had partnered with telecommunications companies. As the world had become more wired and human interaction became more electronic, the companies that facilitated those communications had joined forces with the government to ensure that none could remain private.[5]

That revelation was the tipping point for Snowden, who began downloading documents that would demonstrate the pervasiveness of the NSA's surveillance apparatus. After transferring to Hawaii from Maryland, Snowden said, he took a pay cut to join defense contractor Booz Allen Hamilton so he could obtain the last documents he needed before he went public.[6]

By May 20, 2013, Snowden was ready. That day, he hopped on a flight to Hong Kong. From there, he arranged to meet with Greenwald and Poitras. Neither knew anything about Snowden aside from the fact that he had access to a stunning collection of information that he was prepared to hand over.* He'd already given them a taste, including the Verizon order from the FISA court and a document outlining the Prism program, through which the NSA had tapped directly into the servers of nine major telecommunications companies. But there was so much more to come.

The trove of data and documents that Snowden handed over to Greenwald and Poitras, reported in a steady, piecemeal fashion that Greenwald described as a "journalistic version of shock and awe," revealed a surveillance state run amok.[7] By using XKeyscore, the NSA could track with impunity the information gleaned through its Upstream collection program, including searching through e-mails, checking browser histories, and monitoring "nearly everything a typical user does on the Internet," with no authorization needed.[8] With the Boundless Informant program, the NSA was able to closely track and quantify how much information it was accumulating, a capability the agency had told Congress it didn't have.[9] Snowden revealed extensive spying by the United States on its allies, triggering

* Snowden first reached out to Greenwald on December 1, 2012, under the pseudonym Cincinnatus, promising information and urging Greenwald to start using an e-mail encryption program, even sending tutorial videos. Greenwald brushed him off and didn't learn Cincinnatus's true identity until he was in Hong Kong meeting with Snowden (Greenwald, 7–8, 82).

condemnation from around the world. And many of America's allies had their own secrets laid bare, such as a similar program in Britain with which the country was surveilling and collecting information about its citizens' phone and Internet activity.[10] The Pentagon claimed Snowden downloaded 1.7 million files, which would make it the largest theft of classified information in American history.[11]

Snowden was insistent that he not keep his identity a secret. He wanted the world to know why he'd done what he did. "I have no intention of hiding who I am because I have done nothing wrong," he said. On June 9, after several days of articles in the *Guardian* and the *Washington Post* showed America the tip of the iceberg, he went public.[12]

"I think that the public is owed an explanation of the motivations behind the people who make these disclosures that are outside the democratic model," Snowden said in a video Poitras recorded of Greenwald's interview in Snowden's Hong Kong hotel room. As an infrastructure analyst in a position of "privileged access," Snowden was exposed on a regular basis to vast quantities of "disturbing" information that he began to view as flagrant abuses by the NSA. Snowden's motivation was to show how, in the name of national security, the NSA had increased the intelligence-gathering capabilities that were initially targeted at foreign intelligence to take in the domestic communications of Americans at large "by default."

"Even if you're not doing anything wrong, you're being watched and recorded," he said. "It's getting to the point [where] you don't have to have done anything wrong. You simply have to eventually fall under suspicion from somebody, even by a wrong call, and then they can use the system to go back in time and scrutinize every decision you've ever made, every friend you've ever discussed something with, and attack you on that basis to sort of derive suspicion from an innocent life and paint anyone in the context of a wrongdoer." Snowden said the public needed the opportunity to decide for itself whether the NSA programs were right or wrong. A passionate believer in Internet freedom, Snowden had already made that decision for himself. "I don't want to live in a world where there's no privacy and therefore no room for intellectual exploration and creativity," Snowden told Greenwald and Poitras.[13]

Greenwald noted that for the first few days of news coverage about the still-anonymous Snowden's revelations, the focus was on the outrageous actions of the United States government, which was revealed to have been spying on innocent Americans after denying the existence of such surveillance programs. But once Snowden's anonymity was gone, the focus shifted to him. And once he entered the spotlight, the tone of the discussion changed dramatically. "The story was no longer that reporters had exposed serious NSA abuses, but that an American working for the government had 'betrayed' his obligations, committed crimes, and then 'fled to China,'" Greenwald wrote in his 2014 book, *No Place to Hide*.[14]

Snowden is adamant that he vetted every document he turned over to ensure that no one would be harmed as a result of its disclosure. While he has expressed admiration for Manning, he cited this decision as a significant difference between them.[15] But that has done nothing to temper the firestorm of criticism from US leaders, pundits, and others who view him as a traitor who undermined America's security in the age of terror.

The disapproval of Snowden's actions was swift and fierce in Washington's corridors of power. Among those who used the words *traitor* or *treason* to describe Snowden and his actions were House Speaker John Boehner, Senator Bill Nelson, and Senator Dianne Feinstein, who at the time chaired the Senate Intelligence Committee that oversaw the programs Snowden had unmasked. "Edward Snowden is not a whistle-blower. What Edward Snowden did amounts to an act of treason," Nelson wrote.[16] Secretary of State John Kerry said Snowden was a coward and traitor who had "betrayed his country," while his predecessor, Hillary Clinton, cast aspersions on him for taking refuge in Russia and Hong Kong.[17] Some critics would suggest or allege outright that Snowden was a spy. Former CIA director James Woolsey even advocated that Snowden be tried for treason and "hanged by his neck until he is dead" if convicted.[18]

However, Snowden has no shortage of supporters as well. Many were outraged by the extent of the government eavesdropping he revealed, and praised him as a hero and patriot for putting his freedom on the line to tell Americans the truth about what their government was doing. Ellsberg described Snowden as a hero who could help reverse an "executive coup" against the Constitution. "In my estimation, there has not been in American history a more important leak than Edward Snowden's release of NSA material—and that definitely includes the Pentagon Papers forty years ago," Ellsberg wrote in the *Guardian*.[19] *Washington Post* columnist Ezra Klein called Snowden a patriot, writing, "[I]t's hard to escape the conclusion that Snowden did the country a real service."[20] Tens of thousands have signed an online petition demanding that Snowden be pardoned.

Snowden's revelations sparked what many believed to be a long-overdue conversation and convinced many Americans, even in Congress, that their country had gone too far. The efforts to steer the United States away from that path brought unlikely allies together in Washington. Michigan congressmen Justin Amash, a Tea Party Republican, and John Conyers, a liberal Democrat, cosponsored legislation aimed at defunding NSA programs and curbing what they considered the agency's abuses. "He told us what we need to know," Amash said of Snowden.[21]

Snowden told Greenwald and Poitras that he didn't expect to see home again. If he does, he will no doubt also see the inside of a federal prison. Snowden never had any illusions about the likelihood that he'd face indictment. And that expectation predictably came true in June 2014, within days of his public outing of himself. To his supporters, it must seem only fitting that the federal criminal charges Snowden faces were brought under the 1917 Espionage Act, the World War I–era law that has long been a byword for government oppression in America.*

Jesselyn Radack, an attorney for Snowden, partly justified his refusal to return to America to face his charges on the grounds that he would not be able to receive a fair trial under the Espionage Act. To those who say Snowden "should turn himself in, mount a solid defense, and all will be righted at trial," Radack said, "That's a fantasy." Radack described the Espionage Act as an "arcane" law designed to be used against spies, constructed in such a way as to prevent whistle-blowers accused of leaking classified information from properly defending themselves. "The motive and intent of the whistle-blower are irrelevant. And there is no whistle-blower defense, meaning the public value of the material disclosed does not matter all," Radack wrote in the *Wall Street Journal*.[22]

Instead of coming home to face his charges, the world's most famous fugitive languishes in Russia. Snowden applied for asylum in twenty-one countries, ending up in Russia almost by default.[23] Snowden found himself stuck in Moscow's Sheremetyevo International Airport on June 23, 2013, after arriving from Hong Kong. He was scheduled to fly from Russia to Cuba, but he was denied passage after the State Department revoked his passport. Rather than risk traveling to a Latin American country, where the US government would have easier access to him—Bolivia, Ecuador, Nicaragua, and Venezuela all offered him permanent asylum—Snowden accepted an offer of temporary asylum in Russia.[24] It is in Russia where he remains today, uncertain of when or if he'll ever be able to return home as a free man.

In their first meeting, Snowden told Greenwald that his biggest fear was that his disclosures would be met with apathy by the American people—that he was throwing everything in his life away for nothing. As Greenwald, a passionate advocate for privacy rights, wrote, that has been the furthest thing from the case.[25] Thanks to Snowden, Americans are debating the merits of privacy and the limits of government power to an extent never before seen since the advent of the Information Age. It is a debate that may rage on for generations. The debate over whether Snowden is a patriot or a traitor will likely last for just as long.

* See chapters 7 and 8 for more on the Espionage Act.

Notes

Introduction

1 Kidd, Thomas S. 2011. *Patrick Henry: First Among Patriots*. New York: Basic Books, 51–52.

2 Edmund Pendleton to James Madison, April 21, 1790.

3 Wilson, James, and McKean, Thomas. 1792. *Commentaries on the Constitution of the United States of America, With That Constitution Prefixed, in Which are Unfolded, the Principles of Free Government, and the Superior Advantages of Republicanism Demonstrated*. Philadelphia: T. Lloyd, 93–94.

4 *The Federalist*, No. 43.

Chapter 1: The Unauthorized Peacemaker

1 Tolles, Frederick B. 1953. *George Logan of Philadelphia*. New York: Oxford University Press, 3.

2 Thomas Jefferson to Thomas Mann Randolph, July 28, 1793.

3 Tolles, 39.

4 Logan, Deborah N. 1899. *Memoir of Dr. George Logan of Stenton*. Philadelphia: The Historical Society of Pennsylvania, 16.

5 Tolles, 107.

6 Logan, 54–56.

7 Ibid., 54–57.

8 Ibid., 57.

9 Ibid., 61–63.

10 Ibid., 62–63.

11 Tolles, 158–59.

12 Ibid., 159–60.

13 Ford, Worthington C., ed. 1914. "Letters of William Vans Murray to John Quincy Adams, 1797–1803." Washington, DC, 448–49. (Reprinted from the *Annual Report of the American Historical Association for 1912*, pages 341-715.)

14 Tolles, 63, 129.

15 Ibid., 161.

16 Ibid., 163.

17 Logan, 64–65.

18 *A Collection of State Papers Relative to the War Against France Now Carrying On by Great Britain and the Several Other European Powers*, Vol. VIII. 1800. London: S. Gosnell, 214–15.

19 Tolles, 164.

20 *A Collection of State Papers Relative to the War Against France*, 214–15.
21 Tolles, 164–66; Logan, 65, 130–31.
22 Logan, 91.
23 Ibid., 65–66.
24 Tolles, 166.
25 Logan, 67.
26 Logan, 79–80; Tolles, 169.
27 Adams, Charles F., ed. 1852. *The Works of John Adams, Second President of the United States*, Vol. VIII. Boston: Little, Brown and Company, 615.
28 James Lloyd to George Washington, June 18, 1798.
29 Logan, 59–60.
30 Thomas Jefferson to James Madison, June 21, 1798; Logan, 56.
31 Thomas Jefferson to Edmund Pendleton, January 29, 1799.
32 Logan, 54.
33 Thomas Jefferson to James Madison, June 21, 1798.
34 Logan, 55–56.
35 Ibid., 59.
36 Ibid., 75–76.
37 Ibid., 72.
38 Tolles, 172–73.
39 Ibid., 166–67.
40 Tolles, Frederick. "Unofficial Ambassador: George Logan's Mission to France, 1798," *The William and Mary Quarterly*, Third Series, Vol. 7, No. 1, January 1950.
41 Logan, 69.
42 Thomas Jefferson to George Logan, October 3, 1813.
43 Logan, 85.
44 Gibbs, George. 1846. *Memoirs of the Administrations of Washington and John Adams*, Vol. II. New York: William Van Norden, Printer, 192–93.
45 McCullough, David. 2001. *John Adams*. New York: Simon & Schuster, 516.
46 *American State Papers: Foreign Relations*. 2: 236–37.
47 Logan, 86.
48 George Washington's notes on an interview with George Logan and Robert Blackwell, November 13, 1798.
49 George Washington to William Vans Murray, December 26, 1798.
50 *Annals of Congress*, House of Representatives, 5th Congress, 3rd Session, 2421.
51 Ibid., 2422.
52 *Annals of Congress*, Senate, 5th Congress, 3rd Session, 2192.
53 Gibbs, 175.
54 *Annals of Congress*, House of Representatives, 5th Congress, 3rd Session, 2489.
55 Ibid., 2584.
56 Ibid., 2493–95.
57 Ibid., 2496.
58 *Annals of Congress*, House of Representatives, 5th Congress, 3rd Session, 2529.
59 Ibid., 2603.
60 Ibid., 2609.

61 Ibid., 2504.
62 Ibid., 2524.
63 Ibid., 2587.
64 Ibid., 2499.
65 Ibid., 2495.
66 Ibid., 2602.
67 Ibid., 2703.
68 Ibid., 2639.
69 Ibid., 2596.
70 Ibid., 2707.
71 Logan, 89.
72 Ibid., 89–93.
73 *Annals of Congress*, House of Representatives, 5th Congress, 3rd Session, 2620.
74 *Annals of Congress*, House of Representatives, 5th Congress, 3rd Session, 2678.
75 Tolles, 231.
76 George Logan to James Madison, January 10, 1810.
77 James Madison to George Logan, January 19, 1810.
78 George Logan to James Madison, January 14, 1810. James Madison to George Logan, January 19, 1810.
79 George Logan to James Madison, July 4, 1813.
80 Paullin, Charles O., and Frederic L. Paxson. 1914. *Guide to the Materials in the London Archives for the History of the United States since 1783*. Washington, DC: Carnegie Institution of Washington, 210.
81 Tolles, 293.
82 George Logan to Thomas Jefferson, October 9, 1813.
83 Logan, 116.
84 George Logan to James Madison, July 4, 1813.
85 George Logan to Thomas Jefferson, October 9, 1813.
86 George Logan to Thomas Jefferson, September 18, 1813.
87 George Logan to James Madison, January 18, 1813.
88 George Logan to Thomas Jefferson, September 18, 1813.
89 Thomas Jefferson to George Logan, October 3, 1813.
90 Warren, Charles. 1942. *Odd Byways in American History*. Cambridge: Harvard University Press, 170–74.
91 Vagts, Detley F. "The Logan Act: Paper Tiger or Sleeping Giant?," *The American Journal of International Law*, Vol. 60, No. 2, April 1966.

Chapter 2: Speech Becomes Sedition

1 Belt, Gordon T. "The Sedition Act of 1798: A Brief History of Arrests, Indictments, Mistreatment & Abuse," First Amendment Center.
2 Thomas Jefferson to William Stephens Smith, November 13, 1787.
3 Tagg, James. 1991. *Benjamin Franklin Bache and the Philadelphia Aurora*. Philadelphia: University of Pennsylvania Press, 1, 23, 48, 56.
4 Ford, 489–90.

5 Tagg, 86; Smith, Jeffery Alan. 1990. *Franklin and Bache: Envisioning the Enlightened Republic*. New York: Oxford University Press, 137.
6 Church, Forrest. 2007. *So Help Me God: The Founding Fathers and the First Great Battle Over Church and State*. Orlando, FL: Harcourt, 177.
7 Nelson, William, ed. 1895. *Documents Relating to the Colonial History of the State of New Jersey*, Vol. XII. Patterson, NJ: The Press Printing and Publishing Co., 213.
8 Pasley, Jeffrey L. 2001. *The Tyranny of Printers: Newspaper Politics in the Early American Republic*. Charlottesville: University Press of Virginia, 98.
9 Thomas Jefferson to James Madison, April 26, 1798.
10 Tagg, 370.
11 Ibid., 342.
12 Ibid., 370.
13 Ibid., 386–87
14 Rosenfeld, Richard N. 1997. *American Aurora: A Democratic-Republic Returns: The Suppressed History of Our Nation's Beginnings and Heroic Newspaper that Tried to Report It*. New York: St. Martin's Press, 170.
15 Ibid., 190.
16 Thomas Jefferson to James Madison, April 26, 1798.
17 Tagg, 370.
18 *Annals of Congress*, House of Representatives, 5th Congress, 2nd Session, 2093–98.
19 Ibid., 2098.
20 Ibid., 2107–09.
21 Ibid., 2106.
22 Ibid., 2134.
23 Rosenfeld, 188, 191, 195.
24 Ibid., 197.
25 Humphrey, Carol Sue. 1996. *The Press of the Young Republic, 1783–1833*. Westport, CT: Greenwood Press, 61.
26 Stone, Geoffrey R. 2004. *Perilous Times: Free Speech in Wartime from the Sedition Act of 1798 to the War on Terrorism*. New York: W. W. Norton & Co., 46.
27 Tagg, 397; Pasley, 103.
28 Tise, Larry E. 1998. *The American Counterrevolution: A Retreat from Liberty, 1783–1800*. Mechanicsburg, PA: Stackpole Books, 24.
29 Little, Nigel. 2008. *Transoceanic Radical, William Duane: National Identity and Empire, 1760–1835*. New York: Routledge, Taylor & Francis Group, 62, 65.
30 Tise, 29.
31 Ibid., 29.
32 Ibid., 284–85.
33 Ibid., 285.
34 Smith, James Morton. 1956. *Freedom's Fetters: The Alien and Sedition Laws and American Civil Liberties*. Ithaca, NY: Cornell University Press, 287.
35 Ibid., 295.
36 Phillips, Kim Tousley. 1989. *William Duane, Radical Journalist in the Age of Jefferson*. New York: Garland, 87.
37 Tise, 287.

38 Smith, 299.
39 John Adams to Timothy Pickering, August 1, 1799.
40 Adams, Charles Francis, ed. 1852. *The Works of John Adams, Second President of the United States*, Vol. VII. Boston: Little, Brown and Company, 56.
41 Smith, 301–03.
42 Thomas Jefferson to William Duane, May 23, 1801.
43 Little, 124–26.
44 Pasley, 289.
45 Ibid., 90.
46 Durey, Michael. 1990. *With the Hammer of Truth: James Thompson Callender and America's Early National Heroes*. Charlottesville: University Press of Virginia, 43–44.
47 Tise, 27, 52, 254.
48 Ibid., 255.
49 Rosenfeld, 189.
50 Smith, 338.
51 Ibid., 339–40.
52 Ibid., 341.
53 Steiner, Bernard C. 1907. *The Life and Correspondence of James McHenry, Secretary of War Under Washington and Adams*. Cleveland: The Burrows Brothers Company, 203.
54 Smith, 344.
55 Ibid., 345–46.
56 Ibid., 351.
57 Tise, 421.
58 Ibid., 420–21.
59 Tise, 421; Ames, Fisher. 1854. *Works of Fisher Ames: With a Selection from His Speeches and Correspondence*. Boston: Little, Brown and Company, 247; Warren, Charles. 1931. *Jacobin and Junto; or, Early American Politics as Viewed in the Diary of Dr. Nathaniel Ames, 1758–1822*. Cambridge: Harvard University Press, 108.
60 Warren, 109.

Chapter 3: The Federalists' Last Stand

1 Quincy, Edmund. 1867. *Life of Josiah Quincy of Massachusetts*. Boston: Ticknor and Fields, 358.
2 Wood, Gordon S. 2009. *Empire of Liberty: A History of the Early Republic, 1789–1815*. Cary, NC: Oxford University Press, 666.
3 Allison, Robert J. 2005. *Stephen Decatur: American Naval Hero, 1779–1820*. Amherst: University of Massachusetts Press, 135.
4 Brannan, John. 1971. *Official Letters of the Military and Naval Officers of the United States, During the War with Great Britain in the Years 1812, '13, '14, and '15*. New York: Arno Press, 288.
5 Mayo, Eduardo Jimenez, and Brown, Chris N., eds. 2011. *Utmost Gallantry: The US and Royal Navies at Sea in the War of 1812*. Annapolis, MD: Naval Institute Press, 159.
6 Morison, Samuel E. 1970. *Dissent in Three American Wars*. Cambridge: Harvard University Press, 17–18.

7 Carey, Matthew. 1817. *The Olive Branch: Or, Faults on Both Sides, Federal and Democratic. A Serious Appeal on the Necessity of Mutual Forgiveness and Harmony*, 8th ed. Philadelphia: M. Carey and Son, 348.
8 Adams, Henry, ed. 1877. *Documents Relating to New-England Federalism, 1800–1815*. Boston: Little, Brown and Company, 339–41.
9 Parsons, Theophilus. 1859. *Memoir of Theophilus Parsons, Chief Justice of the Supreme Judicial Court of Massachusetts, With Notices of Some of His Contemporaries*. Boston: Ticknor and Fields, 46–47; Brown, Charles R. 1915. *The Northern Confederacy: According to the Plans of the "Essex Junto" 1796–1814*. Princeton, NJ: Princeton University Press, 7–10.
10 Brown, 32; Thomas Jefferson to Louis H. Girardin, December 21, 1814.
11 Plumer, William, Jr. 1857. *The Life of William Plumer*. Boston: Phillips, Sampson and Company, 298–300.
12 Clarfield, Gerard H. 1980. *Timothy Pickering and the American Republic*. Pittsburgh: University of Pittsburgh Press, 225–27.
13 Chernow, Ron. 2004. *Alexander Hamilton*. New York: Penguin Press, 678; Plumer, 298–300.
14 Ford, Worthington C., ed. 1917. *Writings of John Quincy Adams, Vol. VII, 1820–1823*. New York: The Macmillan Company, 257–58; Clarfield, 306–07.
15 Wood, 649–50, 664–65.
16 Ibid. 667.
17 James Madison's war message to Congress, June 1, 1812; Hickey, Donald R. 2012. *The War of 1812: A Forgotten Conflict* (Bicentennial Edition). Urbana: University of Illinois Press, 261.
18 Morison, 3.
19 Wood, 669.
20 Banner, James M. 1970. *To the Hartford Convention: The Federalists and the Origins of Party Politics in Massachusetts, 1789–1815*. New York: Knopf, 307, 313; Plumer, 405.
21 Lodge, Henry C. 1878. *Life and Letters of George Cabot*. Boston: Little, Brown and Company, 535.
22 Adams, 407.
23 Banner, 307.
24 Hickey, 261–63.
25 Hickey, 264–65; *American State Papers: Military Affairs*. Vol. 1, 325.
26 James Madison's annual message to Congress, November 4, 1812.
27 Hickey, 266–67.
28 Ibid., 268.
29 Ibid., 271.
30 Ibid., 272.
31 Ibid., 270.
32 Ibid., 272.
33 King, Charles R., ed. 1898. *The Life and Correspondence of Rufus King, Comprising His Letters, Private and Official, His Public Documents and His Speeches, Vol. V, 1807–1816*. New York: G. P. Putnam's Sons, 414.
34 Banner, 320.
35 Hickey, 273; Banner, 314.

36 Banner, 319–22; Hickey, 274, 277.
37 Hickey, 276, 278.
38 Hickey, 277.
39 Banner, 331–33.
40 Hickey, 278–80; Banner, 329.
41 Lodge, 546; Adams, 411–12.
42 Plumer, 420; Hickey, 282.
43 Hickey, 278.
44 John Adams to William Plumer, December 4, 1814.
45 Banner, 335–37; Hickey, 280; Lyman, Theodore, Jr. 1823. *A Short Account of the Hartford Convention, Taken from Official Documents and Addressed to the Fair Minded and the Well Disposed. To Which is Added an Attested Copy of the Secret Journal of that Body.* Boston: O. Everett, 22–36.
46 Otis, Harrison G. 1820. *Letters Developing the Character and Views of the Hartford Convention*. Washington, DC, 380; Adams, 423–24; Banner, 347; Hickey, 281.
47 Dwight, 352–65.
48 Ibid., 366.
49 Ibid., 368–69.
50 Ibid., 377–78.
51 Ibid., 355, 379.
52 Ibid., 382.
53 Brands, H. W. 2005. *Andrew Jackson, His Life and Times*. New York: Doubleday, 230.
54 Lodge, 413.
55 Lyman, 17.
56 Dwight, 4, 402–03.
57 Brown, 117.
58 "Congress," *Long-Island Star*, May 1, 1828.
59 "Consistency of Political Anti-Masonry," *Onondaga Standard* (Syracuse, New York), March 31, 1830.
60 Brown, 113.
61 *Minutes of the Ninth Annual Meeting and Reunion of the United Confederate Veterans*. 1900. New Orleans: Hopkins' Printing Office, 31.

Chapter 4: The Rogue Diplomat

1 Elizabeth Trist to Nicholas P. Trist, February 9, 1821, via Thomas Jefferson Foundation, Inc.
2 Ohrt, Wallace. 1997. *Defiant Peacemaker: Nicholas Trist in the Mexican War*. College Station: Texas A&M University Press, 102; Greenberg, Amy S. 2012. *A Wicked War: Polk, Clay, Lincoln, and the 1846 US Invasion of Mexico*. New York: Alfred A. Knopf, 93, 174.
3 Elizabeth Trist to Nicholas P. Trist, February 9, 1821, via Thomas Jefferson Foundation, Inc.
4 Ohrt, 2, 6–7; Greenberg, 91.
5 Ohrt, 50; Greenberg, 91–92.
6 Mahin, Dean B. 1997. *Olive Branch and Sword: The United States and Mexico, 1845–1848*. Jefferson, NC: McFarland & Co., 8.

7 Ibid., 8.
8 Ohrt, 57.
9 Mahin, 15.
10 Ibid., 9.
11 Ibid., 11–15.
12 Ohrt, 98; Mahin, 40.
13 Howe, Daniel W. 2007. *What Hath God Wrought: The Transformation of America, 1815–1848*. New York: Oxford University Press, 734–35.
14 Merry, Robert W. 2009. *A Country of Vast Designs: James K. Polk, the Mexican War and the Conquest of the American Continent*. New York: Simon & Schuster, 319–20.
15 Ibid., 359.
16 Ibid., 361.
17 Ibid., 366.
18 Polk, James K. 1910. *The Diary of James K. Polk during His Presidency, 1845–1849, Vol. II*. Chicago: A. C. McClurg & Co., 478–79.
19 Polk II, 483; Greenberg, 215.
20 Merry, 366–67.
21 Scott, Winfield. 1864. *Memoirs of Lieut.-General Winfield Scott, LL.D., in Two Volumes, Volume II*. New York: Sheldon & Company, 576; Greenberg, 206.
22 United States. 1848. *The Treaty Between the United States and Mexico: The Proceedings of the Senate Thereon, and Message of the President and Documents Communicated Therewith*. Washington, DC, 121.
23 Ibid., 158.
24 Ibid., 130–31.
25 Greenberg, 207.
26 Merry, 368.
27 Ibid., 368–69.
28 Merry, 370; Polk, James K. 1910. *The Diary of James K. Polk During his Presidency, 1845–1849, Vol. III*. Chicago: A. C. McClurg & Co., 76.
29 Polk III, 76–78.
30 Clary, David A. 2009. *Eagles and Empire: The United States, Mexico, and the Struggle for a Continent*. New York: Bantam Books, 316.
31 Merry, 371–72.
32 Ibid., 372.
33 Ibid., 372.
34 Ohrt, 121–22; Merry, 372–74.
35 Merry, 372–74.
36 Ibid., 382.
37 Ibid., 384.
38 Ibid., 385.
39 Ibid., 385.
40 Greenberg, 218–21.
41 Merry, 386.
42 Ibid., 399.
43 Greenberg, 238; Merry, 398–99.

44 Greenberg, 239.
45 Ohrt, 139–40.
46 Merry, 399.
47 *Treaty*, 243–44.
48 Greenberg, 239.
49 Polk III, 301.
50 Merry, 407.
51 Polk, James K. Message of the President. *Congressional Globe*, 30th Congress, 1st Session, December 7, 1847.
52 Merry, 394–95.
53 Clary, 387.
54 Ohrt, 142–44.
55 Merry, 425; Ohrt, 142–45.
56 Ohrt, 145.
57 Ibid, 146–47.
58 Polk III, 345, 348.
59 Merry, 427.
60 Ibid., 434.
61 Ohrt, 150–51.
62 Mahin, 15.
63 Ohrt, 156–57, 159.
64 Ibid., 160–62.
65 Greenberg, 94.

Chapter 5: The Gray-Eyed Man of Destiny
1 Greene, Lawrence. 1937. *The Filibuster: The Career of William Walker*. Indianapolis: Bobbs Merrill Company, 22–24.
2 Dando-Collins, Stephen. 2008. *Tycoon's War: How Cornelius Vanderbilt Invaded a Country to Overthrow America's Most Famous Military Adventurer*. Cambridge, MA: Da Capo Press, 9.
3 Carr, Albert Z. 1963. *The World and William Walker*. New York: Harper & Row, 23.
4 Ibid.
5 Ibid.
6 Thomas, Jane H. 1897. *Old Days in Nashville, Tenn*. Nashville, TN: Methodist Episcopal Church, South. Barbee & Smith, Agents, 78; Brown, Charles H. 1980. *Agents of Manifest Destiny: The Lives and Times of the Filibusters*. Chapel Hill: University of North Carolina Press, 174.
7 Greene, 24; Thomas, 78.
8 Greene, 25.
9 Brown, 180.
10 Ibid., 180–81.
11 May, Robert E. 1989. *The Southern Dream of a Caribbean Empire, 1854–1861*. Athens: University of Georgia Press, 17–19.
12 May, *The Southern Dream*, 9–11.

13 Polk, James K. 1910. *The Diary of James K. Polk, 1845–1849, Vol. III*. Chicago: A. C. McClurg & Co., 446, 479; Brown, 42–88.
14 May, Robert E. 2002. *Manifest Destiny's Underworld: Filibustering in Antebellum America*. Chapel Hill: University of North Carolina Press, 74–75.
15 Walker, William. 1860. *The War in Nicaragua*. Mobile, AL: S. H. Goetzel & Co., 19–20; Greene, 28–29; Brown, 182.
16 Greene, 29.
17 Walker, 21–22.
18 Brown, 183, 190.
19 Greene, 30.
20 Ibid., 30.
21 Brown, 195.
22 Greene, 31.
23 Wells, William V. 1856. *Walker's Expedition to Nicaragua: A History of the Central American War*. New York: Stringer and Townsend, 26.
24 Scroggs, William O. 1916. *Filibusters and Financiers: The Story of William Walker and His Associates*. New York: Macmillan, 38.
25 Greene, 32.
26 Ibid., 32.
27 Scroggs, 38–39; Wells, 27.
28 Greene, 35.
29 Wells, 27.
30 Greene, 32–33.
31 Ibid.
32 Scroggs, 42; Greene, 38.
33 Greene, 35.
34 Ibid., 41.
35 Ibid., 40–41.
36 Greene, 42–44; Scroggs, 46.
37 Greene, 45; Scroggs, 46–47.
38 Greene, 45–46.
39 Ibid., 47.
40 Walker, 24.
41 Greene, 58–59.
42 Greene, 59–61; Wells, 43.
43 Greene, 62–71.
44 Walker, 47–48.
45 Greene, 79–80; Walker, 50–53; Scroggs, 109.
46 Greene, 90–91.
47 Ibid., 91–92.
48 Greene, 94; Walker, 79–80, 85.
49 Greene, 96–98.
50 Scroggs, 114; Dando-Collins, 84–85.
51 Greene, 100; Scroggs, 114–15; Dando-Collins, 84–93; Doubleday, C. W. 1886. *Reminiscences of the "Filibuster" War in Nicaragua*. New York: G. P. Putnam's Sons / The Knickerbocker Press, 159–61.

52 Greene, 103.
53 Greene, 106–07; Dando-Collins, 101–02.
54 Dando-Collins, 106–07; Greene, 108–09; Walker, 109–10.
55 Greene, 111; Walker, 109–12; Scroggs, 117.
56 Walker, 113; Greene, 117.
57 Greene, 118–20.
58 Ibid., 123.
59 *Index to the Executive Documents, Printed by Order of the Senate of the United States, First and Second Sessions, Thirty-Fourth Congress, 1855–'56.* Washington, DC: A. O. P. Nicholson, Senate Printer, 1856, 34.
60 Greene, 156–57.
61 Dando-Collins, 30–31, 35–36, 43–45, 145.
62 Greene, 106, 124, 161.
63 Greene, 161; Dando-Collins, 30.
64 Greene, 161–62.
65 Ibid, 143.
66 Greene, 163; Brown, 316–17.
67 Brown, 316–17; Greene, 165; Dando-Collins, 157–59; Scroggs, 142.
68 Dando-Collins, 160; Brown, 319.
69 Dando-Collins, 167–68.
70 Ibid., 167, 177–78.
71 Ibid., 177–78.
72 Brown, 322–23; Dando-Collins, 178.
73 Greene, 169.
74 Dando-Collins, 176; Greene, 170.
75 Dando-Collins, 197–99.
76 Greene, 178.
77 Dando-Collins, 205; Brown, 334–5.
78 Brown, 340–42.
79 Ibid., 343.
80 Greene, 191–93.
81 Dando-Collins, 225–26.
82 Brown, 346.
83 Dando-Collins, 229.
84 Brown, 350.
85 May, *Manifest Destiny's Underworld*, 263–64; Dando-Collins, 341; Brown, 352.
86 Walker, 252.
87 Brown, 349.
88 Walker, 253–54.
89 Ibid., 255, 257, 261.
90 Brown, 352.
91 Walker, 266.
92 Greene, 229; Dando-Collins, 240.
93 Scroggs, 255.
94 Greene, 240–42.

95 Ibid., 245–46.
96 Greene, 263; Dando-Collins, 278–83.
97 Greene, 340.
98 Dando-Collins, 262–66.
99 Ibid., 284–86.
100 Ibid., 289, 292–93.
101 Dando-Collins, 289.
102 Brown, 384.
103 Ibid., 392–93, 398.
104 Dando-Collins, 301, 307–08; Brown, 406–07.
105 Dando-Collins, 318–19; Brown, 407.
106 Brown, 407.
107 Walker, 429.
108 Brown, 409.
109 May, *Manifest Destiny's Underworld*, 265.
110 Brown, 409–10.
111 Ibid., 414.
112 Dando-Collins, 322–23.
113 Brown, 419.
114 May, *The Southern Dream*, 114; Greene, 309.
115 May, *The Southern Dream*, 125–26.
116 Ibid., 123.
117 Dando-Collins, 9; Brown, 432.
118 Brown,439–42.
119 Walker, dedication.
120 Dando-Collins, 331; Brown, 450–51.
121 Brown, 451.
122 Dando-Collins, 331; Brown, 452.
123 Brown, 454; Scroggs, 391.
124 Scroggs, 394.
125 Buchanan, James, Annual Message to Congress, December 3, 1860.
126 "Filibusterism Not Buried in the Grave of Walker," *Nashville Union and American*, October 10, 1860.
127 May, *Manifest Destiny's Underworld*, 295–96.
128 Brown, 174.

Chapter 6: Striking the Copperhead
1 Stone, Geoffrey R. 2004. *Perilous Times: Free Speech in Wartime from the Sedition Act of 1798 to the War on Terrorism*. New York: W. W. Norton & Co., 99.
2 Weber, Jennifer L. 2006. *Copperheads: The Rise and Fall of Lincoln's Opponents in the North*. New York: Oxford University Press, 3.
3 Foote, Shelby. 1986. *The Civil War: A Narrative, Fredericksburg to Meridian*. New York: Vintage Books, 630.
4 Weber, 33.

5 Foote, 631.
6 Vallandigham, James L. 1872. *A Life of Clement L. Vallandigham*. Baltimore: Turnbull Brothers, 1–8.
7 J. Vallandigham, 37–39.
8 Vallandigham, Clement L. 1864. *Speeches, Arguments, Addresses, and Letters of Clement L. Vallandigham*. New York: J. Walter & Co., 545.
9 C. Vallandigham, 546.
10 J. Vallandigham, 83; Klement, Frank L. 1998. *The Limits of Dissent: Clement L. Vallandigham and the Civil War*. New York: Fordham University Press, 11–16.
11 Klement, 15, 17–18.
12 Ibid., 9.
13 C. Vallandigham, 133–34.
14 J. Vallandigham, 144.
15 Klement, 53.
16 J. Vallandigham, 141.
17 Klement, 105.
18 Ibid., 110–11.
19 *The Trial of Hon. Clement L. Vallandigham by a Military Commission and the Proceedings Under His Application For a Writ of Habeas Corpus in the Circuit Court of the United States for the Southern District of Ohio*. 1863. Cincinnati: Rickey and Carroll, 7.
20 C. Vallandigham, 44.
21 Klement, 152.
22 *Trial of Hon. Clement L. Vallandigham*, 8, 11–12, 23.
23 Ibid., 14–15.
24 Klement, 156–58.
25 Ibid., 160–61.
26 J. Vallandigham, 260–61; Klement, 159.
27 *Trial of Hon. Clement L. Vallandigham*, 23.
28 Ibid., 26–28.
29 Ibid., 29–30.
30 *Trial of Hon. Clement L. Vallandigham*, 33; Klement, 165.
31 Rehnquist, William H. 1998. *All the Laws But One: Civil Liberties in Wartime*. New York: Knopf, 67; Klement, 51, 257.
32 C. Vallandigham, 256–57.
33 *Trial of Hon. Clement L. Vallandigham*, 41.
34 Ibid., 169–86.
35 Ibid., 270–71.
36 Ibid., 263–69.
37 Stone, 108 (footnote); Klement, 177.
38 Nicolay, John G., and John Hay. 1909. *Abraham Lincoln: A History*, Vol. 7. New York: The Century Co., 341.
39 Stone, 109; Weber, 96.
40 DeRose, Chris. 2014. *The Presidents' War: Six American Presidents and the Civil War that Divided Them*. Guilford, CT: Lyons Press, 272.
41 Klement, 178.

42 Foote, 634.
43 Nicolay, 341; Klement, 181; Stone, 107.
44 "Arrest of Vallandigham," *Cleveland Daily Leader*, May 6, 1863.
45 Weber, 98.
46 Lamers, William M. 1999. *The Edge of Glory: A Biography of General William S. Rosecrans, U.S.A.* Baton Rouge: Louisiana State University Press (Louisiana Paperback Edition, reprinted from 1961), 267; Weber, 98.
47 Weber, 98–99.
48 Ibid., 99.
49 Ibid., 98, 118.
50 Brown, Harry J., and Frederick D. Williams, eds. *The Diary of James A. Garfield, Vol. III: 1875–1877*. East Lansing: Michigan State University Press, 425–26.
51 Klement, 184.
52 Stone, 115.
53 Ibid., 111.
54 Howe, Henry. 1907. *Historical Collections of Ohio: In Two Volumes: An Encyclopedia of the State, Volume I.* Cincinnati: C. J. Krehbiel & Co., 446.
55 Klement, 238–43; Howe, 446.
56 Klement, 243, 246.
57 Weber, 94, 121; Klement, 254, 256.
58 DeRose, 278.
59 Klement, 252; Weber, 121.
60 Klement, 259–60.
61 Ibid., 270.
62 Foote, 634; Klement, 271–72, 276.
63 Klement, 261.
64 Klement, 284; Foote, Shelby. 1986. *The Civil War: A Narrative, Red River to Appomattox*. New York: Vintage Books, 551-52.
65 Klement, 291.
66 Cowden, Joanna D. 2001. *Heaven Will Frown on Such a Cause as This: Six Democrats Who Opposed Lincoln's War*. Lanham, MD: University Press of America, 185.
67 Porter, George H. 1911. *Ohio Politics during the Civil War Period*. New York: Columbia University Press, 230 (footnote).
68 Klement, 305–07.
69 Ibid., 309.

Chapter 7: The Will of the People Undone

1 Constantine, Robert J., ed. 1990. *Letters of Eugene V. Debs, Vol. 1, 1874–1912*. Urbana and Chicago: University of Illinois Press, 276 (footnote); Salvatore, Nick. 1982. *Eugene V. Debs: Citizen and Socialist*. Urbana: University of Illinois Press, 150–51.
2 Miller, Sally M. 1973. *Victor Berger and the Promise of Constructive Socialism, 1910–1920*. Westport, CT: Greenwood Press, 17; *Certified Copy of the Testimony of Victor L. Berger at the Trial of the Case of the United States vs. Berger et al. in the United States District Court for the Northern District of Illinois, Eastern Division*. Washington, DC: Government Printing Office, 1919, 3–4.

3 Miller, 18, 24.
4 Salvatore, 196; *Certified Copy of the Testimony of Victor L. Berger*, 4–5; Miller, 22, 32–33.
5 Murray, Robert K. 1955. *Red Scare: A Study in National Hysteria, 1919–1920.* Minneapolis: University of Minnesota Press, 19; Berger, Victor L. 1912. *Berger's B roadsides*. Milwaukee: Social-Democratic Publishing Company, 205–10.
6 Steffens, Lincoln. "Eugene V. Debs on What the Matter Is in America and What to Do About It," *Everybody's Magazine*. October 1908. (Republished in *Everybody's Magazine, Vol. XIX, July to December 1908*, 461); Constantine, 311, 397.
7 Zumoff, Jacob A. 2014. *The Communist International and US Communism, 1919–1929.* Leiden, The Netherlands: Brill, 289; Salvatore, 226.
8 Miller, 70–71.
9 Ibid., 72.
10 Spargo, John, ed. 1912. *Proceedings of the National Convention of the Socialist Party.* Chicago: The Socialist Party, 234.
11 Miller, 77–84; "Federal Ownership Urged for All Wireless," *New York Times*, April 25, 1912; "Berger Denounces Senate; Asks That It Be Abolished," *Washington Times*, April 27, 1911.
12 Miller, 119–25.
13 Thomas, William H., Jr. 2008. *Unsafe for Democracy: World War I and the US Justice Department's Covert Campaign to Suppress Dissent*. Madison: University of Wisconsin Press, 113–14; Miller, 127.
14 Miller, 148–49.
15 Murray, 20; Miller, 166–67; *Victor L. Berger, Hearings Before the Special Committee, Appointed Under the Authority of House Resolution No. 6 Concerning the Right of Victor L. Berger to Be Sworn In as a Member of the Sixty-Sixth Congress, Vol. II.* 1919. Washington, DC: Government Printing Office, 19; Salvatore, 282, 287.
16 Murray, 13–14.
17 Herbst, Susan. 1994. *Politics at the Margin: Historical Studies of Public Expression Outside the Mainstream*. Cambridge: Cambridge University Press, 131.
18 Teachout, Terry. 2002. *The Skeptic: A Life of H. L. Mencken*. New York: Harper Collins, 145; "A Talk with Mr. Burleson," *The Union Postal Employee*, Vol. XIII, No. 11, November 1917.
19 Miller, 198–99; "The Middle West and La Follette," *Viereck's,* Vol. VII, Number 13, October 31, 1917.
20 Thomas, 113; Miller, 200–01.
21 Miller, 201.
22 Miller, 207–08.
23 Miller, 205–06; Pietrusza, David. 1998. *Judge and Jury: The Life and Times of Judge Kenesaw Mountain Landis*. South Bend, IN: Diamond Communications, 141.
24 Pietrusza, 139.
25 Lehman, Daniel W. 2002. *John Reed and the Writing of Revolution*. Athens: Ohio University Press, 35.
26 Pietrusza, 140–41.

27 Miller, 208–18; Pietrusza, 140–43; *Victor L. Berger, Hearings Before the Special Committee, Appointed Under the Authority of House Resolution No. 6 Concerning the Right of Victor L. Berger to be Sworn in as a Member of the Sixty-Sixth Congress, Vol. II.* 1919. Washington, DC: Government Printing Office, 18–19, 511.
28 Miller, 211–12; "Statement of Berger," *Oklahoma Leader*, February 27, 1919.
29 "Statement of Berger."
30 Miller, 212–13; Nichols, John. 2011. *The "S" Word: A Short History of an American Tradition . . . Socialism.* London, New York: Verso, 149.
31 Miller, 214.
32 *Victor L. Berger, Hearings Before the Special Committee, Appointed Under the Authority of House Resolution No. 6 Concerning the Right of Victor L. Berger to Be Sworn in as a Member of the Sixty-Sixth Congress, Vol. I.* 1919. Washington, DC: Government Printing Office, 41, 146–50, 160.
33 Miller, 214–16; Murray, 226–29; Nichols, 161-62 *Victor L. Berger, Hearings Before the Special Committee*, 41.
34 Miller, 215, 216–17; Murray, 227; Nichols, 162–63.
35 Nichols, 163; Miller, 217.
36 Murray, 229.
37 *Milwaukee Social Democratic Publishing Co. v. Burleson.* 255 US 407. Supreme Court of the United States. 1921.
38 *Schenck v. United States.* 249 US 47. Supreme Court of the United States. 1919.
39 *Milwaukee Social Democratic Publishing Co. v. Burleson.* 255 US 407. Supreme Court of the United States. 1921.
40 *Berger v. United States.* 255 US 22. Supreme Court of the United States. 1921.
41 *Appeal to Reason* (Girard, Kansas), June 4, 1921.
42 "Victor Berger Laid to Rest," *The Lincoln Star* (Nebraska), August 11, 1929; United Press, via *The Anniston Star* (Alabama), August 11, 1929.

Chapter 8: American Bolshevik

1 Rosenstone, Robert A. 1981. *Romantic Revolutionary: A Biography of John Reed* (reprint of 1975 edition). New York: Vintage Books, 12, 14.
2 Morgan, Ted. 2003. *Reds: McCarthyism in Twentieth-Century America.* New York: Random House, 19.
3 Hicks, Granville. 1936. *John Reed: The Making of a Revolutionary.* New York: Macmillan, 18.
4 Rosenstone, 45.
5 Lehman, Daniel W. 2002. *John Reed and the Writing of Revolution.* Athens: Ohio University Press, 11.
6 Rosenstone, 109.
7 Rosenstone, 108–09; Homberger, Eric. 1990. *John Reed.* Manchester: Manchester University Press, 39.
8 Homberger, 41.
9 Rosenstone, 98, 123.

10 Lippmann, Walter. "Legendary John Reed," *The New Republic*. December 26, 1914. (Republished in *The New Republic: A Journal of Opinion, Part 2, Vol. 1, November 7, 1914 to January 30, 1915*. New York: The Republic Publishing Company, Inc.)
11 "War in Paterson," *The Masses*. Vol. 4, No. 9. June 1913.
12 Rosenstone, 120–22.
13 Homberger, 49.
14 Rosenstone, 151, 166, 169.
15 "The Traders' War," *The Masses*. Vol. 5, No. 12. September 1914.
16 Ibid.
17 Rosenstone, 210–11, 229.
18 Ibid., 239–40, 255.
19 "Woodrow Wilson," *The Masses*. Vol. 9, No. 8. June 1917.
20 "Whose War?," *The Masses*. Vol. 9, No. 6. April 1917.
21 Rosenstone, 264.
22 Ibid., 282.
23 "Special Announcement," *The Masses*. Vol. 9, No. 12. October 1917.
24 Reed, John. 1922. *Ten Days That Shook the World* (Famine relief edition). New York: Boni & Liveright, 11–12.
25 Ibid., 17–18.
26 Rosenstone, 285, 292.
27 Reed, 125.
28 Rosenstone, 296.
29 Ibid., 307–08.
30 Ibid., 308, 313.
31 Ibid., 309–10.
32 Ibid., 314.
33 Hicks, 164–65.
34 Rosenstone, 317, 320.
35 Lehman, 175.
36 Hicks, 167.
37 Ibid., 174.
38 Rosenstone, 324.
39 Hicks, 172–74; Rosenstone, 329.
40 "Knit a Straight-Jacket for Your Soldier Boy," *The Masses*. Vol. 9, No. 10. August 1917.
41 Rosenstone, 332–33.
42 Ibid., 335.
43 Morgan, 64–66.
44 *Brewing and Liquor Interests and German Propaganda, Hearings Before a Subcommittee of the Committee on the Judiciary, United States Senate, Sixty-Fifth Congress, Second and Third Sessions*. 1919. Washington, DC: Government Printing Office, 2755–777.
45 *Bolshevik Propaganda, Hearings Before a Subcommittee of the Committee on the Judiciary, United States Senate, Sixty-Fifth Congress, Third Session and Thereafter*. 1919. Washington, DC: Government Printing Office, 465–66.
46 *Bolshevik Propaganda*, 580–90.

47 Ibid., 566, 591.
48 "Plans Bolshevist Bureau Here," *New York Times*, February 22, 1919.
49 Rosenstone, 345.
50 Ibid., 345.
51 Reed (1922), preface, xii.
52 Rosenstone, 349–50.
53 Ibid., 339–40.
54 Homberger, 187.
55 Ibid., 187–89.
56 Rosenstone, 352.
57 Ibid., 354.
58 Ibid., 360.
59 Ibid., 361.
60 Zumoff, Jacob A. 2014. *The Communist International and US Communism, 1919–1929*. Leiden, The Netherlands: Brill, 44.
61 Rosenstone, 367.
62 Rosenstone, 367–68; Homberger, 201.
63 Homberger, 205.
64 Rosenstone, 368.
65 Ibid., 361.
66 Homberger, 207.
67 Rosenstone, 372–74.
68 Ibid., 374–77.
69 Homberger, 212–14.
70 Rosenstone, 379–81.
71 Ibid., 382–84.
72 Ibid., 367.
73 Homberger, 4–5.
74 Goldman, Emma. 1925. *My Disillusionment in Russia*. London: C. W. Daniel, 167–68.
75 Reed (1922), introduction by Vladimir Lenin.

Chapter 9: The Press Goes to War

1 Smith, Richard Norton. 1997. *The Colonel: the Life and Legend of Robert R. McCormick, 1880–1955*. Boston: Houghton Mifflin, 416; "A 'Scoop' Gave Axis Our World War II Plans," *Washington Post*, January 6, 1963; *Chicago Tribune*, June 27, 1950 (reprinted in *The Capital Times* (Madison, Wisconsin), July 1, 1950.
2 Black, Conrad. 2003. *Franklin Delano Roosevelt: Champion of Freedom*. New York: Public Affairs, 634.
3 Wedemeyer, Albert C. 1958. *Wedemeyer Reports!*. New York: Henry Holt & Company, 28–29; "F.D.R.'s War Plans!," *Chicago Tribune*, December 4, 1941.
4 Gaston, James C. 2000. *Planning the American Air War: Four Men and Nine Days in 1941*. Honolulu: University Press of the Pacific (reprint from 1982 edition), 34.
5 "F.D.R.'s War Plans!"

6 Ibid.
7 Ibid.
8 Ibid.
9 "A 'Scoop' Gave Axis Our World War II Plans."
10 Smith, 416.
11 "Reputed Army-Navy Scheme Plans 5-Million-Man AEF," United Press, via *Bradford Evening Star* and *Bradford Daily Record* (Pennsylvania), December 4, 1941.
12 "Release of Army Plans Denounced by Stimson," Associated Press, via *Wilkes-Barre Record* (Pennsylvania), December 5, 1941.
13 Ibid.
14 Winfield, Betty Houchin. 1990. *FDR and the News Media*. Urbana: University of Illinois Press, 178.
15 Ickes, Harold L. 1954. *The Secret Diary of Harold L. Ickes, Vol. 3: The Lowering Clouds, 1939–1941*. New York: Simon & Schuster, 659.
16 Kennedy, David M. 1999. *Freedom from Fear: The American People in Depression and War, 1929–1945*. New York: Oxford University Press, 488.
17 Fleming, Thomas. "The Big Leak." *American Heritage* 38, No. 8. December 1987.
18 Fleming, Thomas J. 2001. *The New Dealers' War: FDR and the War within World War II*. New York: Basic Books, 12; Stevenson, William. 2009. *A Man Called Intrepid: The Incredible WWII Narrative of the Hero Whose Spy Network and Secret Diplomacy Changed the Course of History*. Guilford, CT: Lyons Press (reprint of 1976 edition), 314.
19 Wheeler, Burton K. 1962. *Yankee from the West: The Candid, Turbulent Life Story of the Yankee-born US Senator from Montana*. Garden City, NY: Doubleday, 36.
20 Ryan, James G., and Leonard Schlup, eds. 2006. *Historical Dictionary of the 1940s*. New York: Routledge, 471.
21 Shirer, William L. 1990. *The Rise and Fall of the Third Reich: A History of Nazi Germany*. New York: Simon & Schuster Paperbacks (reprint), 894–95; "The Big Leak."
22 *Chicago Tribune*, December 8, 1941; Smith, 419.
23 Wheeler, 32–33; "The Big Leak."
24 Wheeler, 32–33.
25 Smith, 418.
26 Wedemeyer, 21.
27 Wedemeyer, 25, 31–32; "The Big Leak."
28 Wedemeyer, 21; "The Big Leak."
29 "The Big Leak."
30 Wedemeyer, 22–43; "The Big Leak."
31 "The Big Leak"; Smith, 417, 562 (footnote).
32 Fleming (*New Dealers' War*), 27–28.
33 "A 'Scoop' Gave Axis Our World War II Plans"; "The Big Leak."
34 "The Big Leak."
35 Wheeler, 36; Fleming (*New Dealers' War*), 28–29.
36 Stevenson, 314; Fleming (*New Dealers' War*), 29.
37 Fleming (*New Dealers' War*), 28–29.
38 Fleming (*New Dealers' War*), 26; Smith, 415; "The Big Leak."

39 Wheeler, 36.
40 Gaston, 100–02; Fleming (*New Dealers' War*), 35–38; "A 'Scoop' Gave Axis Our World War II Plans."
41 Sweeney, Michael S. 2001. *Secrets of Victory: The Office of Censorship and the American Press and Radio in World War II*. Chapel Hill: University of North Carolina Press, 81–82; "The Big Leak"; Smith, 440.
42 Smith, 426–28; Winfield, 179.
43 Rudenstine, David. 1996. *The Day the Presses Stopped: A History of the Pentagon Papers Case*. Berkeley: University of California Press, 19–21.
44 Ibid., 15–16.
45 Ibid., 36–37.
46 Rudenstine, 37–42; Ellsberg, Daniel. 2002. *Secrets: A Memoir of Vietnam and the Pentagon Papers*. New York: Viking. Preface, vii, 295.
47 Ellsberg, vii.
48 Rudenstine, 43, 45–46.
49 Ibid., 51, 52–53, 57–58, 61.
50 Ellsberg, ix; Nixon, Richard M. 1978. *RN: The Memoirs of Richard Nixon*. New York: Grosset & Dunlap, 326–27.
51 Nixon, 511.
52 Ibid., 509.
53 Rudenstine, 107, 185–86.
54 Ibid., 143–44, 169–72.
55 *New York Times Co. v. United States*. 403 US 713. Supreme Court of the United States. 1971.
56 Rudenstine, 326, 342; *New York Times Co. v. United States*.
57 Nixon, 511.
58 "Edward Snowden Just Got a New Job," *National Journal*, January 14, 2014.

Chapter 10: The Road to McCarthyism

1 "See It Now," CBS. March 9, 1954.
2 "US Supreme Court Upholds Convictions of Top Communists," Associated Press via *Oregon Statesman*. June 5, 1951.
3 *Dennis v. United States*. 341 US 494. Supreme Court of the United States. 1951.
4 Heale, M. J. 1990. *American Anticommunism: Combating the Enemy Within, 1830–1970*. Baltimore: Johns Hopkins University Press, 131.
5 Belknap, Michal R. 1977. *Cold War Political Justice: The Smith Act, the Communist Party, and American Civil Liberties*. Westport, CT: Greenwood Press, 40.
6 Morgan, Ted. 2003. *Reds: McCarthyism in Twentieth-Century America*. New York: Random House, 299.
7 Dennis, Peggy 1977. *The Autobiography of an American Communist: A Personal View of a Political Life, 1925–1975*. Westport, CT: Lawrence Hill & Co., 162–64.
8 Ibid., 191.
9 Belknap, 81.
10 Belknap, 64–67.

11 Ibid., 82.
12 Powers, Richard G. 1987. *Secrecy and Power: The Life of J. Edgar Hoover*. New York: Free Press, 556.
13 "Six Top Reds Post $5,000 Bonds," Associated Press via *Tucson Daily Citizen*, July 21, 1948.
14 Dennis, Eugene. 1948. *"Dangerous Thoughts": The Case of the Indicted Twelve*. New York: New Century Publishers, 3, 7, 8, 9.
15 Schrecker, 198.
16 Morgan, 315.
17 Belknap, 107.
18 Ibid., 71–78.
19 Ibid., 60.
20 "Truman Claims New York; Dewey in Boston Tonight," *News-Herald* (Franklin, Pennsylvania), October 18, 1948.
21 Morgan, 315; Belknap, 104.
22 Belknap, 79.
23 P. Dennis, 168–71.
24 Belknap, 65.
25 Schrecker, 185.
26 P. Dennis, 177.
27 Ibid., 83, 85.
28 Ibid., 83.
29 Stone, Geoffrey R. 2004. *Perilous Times: Free Speech in Wartime from the Sedition Act of 1798 to the War on Terrorism*. New York: W. W. Norton & Co., 397.
30 Belknap, 86.
31 Schrecker, 194.
32 Ibid., 194.
33 Belknap, 83.
34 Belknap, 89; P. Dennis, 183.
35 P. Dennis, 178, 182.
36 Belknap, 80, 106.
37 Johanningsmeier, Edward P. 1994. *Forging American Communism: The Life of William Z. Foster*. Princeton, NJ: Princeton University Press, 325.
38 Belknap, 94, 98.
39 Ibid., 100.
40 Ibid., 101, 102–03.
41 P. Dennis, 180; Belknap, 95–96.
42 P. Dennis, 181.
43 Morgan, 315.
44 Belknap, 109–10; Martelle, Scott. 2011. *The Fear Within: Spies, Commies, and American Democracy on Trial*. Piscataway, NJ: Rutgers University Press, 213–14.
45 Belknap, 110–11.
46 Ibid., 112.
47 Martelle, 216.

48 "Jurist in Communist Trial Is Voted 'Man of the Year,'" Associated Press, via *Lubbock Avalanche-Journal*, December 25, 1949.
49 Stone, 399.
50 Belknap, 126–31.
51 *Dennis v. United States.*
52 Ibid.
53 Ibid.
54 Ibid.
55 Ibid.
56 Belknap, 144.
57 Ibid., 144.
58 Morgan, 319.
59 Belknap, 153.
60 Ibid., 152–56.
61 Ibid., 156.
62 Ibid., 245.
63 Martelle, 251.
64 Ibid., 252.
65 Belknap, 245.
66 Martelle, 252.
67 *Yates v. United States*. 354 US 298. Supreme Court of the United States. 1957.
68 *Yates v. United States.*
69 Ibid.
70 Ibid.
71 Ibid.
72 Belknap, 259.
73 Ibid., 260.
74 Belknap, 252.
75 Ibid., 254.
76 Ibid., 157, 169.
77 Ibid., 188–206.

Chapter 11: The Chennault Affair

1 Hughes, Ken. 2014. *Chasing Shadows: The Nixon Tapes, the Chennault Affair, and the Origins of Watergate*. Charlottesville: University of Virginia Press, 7.
2 Chennault, Anna. 1980. *The Education of Anna*. New York: Times Books, 163–68.
3 Ibid., 170.
4 Lyndon Johnson's Address to the Nation. March 31, 1968. LBJ Presidential Library.
5 Hughes, 11.
6 Safire, William. 1975. *Before the Fall: An Inside View of the Pre-Watergate White House*. Garden City, NY: Doubleday, 89; Hughes, 8–9.
7 Chennault, 174–75.
8 Bui, Diem, and David Chanoff. 1987. *In the Jaws of History*. Boston: Houghton Mifflin, 236–37.

9 Chennault, 174–75.
10 Hughes, 11–12.
11 Ibid., 12.
12 Ibid., 10, 12.
13 Diem, 239.
14 Hughes, 19–20.
15 Ibid., 4.
16 Ibid., 26–29.
17 Lyndon Johnson, Hubert Humphrey, Richard Nixon, and George Wallace, Tape 6810.04, Conversation 13547. October 16, 1968. University of Virginia, Miller Center, Presidential Recordings Program.
18 Nixon, Richard M. 1978. *RN: The Memoirs of Richard Nixon*. New York: Grosset & Dunlap, 326–27.
19 Lyndon Johnson and Everett Dirksen, Tape 6810.11, Conversation 13617. October 31, 1968. University of Virginia, Miller Center, Presidential Recordings Program.
20 Hughes, 34–35.
21 Hughes, 5–6; Dallek, Robert. 1998. *Flawed Giant: Lyndon Johnson and His Times, 1961–1973*. New York: Oxford University Press, 585.
22 Dallek, 587; Hughes, 6, 37; Diem, 244.
23 Chennault, 186.
24 Dallek, 586.
25 Clifford, 583.
26 Lyndon Johnson and Richard Russell, Tape WH6810.10, Conversation 13612. October 30, 1968. University of Virginia, Miller Center, Presidential Recordings Program.
27 Clifford, 592.
28 US Department of State, Office of the Historian; Foreign Relations of the United States, 1964–1968, Vol. VII, Document 166.
29 Lyndon Johnson and Everett Dirksen, Tape WH6810.11, Conversation 13614. October 31, 1968. University of Virginia, Miller Center, Presidential Recordings Program; Lyndon Johnson and Everett Dirksen, Tape WH6810.11, Conversation 13617. October 31, 1968. University of Virginia, Miller Center, Presidential Recordings Program.
30 Lyndon Johnson and Hubert Humphrey, Tape WH6810.11, Conversation 13620. October 31, 1968. University of Virginia, Miller Center, Presidential Recordings Program.
31 DeLoach, Cartha. 1995. *Hoover's FBI: The Inside Story by Hoover's Trusted Lieutenant*. Washington: Regnery Publishing, 397.
32 "Johnson Calls for Prompt Negotiations," United Press International via *The Times Record* (Troy, New York), November 1, 1968.
33 Chennault, 190–91.
34 DeLoach, 398; Hughes, 39.
35 "Thieu Says South Viets Will Skip Paris Talks," Associated Press, via Colorado Springs *Gazette-Telegraph*, November 2, 1968; "LBJ Halts All Attacks on North," *New York Times* News Service, via *The Sun* (San Bernardino, California), November 1, 1968.

36 Summers, Anthony, and Robbyn Swan. 2000. *The Arrogance of Power: The Secret World of Richard Nixon*. New York: Viking, 302.
37 Lyndon Johnson and Everett Dirksen, Tape WH6811.01, Conversation 13706. November 2, 1968. University of Virginia, Miller Center, Presidential Recordings Program.
38 Lyndon Johnson and George Smathers, Tape WH6811.02, Conversation 13708. November 3, 1968. University of Virginia, Miller Center, Presidential Recordings Program; Hughes, 51.
39 Lyndon Johnson and Richard Nixon, Tape WH6811.02, Conversation 13710. November 3, 1968. University of Virginia, Miller Center, Presidential Recordings Program.
40 Hughes, 52.
41 Summers, 307.
42 Lyndon Johnson and Cartha DeLoach, Tape WH6811.04, Conversation 13730. November 12, 1968. University of Virginia, Miller Center, Presidential Recordings Program; DeLoach, 405–06.
43 Summers, 303–04.
44 Ibid., 304–05.
45 Chennault, 243.
46 Summers, xiv, 306.
47 Dallek, 591.
48 Lyndon Johnson and George Smathers, Tape WH6811.02, Conversation 13708. November 3, 1968. University of Virginia, Miller Center, Presidential Recordings Program.
49 Hughes, 67.
50 Hughes, 44–45; Dallek, 591.
51 Summers, 305.
52 Witcover, Jules. 2005. *The Making of an Ink-Stained Wretch: Half a Century Pounding the Political Beat*. Baltimore: The Johns Hopkins University Press, 131.
53 Humphrey, Hubert H. 1991. *Education of a Public Man: My Life and Politics*. Minneapolis: University of Minnesota Press, ProQuest ebrary, xix.
54 Hughes, 2–3.
55 Ibid., 68, 160.
56 Johnson, Lyndon B. 1971. *The Vantage Point: Perspectives of the Presidency, 1963–1969*. New York: Holt, Rinehart and Winston, 517–18.
57 Summers, 302.
58 Witcover, 131.
59 Summers, 299.

Chapter 12: Arms for Hostages and Money for Freedom Fighters

1 Liman, Arthur. 1998. *Lawyer: A Life of Counsel and Controversy*. New York: Public Affairs, 318.
2 Brands, H. W. 2015. *Reagan: The Life*. New York: Doubleday, 547.
3 Brands, 557.

4 Draper, Theodore. 1991. *A Very Thin Line: The Iran-Contra Affairs*. New York: Hill and Wang, 33.
5 Ibid., 77.
6 Draper, 37, 40; *Report of the Congressional Committees Investigating the Iran-Contra Affair*. Washington, DC. 1987, 59.
7 Draper, 55, 67.
8 Ibid., 80.
9 Walsh, Lawrence E. 1997. *Firewall: The Iran-Contra Conspiracy and Cover-Up*. New York: W. W. Norton & Co., 19; Draper, 81–82.
10 Draper, 83.
11 Brands, 548.
12 Woodward, Bob. 2005. *Veil: The Secret Wars of the CIA, 1981–1987*. New York: Simon & Schuster Paperbacks (reprint of 1987 edition), 408.
13 Kornbluh, Peter, and Bryne, Malcolm. 1993. *The Iran-Contra Scandal: The Declassified History*. New York: New Press, 220–26.
14 Draper, 150–51.
15 Byrne, Malcolm. 2014. *Iran-Contra: Reagan's Scandal and the Unchecked Abuse of Presidential Power*. Lawrence: University Press of Kansas, 61–62.
16 Draper, 128.
17 *Report of the Congressional Committees*, 526.
18 Ibid., 199.
19 Draper, 129–34; Byrne, 63.
20 Byrne, 63–64; Draper, 133.
21 Byrne, 64; Draper, 137–41.
22 Draper, 140–41.
23 Ibid., 142, 145, 156.
24 Draper, 142–44; Byrne, 67.
25 Draper, 143.
26 Byrne, 69.
27 *Report of the Congressional Committees*, 167.
28 Reagan, Ronald. 2007. *The Reagan Diaries*. New York: HarperCollins, 343.
29 Draper, 156–57.
30 Brands, 549.
31 Draper, 167–69; Byrne, 71.
32 Woodward, 415.
33 Draper, 169–70.
34 Ibid., 170–71.
35 Ibid., 170.
36 Ibid., 184–92.
37 Ibid., 193.
38 Ibid., 193–94.
39 Ibid., 195–96.
40 Byrne, 103.
41 Woodward, 424.

42 Kornbluh, 231.
43 Woodward, 425.
44 Kornbluh, 231.
45 Draper, 215.
46 Byrne, 145; Draper, 239.
47 Byrne, 106–07, 301; Draper, 226–28; *Final Report of the Independent Counsel for Iran/Contra Matters, Vol. I: Investigations and Prosecutions*. Chapter 24.
48 Byrne, 163.
49 *Report of the Congressional Committees*, 269–70.
50 Ibid., 271.
51 Ibid., 216.
52 Ibid., 271.
53 Ibid., 216.
54 Kornbluh, 232–35; Byrne, 158; Draper, 239–40.
55 Woodward, 442–43.
56 Draper, 289; Byrne, 165.
57 Kornbluh, 319–23.
58 Draper, 290–92.
59 Byrne, 188–89.
60 Byrne, 190; Draper, 314.
61 Byrne, 192.
62 Draper, 315–17.
63 Byrne, 197.
64 Draper, 321–22.
65 Ibid., 321, 326.
66 Ibid., 323.
67 Byrne, 202–03.
68 Byrne, 203; Draper, 325–26.
69 Byrne, 206; Draper, 380.
70 Byrne, 238; Draper, 377–79.
71 Draper, 382.
72 Ibid., 375.
73 Draper, 382–83; Kornbluh, 237–39.
74 Kornbluh, 237–39; *Final Report of the Independent Counsel*, The Underlying Facts.
75 *Report of the Congressional Committees*, 250; Draper, 396.
76 Draper, 399–400.
77 Kornbluh, 302–03; Draper, 451.
78 Draper, 459.
79 Ibid., 352–53, 355.
80 North, Oliver. 1992. *Under Fire: An American Story*. New York: HarperCollins, 8.
81 Draper, 112–13, 345.
82 Ibid., 346–50.
83 Draper, 452, 457.
84 Brands, 612.

85 Reagan, 450.
86 Brands, 615–16.
87 Ibid., 617.
88 Walsh, 3.
89 Reagan, 374–75.
90 Ibid., 381.
91 Brands, 619–28.
92 Byrne, 269.
93 Draper, 506.
94 North, 12.
95 Byrne, 271–72.
96 Reagan, 453.
97 Byrne, 278.
98 North, 6.
99 Woodward, 509.
100 Brands, 559.
101 *Final Report of the Independent Counsel for Iran/Contra Matters, Vol. I: Investigations and Prosecutions*. Chapter 3.
102 Brands, 663.
103 *Report of the Congressional Committees*, 555.
104 Byrne, 299.
105 North, 14–15; Walsh, 24.
106 North, 10.
107 Draper, 297.
108 "Iran-Contra Hearings: 'Head High and Shoulders Straight'; North and the Chair of Command: When to Be a Scapegoat and When Not," *New York Times*, July 10, 1987.
109 Draper, 34.
110 North, 345–46.
111 *Report of the Congressional Committees*, 11, 21–22.
112 Walsh, 31.
113 Byrne, 222, 315.
114 Ibid., 315–16.
115 "Watergate's Shadow on the Bush Presidency," *The Washington Post Magazine*. June 20, 1999.

Epilogue: A Right to Know

1 "Whistle-Blower Edward Snowden Talks to *South China Morning Post*," *South China Morning Post*, June 12, 2013
2 "Edward Snowden: The Whistle-Blower Behind the NSA Surveillance Revelations," *Guardian*, June 11, 2013.
3 Ibid.
4 Greenwald, Glenn. 2014. *No Place to Hide: Edward Snowden, the NSA, and the US Surveillance State*. New York: Metropolitan Books, 43.
5 Ibid., 47.

6 Ibid., 48.
7 Ibid., 52.
8 "Edward Snowden NSA Files: Secret Surveillance and Our Revelations So Far," *Guardian,* August 21, 2013.
9 "Boundless Informant: The NSA's Secret Tool to Track Global Surveillance Data," *Guardian,* June 11, 2013.
10 "GCHQ Taps Fibre-Optic Cables for Secret Access to World's Communications," *Guardian,* June 21, 2013.
11 "Pentagon Says Snowden Took Most US Secrets Ever: Rogers," *Bloomberg Business,* January 9, 2014.
12 "Edward Snowden: The Whistle-Blower Behind the NSA Surveillance Revelations."
13 Ibid.
14 Greenwald, 89.
15 "Edward Snowden: The Whistle-Blower Behind the NSA Surveillance Revelations."
16 "This Man Is a Traitor," *New York Daily News,* June 11, 2013.
17 "Kerry: Snowden a 'Coward' and 'Traitor,'" NBC News, May 28, 2014; "Hillary Clinton: Edward Snowden's Leaks Helped Terrorists," *National Journal,* April 25, 2014.
18 "Ex-CIA Director: Snowden Should Be 'Hanged' If Convicted for Treason," Fox News Channel, December 17, 2013.
19 "Edward Snowden: Saving Us from the United Stasi of America," *Guardian,* June 10, 2013.
20 "Edward Snowden, Patriot," *Washington Post,* August 9, 2013.
21 "Amash Insists Snowden 'Told Us What We Need to Know,'" *Washington Post,* August 4, 2013.
22 "Jesselyn Radack: Why Edward Snowden Wouldn't Get a Fair Trial," *Wall Street Journal,* January 21, 2014.
23 "Edward Snowden Asylum: Countries Approached and Their Responses," *Guardian,* July 4, 2013.
24 "Did Edward Snowden Just Evade the US Justice System?," MSNBC, September 13, 2013.
25 Greenwald, 248.

Acknowledgments

There are many people who provided me with encouragement, support, and assistance while I wrote my first book, and some without whom I never would have been able to complete it.

First and foremost, I don't know how I could have written this book without the love and support of my extraordinary wife, Robyn Nebrich-Duda. For many months, we spent more time apart than either of us would have liked while I researched and wrote. But through it all, she was by my side with words of encouragement, and was an enthusiastic editor whose advice helped make this a better book.

My mother and stepfather, Amy Kruchkoff and Junius Taylor, and my father and stepmother, Paul and Janet Duda, have given me their love and support not only through the writing of this book but throughout my life. For that I owe them more gratitude than I can ever repay.

At every step of the process, my brother, David Duda, was there for me to bounce ideas off of and to read this book while it was a work in progress. As a fellow lover of history, I relied on David's opinions and advice as I wrote. He and his wife, Audrey Peck, my dear sister-in-law, were sources of constant encouragement.

No one did more to help this book become a reality than my good friend Chris DeRose, who opened the door to this opportunity and helped me achieve a lifelong dream by recommending me to Lyons Press. A talented author of history whose work has been an inspiration, Chris provided invaluable advice that helped me write this book and navigate the publishing world, oftentimes during our bar trivia team's weekly competitions.

My thanks to Keith Wallman of Lyons Press, who took a chance on a first-time author and gave me an opportunity for which I will be eternally grateful. I hope this book is worthy of the trust he placed in me.

My wife's family is too numerous to name individually, but my father-in-law Peter Nebrich and the entire Nebrich clan provided endless support as I wrote. I extend a special thanks to my niece, Madeline Ackley, who provided me with invaluable assistance while I was writing this book.

Many others contributed in many ways, providing encouragement, advice and support. I extend my thanks and gratitude to my friends and family who stood by my side and offered their support, including Sian and Ian Adams, Liz and Ben Barnett, Tim Bourcet, Kate and Ruben Gallego, Erin Hunt and Ari

Grossman, Deborah Kaufman, Hannah and Oran Switzer, Jeff Stapleton, Geoff Woods, the other members of the illustrious bar trivia team, the Blue Comet—who have spent more time than almost anyone else listening to me talk about this book—including Allison and Alex Benezra, Elise and Trey Terry and Jeremy Zegas, and to my colleagues at the *Arizona Capitol Times*.

And to anyone else I've forgotten to name who has assisted me, supported me or helped promote *If This Be Treason*, I extend my thanks.

Index

About the Author

This is the debut book for Jeremy Duda, a thirteen-year veteran of print journalism and an award-winning reporter in the world of Arizona politics and government. At the *Arizona Capitol Times*, which is widely regarded as the premier source of political news in Arizona, he has spent more than six years covering the governor's office beat and other political stories. He has a proven record of breaking high-profile news stories and scooping much larger competitors, developing sources deep inside the often-murky world of politics and government, and providing some of the most comprehensive and insightful reporting on state politics and government. He lives in Phoenix with his wife, Robyn.